# State College

## at

## Framingham

5M-6-65-940607

# Experiential Foundations of Rorschach's Test

# EXPERIENTIAL FOUNDATIONS OF RORSCHACH'S TEST / Ernest G. Schachtel

BASIC BOOKS, INC., PUBLISHERS

*New York / London*

# PREFACE

This book addresses itself primarily to those who are already acquainted with Rorschach's test, to advanced students of the test, and to clinicians using the test or interested in it for other reasons. It is not a manual of instruction or a book for the beginning student. Its aim is to add to the theoretical understanding of the test and, since I am convinced of the close relation between theory and practice, thereby also to its clinical use. If we have a better understanding of the rationale of a score, for example of why a specific determinant has a particular meaning, then we are in a better position to judge in our clinical work whether, to what extent, and in what way this meaning applies or does not apply to a particular response based on this determinant. Thus, my main concern is to contribute to the development of a rationale of the test as a whole and of the most important test scores, namely the determinants, and thereby to the method of test interpretation. Since such a rationale can be developed only in the context of our general psychological and clinical knowledge, the book may also be of some interest to those concerned with the problems of personality and perception and of the psychology of test situations and their effect on the persons tested.

The viewpoint from which the book is written owes its development mainly to psychoanalytic and phenomenological thought. All the material on the test as a whole, on the nature of the data studied by the test, is new; so is the chapter on the form response, with the exception of the section on Dynamic Form Responses which is a condensed version of my article "The Dynamic Perception and the Symbolism of Form." The chapters on shading and on content, symbol, score, and percept are new. The chapters on movement and color responses and on the test situation are based on articles published previously but now out of print. The chapter on the movement responses is largely un-

v

changed. The chapter on the color responses has been revised and added to in the light of my studies on the development of perception.[1] The chapter on the test situation has been enlarged, especially by a section on the role of the social setting of the test situation and of the personality of the tester.[2] The modes of apperception (location scores) are discussed only insofar as the testee's definition of the test situation and certain defensive attitudes influence them.[3]

I want to thank Florine Katz and my wife, Zeborah Schachtel, for their careful reading of the manuscript and for their helpful suggestions and criticism.

E. G. S.

*New York City*
*June 1966*

---

[1] *Metamorphosis*, "On the Development of Affect, Perception, Attention, and Memory" (New York: Basic Books, 1959), pp. 79–248.

[2] I am indebted to the William Alanson White Psychiatric Foundation for permission to use the articles referred to above; all were originally published in *Psychiatry*, as follows: "The Dynamic Perception and the Symbolism of Form," *Psychiatry*, 4 (1941), 79–96; "On Color and Affect," *Psychiatry*, 6 (1943), 393–409; "Subjective Definitions of the Rorschach Test Situation and Their Effect on Test Performance," *Psychiatry*, 8 (1945), 419–448; and "Projection and Its Relation to Character Attitudes and Creativity in the Kinesthetic Responses," *Psychiatry*, 13 (1950), 69–100.

[3] For a fuller discussion of the apperceptive modes, see, aside from Rorschach's book, Albert Furrer, *Der Auffassungsvorgang beim Rorschach's schen psychodiagnostischen Versuch* (Zürich, 1930); Laurence Hemmendinger, "Developmental Theory and the Rorschach Method," in Maria A. Rickers-Ovsiankina, ed., *Rorschach Psychology* (New York: John Wiley and Sons, 1960), pp. 58–79; Gertrude Meili-Dworetzki, "The Development of Perception in the Rorschach," in Bruno Klopfer *et al.*, *Developments in the Rorschach Technique* (Yonkers-on-Hudson: World Book Company, 1956), II, 104–148.

# CONTENTS

# Experiential Foundations of Rorschach's Test

# 1 / INTRODUCTION

The main purpose of this book is to contribute to the understanding of Rorschach's test. Despite the wealth of stimulating thoughts and implications contained in his book, Rorschach felt that the results of his "experiment" were predominantly empirical observations and that its theoretical foundations were, "for the most part, still quite incomplete." [1] Of the extensive literature on the test, by far the greatest part has been devoted to adding to these empirical observations and to refinements of technique; relatively few attempts have been made to inquire into the rationale of the test and to contribute to its theoretical foundations. This is all the more surprising since Rorschach's test and his book offer, among other things, so far as I know, the first major contribution to the problem of perception and personality, which, in the past twenty or thirty years, has become one of the foremost issues in psychology. Thus the gap between empirical observations and theoretical understanding, though somewhat narrower than in 1921, when Rorschach's book was published, is quite large.

The attempt to increase our understanding of the foundations of the test seems important to me for several reasons. For the psychologist interested in theory, the phenomena occurring during a Rorschach test raise a wealth of questions and open up possibilities of approaching the solution of these questions because they contain data that are not accessible as readily and in such variety and abundance to other methods of observation. Any improvement of our understanding of the rationale of

---

[1] Hermann Rorschach, *Psychodiagnostics* [English edition] (Berne: Hans Huber, 1942), p. 13.

1

the test is likely to contribute to the relevant formulation of these questions and to their eventual solution. It is likely to contribute even more to the *clinician's* use of the test. One can achieve some competence in the use of the test with the mere knowledge of the empirical findings that certain scores or combinations of scores tend to indicate certain types of pathology, certain tendencies, and certain assets and limitations in the personality of the testee. But such competence and such use of the test remain blind in the sense that they do not derive from an understanding of *why* the scores mean or indicate what they are supposed to indicate. This situation resembles a diagnosis on the basis of symptoms without understanding the nature of the connection between the symptom and the condition it usually indicates. The word "usually" is important here; without understanding the connection between symptom and the condition empirically found with it, one cannot know when what seems on the surface to be the same symptom does *not* indicate the same condition.

The empirical "validation" of the symptomatic significance of certain Rorschach scores does not differ in principle from some of the validation on which much folk wisdom rests, namely, on recurrent experience of a relation between two factors, a score and a trait or tendency, a dream symbol or content and its "meaning." The main difference is that we now have statistical methods that tell us when to accept such a relationship as valid but that do not exclude the possibility that in any particular case it may not be valid. No amount of validation of Rorschach-test-score meanings can substitute for the understanding of what goes on in the test and in its interpretation.

The use of the test will be most fruitful if we understand fully the nature of the data we are studying in a Rorschach protocol and if we understand, furthermore, the nature of what we are doing when we score and interpret a protocol. This implies that we know what the processes are that lead to a response; which of these processes we single out and which we omit; what we emphasize and what we neglect when we assign a score to a response; and exactly what we do, what we assume and why we assume it, when we interpret a score or a psychogram, a response, a sequence of responses, or a total test protocol. We are far from knowing all this, and probably we shall never know it fully. But every step that increases our knowledge, limited though it is destined to be, will add to our understanding of the test and improve our capacity to use it intelligently. On the other hand, to use the test without the serious attempt to understand as much as possible of its rationale is tempting as well as dangerous.

It is tempting especially to the beginner, but also to the expert, insofar as it may give one a spurious feeling of security to rely on a fixed meaning of a particular score or a particular symbol (as is done in much of content interpretation) he has learned from an authority—a teacher or a book. It is more difficult if one has always to examine anew whether such meaning really applies to the concrete response before him. This does not mean, of course, that a statistically valid relation between a particular score and a particular meaning is without value. It only means that it still requires judgment to decide whether the usual meaning applies in a particular case.

If blind dependence on learned meanings of scores and the like is one danger, the development of an esoteric Rorschach language and Rorschach psychology, not or insufficiently connected and integrated with our general knowledge of the normal and abnormal psychology of personality and interpersonal relations, is another. The use of such an esoteric language and of a special Rorschach psychology entails the danger that it does not communicate meaningfully to other people, and not even to other psychologists and psychiatrists. Sometimes it does not even communicate to the person who uses it because his sense of understanding the meaning of this esoteric language is spurious even though it may be comforting and reassuring. Similarly, excessive refinements of "technique," if not founded on advances in theory and validated by empirical data and concrete understanding, may foster a tendency to confuse the matter to be studied with the method used for the study and to mistake complicated and impressive scores and tabulations for better and more subtle understanding.[2]

In the following chapters, I shall attempt to develop hypotheses that I hope may contribute to a better understanding of the nature of some of the data we study in Rorschach's test, of some of the methods by which we can study them, and thus of the rationale of the test. This attempt will include an examination of some of the reasons various scores have a particular meaning, why these meanings vary within a certain range, and what some of the limitations of the applicability of

---

[2] For a more detailed critique of this latter tendency in the social sciences in general, see C. Wright Mills, *The Sociological Imagination* (New York: Oxford University Press, 1959), especially the chapter "Abstracted Empiricism," pp. 50–75.

these meanings are so far as their use for diagnostic evaluation of the more enduring dynamics, trends, and traits of a particular personality is concerned. I also hope to draw the reader's attention to some data that are omitted by the traditional scores and methods of interpretation, but that I believe can furnish significant insights into the testee's personality structure. I call the main approach I use for the understanding of these problems "experiential" because it consists mostly in the attempt to reconstruct, to understand, and to make more explicit the experiences that the testee underwent in taking the test and his reaction to these experiences, specifically his way of approaching or avoiding and of handling the experience of the inkblots in the context of the test task. By "experience" I mean conscious as well as unconscious and only vaguely or peripherally conscious experiences.

How the testee experiences, his "apparatus for experiencing," was also the focus of Rorschach's interest and is of central significance in his book.[3] Long before he wrote his book and throughout his life, he was interested in the differing ways in which different people see and experience a painting. When visiting an art exhibition, he would try to imagine how one or another person of his acquaintance would feel when looking at a certain painting.[4] Though I question whether the experience type—in Rorschach's technical sense of the word, namely, the numerical relation of movement to color responses[5]—is the main representative of the person's way of experiencing, I do believe that the various determinants (form, color, movement, shading) represent different perceptual and experiential attitudes, as I shall try to show later, and that the relative strength of and the type of fluctuation among these attitudes are significant indicators of the person's way of experiencing.

This way of experiencing refers primarily to the testee's experience and perception of the inkblots, which also was the main focus of Ror-

[3] Rorschach, *op. cit.*, p. 87. In the original German text, the sentence referring to the "experience type" is not only italicized, but the word *Erlebnistypus* is emphasized by bold type not used anywhere else in the text (4th German edition [1941], p. 82). The English translation omits both the italics and this unique emphasis.

[4] Henri Ellenberger, "The Life and Work of Hermann Rorschach," *Bulletin of the Menninger Clinic*, 18 (1954), 173–219, pp. 191, 196.

[5] By "movement responses," Rorschach means those interpretations of the blot that are determined by its form plus kinesthetic factors, usually people perceived as moving or in a certain posture; they will be discussed in detail in Chapter 9. By "color responses," he means responses that are determined either solely by the color of the blot or by a combination of its color and its form; they will be discussed in Chapter 8.

schach's interest. But the experience of the inkblots takes place in the context of a *task,* namely, the test task: to say what the blots might be. The posing of this task forces the testee—or at least most testees—to come to terms in some way with the inkblots, to look at them and to deal with them in accordance with the task. If they saw them outside a task situation, many would not pay any attention to them; others would deal with them in different ways; probably only relatively few would become interested in them. Hence, what the task means to the testees will have a significant influence on the quality of their encounter with the blots, on the way they experience them and deal with them. Rorschach was aware of this when he observed that some testees took the test very seriously and that for some the test is work, whereas for others it is play.[6] The weight of the task will cause some testees to experience the blots in a much more constrained way than do others for whom the task aspect looms less forbidding and who, therefore, are freer to experience and play with the inkblots. Indeed, it is possible and occurs quite frequently that the testee's experience of an inkblot and his reaction to the task aspect of the test are difficult for him to reconcile. If he did not have to come up with what he feels is a suitable answer to the tester's question "What might this be?", he might either have a different experience of the inkblot or he might not feel constrained to screen out, consciously or unconsciously, some aspects of experience of the blot he may have but may cut short or reject as unsuitable for the fulfillment of the task.

Hence, in the test performance and in the responses that make up this performance, we deal not just with the testee's encounter with and experience of the inkblots, but with this encounter in the context of the test task, that is to say, also with his experience of the test task and of what he feels he has to do in order to deal with this task. As will be shown later, some of Rorschach's method of interpreting the test score, especially his concept of sequence, often deals with the reaction to the task aspect, even though he does not state this explicitly.

The test task is, in turn, part of the total test situation and its setting. This, too, is part of the testee's experience, and with this, too, he deals in responding or not responding and in the particular way he responds to the inkblots. In the attempt to reconstruct the testee's way of experiencing and his reactions to it, all these factors have to be included and

---

[6] *Op. cit.,* pp. 43, 57, 81.

kept in mind. Their totality is what I mean by the testee's experience of the inkblots and the test. It is impossible, of course, to know and encompass all this totality by studying a test performance or its protocol. Nevertheless, most test performances give sufficient clues to enable us to reconstruct important parts of the testee's experience and of his dealing with it and thus to see significant aspects of his personality structure. The complexity of Rorschach's test, which will have become apparent from what has been described here, far from being an obstacle to its clinical use is indeed an asset because it allows us to observe different levels of functioning and ways of experiencing, their rigidity or flexibility, and their consistency or scatteredness.

The complexity of the test is also one of the reasons neither the experiential approach by itself nor any other approach can explain *all* the phenomena occurring in the test and why in interpreting tests a variety of methods is usually used, even though the interpreter may not be aware of the methodological differences between the various viewpoints from which he evaluates a response and a whole test protocol. Thus, a good W response of a high F + % [7] may be viewed as an *achievement* that permits conclusions regarding certain intellectual *abilities* or certain intellectual processes enabling the person to make such an achievement. Rorschach considers the W responses in this way when he uses them as an indicator of the capacities for abstraction and for imagination. But he also uses the W as an indicator of a special kind of *motivation,* of conscious or unconscious *willing,* that is to say, as pointing to dynamic factors in the personality structure. These, in turn, may be related to the way in which the testee experiences and defines the test task and the test situation. It would be an interesting task—which, to my knowledge, has not yet been undertaken—to study systematically the various implicit methodological procedures and assumptions that underly Rorschach's and others' ways of using and interpreting his test and thus to make these procedures and assumptions explicit.

This book attempts to do this mainly for the experiential approach which, depending on what one wants to find out from a test, has to be supplemented by other approaches. For example, in clinical use of the

---

[7] By W (or whole) response, Rorschach means a response to the entire inkblot, as contrasted to responses referring to parts of an inkblot. By F + %, Rorschach refers to the percentage of well-seen or acceptable F, or form, responses in relation to the total number of all those responses that are determined by the form of the blot only. The form responses will be discussed in Chapter 7.

test, one generally will also want to get some impression of the degree and quality of the testee's intelligence. Hence, one will also look at such factors as W, F +, and F − from the viewpoint of the level of intellectual achievement, not only from the viewpoint of the experiential meaning of W, F +, and F −. If, then, one should find, for example, one or two excellently seen F + responses while the other form responses are mostly mediocre or poor, one might conclude that the testee must have the potential for the kind of intellectual achievement represented by such an excellent F +, but that something seems to interfere with his functioning more frequently at this level. To find what it is that interferes, one might turn to an analysis of his thought processes as reflected in the test and to the experiential approach. The latter may help us to see something about the testee's experience of his uneven performance and his reaction to it or about the lack of awareness of it. It may also help us to understand what interfered with his thought processes and why and, possibly, why this interference occurred at one point and not at another. In reality, intellectual functioning and total experience are not separated so neatly as they have been here for the sake of illustrating the difference between the experiential approach and the method of gauging intelligence from achievement, which is essentially also the method used in intelligence tests.

## 2 / THE NATURE OF THE TEST DATA
### I. THE PROJECTION HYPOTHESIS; THE
### PERCEPTION-ASSOCIATION HYPOTHESIS

The richness as well as the complexity of the *data* elicited by Rorschach's test is due to the many processes set in motion in the testee when he reacts to the task posed by the test. These processes comprise his reactions to the total test situation, including the personality and the behavior of the tester, and to the real or imagined expectations of the tester as to what the testee is to do; they comprise the testee's thoughts and phantasies as to what conclusions the tester, and other people significant to the testee, may arrive at on the basis of his test performance, or his indifference to these conclusions; the expectations the testee has with regard to himself, his thoughts about the impression he would like to create, impulses deriving from his self-image that are mobilized by the test situation; they usually comprise both attempts to realize some self-ideal and attempts to counteract, to conceal, or—sometimes— defiantly to express what might be called his negative self-image, which —like the self-ideal—may be closely (realistically) or distantly (unrealistically) related to his basic personality. These are examples of some of the processes that enter into and make up the testee's subjective definition of the Rorschach test situation, which is never fully conscious and articulate, is different in each testee, and is a major factor influencing the test performance and the test "results." [1]

It is within this setting that the testee's encounter with the Rorschach inkblots takes place, an encounter which in itself is a complex process and, together with the total test situation, sets in motion complex reac-

---

[1] More about this in Chapter 12.

8

tions. The nature of this encounter determines how the testee experiences the inkblots and how he reacts to them, especially insofar as his reactions result in test "responses," in the narrower sense of the word. In this sense a response may be defined as the verbal communication by the testee to the tester that the testee offers as one of his solutions (or the solution) of the test task with regard to a particular inkblot, namely, the task to say what the blot could be, what it might look like. Of course, most testees have and also give responses other than those in the sense just defined. They express like and dislike of the blots, puzzlement, groping, requests for direction, for reassurance or approval; criticism of the blots, the test, the tester; self-criticism and self-approval; and so forth. These responses are significant, too, in the wider sense of the word. They may reveal something about the testee's experience and definition of the test situation or about the genesis of, and the testee's feeling concerning, a particular response,[2] or about both. The responses and the processes leading to them can be separated only by an artificial abstraction from the processes going on in the testee's experience of the total test situation, and they are constantly codetermined by the total test situation. Nevertheless, it is useful to make this abstraction; but it should be made consciously and not, as most of the Rorschach literature does, without awareness of the significance of the test situation.

Before examining in detail the nature of the data we study in Rorschach's test and the means by which we study them, especially in the experiential approach, I want to review briefly two answers given to this problem, one primarily in much of the American literature on the test, the other by Rorschach. In the American literature it has become customary to classify Rorschach's diagnostic method as one of the so-called projective techniques, together with such diverse methods as word association, graphology, Szondi's test, the Thematic Apperception Test, the Four-Picture Test, the Bender Visual-Motor Gestalt Test, Finger Painting, Human Figure Drawing, the House-Tree-Person Test, Sentence Completion, the Mosaic Test, the Make A Picture Story (MAPS) Test, Psychodrama, the Blacky Picture Test, Mira's Myokinetic method, Rosenzweig's Picture-Frustration study, the study of expressive movements, L. Murphy's miniature life-toy technique, the World Test, and others.[3] Such classification, of course, always implies a

---

[2] When the word "response" is used without qualification in this book, it refers to the response in the above-defined, narrower sense of the word.

[3] New ones, and variations of those mentioned above, are constantly being

statement about the nature of the method so classified. The concept of projection, as originally developed by Freud, plays no important role in any of the "projective" techniques.[4] Freud used the term as meaning the mistaken attribution of a quality or trait of which one is not aware in himself onto others, thereby distorting reality. Originally, he felt that this mechanism played quite generally a very important role in shaping man's picture of the world;[5] later he restricted the concept to those cases in which projection served the purpose of defense, namely, the defense of externalizing that which is too difficult, dangerous, and anxiety-arousing to deal with as a quality of oneself.[6] But even when one uses the term "projection," as I do, in the wider sense of the *attribution of qualities, feelings, attitudes, experiences, and strivings of one's own to objects (people or things) of the environment,* regardless of whether one is aware of them in himself and regardless of whether the projection leads to a distortion of reality or not, projection in this wider sense of the word plays no role at all in most of the so-called projective techniques.[7] In Rorschach's test it plays a role mainly in the kinesthetic responses and in some dynamic form responses, but not in the majority of responses, nor is it the only significant aspect of the kinesthetic and dynamic form responses. In other words, only a small fraction of the many processes underlying Rorschach responses are of a projective nature.

What the so-called projective techniques do have in common is (1) their diagnostic (in the widest sense of the word) aim, which they share with other personality tests, (2) the fact that they pursue this aim by attempting to elicit behavior characteristic of the individual personality, (3) that they do so by not limiting the person's choice or possibility (even where it is not a conscious choice) of ways of behaving in

---

added. For a survey see Harold H. Anderson and Gladys L. Anderson, *An Introduction to Projective Techniques* (New York: Prentice-Hall, 1951); Lawrence K. Frank, *Projective Methods* (Springfield, Ill.: Charles C Thomas, 1948). For a recent attempt at classification: Gardner Lindzey, "On the Classification of Projective Techniques," *Psychological Bulletin,* 56 (1959), 158–168.

[4] This has been pointed out also by Murray. See Henry A. Murray in Anderson and Anderson, *op. cit.,* pp. xii–xiii.

[5] See *Totem and Taboo* (1912–13) [Standard Edition (London: Hogarth Press)], XIII, 64.

[6] *Metapsychological Supplement to the Theory of Dreams* (1916) [Standard Edition], XIV, 223–224; *Beyond the Pleasure Principle* (1920) [Standard Edition], XVIII, 29.

[7] For instance, in word association, Bender Visual-Motor Gestalt Test, Finger Painting, Mosaic Test, Mira's Myokinetic psychodiagnosis, graphology, the study of expressive movements.

producing the desired behavior sample to be studied (the test responses, the sample of handwriting, or other expressive movement), and (4) that this usually involves the explicit or implicit communication that there is no "right" or "wrong" response.[8]

To equate individually characteristic behavior with projection and call methods aimed at eliciting relatively free samples of such behavior projective widens the term "projection" to a point where it loses all of its specific meaning and invites misunderstanding by using the same word in two or more different meanings.

Only a few of the many authors who classify Rorschach's test as projective state explicitly why they do so and what they mean by it. Rapaport, who considers Rorschach's test closely approaching the ideal of a projective test, makes it clear that he uses projection in a sense different from the original psychoanalytic meaning of the term. According to him, the "projective hypothesis" implied in the projective procedures is that any and all behavior of a person reveals his individual personality.[9] Projection is hence synonymous with individually characteristic behavior, and projective procedures attempt to study the individual person by observing, and drawing inferences and conclusions from, such behavior. Rapaport points out quite rightly that in this sense of the word the case history is just as much a projective procedure as are the projective tests. According to him, "the concept of projection as used in projective procedures is . . . formed on the pattern of projector and screen." [10]

----

[8] Exceptions to this are Mira's Myokinetic psychodiagnosis where the task is to draw, blindfolded, ten 5-cm-long parallel lines as closely together as possible, and the Bender Visual-Motor Gestalt Test, where the instructions are to copy some designs. This implies that the "right" response is to produce an accurate copy, especially if the tester amplifies this instruction, as for example Halpern does, by telling the testee to copy them "as well as he can" (Florence Halpern in Anderson and Anderson, *op. cit.*, p. 325). This emphasizes and narrows the kind of task implicit also in some of the other "projective techniques," namely, that the response should be "fitting": in the Rorschach it should be a *likeness* to the inkblot, in the various picture tests, and in the sentence-completion test it should fit the pictures or the beginning of the sentence. But while such likeness or fit can be achieved in many different ways, there is only one perfect solution for the task to copy something as well as one can, and the direction of the effort required in Mira's technique is defined with mathematical precision. The fact that the defined goal of these tasks leaves little or no leeway does not, of course, mean that the ways in which testees respond to them are not widely varying, individually characteristic and diagnostically differentiating. The strained attempt at a literally "perfect" solution is just as valuable a diagnostic indication as a more relaxed attitude.

[9] David Rapaport, *Diagnostic Psychological Testing* (Chicago: The Year Book Publishers, 1946), II, 6–12.

[10] *Ibid.*, p. 7.

Whether the classification of Rorschach's test as projective is based on such an explicit definition of the concept of projection or whether, as is sometimes the case, "projective" is used merely as a convenient label with more or less vague connotations, the mere fact that it is thus classified tends, as does any classification or labeling, to influence and bend the articulate or inarticulate ideas of those who use such a label in a certain direction. It is especially important to examine the direction of such bents when they are not made explicit. An implicit or even unconscious assumption often influences in an obscure way what we do and think more than does an articulate and explicit one. The projection hypothesis made explicit by Rapaport, and probably implicit in the use of the term by many others, may lead to the faulty assumption that the testee, rather than *encountering* something and somebody in the world and experiencing and interacting with what he encounters, is faced with a blank screen on which he projects only his own subjectivity. Such a view is approximated by those who believe that the Rorschach inkblots are "unstructured" and by those who use the test without taking into account the social context in which it is used and the personality and behavior of the tester but act, explicitly or implicitly, on an assumption parallel to Freud's that the analyst is a blank and neutral mirror. Actually, it is the *encounter* of the testee with the inkblots in the setting of the test situation, and his experience of, and reactions to, this encounter that we study when interpreting a Rorschach record.

What is the nature of the processes taking place in the testee when he encounters and responds to the inkblots by telling us what they look like to him? Rorschach expressed a definite conviction about this question, even though in general he felt that the theoretical foundations for his experiment were quite incomplete. He held that the process resulting in a response is of the general order of perception and apperception (*Wahrnehmung und Auffassung*) and that, "since [according to Bleuler's theory of perception quoted by Rorschach] perception can be called an associative integration of available engrams (memory images) with recent complexes of sensations," the interpretation of the inkblots (i.e., the responses) "may be called a perception in which the effort of integration of sensation complex with engram is so great that it is realized consciously as an integrative effort." [11] He goes on to point out that the responses of some groups of people are not interpretations

---

[11] *Op. cit.*, pp. 13, 16–17. I have changed the translation of the English edition somewhat to approximate more closely the meaning of the original German text.

of the blots but perceptions in the usual sense of the word. He considers the difference between perception and interpretation to be one of degree rather than of kind and concludes that interpretation of the blot is only a special kind of perception and that therefore there can be no doubt that it is justified to designate his experiment as a test of perception (i.e., of individual differences in perception).[12] Whether one agrees with Bleuler's and Rorschach's concept of perception or not, it is clear that the processes of perceiving the inkblot, of associating remembered ideas and images and trying to integrate them with the inkblot (i.e., to restructure the perception of the inkblot in the light of these images), and, conversely, to try out these images for "fit" (congruence) with the inkblot play a decisive role in the typical "normal" Rorschach response.[13] These are essentially the same processes that Rorschach had in mind when he came to the conclusion that the responses to his blots are based on perception.[14]

However, perception, association, and the integration of a fitting association with the restructured inkblot lead to a "private" solution of the test task; but in order to become a response this solution has to be communicated to the tester. Hence, *communication* is the final step in the response process. The fact that the testee has to communicate his response to the tester constitutes the decisive difference between private percepts, associations, thoughts, and a test task which has to be met within the *interpersonal* test situation. This fact, in varying degrees and ways, plays a significant, co-determining role in the processes of perceiving, associating, and selecting a suitable association, because the testee knows that eventually he will have to tell the tester what he thinks the inkblot could be. The impending communication of the response thus casts its shadows—and its lights—ahead, as it were, into the ongoing process of taking in the inkblots and trying to find a likeness to them. The *style* of the communication, in addition to the perceptual qualities and the content of the response, will often reveal something about the way in which the testee experienced the fact that he has to *give* the response to the tester.[15]

---

[12] *Ibid.*, p. 18.

[13] In some responses, occurring most frequently in pathology, there is a short-circuiting of these processes so that one or the other step may be missing, especially the "trying out for congruence."

[14] They are also the processes considered decisive for the rationale of Rorschach's test by Rapaport (*op. cit.*, pp. 89–94).

[15] Style of communication is a concept different from Rapaport's concept of *verbalization*. It refers to the testee's general style of speech as well as to the

People differ a great deal in the way in which the eventual communication of the response affects their search for and finding of responses. They also differ greatly in their criteria for congruence of an image with the blot and in the rigor, rigidity, or flexibility with which they apply these criteria. These differences, in turn, may be related to the differences in their experience and definition of the test situation. The process of selection or rejection of an image as a suitable response may be so rapid as to be not in awareness, as in some "intuitive" and often quite brilliant and original responses, or it may become painfully laborious and highly conscious, as is often the case in depressive and in obsessive patients. Also, this may fluctuate within one and the same record.

While association plays a significant role in the genesis of a Rorschach response, it would be wrong to classify Rorschach's test as an association technique, as Lindzey does.[16] The test task is not, as he erroneously assumes, to respond to the inkblots with the first image or percept that comes to the testee's mind, but to say what the blot could be, what it might look like. The task is to find a *likeness* to the blot and it is left to the testee whether he wants to meet this task by telling the first image that comes to his mind or whether he wants to use his judgment and to take his time to find a fitting likeness, or to select from the images and ideas that occur to him the most fitting ones. As Rorschach said very pointedly, "the test does not induce a 'free flow from the subconscious' but requires adaptation to external stimuli, an action of the 'fonction du réel.'"[17] The most valuable material elicited by the test would be lost if it did not permit the tester to see how the perceptual, judgmental, and associative factors are interwoven in the process leading to the response, how much or how little critical judgment the testee exercises, and whether in such judgment the testee acts like a severe taskmaster and critic or like a craftsman finding satisfaction in his work, whether he gives himself to the free play of trying out various images, testing them against the reality of the inkblot, or whether there is a short-circuiting due to the pressure of an instantaneous association

---

specific style in response to the interpersonal aspects of the test situation. Rapaport's analysis of verbalization refers mainly to the thought processes in the course of associating to the inkblots and integrating association and percept. Compare Rapaport, *op. cit.*, pp. 324–366.

[16] Lindzey, *op. cit.*, p. 163.

[17] *Op. cit.*, p. 123, translation slightly changed to make it correspond more closely to the original text. See also Schafer, who emphasizes rightly the interplay of reality-testing with free phantasy. Roy Schafer, *Psychoanalytic Interpretation in Rorschach Testing* (New York: Grune & Stratton, 1954), pp. 76–77.

which precludes any judgment. There are, of course, many more ways in which association, perception, and critical, selective judgment interplay with one another and many gradations of the examples given which may shade into one another.

The conscious effort in finding a likeness to the inkblot, and the decision concerning the congruence of memory image or concept with the inkblot, distinguishes the average interpretation of an inkblot from the recognition of an object seen in everyday life. The active, structuring, and organizing processes in perceiving the inkblot and in deciding whether or not it looks like some remembered object play a much greater role in arriving at a Rorschach response than they do in *recognizing* a familiar object where the memory of the object, usually, is readily available and carries immediate conviction. In recognizing the object before me as my desk I do not have to search my memory and am not even aware that such recognition would not be possible without the activation of a memory.

Conscious effort in everyday perception does occur, however, as soon as there are obstacles to ready recognition. Such obstacles may arise, for example, from poor visibility, from an impairment of perception due to toxic conditions or to extreme fatigue, or from the perceiver's unfamiliarity with a new and strange object. If somebody walking along a road on a foggy day tries to decide what an object dimly perceived in the distance might be, he may quite consciously ask himself whether the few features of this object that are vaguely visible make it more likely that it is a tree, or a house, or a car. His decision will rest on a conscious effort to structure and give meaning to the object by comparing its few and vaguely perceived features with those of objects familiar from previous experience. The consciousness of assimilative effort, thus, is present in this case as it is in most interpretations of the Rorschach inkblots.

There is, however, an important difference between perception in the Rorschach situation and that under conditions of poor visibility or in seeing an unfamiliar object. In these latter cases the perceiver knows that it is a real object he sees and he is in doubt only about what it might be. In the Rorschach situation most people are aware that they are looking at inkblots only and not at "real" objects or at representations of real objects. The situations in which unfamiliar or unclearly seen objects are encountered usually furnish definite clues to the perceiver as to what general kind of object it might be. This is not so in the Rorschach situation. A likeness to the inkblots might be found in any

area of human experience and imagination. The situation does not limit
the areas in which to search. This freedom from limitations other than
those imposed by the features of the blots to which a likeness has to be
found may arouse the anxiety, insecurity, helplessness, doubt, and other
similar feelings to which man is prone when confronted with the wide-
open, limitless, the unknown, and thrown on his own resources without
any guidance.

But the greater scope of possible choice, which may arouse uneasiness and anxiety, may also lead to a richer, more spontaneous and creative response than in everyday perception of unknown or poorly visible
objects. This freedom of the Rorschach-test situation increases the
range of possibilities of "what the inkblot might be" in two significant
ways, each of which leads to a far greater variety of possible percepts
than pictures or reality would lend themselves to. First, the delimiting
and emphasizing process, which is present in every act of perception,
has far more possibilities in the encounter with the Rorschach blots
than in an encounter with the "reality" environment. Second, the range
of associations (content) to choose from is much wider in the Rorschach
situation than in everyday perception.

The greater range of structuring (delimiting and emphasizing) possibilities is due to the fact that the inkblot need not be taken as one
object or group of objects, that is as a unit (W response), but that the
testee is free to delimit any area within any of the inkblots and to respond to that area (D, Dd, and S responses), and that for each area
thus delimited he is free to focus on any aspect of it that he chooses or
is impressed by. In usual reality perception, the environment is structured into definite "reality" objects and their interrelations (the street,
the people on it, the houses, the cars, this particular person, this show-
window, etc.). The perceiver in the constantly changing, developing,
and shifting process of perception will focus now on one object, now on
another; but the units singled out by him are usually limited to the
objective units of reality or some aspect of them (this house, the color
of its brick wall, the door of the house, etc.). In the inkblots, while their
structure, spatial arrangement, color, and shading make it probable
that some parts (D) will be more readily singled out as "units" for
interpretation than others (Dd and S), the choice of how to delimit the
percept, and what aspect of it to emphasize, is still left to a much
greater extent to the perceiver than is the case in the object structure of
reality. The quality of this structuring process may vary widely: it may
be hesitant, tentative, groping, bewildered, anxious, unseeing, vague,

impulsive, forceful, patient, impatient, searching, laborious, intuitive, playful, indolent, actively curious, explorative, absorbed, bored, annoyed, stymied, dutiful, spontaneous, dreamy, critical, and so forth. But, whatever the quality of the testee's attempts to structure the blot, the typical Rorschach perception is a more *active* structuring process than is the typical everyday perception. More is left to the activity of the testee, to his conscious or unconscious inclination, his choice and decision, than in the perception of his environment, and also more than if we present him with more or less realistic pictures, as is done in the Thematic Apperception Test or in the Four-Picture Test, where the objects shown on the pictures are familiar and usually only their individual qualities and their relation to each other may be seen in a variety of ways.

The greater amount of active structuring in the testee's perception of the inkblot, as compared with his perception of an object of reality, goes together with and is inseparable from the *wider range of associations* (memory images) from which to choose a likeness. In everyday perception of a dimly seen or an unfamiliar object, the perceiver knows that he is confronted with a real object and, furthermore, the context of the situation together with the visible features of the object furnish many clues as to what kind of object it is likely to be or, at least, to what general class of objects it might belong. The expectations the perceiver forms on the basis of such clues and of his past experience drastically limit the range of associations among which to search for an answer to his question what this strange or only vaguely perceived object is likely to be. In the Rorschach situation such cues are absent. As a result, there are no limitations of the range of associations from which to choose an answer to the question "What might this be?" except those given by the features of the inkblot the object has to resemble.

Most testees are aware that the inkblots might resemble anything. A few believe that they are supposed to represent a definite object, but even they, as a rule, do not form definite ideas as to what kind or class of object they are supposed to "discover" in the inkblots. Usually, they merely suspect that there are definite "right" answers to the test question.[18]

The absence of limitations to the range of associations from which to

----

[18] An exception to this, which I have found sometimes among testees with a pseudo-psychoanalytic sophistication, is the idea that they are supposed to find likenesses of sexual organs. But this idea does not take the form, in my experience, that this is the only thing they are supposed to find.

choose a likeness to the inkblots has two implications. First, it offers an opportunity to study major *themes* toward which the process of associations tends to flow. Second, it permits us to study what limitations the testee imposes on the free range of associations from which to choose fitting images. Such limitations may take the form of a general, pervasive, automatic, defensive regimentation which altogether fetters the freedom and flexibility of the associative processes and often prevents the emergence of personally significant themes as well as the free play of phantasy. They may derive occasionally from a belief that the inkblots are *supposed* to resemble a definite object and that the testee's task is to find it. Or they may be linked more closely to the interpersonal aspects of the test situation and stem from the testee's feeling that the tester would disapprove of certain response contents, such as sexual content, or that certain types of content are more desirable than others.

Limitations of the range of associations may also be due to limitations of intelligence or of the range of the testee's experiences and to lack of motivation to cooperate in the test situation or to conscious or unconscious resistance against the test situation. The range of experience, in turn, depends on socioeconomic and intellectual factors and on those personality factors which determine the degree and quality of active interest and exploratory drives. Motivation to cooperate, too, may be partly determined by socioeconomic factors.

In the genesis of many, but not of all, Rorschach responses there occurs a phase in which the testee makes a conscious, selective, critical decision whether a percept that has come to his mind is or is not suitable as a response to fulfill the Rorschach task and to be communicated to the tester. In this phase the testee's conscious or unconscious definition of the test situation and of its interpersonal aspects plays an especially important role. However, the phases of perceptual structuring, associating, and tentative judgment as to the fitness of a percept to be communicated to the tester do not necessarily or even usually follow each other in time. They alternate and merge with each other and the subjective meaning of the test situation influences all of them. When there is a final decision to give a response, the testee usually does not experience this as a separate act of decision-making, except sometimes where there has been considerable doubt and hesitation as, for example, in obsessional patients or in people with marked feelings of inadequacy.

# 3/ THE NATURE OF THE TEST DATA

### II. THE EXPERIENTIAL DIMENSIONS;
### QUALITIES OF THE RORSCHACH INKBLOTS

We can give a fairly correct description of the processes underlying Rorschach responses by speaking of perception, memory, association, critical judgment as to likeness, and communication. However, this description remains rather abstract and lifeless and does not do full justice to the *experiential* meaning and range of these processes. Rorschach thought that from his test he could draw conclusions not about the content of a person's experiences but about his individually characteristic way of experiencing. He felt that "at first glance . . . [it] may appear absurd" to draw such far-reaching conclusions from the results of "so simple an experiment." [1] But I think we have to agree with him that it is not at all absurd. Experience is mediated through our perceptions of the world around us and of our inner life. Since perceptual, memory, associative, and other thought processes enter into each perception and each response, something of the experiential quality of these processes may be expected to become apparent directly in the responses or by means of a suitable analysis of the responses.

By the experiential dimensions of the testee's reactions to the Rorschach inkblots I do not mean anything *separate* from his perception of the blots or from the memory images and ideas associated with and co-determining his perception. Rather, I want to emphasize qualities of his experience in encountering the inkblots and the testing situation which, while exercising a determining influence on his percepts and partly reflected in the traditional scoring categories, nevertheless are not fully "caught" in these scoring categories.

---

[1] Rorschach, *op. cit.*, pp. 86–87.

In order to describe more fully what happens in the testee's "perception" of the inkblots, several questions have to be raised: What does the testee experience in his encounter with the inkblots and the test situation? What is his way of experiencing this encounter? How much does he permit himself to experience, or how little? How deeply and how fully does he enter into this encounter, or how detached does he try and succeed to remain from it? How varied or how stereotyped is his experience? What layers of his personality and what levels and types of mental functioning become involved in it and at what point in the encounter with each single inkblot and with the entire series of ten inkblots? To answer such questions it is necessary, first, to consider the general qualities of the inkblots and some implications of these qualities for the experiential dimension of perception.

## General Experiential Qualities of the Inkblots

The most important quality of the inkblots is their *unfamiliar structure*. They are not unstructured, as is sometimes assumed in the literature. But their structure is unfamiliar; it does not correspond closely and accurately to any familiar object. They are, as Rorschach puts it, "accidental forms"—neither purposive, as most manmade objects are, nor part of nature, organic or inorganic. They are different, thus, from the vast majority of objects in man's environment that are either made to serve a purpose or have developed as part of the natural world. There are no ready clichés for them.[2] Their unfamiliar structure makes it possible to see (structure) them in many different ways, by emphasizing some, ignoring or de-emphasizing other aspects of their structural Gestalt and their coloration or shading.

The absence for the inkblots of ready labels such as we have for the familiar objects of our environment has two consequences. First, the individual differences in perception, usually obscured by the common language labels, become more apparent; second, these differences are enhanced because in giving a response the active, structuring processes in perception are increased in comparison with ordinary, everyday perception. While these two factors overlap, they are not identical. Two people do not see a table or a chair in the same way, and this holds true

---

[2] Some blots or parts of blots, however, more closely approach a representational, pictorial quality than others, especially blot V and the lateral "animal" figure on blot VIII. They stimulate the "popular" responses (P).

even more for seeing a person, a face, a tree, a landscape. This becomes apparent very readily when one compares portraits of the same person by two different painters or the same landscape painted by two different painters. It also becomes apparent when one asks two people to describe a room they have just seen, or the same person or landscape, or even a simple object, like a flower. Their descriptions will reveal many differences in what they saw and what they failed to see and in the way they saw it, even if we discount the differences in their linguistic ability to describe something. But, usually, many individual differences in perception remain unnoticed because we do not pay much attention to what we or others see or fail to see and we do not ask them to describe it. And even when we do get a description of what two people saw, e.g., in looking at the same person or house, considerable individual differences in perception will be obscured by the identical word labels we use in talking about what we have seen, such as the dining room table, A's living room, our acquaintance Mr. X, the view from the bridge in B-town, a rose, etc. Furthermore, there are very many quite marked as well as subtle differences in perception which do not become apparent because even the richest language cannot readily describe them, much less the more limited vocabulary of everyday speech.

Since there are no ready labels for the inkblots, the testee's responses will usually make apparent what he has seen and what he has not seen or not mentioned, which features of the blot his responses emphasize and which they neglect. In addition to that, the confrontation with the unfamiliar inkblot forces the testee—or at least most testees—to look more carefully than he is likely to do in the mere registering of the familiar objects of his usual environment. This, in itself, makes for an increased activation of the perceptual process and, finally, since the structure of the inkblot offers many possibilities, the structuring and organizing aspects of perception are accentuated.

The absence of the cliché label, thus, tends to force the testee really to look and see rather than to repeat what he has learned and knows, as he does in everyday recognition. But while the absence of a label is one important experiential quality of the inkblots, the implications of this negative quality do not exhaust the significance of the inkblots' unfamiliar structure.

The unfamiliar structure also has the *positive impact of the unknown.* The unknown, the phantastic—that which is not part of, is different from, the routine of everyday life—confronts the person who encounters the inkblots. The extremely strong and prevalent tendency to experience stereotypes in our dealings with our human and nonhuman environment and to react to these stereotypes in a routine stereotyped way has the effect that the world, the other person, is not encountered with our own full personality, that therefore it does not add significantly to our experience and does not lead to growth, to a deepening and enriching of our life. Hence the emptiness of so many lives, which people fail to notice only because it is covered by a thousand activities and because a more meaningful way of life is unknown to them. While in every moment of life and in every person and every part of nature that which could touch and enrich our own life is present if only we are sufficiently open and ready to experience it, most objects of our environment can also be perceived as the cliché, the stereotype that the culture has made of them, that we have learned to use and that precludes an encounter which will add significantly to our experience and our life. The experiential significance of the inkblots lies in the fact that their phantastic and unknown quality presents a powerful appeal to encounter them, to experience them freshly because the ready label of routine "recognition" is not offered by them and therefore the possibility to dispose of them by transforming them into clichés is made more difficult. In other words, by striking at the empty shell of cliché recognition, the inkblots speak to something deeper in the person; they invite him to go to that depth where his own resources are, his resources for being a person of his own, capable of relating in a personally meaningful way to the new and unknown that cannot so easily be "handled" by routine procedures.

Such encounters with the unfamiliar, the unknown are of crucial significance for man's entire life and development. Rorschach's test, by activating on a small scale the various, individually differing experiences and reactions involved in such an encounter, renders some of them observable, in degrees varying with each testee. The significance of the encounter with the unknown is based on man's basic capacity of *openness toward the world,* which distinguishes his world from the much more closed world in which even the higher animals live. The encounter with the unknown, the new, the unfamiliar is apt to reveal how much of this openness, usually at its peak in childhood, man has maintained or how much he lives in a closed world, protecting himself from such encounters. These two possibilities are based on the fact that to man the unknown is both frightening, so that he wants to flee from it, and challenging, inviting exploration. Whether the anxiety aroused by the unknown wins out over the wish to expand one's relatedness in the encounter with the unfamiliar or whether the anxiety is overcome by this wish decides the fate of man's basic openness toward the world.[3] Similarly, the small "world" of the Rorschach inkblots invites exploration and the test instruction "What might this be?" asks for it. While practically all testees understand this explicit question, the unspoken invitation presented by the strange, unfamiliar, phantastic inkblots is heard and accepted by some, unheard or avoided by others. Some feel intrigued by the inkblots and welcome their challenge, others feel consciously or unconsciously frightened by them; they feel like a fish out of water when asked to leave the secure and "known" world of familiar objects[4] of their environment for the strange and ambiguous world of the inkblots.

Their ambiguity offers practically countless *possibilities* of perceiving them and, in responding, giving definite form to one or another of these possibilities. In this respect they confront the testee with a freedom of choice and with the predicament of this very freedom. This touches upon a basic condition of human existence that was a major subject of Kierkegaard's thought. He wrote that anxiety is the dizziness of freedom arising when freedom looks into the abyss of its own possibilities and grasps at finiteness in order to find a hold in it. But in trying to find a hold in the finite freedom loses itself.[5] Man is confronted throughout his life with many possibilities of how and what he could or might be or do. He can play with some of these possibilities; indeed, he has to play with them as most children do in order to arrive at choices. But if he does not go beyond this, his play becomes idle, as it often does in our daydreams. This may arouse the anxiety of bypassing life. If we do make choices and act on them we give up part of the freedom of unlimited possibility. And if the choice becomes a protection against the ever-

---

[3] The crucial role of the encounter with the unknown and its implications for human development are discussed in detail by Ernest Schachtel, *Metamorphosis: On the Development of Affect, Perception, Attention and Memory* (New York: Basic Books, 1959), pp. 150–154, 183–209.

[4] Of course the "familiarity" of even the most familiar object is due only to the fact that usually we approach it from the same inner perspective, hence do not discover the inexhaustible depth and variety of unfamiliar aspects under which it may be seen. To discover these other aspects is the work of creative experience such as is found among the great painters, poets, scientists, as well as among all those others who have preserved and expanded the child's capacity for wonder and discovery.

[5] Sören Kierkegaard, *Der Begriff der Angst* [*The concept of dread*] (Jena: Eugen Diederichs), pp. 56–57.

renewed challenge of the freedom of being able to live, think, act in ways other than the accustomed ones of social role, habit, custom, routine, then we may experience the anxiety of unlived life, of being dead while we are still living.[6]

In some respects, the miniature world of the unfamiliar, ambiguous inkblots resembles this situation in that the test task poses a question to which there is no "correct" answer although there are a thousand answers. Even after the testee has given a response to the question, it still remains open because it is possible to give innumerable other "answers." The testee, confronted with the "abyss" of the possibilities of the inkblot, has to decide which of the possible answers he will give and at which point he feels that he has met the task to his satisfaction even though he may be aware of the fact—not all testees are—that there remain many other possibilities. For quite a few people this decision is practically impossible to make, at least without the real or imagined approval of the tester.

While the unfamiliar structure of the inkblots activates the individual tendencies connected with the encounter with the unknown, the unknown "world" of the inkblots differs from the real world, and the encounter with them differs from that with the unknown in life in the real world. The main difference lies in the fact that the inkblots have to be dealt with in thought and phantasy only. But the man who ventures into the jungle, the traveler who goes beyond the sightseeing routine and really encounters people and ways of life different from the familiar ones, or the person who fully and openly encounters another person has to meet such reality with action, not only with thought. The inkblots remain inkblots, they do not change or react; but the unknown in life, the unknown in other people or in nature is capable of affecting and does affect our life profoundly. The described difference between the inkblots and reality is not an absolute, but a relative one because the inkblots are encountered in the test situation where the reactions, while taking place in thought and phantasy only, have to be *communicated* to another person, the tester, and this communication, depending on the various social contexts in which the testing takes place, may be

---

[6] Tolstoy's story "The Death of Ivan Ilyitch" is a masterly, compelling description of how impending death arouses this anxiety in the sudden realization of a man that his life has been spent hiding behind the respectability of his socially approved role while actually being deaf and blind to the life around him, to others, and how in the anguish of this realization his life is transformed in his struggle with and eventual acceptance of death.

felt by many testees to have important repercussions on their lives.[7] If
the testee responded to the inkblots only privately, without ever showing his responses to anybody else, they would still be individually characteristic of him, but probably different in some ways from those given
in an actual test situation.[8]

Even though the difference between the unfamiliar in the inkblots
and the unfamiliar in reality is not an absolute one, its significance becomes palpable in the type of testee who enjoys exploring the world of
the inkblots by letting his imagination play with their many possibilities
and who, without a feeling of pressure to have to produce something,
allows his ideas and associations to take over, temporarily permitting
his thoughts to take leave of the task of adaptation to life in reality.[9]
This same person may flee from, or experience severe anxiety in, the
encounter with the unknown in reality. On the other hand, to people
who lack or are inhibited in the capacity for such imaginative play, the
encounter with the inkblots may be as disquieting as the exposure to
the unknown in reality. And for those who habitually avoid the unknown—and there are many who do this and many ways of doing it—
the test situation constitutes a pressure which forces them to come to
grips in some way with the unfamiliar; this enforced contact may cause
anxiety, bewilderment, momentary disorientation and may mobilize
more or less massive defenses.

That imaginative people are stimulated by and enjoy the temporary
sojourn in the unfamiliar world of the inkblots is a consequence also of
the *phantastic quality* of the inkblots, more pronounced in some than in
others, but present in all of them. This quality is related to their unfamiliarity and strangeness yet does not coincide with them. It would be

---

[7] The above-discussed relation of the Rorschach-test situation to actual life
situations resembles that of the Szondi test. There the testee is asked which of the
people whose photographs he is shown he likes best and which he dislikes most.
To *act* on such preferences and dislikes by choices in life has much more far-
reaching consequences than to express them in relation to photographs. Yet, to
communicate the preferences or dislikes to the tester involves for the testee real
or imagined consequences different both from actual choices in life and from
private selection of the preferred or rejected photographs. This is one reason
self-administration, both in Rorschach's and Szondi's test, probably would lead
to results different from those obtained when the test is given by another person.
Compare S. Deri, *Introduction to the Szondi Test* (New York: Grune & Stratton,
1949), pp. 10–11.

[8] The degree of such differences would show significant interindividual variations.

[9] Rorschach has described this type of person more fully in his chapter on
"Imagination," *op. cit.*, pp. 102–104.

diminished or destroyed if they were more neat either in clarity of out-line, in symmetry, or in color and shading. More uniform, flat, and neat surface colors, both in the chromatic and achromatic cards, would take away from the blots much of the challenge of the unknown, to some people of the mysterious, created by the subtle gradations of shading and depth, in some parts merging gradually into each other, in others set off against each other in sharper contrast. The phantastic quality of the blots plays probably the most important role in making people think that the test is one of imagination. Rorschach thought that this idea was held by almost all subjects, so that it could be considered practically "a condition of the experiment." To some extent this has changed with the wide dissemination of information and misinforma-tion on the test by popular and scientific periodicals and by word of mouth. But what has remained, no matter whether the testee is familiar or unfamiliar with the purpose of the test, is the fact that the blots by their very nature invite the play of imagination and phantasy.

Rorschach points out that the inkblots must have a *picturelike* (*bild-haft*) quality[10] without which many testees would reject them as "just an inkblot." One factor in this picturelike quality is their *size* or scale. This is important in several respects: as relative size of the different parts of each inkblot, as relative size of the inkblot in relation to the size of the card, and as absolute size of the blot. The main component parts of the inkblots (the D) should not be disproportionate in size but should show a certain balance, otherwise the picturelike effect of the cards would be diminished or destroyed. So far as the absolute size of the blots is concerned, I want to consider primarily the requirement that neither the inkblot as a whole nor its major parts (D) should be below a certain minimal size. This point may be illustrated by a refer-ence to painting. If we compare miniature portraits, no matter how skillfully and delicately executed, with larger portraits, we notice that they do not speak to us in the same way. No miniature portrait touches us with the power, profundity, and truly human quality with which a portrait of average size by any of such great painters as Rembrandt, Leonardo, Holbein, or, among more recent painters, by Cézanne or van Gogh will speak to us. In fact, the great masters, so far as I know, did not paint miniature portraits although they sometimes drew plants, bugs, and the like, in tiny sizes (e.g., Leonardo, Dürer) with attention

---

10 *Op. cit.* [German edition], p. 15.

to minute detail. But these drawings were more in the nature of exercises. If a painting is to affect the beholder on a profound level it has to be above a minimal size; it must not be a miniature. We might say that it has to be within the "human scale," neither below nor above. By human scale I do not mean, of course, the measurements of the human body. Most portraits by the great masters are smaller than life size and yet able to convey about a human being the profoundest truth that can be conveyed. I mean the scale within which the full range of human feelings can be spoken to and respond. This scale probably has an optimum range which will be different in a portrait, in a landscape, and in an inkblot. The inkblot, too, loses its power to speak to a certain depth in the average perceiver if its size goes either below or above a certain scale.

This has a bearing on the meaning of some, not all, Dd responses. Where there is a marked emphasis on the Dd, or where for other reasons they occur where one would expect a W or D response, the tester should consider whether and for what reason the testee avoids the impact of the whole inkblot or of its larger details. Also relevant in this context is Binder's observation that the chiaroscuro (Hell-Dunkel) determinant, i.e., the perception of diffuse darkness, occurs usually only in relatively large areas of the inkblots. A tiny black area cannot be perceived, by most people, with the dysphoric implications of darkness.[11]

While Rorschach does not mention the size of the inkblots, he points out two other requirements that, in his opinion, are essential for the required picturelike quality: they should be relatively *simple,* and their arrangement in the space of the card should meet certain conditions of *spatial rhythm (Raumrhythmik)* of which their *symmetry* is a major one.[12] Both these factors are important especially for the experiential dimension of the testee's reactions. A too-complicated inkblot might stimulate confused, chaotic impressions and percepts[13] and would not

---

[11] Hans Binder, *Die Helldunkeldeutungen im psychodiagnostischen Experiment von Rorschach* (Zürich: Art. Institut Orell Füssli, 1932), pp. 30–31. For some other experiential aspects of size in Rorschach responses compare Roland Kuhn, *Maskendeutungen im Rorschachschen Versuch* [2nd edition] (Basel and New York: S. Karger, 1954), pp. 41–42, first published in *Monatsschrift für Psychiatrie und Neurologie,* 107 and 109 (1944).

[12] Beyond the role of the spatial rhythm of the blots in contributing to their "picturelike" quality, the testee's individual experience of the *spatial dynamics* and *structure* of the various inkblots often reveals significant aspects of his individual, experiential life-space. See below, pp. 33–41.

[13] The inkblots vary in the degree of their simplicity and complicatedness.

permit sufficient possibilities for the organizing, structuring tendencies in perception.

The symmetry of the blots, as Rorschach mentioned, facilitates "the interpretation of whole scenes." [14] I believe that the most significant point in these interpretations relates to the appearance of similar figures on both sides of the blot, especially in cards I, II, III, VII, VIII, IX, and X. These lend themselves readily to human or animal percepts and offer the opportunity to see some kind of relationship between the two figures. The presence or absence and the quality of such a relationship can be of diagnostic significance, as can the fact that some testees refer in their responses only to one of the two figures right and left of the central axis.

The symmetry also makes possible, and very often leads to, an unconscious identification with the inkblot. This is a result of the fact that the approximately, but never exactly, symmetrical arrangement of the two sides of the blots in conjunction with the presence of a central axis (both results of the folding of the inkblots in producing them) creates a semblance of organic forms and more especially of the anatomy of the vertebrates. Many testees actually perceive a vertebral column or spinal cord in the central axis of some of the inkblots; many others, without giving such an explicit response, make unconscious identifications of their own body image with the blot. The specific quality of such identifications often can be inferred from the way in which the central axis is perceived, by itself as well as in relation to the lateral parts. R. Kuhn seems to assume a basic trend in people to identify unconsciously with the central axis or figure, while the lateral figures are (unconsciously) felt to represent the environment. He reports that if a testee gives more responses to the central than to the lateral areas of the blot, he will be inclined to hold on more to himself; if his responses to the lateral areas are more numerous he will tend to hold on more to the world around him.[15] I doubt that the relative proportion of axial and lateral responses

---

[14] *Op. cit.*, p. 15.

[15] Kuhn, *op. cit.*, pp. 40–41. Similarly, Booth, in a comparative study of 60 patients suffering from arterial hypertension (V, or vascular, type) and 60 patients suffering from arthritis or Parkinsonism (L, or locomotor, type), reports that the L type tended to give more responses centered in the vertical axis while the V type gave more responses to lateral parts of the blot. He describes the L types as relying more on individual initiative and action, on self-assertion, and as "more concerned with what they want to do than what is given to them from the outside" and "determined more by the prompting of their inner selves than by the object world around them." In contrast, the V type "depends primarily on the . . . conditions of his environment as determinants of his conduct." Booth considers

is always a reliable indicator of these tendencies. A concrete analysis of the experiential meaning of the center and the sides of each blot for each testee and of the relation of the center to the sides appears to me a more promising procedure.[16]

The symmetry of the inkblots often becomes the object of comments and descriptions by testees, and it is safe to assume that it is noticed by all testees. Some of these comments, particularly frequently by obsessive-compulsive people, concern the fact that the symmetry is not completely exact: one side of the blot has a little protruberance not found on the other side, or the shading on one side is slightly different from that on the other side, etc. This "inexactness" is also true of all organic nature and of art (except most architecture and ornament). The symmetry of animals and plants is never exact; one side of the human face, for example, always is slightly different from the other; one side of a leaf is not the same as the other. Only in geometry, in crystals, and in manmade objects do we encounter exact symmetry, not in anything alive. The human perception of balance, visual and otherwise, of which the perception of symmetry is an outstanding, although not the only example, is not concerned with small deviations but directed toward the over-all, total feeling of balance or imbalance. Hence, the Rorschach blots are perceived as balanced and symmetrical. As soon as small asymmetries are noted, the perceiver's relation to the inkblot has undergone a change. He is no longer receptive to the over-all impact of the blot but examines it critically with a small focus, hunting as it were for "mistakes." Some testees, indeed, comment on these asymmetries as though they had caught the tester or the "designer" of the blots in a mistake, while others may feel that their alertness or brightness is being tested by watching whether or not they will discover these small deviations from exact symmetry.

---

the relation between axial and lateral responses and the quality of the axial responses a more basic indicator of introversion (the L type) and extroversion (the V type) than Rorschach's experience type (*Erlebnistypus*). Gotthard Booth, "Organ Function and Form Perception," *Psychosomatic Medicine*, 8 (1946), 367–385, 368, 370–377. Both Kuhn's and Booth's studies would seem to presuppose that the testee unconsciously *always* tends to identify the center of the blot with himself and the sides with the environment. However, I have observed many responses in which the testee clearly identifies with a lateral area while the axial area represents somebody else. For instance, in Rorschach's study of Oberholzer's patient the axis represents the magical power and strength of the father to which the patient, identified with the lateral parts of the blot, clings. Rorschach, *op. cit.*, pp. 211–12. Of course, there also can be multiple identifications.

[16] For this and other problems concerning the meaning of axial and lateral responses see also below, pp. 38–41.

The "inexactness," the lack of uniformity of the inkblots is not confined to their symmetry, but it is a significant and pervasive quality which distinguishes their form and their nuances of color and shading from the machine-made products of man as well as from his geometric and diagrammatic abstractions. The contours of the blots curve and curl in countless different ways, as do the organic forms of nature, and in some respects even more than natural objects. Their colors and shadings resemble anything but the uniform coats of paint applied by man to objects of his manufacture, and most of the colored or shaded details of the blots show more gradations of hue and intensity than, say, a leaf, a blade of grass, and many other natural, organic or inorganic objects. Their accidental shape, coloring, and shading is a significant quality, the opposite of exactness, that is essential for their unfamiliarity and ambiguity.

It is no accident that the described general qualities of the inkblots do not refer to objects in the sense of something existing independently of human experience but to objects which are part of the human world. They are qualities perceived from the human perspective, by an experiencing being. Therefore, they also would elude the attempt to describe them, in terms of a stimulus-response psychology, as having such-and-such physical or chemical properties that excite such-and-such electrochemical processes in the nervous system. They are meaningful only when viewed from the perspective of the relatedness of the experiencing person to the object experienced. This is obvious for such qualities as unknown, unfamiliar, phantastic, pictorial. But it applies also to such qualities as symmetry, balance, size, having a central axis. They could be described partly in terms of geometric space but, in such a description, would lose the meaning they have in our context.[17] This also holds true for the significant structural and other perceptual qualities which are not common to all ten blots. They may be peculiar to a single blot or they may be present, in varying degrees and configurations, in several of them. We shall now consider some of these qualities peculiar to the *individual inkblots* and some typical reactions to them.

---

[17] For the principle involved in the distinction between geometric, physical, or chemical qualities on the one hand, and experiential qualities on the other, compare Erwin W. Straus, "Aesthesiology and Hallucinations," in *Existence*, ed. Rollo May, Ernest Angel, Henri F. Ellenberger (New York: Basic Books, 1958), pp. 139–169.

### Experiential Qualities of the Individual Inkblots

Rorschach realized that the conditions for responding vary according to the different qualities of the blots. He discusses these differences in terms of the degree of difficulty of finding responses to the individual blots, the degree of difficulty for W responses, the relative strength of the stimulus for F as compared with M responses, the presence or absence of color and of striking white space. He also mentions certain differences in aesthetic appeal, namely, that card IV was generally felt to be beautiful by his subjects, that card VIII is harmonious in color and form, card IX inharmonious.[18] Of course, the facts that all blots have a form, that some are colored, that all show different kinds of shading, and that the dynamic structures of some of them, in varying degrees, act as stimuluses for movement responses are the basis of their most important, experiential qualities. The testee's reaction to these qualities is represented, to a large extent, by the determinant scores. Their experiential meaning will be discussed in detail later on.[19] Here I want to call attention to some other experiential qualities of the various inkblots which are not reflected in the usual determinant scores.

Some authors, especially interested in the interpretation of content, discuss card IV as the "father card" and card VII as the "mother card." [20] If such "meanings" of Rorschach blots are assumed to be inher-

---

[18] Rorschach, *op. cit.*, p. 52. Other investigators have taken up some of these problems more systematically; compare for example Bernard Meer, "The Relative Difficulty of the Rorschach Cards," *Journal of Projective Techniques*, 19 (1955), 43–53; E. Earl Baughman, "An Experimental Analysis of the Relationship between Stimulus Structure and Behavior on the Rorschach," *Journal of Projective Techniques*, 23 (1959), 134–183 (deals mainly with the effect of eliminating shading nuances and color, of pure outline, and of reversal of black and white); Maxwell I. Schleifer and A. William Hire, "Stimulus Value of Rorschach Inkblots Expressed as Trait and Affective Characteristics," *Journal of Projective Techniques*, 24 (1960), 164–170 (deals with subjects' choices from a multiple-choice word list, intended to be descriptive of the emotional quality of the various inkblots).

[19] See Chapters 6–10.

[20] Ephraim Rosen, "Symbolic Meanings in the Rorschach Cards: A Statistical Study," *Journal of Clinical Psychology*, 7 (1951), 239–244; Fred Brown, "An Exploratory Study of Dynamic Factors in the Content of the Rorschach Protocol," *Journal of Projective Techniques*, 17 (1953), 251–279; I. O. Sims, "An Approach to the Study of the Stimulus Significance of the Rorschach Ink Blots," *Journal of Projective Techniques*, 24 (1960), 64–66. Richards asserts that the testee's perception of the two dominant figures in cards II and III reveals his unconscious (II) and conscious (III) perception of the relation between his parents, that the testees react to card V "as to themselves or their concept of themselves," and also mentions the "father" and "mother" cards (IV and VII); T. W. Richards, "Personal

ent in the objective stimulus of the blot or to be regularly "read" into the card by the testee, such an assumption will lead to faulty interpretations. The reasons for these misinterpretations are mainly two: One is the assumption that all testees will perceive a big man or such visual qualities as massiveness, powerfulness, possibly an aggressive stance, or threatening darkness in card IV; the other is the additional assumption that these qualities will be associated by the testee with feelings about his or her father. Similarly, the assumption is made that card VII will be perceived as a woman and/or as feminine, delicate, etc., and that these qualities will be associated by the testee with feelings about his or her mother. However, while qualities such as massiveness or delicacy can be seen and often are seen in cards IV and VII respectively, they are not seen by everybody. I doubt, for example, that Rorschach's subjects who felt card IV to be beautiful,[21] or some other testees who were intrigued by its "mysteriousness" reacted necessarily to a "masculine-aggressive-father" complex; or that people who give the response "children" or "rabbits" or "thunderclouds" to card VII experience this blot as feminine or react necessarily to a complex of feelings (conscious or unconscious) about their mother. While one often finds reactions of anxiety to card IV, these may derive from experiences other than the testee's relation to the father. In many American families in which the mother has the dominant role and the father is either the weaker personality or remote from the family, the anxiety may indeed have to do with the testee's relation to the mother. Even when a man is seen in card IV and women in card VII, the attributes the testee may give to the man (such as threatening, clumsy, big feet, puny arms, etc.) or to the women (delicate, stubborn, cute, aggressive, etc.) do not necessarily refer to the way in which he consciously perceives or unconsciously experiences his father or mother. I am convinced that it is misleading to assume that any specific content can be assigned to any particular card and serve as the basis for the assumption that, whatever the testee's reaction, it will have some relation to this assumed "meaning" of the inkblot.

---

Significance of Rorschach Figures," *Journal of Projective Techniques,* 22 (1958), 97–101. While these authors do not claim that card IV and card VII are always the father and mother cards, respectively, the belief that this "meaning" of cards IV and VII can be assumed regularly is widespread. In many years of teaching advanced students of Rorschach, I have been told by a great number of them that they have been taught this. I do not know to what extent these reports are reliable and to what extent the student's need for a fixed meaning may lead to a distortion of what he has been taught.

[21] Rorschach, *op. cit.,* p. 52.

Instead, it is more fruitful to examine the distinctive perceptual qualities of the various blots and significant and typical reactions to these qualities.[22] The structural and other perceptual qualities in which the various inkblots differ from each other are best described by arranging them around certain *perceptual themes* each of which, in turn, may be thought of as extending between two opposite poles. Many of these themes are linked to the *form* structure of various blots. However, most of them have at the same time to do with the perception of the distribution of *mass* and *expanse*. This factor has not been taken into account by the Rorschach literature, although it plays a role in many form responses as well as in the other determinants.

One perceptual theme ranges between the poles *unity* and *dispersal* or *fragmentation*. Unity is an important element of the "picturelike quality" that Rorschach considers essential for his inkblots. The quality of unity has some relation to, but is not identical with, the readiness with which the blot lends itself to W responses. If one looks at the inkblots without any attempt to find an answer to the test question "What might this be?," they all have unity; they all, indeed, have a picturelike quality, and one of the essential elements of a picture is that it have unity. But the *degree* of unity, its compellingness, varies from one blot to another. Without attempting to suggest a scale of degrees of unity, I would say that I, II, IV, V, VI, VIII, and even IX[23] have considerable unity, VII occupies perhaps an intermediate position, and III and X tend more toward dispersal. Card III, however, has a unique position on the continuum of unity and fragmentation, because of the separation between the torso and leg of the two popular human figures. As soon as the leg is seen as part of the body, as it is in the popular response, the separation is disregarded or de-emphasized and the blot, or at least the two figures, is usually seen with a feeling of unity. When the popular leg part is not seen as a leg, this is usually due to perceptual emphasis on the separation. Rorschach comments that prob-

---

[22] A purely objective exploration of the different structure of each inkblot has been suggested by Rudolf Arnheim, "Perceptual and Aesthetic Aspects of the Movement Response," *Journal of Personality,* 19 (1951), 265–281. Klein and Arnheim have given an example of it in an analysis of card I; Abraham Klein and Rudolf Arnheim, "Perceptual Analysis of a Rorschach Card," *Journal of Personality,* 22 (1953), 60–70. While their statement that "the stimulus in itself is a perceptual thing that can be defined objectively by measurable shape, size, proportion, orientation, color, etc." is quite true, their own analysis does not rely on objective measurement but much more on what I would call the human perspective, and rightly so.

[23] Even though Rorschach considered IX as lacking harmoniousness both in color and in form, it nevertheless has unity. But it is difficult to find a W for it.

ably kinesthetic perception is necessary to enable the testee to overlook this separation.[24] This establishes a link between the capacity to see the figures as alive and the experience of unity. The feeling of fragmentation, indeed, often goes together with the feeling of some impairment of full aliveness.

A different distribution results if we do not consider the question of unity versus dispersal, but the ease or difficulty with which the blots lend themselves to W responses.[25] Then V, I, VII, II lend themselves, approximately in this rank order, relatively easily to W responses, while it is more difficult to find W for X, IX, III, VIII, VI and IV.[26] The two distributions overlap, especially at their extreme poles. Thus, V lends itself most readily to a W response and probably has the most compelling unity, while X is both the most dispersed and the most difficult for W.

The described differences between the various inkblots are important for the interpretation of Rorschach records. A good W response to a blot which facilitates the giving of W responses has a different weight than a good W to a blot that makes it difficult to find a W. Similarly, the meaning of a testee's sensitivity to unity and dispersal has to be evaluated differently if he experiences unity in a rather dispersed blot than if he perceives it in a blot with strong inherent unity. To experience mainly fragmentation in a strongly unified blot is likely to point to some pathology, while dispersal perceived in X need not have this meaning.

The *meaning* of special sensitivity to the unity-fragmentation continuum is different from the meaning of W as compared with D or Dd, yet has some relation to it. The compulsion to give W responses to all ten blots, sometimes as many as possible, is an often-observed phenomenon. It may point to intellectual ambition or to a narrow and exacting subjective definition of the test task which, in turn, may be a result of an authoritarian attitude of the testee in which the submission to a strict authority in the sense of wanting to excel in the eyes of the au-

---

[24] *Op. cit.*, p. 25.

[25] W is used in this context in Beck's sense: a response which is given to the entire inkblot, also in III, where Rorschach scored W even if the red areas were not included. As soon as one considers Klopfer's cut-off W as a whole response, it becomes, of course, much easier to give whole responses to II, III, IV, and VI than if one scores according to Rorschach or Beck.

[26] Neither the classification according to unity or dispersal of the blot, nor that according to ease or difficulty of finding W, rests on statistical data. The former is based on a perceptual analysis of the blots and on occasionally obtained reactions of testees, the latter on an over-all impression based on clinical experience.

thority or the wish to be like such an authority may predominate. These testees may feel distress and a sense of frustration or failure if they cannot live up to such an ambitious and inflexible goal. However, in some testees one encounters a qualitatively different distress or uneasiness when they experience a blot as being fragmented and lacking in unity. Their preoccupation with and sensitivity to unity and the lack of it are not due to an ambition to find W. These are often people who, usually unconsciously, feel or fear that *they* are not "whole," have no unity, are fragmented, disperse their energies and talents, are pulled in different directions by their conflicts, or have not been able to find goals and give direction to their lives. Unity, for them, becomes a vital matter rather than an ambitious intellectual achievement; lack of unity a threat to the core of their personalities rather than a failure in an assigned (or self-assigned) task. They project these feelings onto the inkblots just as they may have a heightened experience of chaos and disorder in their environment. They are not aware of this process of projection and usually also not, or not fully, of the feared lack of unity in themselves. Often they may depend on their environment—including the transient environment constituted by the Rorschach blots—to provide a unity they do not feel sure of in themselves. In these people, the "energy of associative activity" and the special sort of volition considered by Rorschach as the primary prerequisites of the W response[27] may have their source not only in a certain ambition but also in a vital need for unity. Of course, the two are not mutually exclusive. However, the described need for unity in no way guarantees the production of W. In fact, where the feeling of lack of unity is strong, it may interfere with the ability to produce good W.[28]

The theme of unity bears some relation to two other themes, those of

---

[27] Rorschach, *op. cit.*, p. 59.

[28] It would be an interesting task for research to investigate systematically, on the basis of clinical material, the quality of the various inkblots and of reactions to them with regard to (1) the degree of unity, (2) the ease or difficulty with which they elicit W responses, (3) the differential meaning of sensitivity to unity and fragmentation as compared with W production. Obviously, in such research the important qualitative differences of different W and their different meanings have to be taken into account. Compare to the latter point the significant contributions of Albert Furrer, *Der Auffassungsvorgang beim Rorschach'schen psychodiagnostischen Versuch* (Zürich: Buchdruckerei zur Alten Universität, 1930), and Roland Kuhn, "Some Problems Concerning the Psychological Implications of Rorschach's Form Interpretation Test" in Maria A. Rickers-Ovsiankina (ed.), *Rorschach Psychology* (New York and London: John Wiley & Sons, 1960), pp. 319–340, 332–334; in the same book also Laurence Hemmendinger, "Developmental Theory and Rorschach Method," pp. 58–79.

*connectedness* versus *separateness* and *solidity* (or *holding together*) versus *fragility* (or *falling apart*). In "unity," the blot is perceived essentially as *one* coherent thing or scene or, in a lesser degree of unity, as a collection of things, for example the responses "butterfly collection" or "aquarium" to card X. In "connectedness" the unity exists only by virtue of *links* between different parts or because different parts touch each other at some point. The blots which, because of their structure, are most likely to elicit responses bearing on the theme of connectedness are VIII, X, and VII, rarely I and II. I have encountered the theme of connectedness in IV, V, VI, and IX only rarely; their intrinsic structure does not stimulate the perception of this theme. It occurs in III, as already discussed, with regard to the separation between the leg and torso details of the two popular human figures. VIII, X, and VII have clearly set-off D areas all or (in X) many of which touch at a relatively small point other D areas. Some testees explicitly comment on the flimsiness of these connections or, less frequently, on their strength; or they may carefully inspect card X to find out whether or not everything is connected with everything else. In card VIII, they may comment that only a thin thread seems to connect the blue with the bottom red and orange areas, or they may compare this connecting link with the ones provided by the popular "animals" whose feet touch on both the bottom pink-orange area and the top gray area. They may find all these connections not solid enough, or—as one testee did—feel that the "inner" link is too weak, but that the figure is held together by the two animals. In this case, the testee suffered from a lack of wholeness in himself and tried to compensate for this by relying on his family and on a compulsive order that he imposed on his activities as well as on certain objects and arrangements in his environment; these had to supply a unity, a stable framework without which he felt uneasy. Similarly, he had hoped that, by founding a family, his life would acquire a direction, meaning, and unity it lacked. But his hope was not fulfilled and turned out to be a demand and burden on his family. The *search for connectedness*, especially in X, often expresses a dependent attachment to others and a neurotic fear of separation which may go back to an original trauma or fear of separation from the mother.

The theme of *solidity* (holding together) versus *fragility* or *precariousness*, like the theme of unity, usually expresses a concern about the testee's own feeling of strength or fragility which may be projected on the environment in which he lives; it also may have been, early in his life, a significant experience concerning his parents or parent-substitutes, and thus may have come to color his later relations to people as well as becoming part of his self-image. Card VII is the one most likely to elicit this theme from people in whom it plays a significant role. This is due to the narrow links between the bottom detail, the two lateral details immediately above, and the two details on top of these. The blot lends itself to be seen as an organic whole, e.g., two people. In this case the narrow links are usually perceived as the neck and waist of the person and not as particularly fragile. However, when the upper four D are seen as resting on the lower D, or when each D is seen as relatively independent of the others, the emphasis may (but need not) shift to fragility or precariousness, e.g., "two people precariously seated on a rock," or, "four rocks balanced on top of another rock." The connections between the various D in VIII or X are also sometimes perceived as fragile or brittle.

Solidity (or massiveness) may also contrast with *hollowness* or *emptiness,* especially in blots with a striking central white area, such as II and VII. When these S areas are perceived not as background or as separate figures but as hollowness of the whole figure, it points to the testee's sensitivity to the theme solidity versus hollowness. A related phenomenon is the occasionally occurring percept of the central axis as hollow, e.g. in VI.

*Massiveness,* most frequently experienced in card IV, may also contrast with *delicacy,* the perception of which may be stimulated by the forms of card VII, the color of card VIII, the form and/or colors of card X. In this pair of opposites the value emphasis of massiveness often is not on the positive feeling of desirable solidity, but on a negative tone of clumsiness or threat, while delicacy, in contrast to fragility, acquires a positive meaning.

The perception of *stability,* often related to that of solidity, is an instance of another group of themes. What they have in common is the importance to them of a basic fact in human perception and human life: that man perceives himself and the objects of his environment in implicit reference to the gravitational field in which he lives and to his own body and its upright posture with its emphasis on the vertical axis (symbolized by the human spine) and balance around this axis. The occurrence of these themes, too, varies not only in accordance with their significance for different people but also with the degree to which the particular structure of some inkblots is more apt to activate these themes than is the structure of other blots. The theme of stability versus precariousness is linked to the perception of the gravitational field and is often stimulated by card VII, in which the people are seen by some as precariously balanced while this idea does not occur to the majority of testees.

Another form in which the theme of stableness or unstableness occurs is the perceptual emphasis on the presence or absence of a solid, firm *basis* or *fundament.* The structure of cards VI, VII, and IX is particularly likely to evoke this theme, VI and IX because they have a solid base (the large lower D in VI, the pink bottom D in IX), VII because it, too, has a large D base but one which "rests" on the ground only with the center of its bottom edge and curves slightly upward from the center on both sides. Occasionally one encounters this theme also in IV and V. Some testees remark that the "feet" of the human figure in card IV do not stand on the ground but, in relation to the bottom center D, are up in the air. Some of them will account for this by seeing the figure as seated on the bottom center D, with feet dangling, thus furnishing a basis, while others will emphasize more the lack of something to stand on. Even those who see the figure as seated with feet dangling express in such a response their feeling that the feet are up in the air. This contrasts with the more usual perception in which the figure is seen as standing, walking, or jumping up and down. The contrast is significant since the latter percepts lack the concern with the ground to stand on while the former may be due to such a concern. It is even more striking when the question of a base or ground to stand on comes up in card V, where it is rare. Yet I have observed it in a few records where the testee expressed the feeling that the animal or person, seen in the whole or in the center D of V, had nothing to stand on.[29] The perceptual preoccupation with the presence or absence, stability or lability of the *base* usually points to the testee's feelings of insecurity which take the form of concern, doubt, fear regarding whether he has a firm ground to stand on or whether he can stand firmly on his own feet. He may or may not be aware of these feelings.

The significance of the gravitational field and man's upright posture also applies to the perception of the *central axis* of the blots and *its relation to the lateral areas.*[30] The axis, or median detail (mD), is more

---

[29] This, of course, is a very different percept from the frequent one in which V is seen as a bat, bird, or butterfly flying.

[30] For some comments on the general axial and symmetrical structure of all

prominent in some blots than in others, especially in IV, VI, VIII, IX, and—the center figure rather than the center line—in I. In II the center line is fairly prominent but discontinuous; in VII it is quite prominent but limited to the lower third of the blot, while between the two upper thirds there is a striking white space. In III and X it is less pronounced. In V the structure of the blot invites W responses (the popular bat or butterfly) more strongly than in any other blot, and where the testee responds to this quality there is usually no separate emphasis on the center, except on its upper and lower projections (head and feet; or the "tail" of the swallowtail butterfly). Hence it is of interest when the center line or figure assumes a special role, either as a separate figure or in dynamic tension with the lateral parts of the W figure. These differences in the structure of the blots affect the frequency and significance of responses dealing with the center axis by itself as well as in its relation to the sides.

In the blots in which the median detail or axis is prominent the testee often identifies, consciously or unconsciously, with it. He may do so by identifying his whole person or his inner core, his—figurative or literal —backbone, i.e., his own central axis, with the mD. Whether he does one or the other depends partly on the structure of the mD. For example, the central "human figure" in card I often leads to an identification of the whole person with this figure. However, even where no human figure is seen but, e.g., a spinal column or a pole, the testee may identify his whole person with these percepts, sometimes in the *pars-pro-toto* mode frequent in primary process thought; or he may identify his backbone with the mD, while the rest of the blot may be omitted or experienced, vaguely and hardly ever explicitly, as his body on either side of the backbone.

Whenever there is reason to assume such identifications,[31] two questions should be examined. First, how is the quality of the mD perceived; second, what is the quality of the relation between the mD and the lateral areas of the blot?

The mD of card VI, for example, may be perceived as solid, as a

---

ten inkblots and its implications see above, pp. 28–29. Since the frequent identification of the testee with the axial and of his environment with the lateral areas has been discussed there, it will not be repeated in the following examination of the significance of axial responses.

[31] As already mentioned, these identifications are usually unconscious. Even where there is a dim or clear awareness of them, they are hardly ever explicitly communicated by the testee.

backbone, or otherwise analogous to vertebrate structure. Its relation to the lateral parts, consciously or unconsciously, may be that it gives hold and firmness to them, holds them upright. Similarly, in card I, the central figure in the popular response is seen as the body, the lateral areas as the wings of a butterfly, bat, or bird, or sometimes as a person with the lateral areas as wings, e.g., of an angel or of the statue "Winged Victory." In these examples, too, the central figure is actually seen as the center, the most important part anatomically, that holds everything together or to which the wings are "attached." However, even when the central D of I is seen as (the body of) a person, its relation to the lateral areas may differ considerably from the popular response. It may be perceived as small, weak, helpless, and the lateral D as big, large, powerful, sometimes as doing something to the center figure—lifting it up, dragging it away, pulling at it in opposite directions, or (without explicit activity) as having power over it. Often in such responses the testee identifies with the central figure as a child (himself as a child) while the lateral figures may be symbols of parents or parent-substitutes.[32]

In other axial responses the mD may be seen as hollow or weak rather than solid and strong, e.g., as a tube, or as soft, or as indicating a rift or split between the two lateral parts where they do not hold together well. Or it may be seen as something separating or dividing the two lateral parts, such as a tunnel, a valley, a gorge, or a river. It may have both dividing and uniting functions, as for instance a seam or a zipper. Or it may be perceived as a solid object used to sever the two parts, often with aggressive or destructive implications, such as a knife, a dagger, the path of a bullet.

Furthermore, the center may be seen as shielded, protected, surrounded, or else as oppressed, closed in, or caught by the sides, rather than as supporting and being the source of strength and stability. The perception of a soft, vulnerable, or weak center being shielded by a tougher or stronger outside may represent a particular kind of defensive armor in which an unconscious aspect of the body image may resemble the structure of a shellfish or crustacean rather than of a vertebrate. Emphasis on the protective, shielding, barrier quality of the body envelope (skin, fur, armor, etc.), of course, can and does occur also where the central axis is perceived as vertebrate. As mentioned before, the lateral figures may be perceived as holding the center together

---

[32] Another meaning may be the center as the weak ego in the grip of strong, conflicting drives. The two meanings are not mutually exclusive.

rather than the center supplying solidity and unity to the whole. Or they may be seen as clinging to the center for support or otherwise being dependent on it, and the testee, as in Oberholzer's patient, may be identified with their dependence.

I do not want to interpret here in detail the various qualities and relations of axis,[33] lateral areas, and periphery. Instead, I want to mention briefly some other themes related to the qualities of the various inkblots. They may be designated as directedness versus diffusion; focused or unfocused; smoothness, evenness versus raggedness, jaggedness; fluid versus angular lines; openness versus closedness; shelter versus oppression; pointedness versus roundness; completeness versus incompleteness; viable space and freedom to move versus crowdedness and collision (especially in card X). Another theme is that of definiteness versus indefiniteness, formlessness, elusiveness.[34] All the structural qualities of the blots (and the emphasis they receive in test responses) mentioned so far concern their form and structure. There are other qualities (e.g., of color or shading or texture) that also are significant. For example: softness versus hardness (of texture); dryness versus wetness; smoothness (pleasant tone) versus sliminess (unpleasant tone); warmth versus coldness (of color or of texture); lightness versus darkness.[35] Phenomenological, clinical, and statistical exploration of the various perceptual themes, of their relation to particular blots or areas of blots, and of their significance is a largely unexplored and promising field for research.[36]

---

[33] The perceptual quality of the axis sometimes also plays a significant role in axial responses with sexual content. These occur frequently in cards II, VI, VII, not quite so frequently in IV, VIII, IX. Where the male genital is seen, the axis is usually perceived as firm; where the female genital is seen in the axis it is perceived as a cleft and soft. This is not of particular significance where it is suggested by the axial structure of the blot. But it does become significant where the percept runs counter to the essential structure of the blot, as when the male genital is seen in the lower axis of II or VII, or the female in the top axial D of II. The interpretation of confusion of sexual identity is not always correct in these cases, although often it may be. But it omits the significant element of what the response may suggest about the testee's concrete experience of and identification with these different axial qualities. It should alert the tester to pay careful attention to related axial responses, whether their content is sexual or not.

[34] These can be qualities of the blots experienced by the testee as well as qualities of his response of which he may not be aware. These two possibilities do not exclude each other. Concerning responses with vague form level compare below, pp. 106, 117–118.

[35] On the significance of darkness see Binder, *op. cit.* Reactions to darkness are stimulated especially by cards IV, V, and I.

[36] Loiselle and Kleinschmidt have touched on it in their paper on the stimulus value of the Rorschach blots. But most of the categories they used do not relate at

There are some generally valid requirements and some rules of thumb for the *interpretation* of *perceptual themes* such as those mentioned earlier. Any interpretation should be made only in the context of the over-all picture emerging from the test material. In many interpretations it is important to try to find out with which area of the blot the testee identifies himself or, if there are multiple identifications, which is likely to be conscious or unconscious and which is of more basic importance in the structure of the personality. As a rule of thumb one may assume that the *recurrence* of a similar perceptual quality and of similar dynamic relations points to the importance of the trend expressed in these percepts. Similarly, a sensitivity to very slight structural or other qualities of the blot is often more significant than the more popular reactions to very obvious qualities. Of particular significance is the kind of originality that *reverses* a commonly or frequently perceived quality of the blot. Such a percept runs counter to the essential structure of the blot. For example, card V is probably the card with most unity, offering the most compelling and easily seen W, in the popular bat, butterfly, or bird responses. Usually there is no special articulation of the central axis which, in these responses, is implicitly assumed to be the body of the flying creature, sometimes with explicitly mentioned antennae or ears at the top and legs or a tail at the bottom center. If the wings are seen as disproportionately large, the percept shifts in the direction of less unity and, possibly, an implicit strain on the center axis which becomes explicit if the wings are perceived as too heavy for the body. If, however, this blot is seen as split in the center, or falling apart, this runs counter to the structure of the blot, hence indicates a very significant and strong trend in the testee to experience himself as torn apart or falling apart and finding no central support in himself. Thus, a borderline schizophrenic woman gave the response: "This just suggests to me an impression of disintegration, falling in two, feet going to buckle," and added in the inquiry: "Not a bird, nothing that can fly, perhaps a rabbit. Not an impression of wings. Something that comes out of the body and is splitting it."

---

all or not directly to structural qualities of the blots such as those discussed here. Many refer to physiognomic characterizations, and some of these are only distantly, indirectly, or tenuously related to the qualities of the blot. Robert H. Loiselle and Ann Kleinschmidt, "A Comparison of the Stimulus Value of the Rorschach Ink Blots and Their Percepts," *Journal of Projective Techniques*, 27 (1963), 191–194.

What does the testee experience when he encounters the inkblots in the test situation? It is not possible to know or describe the full experiential range of reactions occurring in people who take Rorschach's test. At this point, I shall consider only the experiential dimension of some significant ways in which testees react to the encounter with the inkblots, emphasizing especially the reactions to the unfamiliar structure of the inkblots, to the quality of the unknown, and to the absence of rules and guideposts in the test situation. Actually, when analyzing the experiential quality of the encounter of the testee with an inkblot one can separate only artificially the subjective from the objective sides of this encounter, the testee's reactions from the qualities of the inkblot. The ways in which the objects of the world, in this case a series of inkblots, are experienced by man depend on the manner of his approach: The richer, more many-sided, and open toward the world the perceiver is, the richer, more varied, and alive will be the object world he encounters. The object will reveal itself fully only to the person who turns to it fully, with all his sensibilities and capacities. Conversely, the person who represses much of his own inner reality equally has to shut out by selective inattention or other mechanisms of avoidance those aspects of reality outside him which might touch on that which he represses. The person whose sensibilities have been starved and impoverished is no longer able to see the full range of the world accessible to man. Thus, man and his world cannot ever be separated, but can be understood only in their interrelation. Man can experience the world only in his own, the human, ways; this is as true of his scientific attempts to under-

43

stand or manipulate the world as it is, in a different way, of his immediate sensory experience.

Expressed in the most general way, the reactions of testees range all the way from a full encounter with the inkblots in which the whole personality with all its layers is engaged on a wide range of levels of functioning, resulting in a considerable variety and flexibility of experiences and responses, to an almost complete avoidance of the encounter either by rejection of the test task or, more frequently, by the mobilization of massive defenses against all but the most superficial, stereotyped, and rigidly controlled reactions. Most testees' reactions lie somewhere between these two extremes and, in addition, fluctuate between a more complete and profound experience in some and a more superficial one in other responses, with individually varying, characteristic types of sensibilities, defenses, and ways of coping with the task before them.

The implications of this experiential range for the perceptual and associative processes stimulated by the test task may be clarified and illustrated by considering various types of reactions. From these illustrations it will also become more apparent that perception and association are not clearly separated in reality but that what we see is already co-determined by our associative bent (expectations, structural emphases of total experience of reality, idiosyncratic perspectives and preoccupations, etc.) and what we associate is co-determined by the individually characteristic way in which we are impressed by the environing world. Or, more accurately, both perception and association bear the stamp of the individually characteristic way of experiencing and reacting to experience, of relating to world and self.

To *perceive* the inkblots fully requires, as does the full perception of *any* object, that the perceiver be open and receptive and that he turn fully toward them, not only with part of his personality, not only for example with detached, critical observation and judgment, but with all his sensibilities, thoughts, and feelings, so that all chords of his being are receptive to and may be touched or struck by and respond to the impact of the inkblot.[1]

Openness and receptivity must not be confused with passivity. In visual perception the latter means being passively impinged upon, while the former mean being turned toward, tuned in on, attentive to.

---

[1] For a more detailed discussion of the concept of turning fully to the perceptual object compare Schachtel, *op. cit.*, pp. 180–181, 220–235.

Open, receptive attention differs also from looking *for* something and from wanting to impose one's own thoughts, principles, categories, or wishes rather than letting the object speak for itself. Freud deals with this difference when he recommends that the psychoanalyst, in listening to the patient, maintain an "evenly suspended attention," [2] and contrasts it with deliberate, concentrated attention that wants to retain.

The visual impressions of the inkblots, openly received, will touch upon memories and sensibilities which resonate in the associations to the inkblot. This again differs both from passivity, which is bound to the immediately striking stimulus, and from strained activity, which wants to dispose of the impression by quickly categorizing it.[3]

Openness, receptivity, and full responsiveness are not possible if, for instance, the testee feels under great pressure to produce as many responses as possible and to do so as quickly as possible; or if he feels that his responses should meet a strict standard of exact likeness; or if he feels that he should be at all times completely matter-of-fact, "objective," and not have any feelings about the inkblots; or that he must see only things "which are completely acceptable to everyday conventional logic." [4] These are examples of fairly frequent, rather concrete, and specific subjective definitions of the test task which are apt to interfere with a rich, varied, flexible, or profoundly meaningful perception of the inkblots, and with the free play of the associative process.

There are other, more subtle, pervasive, and generalized pressures that, in many testees, interfere with a full perception of the inkblot and often with a full perception of the world around them. In order to perceive anything fully, one has to let the object of perception *be*, be-

---

[2] Sigmund Freud, *Recommendations for Physicians on the Psychonalytic Method of Treatment* [Standard Edition], XII, 111–112. These differences in the quality of attention are, in Freud's theoretical model, the consequence of different distributions of attention-cathexis which lead to different qualities of experience. For a discussion of these two types of attention (in relation to the perception of subliminal stimuli) compare Morris Eagle, "Personality Correlates of Sensitivity to Subliminal Stimulation," *Journal of Nervous and Mental Disease*, 134 (1962), 1–17, with further references, especially to Klein's work. Compare also my concept of *oscillation* between these two types of attention, below, Chapter 5, pp. 58–61.

[3] This type of strained activity is often found in persons who are basically passive in the sense of a dread of the unknown, of venturing, and who want to restore quickly a closed world of what is familiar to them.

[4] This last requirement, according to Rapaport, is what "normal" testees by and large feel and which he therefore uses as a yardstick to define the normal "reality of the testing situation," deviations from which he considers weaknesses of reality orientation and reality testing implying pathological tendencies. Rapaport, *op. cit.*, p. 329. For a critical discussion of this viewpoint, see below, pp. 61–73.

fore doing anything with it or to it, even if what one does with it is not a physical action but merely a mental labeling or filing away or some other way of not taking it in fully. If one is in a hurry to think or say that this object is such-and-such or is like such-and-such, one is apt to turn away from it with an implicit feeling that this is all there is to it, and one may thereby cut off the possibility of a full encounter with the object. The subjective side of letting the object be is permitting it to have its full impact on one, allowing one's impression of it to develop, letting it "grow" on one, so that one may clearly know and feel what it is like. To many people the familiar objects remain unknown *because* their very familiarity becomes an easy and convenient way of disposing of them. Believing that they know all about them, they quickly turn away from them, thus ossifying them in an unchanging schema of familiarity. If they encounter something new they are likely to "dispose" of it in a similar way, namely, by quickly trying to label it, placing it in some familiar category, rather than staying with it long enough to come to know it more fully for what it is.

These ways of avoiding a full encounter with both the familiar and the new or strange stem from man's universal uneasiness in the face of the unknown, the as-yet pathless. In relation to familiar objects this uneasiness and anxiety usually does not become apparent because the perception of them as being "familiar" has, among other functions, that of preventing an encounter with their unknown aspects, their "other side," their hidden depths; that is to say, the feeling of familiarity can have and often does have a defensive function, in addition to its more predominant and obvious function of recognition. To perceive the unknown in the familiar requires a change of attitude, a fresh approach, an openness instead of the fixed, accustomed perspective that is comparable to the animal's perception, which is predetermined by a relatively closed instinctive organization. And once one does perceive the hitherto unknown in the familiar, one may have to change one's accustomed attitude even more radically, all of which is anxiety-provoking at the same time as it can be a liberating expansion of one's horizon and of one's relation to other people and to the world around one. Thus, the very fact of familiarity functions both as a protective and a restrictive device, offering protection against the anxiety and disquiet of the encounter with the unknown and restricting man's vision and experience to the *status quo*, preventing change of his attitudes and ways of life, expansion of his horizons, deepening of his relatedness to whom and what he already "knows."

The *unfamiliar* object does not offer such ready defenses against the unknown as the familiar does. Thus, it is often more likely to activate anxiety and uneasiness than the desire to explore the unknown and to relate to it with expanding capacities and developing attitudes. The unfamiliar object, in some respects, is potentially capable of renewing and bringing to the fore man's basic situation: of being in the wide-open, the pathless, with few innate patterns to guide him, of having countless possibilities of finding *his* way in and to the world open to him. This situation is both his glory and his predicament; it constitutes his potential richness, his freedom, as well as threatens him with anxiety, from which he may try to escape by protecting himself in a closed but stagnant world of a repertoire of familiar pathways.[5] The phenomena of tolerance and intolerance of ambiguity[6] are special instances of man's ways of coping with this basic situation. The assimilation of the unknown to the known world of man by establishing links between the two may be based on an open approach to the unfamiliar, permitting man to take it in fully, or on a defensively narrowed approach that forces it into the perspective of a preconceived schema. In the Rorschach-test situation a testee's constrictive, subjective definition of the test task often leads to such a limited approach while the testee usually is quite unaware of the defensive function of his approach as well as of the fact that he, not the tester, has defined the task in this particular way. By narrowing down the test task he restricts the ways in which the inkblots may be perceived, thus excluding certain of their aspects as well as preventing them from having all the impact they might have. "Handling" the inkblots and the test task in a certain way is both a means of assimilating them and of shutting out other ways of handling them, and thus has both constructive, assimilating, and defensive avoiding functions. When the way in which they are handled is a rigid one the defensive function is likely to be predominant.

The readiness to feel uneasiness, insecurity, or anxiety in the face of an unfamiliar object is heightened, for many people, in the Rorschach-test situation, because not only is the object encountered strange, phantastic, unfamiliar, but also because no detailed rules and directions are given or readily available as to what to do with this object and how to behave with regard to it. I believe that the sensitivity of Rorschach's

---

[5] Compare Schachtel, *op. cit.*, pp. 70–75, 183–209.

[6] See Else Frenkel-Brunswick, "Intolerance of Ambiguity as an Emotional and Perceptual Personality Variable," in *Perception and Personality*, ed. Jerome S. Bruner and David Krech (Durham, N.C.: Duke University Press, 1949–50), pp. 108–143.

test to anxiety reactions is based mainly on the combined effect of the phantastic, unfamiliar quality of the inkblots and the nondirective structure of the Rorschach-test situation, and only secondarily on the specific stimulus of the pronounced shading of cards IV, VI, and VII, which the Rorschach literature usually treats as the main catalyst of anxiety reactions. The anxiety-arousing quality of the perceptual object and the Rorschach-test situation sometimes leads to an outspoken *orientation shock* when the testee is confronted with the first inkblot, and very often it leads to initial orientation difficulties, which can be manifested in many different ways, among them paucity of response or compensatory over-responsiveness to card I; coartated reaction to card I in contrast to dilation in later cards; comments, remarks, and questions, etc. Similarly, the so-called *color shock* probably is as much due to the fact that with the introduction of color a sudden unexpected change occurs and the testee is again confronted with an unfamiliar, new situation, as it is to the specific quality of the experience of color.

The uneasiness, disquiet, or anxiety the strange world of the inkblots potentially and often actually can arouse in the testee may be warded off or escaped from in a variety of ways. Some typical examples may serve as illustrations. Some schizophrenic patients, shortly before the onset of an acute schizophrenic episode, produce coartated or very coartative Rorschach records with few responses, some of which may be quite vague because of the anxiety these people experience. They belong to the group Rapaport has called the coartated pre-schizophrenic.[7] While their responses, what they see and communicate, are characterized by an impersonal, stereotyped, emotionally seemingly meaningless, neutral quality, occasionally one or another response or reaction in the inquiry will suddenly reveal a percept that is charged with such intense personal meaning as to be in utmost contrast with the bland and uncommunicative quality of the rest of the record. Here we see, then, a quite brittle defense against the depth, the unknown that the world of the inkblots touches upon. It is thin ice on which this kind of person skates, so thin that he hardly dares touch it since the unknown world underneath this thin and brittle surface is experienced as potentially terrifying by these patients. One can feel how desperately they cling to the empty shell of this stereotyped reaction because to lose hold of it means that the nameless terror of the unknown may break

---

[7] Rapaport, *op. cit.*, I, 21.

through and drown them. Their own fear of what lies underneath this thin shell may be equaled or surpassed by the fear that somebody else —the tester—might see this and that they might let him see it.

A very different picture is that of the massive defense to be found in the average, "healthy" coartated or coartative record. These records are very frequent. They have an empty, matter-of-fact, impersonal, rather stereotyped quality without the vagueness of, and usually with a greater number of responses than, the coartated pre-schizophrenic. The people who produce this kind of record usually do not encounter the phantastic, the great, and the unknown in the world of the inkblots or in the real world, just as they do not encounter what may be buried in the depth of their own person. By shutting it out they succeed in avoiding the disquiet that it would cause and that might find them helpless in the moment in which they see beyond the solidly defended if narrow area of their conscious lives. This kind of record raises the question, of quite general interest to the student of the normal and the neurotic personality, at what point the concept of defense changes or loses its meaning, because it becomes difficult to distinguish between the defense and what is being defended. While in some people the relative absence of personally meaningful emotional experience clearly is a defense (e.g., by distance operations, by intellectualization, etc.) of a vulnerable core in them, in others this "defense" has become so massive that they impress us as emotionally dead or as indifferent, empty, or superficial and that, for all practical purposes, it is no longer possible to reach their potential for a greater depth and scope of life. They are the people who suffer not from neurotic symptomatology but, as Erich Fromm has called it, from a "socially patterned defect." [8]

In these records the exposure of the first card to the testee establishes a set which effectively shuts out a personally meaningful encounter with the Rorschach cards. The inkblots may be transformed, for example, into a kind of puzzle and the testee may try to fit the right pieces together, that is, try to find "good" responses without really entering the world of the inkblots. It is a reaction to the whole microcosm of the inkblots, to their quality, which does not fit into the world of this kind of testee and against which he therefore has to shut his eyes.

This and other blanket "defenses" are very different from those of the person who is also disquieted upon encountering the first card and may

---

[8] Erich Fromm, *Man for Himself* (New York: 1947), pp. 221–223.

experience orientation shock, but whose defenses are more flexible, so that he can enter the world of the inkblots after the "shock" of first encountering it has been overcome. He does not react to it by shutting it out altogether; but in exploring this new world he may feel that some of the cards are dangerous to him—this "decision" probably often takes place on the basis of subliminal or peripheral perceptions which do not come to focal awareness—and he may avoid becoming involved with them by means of one kind of defensive reaction or other, while he is free to experience other cards more fully.

The range of such fuller experience is described nowhere more richly or in a more stimulating and thought-provoking way than in Rorschach's discussion of the experience types, especially within the normal range,[9] and their relation to different types and aspects of personality and to various kinds of talents. It is not possible to understand the central significance of the experience type in Rorschach's thought and the bearing it has on many aspects of life without reading his book. There would be no point in summarizing or repeating what is expressed there in a unique way.

We have discussed the testee's reactions to the world of the inkblots mainly from the viewpoint of openness for, versus defense against, the encounter with the inkblots. When the testee is more or less open to encounter the world of the inkblots, i.e., to relate to them on an experiential rather than a mechanical or cliché level, it is possible to see whether he can integrate this experience without getting too disturbed by it or whether it upsets his functioning and to what extent and in what ways it does so. If he can integrate it this will usually be apparent in a certain flexibility and fluctuation of reactions between the two poles of the more stereotyped, routine reaction and the personally meaningful, experiential level of reaction.

These basic ways of reacting, the defensive avoidance of and the openness for the world of the inkblots, are often accompanied by a variety of attitudes and feeling tones which may be significant in the character structure of the testee and which may find expression in responses and behavior in the test situation, e.g., in the phrasing of responses and of remarks, the tone of voice, facial expression, gestures, etc. I want to mention a few typical examples of these attitudes and feeling tones with which some testees react to the unfamiliar and phantastic quality of the inkblots. One group of these reactions consists of

---

[9] Rorschach, *op. cit.*, pp. 72–115.

*feelings of strangeness,* which may take the form of a sense of derealization, of mysteriousness, of puzzlement or bewilderment, of grotesqueness, or may tend more in the direction of feeling that the blots
are nonsensical, that they do not make sense. This latter attitude often
forms the transition to feelings of *annoyance,* irritation, frustration, because the world of the inkblots is not accessible to the testee and he
finds it annoying to be confronted with a situation with which he cannot deal by means of the skills, routines, defenses, and other mechanisms he has developed in coping with life. Often this attitude is found
in people who are inflexible and find it difficult to accept any new situations. The anxiety or helplessness with which a new situation, the unfamiliar world of the inkblots, threatens them is more or less effectively
kept from awareness by means of becoming angry, hostile, annoyed,
irritated. It is diagnostically useful to be alert to these reactions as well
as to the question whether they are consciously and openly expressed,
whether they form an observable undercurrent of which the testee may
not be aware, whether they find no expression and lead to feelings of
frustration and being stymied, or whether only actual helplessness and
anxiety are apparent. Another group of reactions may be described as
*fascination* by the inkblots. This sometimes may take the form of becoming absorbed in them in a dreamlike way, as is characteristic of
some, usually markedly introversive, people who find pleasure in wan-
dering in this land of phantasy and, in some more extreme cases, almost
get lost in it to such an extent that their sense of reality is temporarily
diminished.

The encounter with the inkblot world takes place within the test situation and therefore the reactions to this encounter can be understood
correctly only if the interpersonal aspects of the test situation are also
taken into account. They will be discussed more fully later on. However, it is necessary at this point to discuss briefly the way in which the
qualities of the perceptual object and the interpersonal relations in the
test situation mesh in leading to the specific reactions of the testee.
The personal meaning the test situation has for the testee may hinder or
help his capacity to experience the world of the inkblots fully and in a
personally meaningful way. Also, the test situation and its subjective
definition by the testee may be used by him to *rationalize,* consciously
or unconsciously, his way of reacting to the inkblots. A significant aspect of such rationalizations is the conscious or unconscious tendency of
some testees to shift the responsibility for their reactions onto the test
situation, the tester, or the inkblots. Other testees assume responsibility

for their reactions and then do not need to use the test situation as a rationalization. These various possibilities may be combined; e.g., a testee may be hindered by the test situation from experiencing the ink-blots fully and may proceed to rationalize his sense of failure or dissatisfaction by assumptions concerning the tester or test task, by feeling, for instance, that he was *supposed* to react in a certain way and that this made it more difficult for him.

When uneasiness in the face of the unknown inkblot primarily mobilizes defenses and results in the avoidance of a full encounter, this often influences the quality of *time* experience and changes the experiential structure of time in which the testee lives during the test situation. For example, one typical change is in the direction of "wanting to be done with it" rather than living in the open flux of fulfilled time which receives its meaning from the developing relatedness to the inkblot in the process of assimilating it. Just as the testee, in these cases, wants to "dispose" of the inkblot rather than experience it fully, so he also wants to "get over with the test task" rather than engage in it fully. This does not necessarily mean that the testee will deal more rapidly with the test task in terms of abstract time measurement. It may have this effect in some testees, who by quick and superficial handling of the whole test succeed in avoiding a meaningful encounter with the inkblots. But it very often has the opposite effect: the wish to "get it over with" may lead to increased uneasiness and doubt because the testee registers somewhere that he has not really dealt with the situation but is avoiding it and thus, while wanting to get done with it, can never feel satisfied that he has done what he feels he is "supposed" to do. Thus, the "empty" time of avoidance may stretch out excessively and yet be characterized by the testee's experience of wishing to be past, rather than in, the ongoing time of the test experience.[10] The general tendency of a person to want to be *past*, rather than *in* ongoing temporal experiences usually goes with the wish to get rid of rather than to relate to a world that is felt to be disturbing, threatening, disquieting.[11] Of course, not

---

[10] Compare the case of Jürg Zünd in Ludwig Binswanger, *Schizophrenie* (Pfullingen: Neske, 1957), particularly pp. 278–279. The described changes in the structure of time can often be seen by qualitative analysis of the testee's test behavior and his responses. While they also affect the "objective" abstract time of his response pattern, merely quantitative time measurements usually will not be sufficient to make the structure of such experiential time palpable.

[11] To the general problem of time in Rorschach's test compare also Kuhn, *Maskendeutungen im Rorschachschen Versuch*, pp. 43–45.

every person who would like to be done with, or rid of, taking a Rorschach test suffers from such a general and basic wish to abolish the world or create greater distance between self and world. There can be other, nonpathological reasons for disliking psychological tests.[12]

So far we have discussed mainly the experiential dimension of the perceptual processes related to a full perception of the inkblot or an avoidance of such full perception. The perception of the inkblot, together with the task set by the test instructions, sets off an *associative process* which, in turn, affects the subsequent perception of the blot until eventually—sometimes sooner, sometimes later—the interplay of perception and association results in a response. Thus, the quality of the test responses depends not only on the initial openness toward, or partial avoidance of, the impact of the inkblot, but also on the quality of the associative process which (in the actual response) leads to definitive restructuring of the perception. The quality of the associations, in turn, depends partly on what layers of the personality the initial perception (and subsequent ones) have touched, in other words, on how open the testee was toward the inkblot, or how much of his sensibilities and feelings was prevented from being touched by the attitude he adopted in his exploratory relation to the inkblot. But the associations also depend on how open the testee is toward himself, how much or how little he can give free rein to his associations. The testee's openness toward potential associations is determined by such factors as the quality of his goal-directedness in relation to the test task, the freedom versus the rigid channeling of associations in only a few directions, the attitude of willing, or even of forcing, an extreme of which is the cramped search for associations, as contrasted with an attitude of allowing ideas and images to occur to him. Even the last step in the genesis of a response, namely, the decision about which associations are and which are not fitting and suitable likenesses, the critical selection of the response proper from the ideas that have occurred to the testee, casts its shadow ahead on the associative process itself. It influences the degree to which the testee can play with the flow of images and ideas as tentative possibilities and the extent to which he can allow only ideas which conform to certain pre-set requirements, whether of form-accuracy or of permissible content.

---

[12] Compare Rexroth's satire on psychological testing, "My Head Gets Tooken Apart," in Kenneth Rexroth, *Bird in the Bush* (New York: New Directions, 1959), pp. 65–74.

The more narrowly and stringently the testee defines the test task, the less likely is it that he will be able to give free rein to the flow of associations. Rigid repressiveness, too, will narrow and obstruct the flow of associations. If phantasy and imagination are excluded because their products do not obey the laws of everyday conventional logic, the range of associations will be reduced drastically, just as it will if subjective feeling is excluded by an overly detached critical attitude. If the testee feels under great pressure to produce, the freedom necessary for the free play of thoughts and images and for any creative endeavor will be lacking and, again, the flow of associations will be obstructed. In this respect, it does not make much difference whether the testee feels that the pressure to produce comes from outside, from the tester, or from himself, from his own ambition to produce a great deal or something excellent. In either case, the strained attitude of willing is likely to interfere with that openness toward himself and his ideas which allows a free play of ideas and associations. On the other hand, some testees indulge in completely "free" association, thus losing touch with the reality of the inkblot and of the test task to find a likeness to the inkblot.

An obstacle to an optimal performance may also be created by a testee's conscious or unconscious fears that his responses may reveal something about him that must not be revealed to others or that he does not want to become aware of. Such a fear may be even more crippling to the free play of his mental activities if it is not concerned with anything specific that he wants to hide from others but is a vague and indeterminate anxiety or feeling of shame which is apt to result in a general, defensive constriction.

# 5 / THE RELATION OF THE EXPERIENTIAL QUALITIES TO SOME GENERAL PSYCHOLOGICAL CONCEPTS

The experiential range of the testee's responses depends, as we have seen, on how fully or superficially he gets in touch with the inkblot; this, in turn, depends both on his openness toward the inkblot and—in the freedom or constriction of associations—on his openness toward himself: on the quality of his being in touch, perceptually, with the inkblot and, in his access or lack of access to a wide range of responsiveness and associations, with himself. To gain a fuller understanding of the meaning and the implications of this statement, its relations to some general psychological problems and their bearing on Rorschach's test have to be considered, namely, the problems of repression, play, activity and passivity, normalcy, reality-testing and adaptation, phantasy, physiognomic perception, and creativity.

In Rorschach's book the problem of *repression* is discussed explicitly only in connection with the phenomenon of color shock, which he considered an indication of neurotic repression of affect.[1] Probably this is due to the fact that, at the time Rorschach wrote his book, the more far-reaching problem of characterological defenses had not yet come to the fore. Actually, Rorschach's concept of coartation and coartativeness (sometimes translated "constriction") has a closer and more important bearing on characterological defenses and on repression as a function of character than does color shock, which may or may not occur in the

---

[1] Rorschach, *op. cit.*, p. 35. The English edition incorrectly translates Rorschach's *Affektverdränger* (affect repressors) as "emotion suppressors." To suppress (*unterdrücken*) is something different, more conscious or, at least, accessible to consciousness than to repress, which translates Freud's term *verdrängen.*

coartated records of certain character neuroses in which the repression of affect plays a very significant role.[2] The neurotically constricted Rorschach performance is the result of an attitude which restricted the testee to a superficial, rigidly controlled, or otherwise largely intellectual, often quite stereotyped approach. Such an attitude precludes a more meaningful perception of the blot, the full exercise of the testee's sensibilities, and his access to associations and images stemming from more central layers of his personality. It is indicative not so much of a repression of specific unconscious drives or ideas as of a general, characterological repressiveness which tends to stifle the whole personality and to result in a stagnation of life.[3]

In examining repression there arise not only the questions what specific affect, drive, or idea has been repressed, but also the questions of how tightly closed and rigid or how permeable and loose the borders between conscious and preconscious, preconscious and unconscious are and how pervasive the repressive system is. Freud touched on this problem when he remarked that probably the artist has a constitutional "laxity" of repression (*Lockerheit der Verdrängungen*).[4] This laxity of repression or, as I prefer to call it, of general repressiveness, is a prerequisite of what Rorschach calls the "loosening of associations,"[5] which he contrasts with stereotyped associations[6] and considers necessary for the production of W and M responses.

Such general repressiveness cannot be clearly separated from, and shades gradually into, the impoverishment and stunting of the capacity for sensory experience and for mental and emotional openness, spontaneity, live interest and responsiveness, a phenomenon characteristic of very many adults of our time. It leads to a shrinking of the interest in expanding and deepening one's contact and relatedness to the world,

---

[2] This does not imply that coartation is always due to repression or to a character neurosis.

[3] Such general repressiveness can be, and often is, the end result of the earlier repression of specific, important feelings and tendencies.

[4] *Introductory Lectures on Psychoanalysis* [Standard Edition], XII, 376.

[5] *Lockerung der Assoziationen* [German edition, pp. 54, 57, 60], translated in the English edition as "freedom of associations" (pp. 58, 62, 65).

[6] Rorschach means by stereotyped associations the predominance of one type of content, namely, a high percentage of animal responses instead of a wider range of content. The rigidity of the coartated record, however, does not always go together with this specific type of content stereotypy, although it often does. Even a wider range of content of responses may go together with a rigidly controlled, detached intellectual approach which may find expression in a coartated or coartative (i.e., tending toward coartation) record.

an interest usually at its peak in early childhood which need not be, but very often is, lost in later years. In these cases, the openness of the child who wants to explore the world around him and exercise all his sensory-motor-affective-intellectual capacities in expanding his relation to the world yields to, and often is stifled by, the stereotyped approach of everyday conventional logic and practicality. This implies both a repression or crippling of, and alienation from, a large part of the person's sensory-motor, emotional, and intellectual capacities and potentialities and a loss of touch with and blindness toward many aspects of the world (other people, nature, and the cultural universe). In terms of the Rorschach-test situation this means that the inkblots will be perceived in a rather stereotyped, clichélike, and shallow fashion and that the associations stimulated by them do not range freely but tend to be confined to what is acceptable to everyday conventional logic and will fit into the schemata of the everyday, closed, conventional world in which the thus-crippled person happens to live, without awareness of the wider potentialities in himself or of the wider and deeper world which transcends his preconceived schemata. On the other hand, where there is little repressiveness and where the border preventing the repressed from coming to awareness is not an impenetrable, rigid wall but is loose and permeable, the testee will be able to give free play to all his capacities in the encounter with the inkblot before him, thereby making available a wide range of possible perceptions and associations.

It is no accident that language speaks of giving free play and of letting come into play when expressing the removal of restrictions over some capacity or impulse and the admission or activation of a capacity in relation to a particular situation, task, or problem. The freedom of play is an essential, though not a sufficient condition for any creative act, including the creative assimilation of the unfamiliar in the expansion of one's relatedness to the world. Such play, which contrasts not with seriousness but with repressiveness, urgent need, too-narrow goal-directedness and regimentation, and with conventional concepts of efficiency, has its prototype in the young child's exploration of and intercourse with the world.[7] In the encounter with the Rorschach inkblots such free play is a condition for a rich, varied, and personally meaningful experience and interpretation of the blots. Its presence or absence and its fluctuations can in many cases be an indication of the experien-

---

[7] Compare "The Development of Focal Attention and the Emergence of Reality" in Schachtel, *op. cit.*, pp. 251–278.

tial range and depth and of the degree and quality of repressiveness of the testee.

The free play with the possibilities offered by the inkblot and the loosening of associations based on the absence of pervasive repressiveness have to be distinguished from the breakdown of repressiveness and of control in acute schizophrenic episodes and in the group described by Rapaport as overideational pre-schizophrenics. While in these people, too, there is a greater openness toward the possibilities of the inkblot than in the typical coartated or coartative record, this openness is often disrupted by the power of the associations, many of which stem from primary process thought. The records of these patients who have retained their pre-morbid intelligence, sensitivity, and talent often show some brilliant, original, well-seen responses; but they also show the effect of the breakdown of controls and of reality-testing in responses which do not take into account the objective features of the inkblot (F−, O− ).

The quality of the testee's encounter with the inkblot, especially his openness toward it or the lack of it, his capacity for imaginative play with it or the absence or impoverishment of this capacity are closely related to the relative proportion and the fluctuation of *activity and passivity* in his approach to the inkblots. I believe that man's visual perception generally oscillates between a more passive attitude (in which the impact of the environment is felt) and a more active attitude (in which he takes hold, perceptually, of the object whose impact he has noticed). This oscillation, usually not in awareness, becomes more readily observable in the encounter with the inkblots, because their unfamiliar and ambiguous quality invites both prolonged and repeated exposure to their impact and prolonged and repeated [8] attempts to structure them so as to give them meaning in the responses to them.

In perception such oscillation becomes more pronounced when we *contemplate* an object in order to take it in fully. This requires first an active turning of attention to the object, then an opening of oneself to its full impact. Such receptive opening toward an object is in itself characterized by the oscillation between letting the total Gestalt or one or another aspect of the object sink in, as it were, affect one's sensibility,

---

[8] By "repeated" I refer to the repeated acts of receptive attention and active structuring while looking at one particular inkblot in the course of responding to it. They may occur in the genesis of each single response, not only when several responses are given to the same inkblot.

and trying to grasp, take hold of the object and its qualities that one has allowed thus to affect one. In prolonged or intensive contemplation there is a constant fluctuation between these more active and more passive attitudes and an interplay in which they both affect the perception of the object and thus change in subtle ways what becomes available to and constitutive of the object as eventually perceived in such contemplation or in other, repeated acts of perception such as may occur, for example, in the interaction with another person and our perception of that person.

In much of everyday perception this oscillation, in individually and situationally varying degrees, tends to be cut short. For example, the (passive) impact of a moving object on the otherwise occupied or idle eye may cause a brief (active) act of attention in order to recognize what it was that struck one's eye; but as soon as a quick glance has achieved recognition, the eye will relinquish the object. Similarly, in more or less automatic orientation in a fairly familiar environment, the oscillation between (passive) impact and (active) taking hold in recognition is very brief. In these examples the cutting short of the perceptual process serves adaptative purposes: if we were to contemplate each object in order to orient ourselves on the way to some goal, we would never get there. On the other hand, if we never contemplated any object our lives would become impoverished indeed. Another kind of short cut may occur when what strikes us in the first visual impact of an object, for example another person, arouses anxiety or fear. Anxiety may disrupt the oscillating process of perception even before the perceiver knows what about the other person and/or in himself caused the anxiety; it may cause him to avoid fuller exposure to the impact of the other person and, thus, freeze the perception at an early and incomplete stage.

In the Rorschach-test situation the test task, to say what the inkblot might be, demands a more active attention from the testee than he might pay to some object he notices in passing with a casual glance. Most testees, as a rule, will therefore turn with more active attention to the inkblots than they would to their everyday environment. But what happens after this first turning-to varies a great deal, especially with regard to the quantity and quality of the oscillation between more active and more passive perceptual attitudes. The optimal, flexible oscillation between active and passive attitude may be interfered with by a variety of factors. Some of these consist of limitations of both the impact of the blot and the range of the active attitude by resorting to certain types of percepts and responses and by avoiding others. For example, where exposure to a blot arouses anxiety, some testees will tend to avoid the total impact of the blot and give either no W response or only a vague one and tend to limit their attention and active structuring to Dd and obvious D areas. The Dd response especially minimizes impact and usually leads to predominantly active structuring on a small scale.[9] The Dd areas are, as a rule, too small to have much impact. Thus, to a testee who is intent on giving responses but in whom the impact of the large dark (gray or black) or colored areas arouses too much anxiety or is disturbing for other reasons, the Dd offer a good way out of his dilemma. Another way of limiting both exposure to and coping with the blot is the tendency of some testees to limit their responses to the most obvious likenesses, that is, to popular or near-popular responses. In doing this they can readily "dispose" of the blot and thus avoid exposure to a longer and more profound or more disturbing impact of the blot as well as the difficulty of more complex, active structuring.

Another interference with optimal oscillation occurs in excessive stimulus-boundedness. In these cases the capacity for active structuring is disturbed either by the temporary situation or habitually. The testee finds it difficult or impossible to shift actively from a particular stimulus configuration and either to gain a different perspective or emphasis or to shift to a different area. Some of the cases in which such stimulus-boundedness is pronounced are reminiscent of Goldstein's observations on the concrete as contrasted with the abstract attitude. The concrete attitude may be said to consist of a tie to a particular simulus configuration, while access to other possibilities—in fact to the whole realm of the possible—is barred or fraught with anxiety.[10]

The pure C response, discussed in more detail later, is characterized

---

[9] Most Dd responses are F or F-dominated, that is, actively structured. Occasionally a colored Dd area may be selected for giving an essentially unstructured C or CF response when the testee tends to avoid the more disturbing impact of a large colored area. However, the Dd C or CF differ from the W or D C or CF responses in that the seeking out of a Dd colored area is in itself an active effort of attention, whereas the C or CF response to a large colored area more usually comes about by giving in to the sheer passive impact of the color, while active coping with the blot is minimized.

[10] Kurt Goldstein, *Human Nature in the Light of Psychopathology* (Cambridge: Harvard University Press, 1947), pp. 53–54.

by the absence of active structuring of the blot. It is a response to the passive impact of the color which may—without oscillation between impingement and active taking hold—lead directly to the association used as the basis of the response.

Rorschach uses the concept of oscillation to describe the free back-and-forth fluctuation between form, movement, and color responses in the course of a test and describes this as characteristic of people who do not repress and are "free of complexes," whereas he considers the restriction of such oscillation a sign of repression.[11] I have used the term "oscillation" to describe the presence or restriction of a process I believe goes on in the microgenesis of many acts of perception and of many Rorschach responses. Probably free oscillation of active and passive perceptual and association processes in the single responses tend to go together with free oscillation, in Rorschach's sense, throughout a Rorschach test. Conversely, restriction of oscillation in the genesis of the single responses is likely to go along with a restriction of free oscillation between the various determinants over the course of an entire test.

The experiential dimension of the testee's reactions to the Rorschach inkblots often tells us, as we have seen, how much or how little he is in touch with the inkblots and with himself or, more accurately, whether his experiential contact with the inkblots and his perceptual experience of them is a superficial one or one in which deeper chords of responsiveness are struck. While the contact with the inkblots is not the same as that with reality, its quality often permits significant inferences about the testee's degree and quality of *relatedness to reality*. The degree and type of relatedness of man to the world is a basic problem of his existence. Insanity means to be out of touch with reality and unable to adapt to it, while sanity requires sufficient contact with reality to enable one to function in it. Hence the significance of a person's capacity for "reality-testing" and of his "adaptation to reality" for psychiatric diagnosis. But the problem of a person's contact with reality is not exhausted with the question whether his "reality-testing" is intact in the sense of freedom from such gross distortions as are found in insanity. Even if he is able to see everyday reality sufficiently clearly to orient himself and to function in it, the question of the shallowness or depth, narrowness or width, rigidity or flexibility, deadness or aliveness of his relatedness to reality—that is, to other people and to the world around

---

[11] Rorschach, *op. cit.*, p. 194.

him—is decisive for the degree of his development and for the fulfillment or lack of it in his life. In the evaluation of a person's relation to reality the observer's concept of what constitutes reality will obviously play a significant role. If by reality he understands the conventional concept of reality implicitly prevalent in a particular social group's way and view of life, he may well arrive at the conclusion that anybody not sharing this view of reality suffers from faulty reality-testing and, to that extent, is "abnormal" or not "well adapted." If, however, he is aware of the fact that there is more to reality than what is perceived by the conventional world view of such a group and that adaptation to such a restricted and—often—sociocentrically distorted view of reality may not be a norm conducive to the optimal realization of a person's potentialities, he will have different criteria for what constitutes reality, normality, mental health, and he will raise the question of *which* "reality" a person should adapt to in order to reach his optimal development.[12]

In the Rorschach literature, reality-testing and adaptation to reality have been connected specifically with the form responses.[13] There is a good reason for this, since the capacity for finding a good form-likeness to the inkblot ( F + ) indeed requires an accurate, hence realistic, perception of the form of the inkblot and critical judgment regarding the likeness of the form of the object associated to the blot. However, an exclusive emphasis on this, like an exclusive emphasis on formal or conventional logic, neglects or overlooks the fact that a very important element in the grasp of reality consists in a person's sensitivity to the emotional atmosphere and to the emotional significance of other people's behavior, their facial and gestural expressions, the nuances of the nonverbal components of their speech (intonations, hesitations, etc.), their way of moving, etc., and that the finest instrument of such sensitivity are the emotional reactions of the perceiver. They are indispensable for accurate reality-testing, provided one is aware of them and what they mean. It is a very widespread pejorative view of affects as being disorganizing and/or primitive forms of behavior which has led to a too-narrow view of intellect and reason as opposed to affect, and of affect as something rather questionable and at best to be tolerated, provided

---

[12] For a more detailed discussion of these problems see Erich Fromm, *The Sane Society* (New York: Rinehart & Co., 1955), pp. 73–74 and throughout, and Schachtel, *Metamorphosis*, pp. 191–192.

[13] Rapaport, *op. cit.*, p. 185; S. J. Beck, *Rorschach's Test* (New York: Grune & Stratton, 1944–45), II, 19–20.

it is properly controlled.[14] Rorschach himself wrote, rightly, that his whole test, not just the giving of form responses, requires adaptation to external stimuli; this he considered an action of the "fonction du réel." [15] Thus, the omission of the color, shading, and movement responses from the problem of reality-testing and its expression in Rorschach's test would lead to grave errors. Actually, competent clinicians know this. But it is important to be aware of the described restrictive undercurrent in the clinical concept of "reality" and its expression in the Rorschach literature.[16]

The reality orientation of a testee often finds expression in his attitude to the reality of the test situation. This reality is given mainly by the purpose of the test as communicated to the testee,[17] by the quality of the inkblots, and by the test instructions. Rorschach kept these to a minimum by handing the inkblot to the testee with the question "What might this be?" The importance of this kind of procedure lies in the fact that by giving both free scope to the testee to structure the situation in his own way and by giving him the responsibility to do so, the tester is

---

[14] Of course I am not advocating uncontrolled impulsiveness, but merely drawing the reader's attention to an undercurrent present in much of the psychological and psychiatric literature. Compare Kurt Goldstein, "On Emotions: Considerations from an Organismic Point of View," *Journal of Psychology*, 31 (1951), 37–49; Schachtel, *op. cit.*, pp. 19–33.

[15] *Op. cit.*, p. 123.

[16] Even in Rapaport's significant contribution to the Rorschach literature, this undercurrent is apparent in the way in which he phrases this problem, although he is quite aware of the positive aspects of a richly and finely modulated emotional reaction. He writes, in discussing the form responses, "formal characteristics and their relationships become our guide in life, and not our affective reactions to the things about us"; and "civilization does not *demand* that all psychological experience be strictly limited to such guidance by formal characteristics; it *allows* also for . . . [appropriate] display of affect and anxiety." (Italics mine.) Rapaport, *op. cit.*, p. 189. In such words as "demands" and "allows," the pejorative view of affect and, ultimately, the influence of a repressive society on our thinking, in psychology as well as in all other areas, become visible. The book has yet to be written which analyzes in what ways and to what extent the social categories of domination, control, suppression, of master and servant pervade and determine man's thinking in general, are built into the language itself, including the technical language of psychology.

[17] The purpose should be stated clearly and truthfully. If the test is used for clinical purposes the testee should be told that it will help in gaining a better picture of the difficulties he suffers from and of the factors in his personality that might cause them. In the literature it is often assumed that all projective techniques are "disguised" so that the testee cannot know the intention of the tester. (See Lindzey, *op. cit.*, p. 159.) If that statement means that the purpose of the test should be withheld from the testee, I disagree with it. Truthfulness is essential in dealings with patients that ultimately serve a psychotherapeutic purpose. Not to state the purpose of the test adds unnecessary stress, doubt, or suspicion to the test situation.

enabled to see more clearly how the testee experiences and responds to the situation. This is important not only because the testee's definition of the test situation gives diagnostically important clues to the dynamics of his character structure, but, as Rapaport pointed out, also because the testee's perception or misperception of the reality of the testing situation permits significant inferences as to the soundness or weakness of his reality-orientation and reality-testing.[18] Such inferences presuppose that the tester have a concept of what constitutes a *normal reality-orientation* to the test situation with which to compare the testee's attitude. Is the true reality of the test situation determined by the way in which the majority of the clinically "normal" population experiences it? And what is this way? Rorschach found that "almost all subjects" believe the test to be one of imagination.[19] Rapaport asserts that "by and large, normal subjects . . . [feel] that they must give responses which are completely acceptable to everyday conventional logic." [20] These two "normal" definitions of the test situation sound very different; perhaps what is completely acceptable to everyday conventional logic leaves no or little room for the play of imagination and phantasy. Are these differing definitions of the normal meaning of the test situation results of cultural differences between the Swiss subjects used by Rorschach and the American subjects used by Rapaport, possibly especially his normal control group, which was taken from the ranks of the Kansas Highway Patrol? [21] Actually, the inkblots are obviously not representational, and the instructions (What *could* or *might* it be?) together with the phantastic appearance of many of the blots imply that no exact and realistic likenesses are called for or, for that matter, exist. These objective conditions of the test situation invite imagination and phantasy.[22] If the testee does not hear this invitation it does not mean that he is "abnormal" in the clinical sense. But it does mean that he restricts the range of the test task by excluding phantasy and imagi-

---

[18] Rapaport, *op. cit.*, p. 329.

[19] Rorschach, *op. cit.*, p. 16. The German word used by Rorschach is *Phantasie*.

[20] *Op. cit.*, p. 329.

[21] *Op. cit.*, I, 28–31.

[22] This is also the opinion of Schafer (*op. cit.*, pp. 76–77). Many American testees understand the test situation in this way, and many a testee who produces a coartated record and/or feels uneasy about his test "achievements" will spontaneously explain that his "lack of imagination" makes the test task difficult for him or accounts for what he feels to be a meager or inadequate performance. Thus, I do not find any evidence for a cultural difference between American and Swiss "normal" subjects so far as the test situation's invitation to phantasy is concerned.

nation. This restriction must not be taken for granted as being "normal," but it raises the question as to its causes, which may be found in such factors as, for example, characterological defenses against a free play of imagination, obsessive concern with accuracy or with the literal meaning of the test task, the testee's sociocultural background, etc.[23] Imagination and phantasy are an important dimension of human reality, of the human world, even if they may not be acceptable to conventional everyday logic.

Actually, imagination is not only closely related to perception but can also be an important part of perception, especially of that attitude of perceptual openness toward the world that enables man to perceive the new in the familiar and to break through the confines of a familiar perspective. Imagination does not form new images out of nothing; it transforms, recombines, varies known images.[24] In doing so, it forms links between a familiar object and something hitherto not connected with it in the perceiver's mind, thus opening new perspectives which may reveal the object in a new light and show a new aspect of it. This imaginative activity in perception is challenged and invited much more by the Rorschach inkblots than by the everyday perception of a familiar environment.

Imaginative testees often give responses which have no counterpart in everyday reality and might not be considered acceptable to everyday logic. Rorschach quotes among his examples of "normal" test results the record of an imaginative, gifted woman who saw in card VIII "A fairy-tale motif, stylized, a fire at the bottom, a buried treasure (blue), the root of the tree under which the treasure is buried (gray), the animals guarding the treasure" (lateral pink). A less elaborate and original response to the center bottom green area of card X is: "Two caterpillars kissing the head of a rabbit." Rapaport would consider such responses "fabulized combinations" and as such deviant. Such an interpretation is understandable—though not correct—only if one shares his assumption that normal persons will understand the test instructions to mean "that they must give responses which are completely acceptable to everyday conventional logic." But the imaginative or the artistically gifted person

---

[23] Very often the factors that cause such a restriction of the reality meaning of the test situation also affect other aspects of the test performance and may cause, for example, coartation, rigidity, stereotypy.

[24] This has been emphasized by Gaston Bachelard, *L'Air et les Songes, Essai sur l'imagination du mouvement* (Paris: Librairie José Corti, 1943), pp. 7–8 and *passim*.

will usually not understand the test instructions as this restrictive and yet be quite normal.

Even more basic than the question of the normality of including or excluding the realm of imagination and phantasy in the range of the normal reality meaning of the test situation is that of the normal level and type of relatedness of testee to inkblot and its implications for the experiential dimensions and the *normality* of the testee's world and for his relatedness to this world. This question concerns the testee's openness and responsiveness to the world and to the inkblots. There, too, if one limits the range of normal responses to those "completely acceptable to everyday conventional logic," he runs the risk of restricting reality-testing to a function of conventional logic, thus excluding the important share of emotional sensitivity and responsiveness in man's grasp of reality. Furthermore, such a definition of the normal response sets a yardstick which implicitly, if not consciously, leads to a definition of normalcy as behavior conforming to the conventionally accepted pattern and of reality as that view of the world which is completely acceptable to conventional everyday logic. This would exclude everything that is creative, penetrates the surface, and touches that which is more real, both in the world and in the person, than the conventional surface and more true than the conventional views. We are dealing here with the crucial problems of what constitutes normality and reality, fundamental to all thinking in psychiatry, psychoanalysis, and the psychology and psychopathology of normality and abnormality.

Two major sources of error and confusion tend to obscure the thinking and the discussion concerned with problems of normality and reality as they converge in the problem of the normal functioning of reality-testing. One is the failure to make explicit, and be aware of, the normative yardstick used for the *concept of normality* and to think through the implications of this yardstick; the other is the equation, often unwittingly taken for granted, of reality with the conventionally accepted reality of a particular sociocultural group and period. One concept of normality takes its yardstick from that fictitious creature, the average man, supposedly a composite of the greatest number of people in a particular society; another from an image of man as a person capable of developing to a stage of maturity, which then serves as the model of normality.[25] Psychoanalytic theory—in all its various schools

---

[25] Of course this does not mean that there is only *one* type of mature person. There are as many ways of being mature as there are ways of reaching maturity.

—has always subscribed to this latter viewpoint, only to arrive at the insight that, according to this yardstick, the majority of people do not arrive at maturity and, in that sense, do not reach full "normality." [26] On the other hand, many psychoanalysts, psychiatrists, and psychologists, when judging reality-testing, implicitly or explicitly restrict their concept of reality to the conventional view of reality prevailing in their culture. Thus, they view reality through the eyes of the greatest number of the population, even though the doctrines and teachers they profess to follow thought that the greatest number of people did not reach maturity and, hence, had a limited and distorted view of reality.

The nature and the implications of these problems, as they affect the diagnostic evaluation of Rorschach responses, may be illustrated and clarified by considering the role of dynamic or *physiognomic perception* (Werner) in the test and in everyday life. Werner contrasts physiognomic perception, which "plays a greater role in the primitive world than in our own," with the "geometrical-technical" type of perception, of which he says that it is the rule in our own world,[27] by which he probably means the world of modern, Western industrial civilization now spreading over the entire globe. He cites much evidence for the prevalence of physiognomic perception, not only among primitive people but also in childhood and in pathological conditions. However, while it is true that physiognomic perception is more obviously prevalent at lower levels of development and functioning (primitive man, childhood, certain types of mental pathology) than at higher ones, this does not mean, as Werner and many others believe, that it represents essentially and always a "lower" stage of development. What is usually overlooked in such an assumption is the fact that physiognomic perception itself is capable of considerable development in its own right, of differentiation and refinement. Art and poetry are to a large extent

---

[26] For a more detailed discussion of this point see Schachtel, *op. cit.*, pp. 247–248. Compare also the interesting observation of Deri who, using the psychoanalytic developmental model, arrived at the conclusion that, according to statistical findings with Szondi's test, the majority of the population is characterized by the "broken ego," an ego-dynamism characteristic of the six-to-nine-year-old child who has discovered that "the path of least resistance is conformity with whatever the environment expects." Deri, *op. cit.*, pp. 224, 227–228.

[27] Heinz Werner, *Comparative Psychology of Mental Development* (revised ed.) (Chicago: Follett Publishing Co., 1948), p. 69. For a penetrating discussion of the problems underlying Werner's concepts of "physiognomic" and "geometric-technical" perception, see Straus' distinction between *Empfinden* and *Wahrnehmen*. Erwin Straus, *Vom Sinn der Sinne* (2nd ed.) (Berlin-Göttingen-Heidelberg: Springer, 1956), pp. 332–419.

based on a physiognomic perception that shows a tremendous advancement over that of the young child. Human physiognomic perception develops not only in the area from which it originally received its name, namely, from the sensitivity to the expressive meaning of the human face, but also in the physiognomic perception of expressive movements, of nature, landscapes, objects, works of art. It is much more pervasive in adult life than Werner assumes; he feels that in the average adult it refers only to other people's faces and bodies. But we perceive landscapes, for example, as austere or gentle; great, majestic, or charming, sweet, soothing; forbidding, cold, indifferent, inhuman, or hospitable and inviting, friendly, warm; infinite, eternal, ageless and timeless, or as inhabited by man and related to his own life cycle; open or oppressive, sheltering or sweeping; hostile, foreboding, ominous, or paradisic, idyllic; turbulent and unquiet, brooding and somber, or quiet and serene; fertile and alive, or barren and dead, and so forth. Unless we are able to perceive the "character" of a landscape in this physiognomic way, it remains a closed book to us, it does not speak to us, we remain unrelated rather than open to it. Compared with such perception, the "geometric-technical" perception of nature is unalive and, rather than deriving from a relatedness in which the whole personality participates, serves only a narrow and specialized perspective: that of orientation in geometric, abstract space and of nature as an object to be used and exploited by man.

Another example of physiognomic perception lies in the artist's or craftman's perception of the material with which he works. The sculptor, for instance, endeavors to do justice to the particular kind of stone or wood or metal with which he works and to let the very essence of this material come to appearance and to its own life in the finished work. The true craftsman, too, is guided in his work as much by the effort to let the sensory quality of a particular material speak in the way germane to it as he is to create an object that will serve its purpose well. Such appreciation of a particular kind of material is likewise physiognomic perception. As we may perceive the essence, the character of a person from the features of his face and the movements of his body, so we perceive the particular character of a material from our visual and tactile experience of it, that is to say, with our open and receptive sensibilities. Such perception is very different from the abstract knowledge that physics and chemistry may give us about the same material; but this difference does not exclude the possibility that there may be a meeting point in the nature of the material where these two different approaches may find a common ground.

In the examples above, the physiognomic perception of landscape or material is a conscious, articulate one. In less articulate forms such perception, or traces of it, occur in all adults, often without their being aware of it because their conscious frame of reference has a different orientation. Also, a great deal of our language expresses such "physiognomic" qualities and is based on physiognomic experience. Actually, the young child's physiognomic perception is usually limited to the relatively few objects in his immediate environment and, for instance, does not extend to landscapes and to works of art. His physiognomic understanding of people, though sensitive and often uncannily accurate in such general categories as friendliness, hostility, condescension, genuineness or artificiality of approach, lacks the differentiation of nuance of which the sensitive and articulate adult is capable. The development of physiognomic perception, provided it is being nourished and cultivated rather than suppressed, goes in the direction of expansion and differentiation, side by side with the development of the abstract, conceptual faculties underlying what Werner calls the geometric-technical type of perception.

I cannot agree with Werner that physiognomic perception is a lower type of mental activity that, while included in the repertoire at the disposal of a more advanced stage of mental development, remains essentially primitive.[28] Rather, it is a *different kind* of perception, characterized by fuller, closer, and deeper relatedness between perceiver and percept, and by a development in its own right, from more primitive to more advanced, differentiated modes of functioning. The relation of physiognomic to geometric-technical perception parallels that of art and poetry to science. Art and poetry are older than science, but this does not mean that they are a lower level of human activity or that they are or remain "primitive" ways of mental functioning.[29]

The capacity for physiognomic perception and for the more detached

---

28 Werner, *op. cit.*, p. 39.

29 Compare especially the work of Cassirer and Langer. Ernst Cassirer, *Philosophy of Symbolic Forms* (New Haven: Yale University Press, 1955); Susanne K. Langer, *Feeling and Form* (New York: Charles Scribner's Sons, 1953); *Philosophy in a New Key* (New York: Mentor Books, 1951). Compare also the psychoanalytic concept, introduced by Kris, of "regression in the service of the ego," which has implications similar to Werner's viewpoint. For a critical discussion of this concept, see Schachtel, *op. cit.*, pp. 237–248.

kind of perception, of which Werner's concept of geometric-technical perception is an example, are essential human capacities, and the insufficient development of either leaves man impoverished in his relatedness to the world.

Applied to Rorschach's test, this means that the "physiognomic perception" of an inkblot and its sensory qualities, *per se,* is neither more primitive than a more detached type of perception, without any apparent feeling tone, nor a phenomenon pointing in the direction of pathology, nor does it imply that the perceiver is not in touch with the reality of the inkblot or of the testing situation. In fact, it may imply that he is *more fully* in touch with reality than is a person whose record is completely lacking in physiognomic responses. Depending on other factors in the response and in the entire Rorschach record, it may also happen that a particular kind of physiognomic response does point to primitive and to pathological tendencies such as faulty reality-testing, distortions, excessive moodiness, etc.

Physiognomic responses occur in all the different determinants. Forms may be perceived, for instance, as inviting or threatening—e.g., as a safe harbor or as one from which it is difficult to sail out into the open sea, as sheltering or oppressive; red color as gay and lively or as violent and hellish; blue color as calm and soothing or as cold and barren; shading as soft texture pleasant to the touch, or as repugnant hairiness, as pleasantly smooth or disgustingly slimy; darkness often is perceived as ominous or in other dysphoric mood nuances; the physiognomic element in movement responses very often is quite apparent in the quality of the movement: energetic or despondent, active or passive, hostile or friendly, etc.

These physiognomic qualities are usually an intrinsic part of the immediate perception of the blot. Of course, there are also cases in which they occur as an afterthought, or as a secondary, fanciful, or intellectual elaboration of an originally more neutral and detached percept. Thus, Binder rightly points out that the "intellectual chiaroscuro responses are the deviant, not naïve behavior of the subject who intellectually contemplates that to which the *average person* [my italics] usually responds feelingly" and he points out the parallel between such behavior and the "intellectual" color responses.[30] The opposite view is expressed

---

[30] Binder, *op. cit.,* pp. 26–27. The responses referred to are Binder's Hd (Helldunkel), for which I use the score Ch (chiaroscuro) and for which there is no exact parallel in Klopfer's or Piotrowski's scoring.

by Rapaport, who asserts that such responses as "inferno" to the lower, center red of card II, or "lake . . . dangerous rocks" to the white space in the middle of card II, indicate "that the subject's associative processes have unduly *elaborated* upon the *original percept* [italics mine] and that a normal subject giving such a response will be immediately prepared to explain that all he really saw was 'rocks' or 'something fiery.' " [31] Actually, both the normal and the abnormal testees giving such physiognomic responses are likely to have had an immediate experience of the red as violent, dangerous, "infernal," and of the blackness surrounding the white and/or of the sharply edged black-white border as threatening or dangerous. Rapaport's normal subject, in denying this, merely supplies a conventional rationalization by which he detaches himself from, and represses, the original immediate experience, a frequent phenomenon in our culture. [32]

The physiognomic quality of a response may be a fully conscious part of a testee's perceptual experience or a vague background feeling, or he may be unaware of it. Also, he may communicate it articulately or only implicitly. When somebody sees "storm clouds" in card VII, he usually communicates implicitly in this response what may be either a quite conscious feeling comparable to seeing dark thunderclouds looming ominously in the sky, or a vague background feeling. The physiognomic perception of color, which has a basic relation to the symptomatic significance of color responses as indicating various kinds of emotional

---

[31] Rapaport, *op. cit.*, p. 332.

[32] Rapaport quotes these two responses as examples of too great distance from the inkblot, caused by the associative elaboration and therefore indicating a pathological weakness of reality-orientation. I feel that this concept of distance can be misleading since dynamically in such physiognomic responses which do not conflict with the stimuli of the inkblot but merely perceive them in a feeling way there is a closer relatedness of perceiver and percept than in a more detached, "objective" response. Even the person who just sees "fire" in a red blot often experiences feelings of pleasant warmth or of excitement or danger or of something violent and destructive. Such feelings may be conscious without necessarily being communicated to the tester, or they may be background or even subliminal feelings of which the testee does not become aware.

Whether the person who gives a physiognomic response is well or mentally sick, normal or abnormal, depends on factors other than the phenomenon of the felt physiognomic percept as such. In the particular examples quoted by Rapaport he goes on to say that the people who gave the response had "the emotion-laden conviction that 'this is what it [the inkblot] really is.' " It is this "loss of distance" from the blot, i.e., the lack of awareness that they are merely interpreting an inkblot, and the assumption that the inkblot is either representational or even really *is* the inferno or the dangerous rocks around the lake, that indicates a pathological weakening of reality orientation.

responsiveness and excitability, is very often quite explicit in such responses as the above-quoted "inferno" to the red in card II. The difference, pointed out by Rorschach, between people who see in a red blot an open wound, rose petals, or a slice of ham, respectively,[33] finds expression largely in the implicit difference of their physiognomic experience of the color red. Very often, the physiognomic perception of color remains merely a background feeling of which the testee may not be aware but which may be observable in such qualities as greater animatedness of the response, more affect-fraught content, etc. I believe that, altogether, there are probably many instances of physiognomic perception of which the testee remains unaware and which either escape the tester's attention or find no expression, just as there are many more instances of physiognomic perception in everyday life than we are aware of and than is generally assumed by our accepted, conventional modes of thought.

One might attempt to tap physiognomic perception of Rorschach's blots directly. One method, although it does not use the concept "physiognomic," is that developed by Rabin and by Loiselle and Kleinschmidt.[34] They asked their subjects to rate the inkblots on twenty-one scales. Each of these scales requires the subject to rate each blot on a continuum between two concepts, supposedly descriptive of the blots, for example beautiful-ugly, happy-sad, kind-cruel, wise-foolish, etc.[35] Of course, this method presents the subject with an induced physiognomic perception rather than exploring the subject's own spontaneous perception. The only conclusion it may permit is that where a subject gives a high, hence definite, rating of a blot (e.g., as definitely "cruel" or definitely "kind"), the aspect rated may seem convincing to the subject, even though he might not have felt it or thought of it by himself. Another limitation is that some of the concepts on these scales, for example "wise-foolish" or "reckless-cautious" seem to have little or no rela-

---

[33] Rorschach, *op. cit.*, pp. 208–209.

[34] Both make use of Osgood *et al.*'s Semantic Differential adapted to explore the meaning of the Rorschach inkblots to people. C. E. Osgood, G. I. Suci, and P. H. Tannenbaum, *The Measurement of Meaning* (Urbana, Ill.: University of Illinois Press, 1957); A. I. Rabin, "A Contribution to the 'Meaning' of Rorschach's Ink Blots via the Semantic Differential," *Journal of Consulting Psychology*, 23 (1959), 368–372; Robert H. Loiselle and Ann Kleinschmidt, "A Comparison of the Stimulus Value of Rorschach Ink Blots and Their Percepts," *Journal of Projective Techniques*, 27 (1963), 191–194, with further references.

[35] Another group was asked to rate their own responses to the ten blots on the same scales. For purposes of our discussion it is not necessary to discuss the details of the technique and the results of Loiselle's and Kleinschmidt's study.

tion to the perceptual qualities of the blots and others a very indirect and distant one, while some (for example hard-soft, large-small, angular-rounded) have a direct relation to the perceptual qualities of some of the blots.

Another method is to ask the subject "What do you feel about this blot?" [36] Both these methods differ drastically from Rorschach's test. They bypass especially Rorschach's crucial intent of using the perception of the inkblot as an instrument to gain some insight into the testee's way of experiencing and adapting to reality. By inquiring about feeling only they eliminate or reduce the attempt to find a likeness to the blot. Their purpose is to find out something about the emotional significance of the blot—Loiselle and Kleinschmidt in the hope of discovering something about the inherent stimulus value of the inkblots, Spiegel in order to learn something about the emotional reactions of particular analytic patients. While both methods elicit primarily physiognomic responses or reactions, they do not permit, by themselves, gauging the significance of such physiognomic experience in relation to the subject's reality orientation as does the spontaneous occurrence of physiognomic responses and, to some extent, their absence in the standard administration of Rorschach's test. But for diagnostic purposes the attempt to elicit physiognomic reactions directly is useful as a supplement to the standard administration. Often, an inquiry about preferences and dislikes of the different inkblots and about the reasons for such positive and negative choices elicits physiognomic descriptions. The direct question "What do you feel about this blot?" can supplement or supplant such choices and is especially useful if in the responses proper physiognomic or similar reactions have been absent.

As mentioned before, physiognomic responses can and do occur in a pathological context. Pathological significance of physiognomic responses is indicated (1) if the responses are absurd, that is, if they do not correspond to and are not compatible with the perceptual qualities of the inkblot, or if, without being absurd, they tend to be F— or vague or extremely idiosyncratic, thus pointing to a disturbance rather than an enrichment of the relatedness to reality in the physiognomic attitude; (2) if they are so numerous that they indicate a lack or a weakening of the capacity for detached critical perception; (3) if there are other in-

---

[36] This method has been used by Spiegel with some psychoanalytic patients to whom she presents the Rorschach blots with the question: "What is the emotional impact of this blot on you?" (Rose Spiegel, oral communication.)

dications, such as a low F + %, very well and very poorly seen F in the same record, or an excessive emphasis of Dd which point to (different types of) weakening of reality-orientation; (4) if the physiognomic qualities perceived by a testee lack variety and are restricted to one or two themes which recur frequently, indicating the predominance of a habitual mood or preoccupation and a lack of flexibility and range of emotional responsiveness; (5) if the response is taken for real, that is, if the testee is convinced that this is what the inkblot "really" is or represents.[37]

---

[37] Like all symptomatic indices and all "rules" of interpretative meaning of a score, the above are not hard and fast rules but have to be applied flexibly, according to the concrete perceptual experience of the testee and the over-all clinical picture emerging from the test data and from whatever other data are available.

# 6 / THE EXPERIENTIAL DIMENSION AND THE DETERMINANTS

Rorschach does not discuss the experiential dimension in the context of the rationale of his test. He felt that the theoretical foundations of the test were, "for the most part, still quite incomplete." [1] He writes about them explicitly in the brief section on "Interpretation of the Figures as Perception" and implicitly in the chapter on "Results" in some of his observations and speculations on intelligence and on the experience type.[2] However, he considered as the most important *result* of his test the fact that it enables us to see *how* a person experiences. "We do not know his experiences: we do know the apparatus with which he receives experiences of subjective and objective nature and to which he subjects his experiences in assimilation of them." [3] This is possible only if the test data themselves furnish significant and illuminating samples of the person's way of experiencing. Indeed, Rorschach's view of what the test shows constitutes a challenge to make more explicit the experiential nature of the processes underlying the test data. Thus, Rorschach's important observation that the extreme predominance, in the coartated and coartative types, of logical discipline is achieved only at the sacrifice of the capacity to experience fully[4] summarizes in one sentence what has been made more explicit in our discussion of openness

---

[1] Rorschach, *op. cit.*, p. 13.

[2] *Ibid.*, pp. 16–18, 56–119 *passim*.

[3] *Ibid.*, p. 87. In the original German text Rorschach does not speak of subjective and objective experiences, but of experiences originating within or without the person, that is to say, inner experiences and experiences concerning the environment [German edition, p. 82].

[4] *Ibid.*, p. 92.

toward or avoidance of the impact of the inkblots, of stringent repressiveness or looseness of repression, of play, of degrees and types of being in touch or out of touch with reality and with oneself, and of the significance of the physiognomic responses. The same problems are touched upon in Rorschach's observation that *intuitive* responses are given almost exclusively by people who have a dilated experience type, in other words, by people in whom the highly conscious logical function has not led to atrophy of the full capacity for experience.[5] Rorschach believed that it is mainly the experience type, i.e., the relation of movement to color responses, that permits one to see how a person experiences and what represents the person's basic experiential attitude. This belief deserves the serious attention and thought of every student of Rorschach's method. While I have some question about his opinion that the importance of the experience type is based primarily on its representation of the relation of extratensive to introversive attitudes, the factors making up the experience type do constitute the core of the test and are of basic significance for the testee's personality, i.e., for his way of approaching, experiencing, and reacting to the world. The reason for this lies in the fact that *all* the determinants, not just color and movement, play a direct or indirect role in the experience type, and that the determinants represent certain basic experiential-perceptual attitudes. The absolute and relative strength and specific quality of these attitudes and their relation to each other show basic aspects of the testee's relation to self and world. In Rorschach's work the experience type has two dimensions. One is the continuum from predominant introversiveness to predominant extratensiveness, represented by the relation of movement to color responses; the other the continuum from coartation to dilation, represented mainly by the relation of form to movement plus color responses. It is true that Rorschach mentions explicitly only the number of movement and color responses "and a few other factors" when he discusses the coartation and dilation of the experience type.[6] But it is clear from his presentation as well as from clinical experience that the significance of the absolute number of M and C responses for the coartation-dilation dimension of the experience type lies mainly in the fact that this number shows implicitly something about the relation

---

[5] *Ibid.*, p. 202.

[6] *Ibid.*, p. 86. The few other factors are mainly the F + %, sequence, and stereotypy (A%); i.e., those factors which can be increased—at least by the normal person—by an effort of will (concentration and logical discipline); pp. 90–92.

of M and C to F responses: Where M + C equals zero, it meant that all responses are form responses, since at the time Rorschach published his book (1921) the only determinants known to him were form, color, and movement.[7] This means that the coartation-dilation dimension of the experience type tells us something about the relation of the emotional capacity for experience (roughly represented by the M and C) to the conscious, critical, logical, intellectual functions (roughly represented by the form responses, especially the F+). The quality of this relation can enhance or stifle the person's capacity for a full experience of reality. As Rorschach put it, "the coartated and . . . coartative types are distinguished by the extreme predominance of those factors which can be increased by direction of conscious attention to them . . . ; these types are distinguished primarily by logical discipline. In achieving this discipline, however, introversive and extratensive features become atrophied; in other words, they sacrifice their ability to experience fully." [8] Rorschach thus was justified in assuming that the experience type pointed to factors of basic, diagnostic relevance. The relevance derives from the central position of the *determinants* in the test.

The determinants refer to the perceptual factors which constitute to the testee the *likeness,* the similarity between the object named in his response and the inkblot, or the part of the inkblot in which he saw the object. The likeness may have been based on the form of the blot, on its color, shading, on kinesthetic factors, or on a combination of two or more of these elements.[9] Hence, the determinants indicate the relative emphasis on these various visual experiences and their sequence in the testee's way of perceiving and interpreting the inkblots. If, as Rorschach believed, the determinants more than any other factor (such as location and content scores) permit a glimpse of the testee's way of experiencing, specific experiential processes and attitudes must play a decisive role in the perceptual acts leading to the emphasis on form, color, movement, or shading in a response. The relation between these

---

[7] He introduced shading as a determinant only later, in his case study of Oberholzer's patient (1922; published first in 1923, reprinted in the second and later editions of his book). Also, the fact that kinesthetic factors other than M and dynamic or physiognomic form responses have a bearing on the question of coartation and dilation was touched upon by Rorschach first in this case study.

[8] *Op. cit.,* p. 92. It is noteworthy that Rorschach continues this passage by noting the resemblance of the "adaptative extratensive" to the coartative type.

[9] There are still other factors which play a role in constituting the likeness between blot and object of response and which are not scored; for instance, distribution of masses, balance, etc.

processes or attitudes and the determinants would give us an important
clue to the *rationale* of the meaning of the determinant scores.

In the following analyses of the major determinants (form, color,
movement, and shading) I shall try to show that *each determinant* usually represents a *perceptual attitude* that is characteristic for the visual
experience resulting in a response based primarily on this determinant.
In other words, each determinant is typically perceived in a particular
kind of relatedness between perceiving subject and world-aspect (environmental object-aspect) seen; this kind of relatedness is different from
that prevailing in a perceptual experience which results in a percept
characterized by a different determinant. The hypothesis I shall develop is that *in perceiving color, form, movement (and shading),
different types of relatedness between perceiver and object perceived
typically prevail,* each type having distinct characteristics of its own.
These types of relatedness differ phenomenologically from each other.
They differ genetically in the sequence in which they appear and develop and in the role they typically play at different stages of genetic
development. They also differ in the role they play in adult perception,
depending on the degree and form in which genetically earlier attitudes
and forms of experience have been transformed, preserved relatively
unchanged, or reactivated ("regression") in different types of personality, in different kinds of mental illness or health, and in the vicissitudes
and fluctuations occurring in temporary shifts and changes of attitude.
By analyzing the typical psychological factors characteristic of man's
attitude in the perception of the various determinants, we may arrive at
a better understanding of why, in Rorschach's test, the various determinants have the meaning Rorschach's and subsequent empirical findings
have suggested. We may also understand better why sometimes what
seemingly is the same determinant may not have the same meaning.

The significance of our hypothesis for the theory of visual perception,
and for the perception of the Rorschach inkblots in particular, will become more clearly apparent if we contemplate it in the context of sensory perception in general, including the senses other than sight. There
too we can raise the question whether the different *senses* and their
*modes of functioning* may be better understood if we study the perceptual attitudes typical for each sense, the ways in which the perceptual
object, the environment is encountered in these attitudes, and in which
way these attitudes and modes of relatedness differ in different senses
and in different modes of functioning of a sense. Erwin Straus has

pointed out that the visual and auditory senses differ not only because they respond to different physical excitations by means of differently functioning organs and because they perceive different objects but also because of the *specific type of relatedness between subject and world* in each of these two senses and because they are different ways of communication between subject and world.[10] This holds true even more strikingly for the olfactory and gustatory as compared with the visual sense; but it also holds true for different modes of functioning of the visual sense. To analyze the kind of relatedness between perceiver and world characteristic of each sense and of different modes of functioning within a sense is an important task of phenomenological psychology.

In the present context, however, I only want to describe briefly two *basic modes of perceptual relatedness* which, roughly, distinguish between the so-called higher and lower senses, but which also differentiate between two different modes of functioning, especially of the higher senses, and which are relevant for the understanding of the rationale of the determinants.[11] They are the subject-centered, or *autocentric,* and the object-centered, or *allocentric,* modes of perception. The main differences between these two modes of perceptual relatedness are the following: "In the *autocentric* mode there is *little or no objectification;* the *emphasis* is on *how and what the person feels;* there is a *close relation,* amounting to a fusion, *between sensory quality and pleasure or unpleasure feelings* (pleasure-unpleasure-boundedness), and the perceiver reacts primarily to something *impinging* on him"; there also is, in some of the autocentric senses, felt organ-localization, i.e., the perceptual experience is *felt* to take place in a specific sense organ (nose, tongue or palate, skin), while this is not so in the usual adult functioning of the allocentric senses. "In the allocentric mode there is *objectification;* the emphasis is on *what the object is like;* there is either no relation or a less pronounced or less direct relation between sensory quality and pleasure-unpleasure feelings . . . ; the perceiver usually *approaches or turns* [*his attention*] *to the object actively* and in doing so opens himself toward it receptively or, figuratively or literally, takes hold of it, tries to 'grasp' it." The distinction between autocentric and allocentric both cuts across and differentiates between the different

---

10 Erwin Straus, *op. cit.,* p. 210.

11 For a detailed discussion of these two basic modes of perceptual relatedness in the various senses, genetically, phenomenologically, and in relation to personality attitudes and dynamics, see chapters 5–10 in Schachtel, *op. cit.,* pp. 81–248.

senses. "It cuts across them [because] developmentally the autocentric mode holds almost exclusive sway at the beginning of life in all the senses of the newborn and, later, the allocentric (higher) senses can and do function also in the autocentric mode, while the autocentric (lower) senses are capable only of a very limited degree of allocentricity. The distinction differentiates between the senses in that the allocentric (higher) senses usually function predominantly in the allocentric mode and are the only ones capable of full-fledged allocentric functioning, while the autocentric (lower) senses always function predominantly in the autocentric mode and are not capable of real allocentric perception." [12]

Rather than giving examples from all the senses, I shall illustrate the differences between autocentric and allocentric perception by comparing briefly the sense of taste with the sense of sight. In order to describe a pure taste experience one has to isolate taste from the natural unity of man's intersensory experience in which taste is intimately linked to smell and touch (sensitivity of palate and tongue to texture and viscosity), and one usually sees what one eats before one tastes it. In the experience of pure taste qualities (sour, sweet, bitter, salty),[13] no object is perceived. The tongue is *made to feel,* passively, these qualities by something that *impinges on it.*[14] But what this something is, what kind of object, of what form or structure, taste does not tell us. Only if the tactile receptors of tongue and palate are called into play may one get some idea of what this something which touches the tongue may be like, and only if one has seen it is he likely to have a full awareness of the object that caused the taste sensation. Actually, the taste receptors react only to liquid stimuli. Food has to be partly liquefied by chewing and by the action of saliva to be tasted. In other words, even if one had an awareness of object structure before tasting food, what he tastes is

---

[12] *Ibid.,* 83–84.

[13] These are the qualities that can be tasted without using the olfactory sense. The perception of most other tastes and flavors depends on the joint functioning of the gustatory and olfactory senses.

[14] The essentially passive perceptual attitude prevalent in the autocentric senses does not preclude the fact that one may pay active attention to *how* something impinging does affect one. For example, in *savoring* a taste active attention is paid to *how* the taste of something *feels* on the tongue. The difference here is between the striking impact, e.g., of the burning sensation on the tongue when one accidentally bites on a peppercorn, which one cannot help noticing, unpleasantly, and the subtle sensation, e.g., of a delicate taste to which one pays attention. Compare Schachtel, *op. cit.,* pp. 65–68 and 112–113.

no longer the same object. There is *no objectification* in the isolated functioning of the sense of *taste;* there is only the nonobjectified sensation of taste. Even if we consider the natural, intersensory experience of tasting food or drink in which gustatory as well as olfactory, tactile, and thermal receptors are involved, while there is some degree of objectification, it is still much lower than in sight and also considerably lower than in manual, active, tactile exploration of an object.

The taste sensation is not only one of sensory quality (sweet, salty, sour, bitter, etc.) but is also usually inextricably linked with pleasure or unpleasure ranging from mildly pleasant, stimulating, to delicious and from mildly unpleasant, irritating, to very disagreeable.[15] Sensory quality, in the sense of taste, usually is *pleasure-unpleasure-bound:* there is a fused experience of taste and pleasure or unpleasure. Furthermore, the gustatory sensation is felt to take place in the mouth, on tongue and palate (felt organ-localization); its quality is that of a bodily, physical sensation: a distinct area of the body is made to feel, passively, a particular way; it is affected by something that causes pleasant or unpleasant sensations on the tongue which have a specific sensory quality.[16]

The physical quality of the sensation, the way the body or part of it is passively affected by the fused experience of sensory quality and pleasure-unpleasure or comfort-discomfort in the autocentric senses is characterized, furthermore, by its *immediacy.*[17] One is directly affected by the sensation, without previous interference of thought, recognition, object-perception. If I bite accidentally on a peppercorn, I feel an immediate burning sensation on my tongue. This sensation may then cause me to think that I must have bitten on and tasted pepper, but the sensation itself takes place whether I know anything about pepper or not, whether I expect or want it or not.

It is a very different experience, indeed, to *see* a peppercorn and to

---

[15] The feeling of disgust which, with great individual differences, is often linked with certain foods or liquids, is an autocentric reaction. However, it usually is not a part of the gustatory experience proper, but often is more closely related to the intimate (oral) tactual contact with an object that is revolting to the person and to already existing biases that, in turn, may be due to early interpersonal experiences in connection with oral behavior.

[16] For traces of objectification in the sense of taste—caused as a rule by a shift of attitude toward object-centeredness—compare Schachtel, *op. cit.,* p. 98, and for the general problem of the relation between shift of attitude and mode of perception, pp. 213–236.

[17] "Immediacy" refers to the experiential quality, not to the measurement of abstract time, just as the psychoanalytic concept of delay does not refer to objective time measurement.

recognize it. Such perception and recognition usually takes place without any particular feeling, in a neutral, neither pleasant nor unpleasant, way.

*Sight,* the highest and most developed of the human senses, is clearly allocentric. It is characterized by *objectification.* We take for granted that to see means to see distinct objects. The main function of sight is recognition of and orientation in the visible environment which—in man—means to recognize, and orient oneself in, a very great variety of different and distinct objects. Sight allows us to grasp many features of any object simultaneously or in very quick succession, more so than does any other sense, and also many more objects, close by as well as far away. In contrast to this, the autocentric senses have a one-dimensional quality. They do not reveal the structure of an object; and the number of objects which, for example, one can taste in one or two seconds is quite limited, usually to one or else to an undifferentiated mixture of several objects experienced as *one* composite taste sensation.

Sight, in order to function fully, requires that we *turn our attention actively* to the object we want to see. Recognition of, orientation among, and exploration of the objects in our environment require some degree of active attention. While sight, as all the senses, also responds to impinging stimuli, e.g., to light, color, or contrast, or to something moving across our field of vision, it requires active attention to recognize what the moving object was that impinged on the eye.

Sight, furthermore, is not *pleasure–unpleasure-bound,* as taste is. The greater part of what the average adult person sees in the course of a day is perceived without particular feelings of pleasure or unpleasure. Seeing the letters or words in a book, the houses on the way to work, etc., takes place most of the time in a neutral atmosphere of orientation. Of course, I do not mean by this that the sense of sight cannot give us the most profound and sublime pleasure or—for that matter—marked displeasure. I want merely to point out that pleasure and unpleasure are not so closely and constantly linked (fused) with sight in adult man as they are with taste and smell (autocentric senses). Also, there is *no felt organ-localization* in sight. While I *know* that I see with my eyes, I do not *experience* or *feel* that the sensation of sight takes place in the eye. The experience is, rather, that *I* see, while in taste or smell I feel that the sensation takes place in my mouth or nose. Only in rare exceptions, for instance when looking straight at the sun, do I feel that a sensation actually takes place in the eye, in this case an unpleasant, slightly painful one: sight is now functioning in the autocentric mode; objectification recedes, the sensation of glaring light becomes predominant, is fused with unpleasure, and is felt *in* the eye. This sensation has the same one-dimensional, physical, bodily quality that we know from the autocentric senses; whereas the pleasure in seeing a beautiful building or a lovely landscape has a much more spiritual quality. In the latter case, we actively take in the sight that pleases us; in exposure to the glare of the sun the eye is passively afflicted by the impinging light, even if the irritation has been caused by turning the eyes deliberately toward the sun.

The brief description of the experiential differences between taste and sight will have to suffice as an illustration of the different modes of relatedness and attitude in autocentric and allocentric perception and of the different way in which the "object" is given to human experience in each of these modes. *Genetically*, two facts are of special significance in the role of the autocentric and allocentric modes of perception in human development. One is that in the neonate and during early infancy the autocentric senses (taste, smell, proprioception, visceroception, and touch)[18] play a much more important role than the allocentric (sight and hearing), while in the adult the reverse is the case. The other fact is that *all* the senses, including sight and hearing, function in the newborn in the autocentric mode, without objectification, mostly reacting passively to impinging stimuli, and largely with pleasure–unpleasure-boundedness.

The differences between the specific qualities of the autocentric and allocentric modes of perception suggest that these two basic perceptual modes are related to Freud's concepts of the pleasure and reality principles. The autocentric mode at first glance seems to function more in accordance with the pleasure principle or, as Freud originally called it, the unpleasure principle;[19] the allocentric mode more in accordance with the reality principle. Similarly, the developmental facts of the early all-but-exclusive predominance of the autocentric perceptual functioning and the very gradual development and eventual

---

[18] Touch is not an autocentric sense in the same way smell and taste are. In adult man, it occupies a curious middle position between the autocentric and allocentric senses, and one of its outstanding characteristics is that, depending on its passive or active functioning, it shifts frequently from the autocentric to the allocentric mode and vice-versa. For a more detailed discussion, see Schachtel, *op. cit.*, pp. 100–103.

[19] Freud, *The Interpretation of Dreams* [Standard Edition], V, 600.

predominance of allocentric perception are reminiscent of Freud's assumptions that in the earliest phase of development the pleasure (unpleasure) principle and its primary processes are the only kind of mental processes; that, furthermore, at that time there are no sensory perceptions but only unpleasure feelings due to excitation by sensory and drive stimuli, and pleasure feelings due to the abolishment or decrease of stimulation. However, while it is true that the perception of reality (which requires objectification) is a late achievement developmentally, the early development does not proceed from the absence of any sensory perception to the predominance of the reality principle, but from the predominance of autocentric perception (which *is* a mode of sensory perception) to that of allocentric perception. I believe that Freud's view has to be modified in four points:

(1) While Freud thought that at first no sensory quality is perceived but that only pleasure and unpleasure are felt in the interior of the psychic apparatus, actually the exteroceptors function from the first day of life (and most of them already in utero) and convey sensory quality as well as give rise to comfort and discomfort feelings. (Fusion of sensory quality and pleasure-unpleasure.)

(2) From birth on the newborn does not wish merely to abolish sensory stimuli, as Freud assumes, but also (increasingly) turns toward them and wants to prolong contact with them.

(3) Pleasure, even in the neonate, consists not only (although predominantly) in the absence or decrease of excitation or in the return to an excitationless state, but also in sensory excitation itself.

(4) Hence pleasure and reality are not intrinsically or inevitably opposed to each other, and the perception of reality does not serve merely as a necessary but unwelcome detour on the way to its abolishment in an excitationless state.[20]

In the development of *sight*, the sense of most immediate relevance to the understanding of Rorschach's test and especially of the rationale of the determinants, the transition from the autocentric to the predominantly allocentric functioning is characterized by a number of gradual changes. Especially significant are the following changes:

1. From a relatively minor role of the sense of sight as compared to touch, taste, smell, proprioception (especially kinesthetic) and viscero-

---

[20] Quoted from Schachtel, *Metamorphosis*, p. 117. The detailed facts and reasons which support the above view are given there, pp. 55–68, 116–165. For Freud's view compare especially his *Formulations Regarding the Two Principles of Mental Functioning* (1911) [Standard Edition], XII, 218–226; and *Instincts and Their Vicissitudes* (1915) [Standard Edition], XIV, 119–121.

ception to a predominant position of sight, a development that continues up to the age of eight or nine years.[21]

2. From *reacting passively to impinging stimuli* to *active turning toward visual stimuli*. This includes

3. the important development *from the unfocused gaze or stare to the focused "looking at"* and to following a moving object with the eye.

4. The change from predominantly wanting to abolish or avoid stimulation, because most or many stimuli are felt as unpleasant or as causing discomfort, to increasing maintenance or seeking out of visual stimuli. This goes together with

5. increasing pleasure and interest in an increasing scope and variety of visual stimuli.

6. The change from the perception only or mostly of light, darkness, color, striking contrasts, and global patterns to the gradual development and refinement of the perception of distinct form and structure.

7. From fusion of sensory quality and pleasure-unpleasure (comfort-discomfort) and lack of distinction of within and without to an increasing separation of within (bodily and other sensations and feelings) and without (an independent, although at first not very differentiated object-world). All the changes mentioned so far contribute to the important development

8. from the rather undifferentiated perception of an impinging and objectless visual field, not experienced as separate from an as-yet undeveloped self, to increasing objectification of gradually expanding variety, distinction, and richness. This also requires the change

9. from undifferentiated total sensations[22] to increasing coordination and experiential separation of the various senses, especially touch and sight.

10. The increasing objectification involves the change from undifferentiated, global object perception to increasing perception of distinct object features (more emphasis on detail, greater accuracy of form perception, distinction of different visual qualities).

11. All these developments contribute to the change from undifferentiated, total re-sensation ("déjà vécu"[23] experience of familiarity) to

[21] Compare Heinz Werner, *op. cit.*, p. 482, with further references.

[22] Compare Werner's "vital sensations," *ibid.*, p. 96, and the author's *Metamorphosis*, pp. 124–129.

[23] Compare Schachtel, *op. cit.*, pp. 158–164.

the increasing importance of re-cognition on the basis of a distinct visual Gestalt with distinct features.

But while sight is the most highly developed sense of man and while the most important quality in the high development of sight is the degree to which it is capable of functioning in the allocentric mode of perception, it would be misleading to assume that adult vision functions only in the allocentric mode. Like the other allocentric senses (hearing and active touch), sight retains and transforms throughout life some of its autocentric past in varying degrees, qualities, and fluctuations. Some of these autocentric factors can and do enrich adult, predominantly allocentric vision. People differ in the relative emphasis of the role of the more allocentric and the more autocentric functioning of sight in their lives and in the flexibility or rigidity with which they shift from one mode to the other and with which they are able to combine both or have to keep them separate, as it were. These differing emphases and ways of functioning are characteristic of the personality; they also fluctuate with changing moods, attitudes, situations, degrees of fatigue, aliveness, alertness. They differ in different states of consciousness, especially of attention and concentration, for instance in receptive openness versus goal-directed, narrowly focused attention; if the latter type of attention is rigidly maintained, the quality of the basic perceptual mode will differ from that of a person in whom receptive openness fluctuates flexibly with more active concentration. The functioning of the basic perceptual modes also differs significantly in various types of illness and health.

The allocentric or autocentric modes of visual perception are a major factor in the perceptual attitudes typical of the perception of some of Rorschach's determinants. Thus, *form* perception tends to be more *allocentric,* the perception of *color* (especially in the C and CF responses) more *autocentric.* This will be shown in greater detail in the following chapters. Also, the significant changes with chronological development from early childhood to adulthood of various factors in Rorschach's test (determinants as well as location scores and quality of W) are to a large extent results of the development of the allocentric mode of perception and the increasing objectification that is the main result of this development.

# 7 / FORM

*Und was in schwankender Erscheinung schwebt,*
*Befestiget mit dauernden Gedanken!*

[And what in wavering apparition gleams
Fix in its place with thoughts that stand forever!]
—Goethe, *Faust*, Prologue in Heaven (Bayard Taylor's translation)[1]

Form is the most important of the determinants as it is the most important aspect of the visible world. Out of Chaos form creates Kosmos. From Aristotle and Plato to Thomas Aquinas, Leonardo, and Goethe form has been recognized as the ordering, structuring principle of the universe perceived by man. But in the world of living organisms this holds true only if form allows for transformation. Where it becomes rigid and unchangeable, it paralyzes rather than structures life. In Rorschach's test, too, we can see that form can be constructive and destructive; constructive insofar as it gives order and structure to the unfamiliar inkblots, destructive when it becomes too paramount, rigid, schematic, or stereotyped and does not allow for flexibility, fluctuation and for openness to the charm, richness, and impact of color. Whether it does one or the other depends on the function it serves in the encounter of the testee with the inkblots.

The importance of form responses in Rorschach's test can be seen from the facts that in the great majority of records form is more frequent than any other determinant and that in many records more than half the responses are form responses. To some extent this is a result of Rorschach's and other scoring systems. Many responses scored F (form) are not exclusively determined by form in the sense of outline, but also by mass and expanse and by the contrast between the color (achromatic or chromatic) of this expanse and that of the white back-

---

[1] Goethe, *Faust* (Modern Library College Editions; New York: Random House, 1950), p. 12.

87

ground or of an adjoining area of the blot. This contrast as such plays a role regardless of whether the specific quality or nuance of color or shading, too, co-determines the percept and the response.[2] Moreover, at the time Rorschach completed his book, responses in which form and shading, or form and kinesthetic factors other than M, determined a response were scored by him as pure form responses. But even after making allowance for distortion due to scoring, form remains the most frequent and most important of the determinants; in most records there are no responses in which form perception does not play some role, either in combination with other determinants or with unscored perceptual factors or as the only determinant.

Similarly, *pure* form perception is a construct which does not usually occur in the perception of our natural environment. It does occur in man's conceptualization of spatial relationships in geometry and trigonometry, and it is approximated in the manmade world of signs such as letters or numerals, and in some designs, especially in diagrams. But while pure form perception is relatively rare, the role of form in man's perception of his visible environment is greater, more varied, and more important than that of any other factor in perception (color, shading, texture, etc.).

In order to arrive at a better understanding of the meaning of form responses in Rorschach's test and of the rationale of their meaning I shall consider, first, the function of form perception in the human sense of sight; second, the most frequent and typical perceptual attitude underlying the giving of form responses; third, the concept of perceptual hold and its relation to the form responses; fourth, the meaning of dynamic form responses; fifth, the problem of delay in the giving of form responses; and sixth, the development of form perception and the form responses of young children. I shall not discuss the scoring of the level of form accuracy (Rorschach's F+ and F− and the various finer differentiations of form level introduced by the Rorschach literature) since this has been dealt with in considerable detail by the literature; but in discussing the rationale of the form response, reference will be made to the adequacy or inadequacy of form perception and of form responses.

---

[2] Compare E. Earl Baughman, "An Experimental Analysis of the Relationship between Stimulus Structure and Behavior on the Rorschach," *Journal of Projective Techniques,* 23 (1959), 134–183.

### Function of Form Perception

Sight is commonly considered the most important and most highly developed sense of man. Aristotle attributed this preferred position of sight to the fact that sight more than any other sense enables man to become aware of the *distinctions* between things,[3] in other words, to recognize the distinguishing features of an object. The fact that sight indeed permits man to perceive many more features and do so more rapidly than any other sense is the basis of its objectifying, allocentric mode of functioning. This objectification rests primarily on the capacity of sight to perceive the *form* and Gestalt of a virtually infinite variety of objects. It is the function of form perception in man to *take hold* of certain salient features of the environment.

Such taking hold requires an *active* perceptual attitude; it requires looking attentively at something rather than merely being struck, passively, by something, as by a strong light or color. In looking at an object the eyes have to focus on it. This means an active organization of the visual field, lifting out of its diffuse impact a particular object which becomes the focus of attention and is set off against a less attended-to background. It means, furthermore, that eye and mind have to pursue the dominant lines, form, and structure of the object which are its distinctive features; they have to take hold of these features, thus establishing a firm perceptual grasp of the object, so that it or its like can be found, seen, and recognized again and, to some extent, recalled at will.[4] The activity in form perception can be quite short-lived, as in recognition of something familiar, or it may be prolonged and attentive, as in trying to take in something new, in orienting oneself in unfamiliar surroundings, or in exploring attentively something of interest. Within such active "looking at" one may be more receptively open to any feature of the object or one may be more actively looking *for* something. These attitudes may fluctuate and alternate. But in either case, the perception of form itself, whether it has caught one's attention or whether one has been looking for it, requires active focusing, structuring, and

---

[3] Aristotle, *Metaphysics* 98D a 26.

[4] Compare the work of von Holst on the active achievements of human visual perception. He shows that objectification and the constancy of the objects necessary for objectification are the result of *active* physiological, nervous, and psychological performance rather than a passive registration of stimuli. Erich von Holst, "Aktive Leistungen der menschlichen Gesichtswahrnehmung," *Studium Generale*, 10 (1957), 231–243.

attention. Form perception objectifies, i.e., transforms the visual field into definite patterns and objects; it structures the visual field.[5] And by means of form man can make representations or pictures of visual objects.

Form perception in man, thus, is an active, abstractive process inherent in the fully developed perceptual function and directed toward taking hold of or fixating definite structures and objects in such a way that they can be re-cognized, recalled, represented, and reconstructed. As Susanne K. Langer has formulated it: "A tendency to organize the sensory field into . . . patterns . . . to perceive forms rather than a flux of light impressions, seems to be inherent in our receptor apparatus. . . . This unconscious appreciation of forms is the primitive root of all abstraction, which in turn is the keynote of rationality. . . . I believe our ingrained habit of seeing *things* and not sense data rests on the fact that we promptly and unconsciously abstract a form from each sensory experience, and use this form to *conceive* the experience as a whole, as a 'thing.'" And in another passage: "The power . . . of regarding everything about a sense-datum as irrelevant except a certain *form* that it embodies, is the most characteristic trait of mankind. It issues in an unconscious, spontaneous process of *abstraction* which goes on all the time in the human mind. . . . *Abstractive seeing* is the foundation of our rationality. . . ."[6]

The human capacity to abstract and take hold of a great variety of forms by means of form perception far exceeds that of even the highest animals. While in many respects different animals surpass man in the sensitivity and acuity of one or another sense modality including, for

---

[5] It also structures the active, tactile field. But this is more pronounced in persons born blind than in seeing people, in whom vision becomes more important than the active, exploratory sense of touch. In complete darkness the active sense of touch, in people with sight rather fumblingly, has to take the place of sight.

[6] Susanne K. Langer, *Philosophy in a New Key* (New York: The New American Library of World Literature, 1951), pp. 72, 58. Langer speaks generally of all sense experiences. Actually, her observations apply only to the allocentric senses and it is no accident that the examples she gives in her discussion are taken from the visual and auditory senses.

A view similar to Langer's has been expressed by Arnheim, who describes (visual) perception as "creative acts of grasping structure" and says that "perceiving a thing means finding form in its structure." Rudolf Arnheim, "Perceptual Abstraction and Art," *Psychological Review*, 54 (1947), 66–82, pp. 70, 75.

I cannot in the present context pursue the wealth of material in the history of ideas witnessing the intrinsic relation between human form perception and human reason. Compare Whyte's "Chronological Survey of Form" in Lancelot Law Whyte (ed.), *Aspects of Form* (New York: Pellegrini & Cudahy, 1951).

example, the much more acute sense of sight of many birds, the human capacity to take hold of the forms of an infinite number and variety of objects is found in no animal.

The abstractive grasp of something definite and essential about the object in form perception is the main basis of man's orientation in the visual environment.[7] The act of selective, attentive visual focusing is constitutive for object perception in man: "it makes what before was part of the total (visual) field into a distinct object for the perceiver," [8] an object of definite form and structure. The more refined and varied man's grasp of the forms of the visible world, the richer his world will be and the greater his capacity for accurate recognition and orientation in the world.

The grasp of form is essential for the objectifying, allocentric mode of perceptual relatedness. The distinguishing feature of man's reality-orientation as compared with that of the animals is that it does not rely primarily on instinctive or on learned recognition of relatively few aspects and signs which are of vital importance in the narrowly circumscribed worlds of the various animals; but that it is potentially unlimited, open to the world, capable of taking in ever-new objects or object features. Form perception has primarily an *adaptive function*, serving the adaptation to the complex world of man and to nature. The degree of richness, variety, and complexity of a man's form perception can be considered an important, although not the only and exclusive, index of the richness and variety of his world and of the accuracy of his grasp of reality. If we follow Langer's thought, form perception is intimately related to *reason*, to man's *rationality*. And reason, certainly, is the most distinctive feature of man's—in contrast to the animals'—adaptation to and orientation in the world.

### Form Perception in Rorschach's Test and the Most Typical Perceptual Attitude Underlying Form Responses

So far we have considered only the general significance of form perception in man's sense of sight. Its relation to form perception in Rorschach's test will become most readily apparent by a brief review of the

---

[7] Compare Hilgard's emphasis on stability and definiteness as the outstanding "goals" of perception. Ernest R. Hilgard, "The Role of Learning in Perception" in *Perception: An Approach to Personality,* ed. Robert R. Blake and Glenn V. Ramsey (New York: The Ronald Press Co., 1951), pp. 95–121. Compare also Erich von Holst, *op. cit.,* concerning the visual constancy phenomena.

[8] E. Schachtel, *op. cit.,* p. 105.

*meaning* of form responses. Rorschach wrote about the form responses mainly from two aspects that are related to each other. His main interest was focused on the *clarity* of form visualization, manifested in percepts with a good likeness to the inkblots and expressed numerically in the F + %, the percentage of well, clearly seen forms. This he found to be a significant component of intelligence, "an indicator of the clarity of . . . associative processes, of the length of the span of attention and the ability to concentrate." [9] The second aspect under which Rorschach considered form responses concerns the level of the personality structure at which they originate. He held them to be the work of *consciousness,* of the conscious function, hence also capable of being improved by conscious effort. They represent "disciplined thinking." [10] These views have been confirmed by the later Rorschach literature, which has paraphrased them in different ways but not fundamentally changed them. Thus Beck considers them as representing intellectual, conscious control,[11] Rapaport as relating to the capacity for formal reasoning.[12] Just as adequate form perception is important for adaptation to reality, so it is also important for finding an accurate likeness to the "reality" of the Rorschach blots. Rapaport[13] finds that form responses are related to the person's "adherence to the demands of reality," Beck to "respect for reality." [14]

While the form responses are indeed a very important factor in assessing a testee's grasp of and adaptation to reality, Rorschach stressed rightly that the whole test, not only the giving of form responses, requires "adaptation to external stimuli, an action of the fonction du réel." [15]

These meanings of the form responses correspond quite well to the role and nature of form perception in man's life discussed before: form perception is to a large extent a function of consciousness, requiring attention to the salient, distinctive features of an object; it is essential for realistic orientation in and adaptation to the complex and infinitely var-

---

[9] *Op. cit.,* p. 57.

[10] *Ibid.,* pp. 209, 213, 67, 119.

[11] S. I. Beck, *Rorschach's Test* (New York: Grune & Stratton, 1944–45), I, 155; II, 19.

[12] Rapaport, *op. cit.,* II, 185.

[13] *Ibid.,* p. 185.

[14] *Ibid.,* II, 19–20.

[15] Rorschach, *op. cit.,* p. 123. (Translation changed slightly to render more closely the meaning of the German text.)

ied world of man; its full development is especially important for the functioning of visual perception in the allocentric mode which is characterized by objectification, that is to say, by seeing the object as existing independently of man, with distinct features of its own. While this is not all there is to form perception, it supports some of the symptomatic significance ascribed by the literature to the form responses, namely, as being related to adaptation to reality, as indicating something about the degree of attention and the quality of intellectual functioning, especially the factor of conscious control or discipline, and as being a function of consciousness.

But since form perception in Rorschach's test is not identical with, although it is related to, form perception in everyday life, which enables us to recognize the familiar and—much more rarely—to discover the new, we must look more closely at the processes leading to a form response and the *typical attitude* of the testee while arriving at an interpretation determined by adequately or well-perceived form (F+).

In most form responses to Rorschach's test (and in most responses in which form is combined with another determinant and is equally or more significant in determining the response), the *active* attitude is even more pronounced than in form perception in general. This becomes apparent when we consider the steps involved in the average form response: (1) Taking in the contours and other form elements of the unfamiliar inkblot requires more active attention than recognition of a familiar object. (2) This first taking hold of the blot features leads to tentative associations of objects that might resemble the inkblot or part of it. (3) A renewed active scrutiny of the blot features takes place in which the image of the object that came to mind during the process of association is tried out for fit, as it were. This usually involves some restructuring of the ambiguous inkblot in which those of its features are emphasized which might constitute likeness with the remembered object. (4) An *active, critical evaluation* of the likeness is made by comparing the form of the restructured inkblot or part of it with that of the object tried out for fit. (5) On the basis of this, the *decision* is made whether this particular association is acceptable to the testee as a response or not. If it is not, the process is repeated with another association.[16]

---

[16] This schematic account is in essential agreement with Rorschach and Rapaport. Rorschach emphasizes the active, conscious "effort of integration" (of memory engram with the present perception of the inkblot), *op. cit.*, p. 17. Rapaport, *op.*

Not all of the described steps in the formation of a form response are perceptual. The process of association, while it usually stays in touch with the requirement of perceptually adequate likeness, i.e., with the perception of the inkblot, may sometimes veer off and lose touch with the blot (e.g., in some of the so-called absurd responses of some schizophrenics or in some persevering responses of organic patients). The *decision* of whether a response is acceptable or not may sometimes be based, entirely or mainly, on factors other than adequate form likeness (e.g., on whether the content will be acceptable). In some testees, making a decision on the basis of which they have to *act*, namely, to communicate the response to the tester, is more a problem of the interpersonal test situation than of the form-adequacy of the response.

The active, *perceptual* attitude concerns the preliminary grasp of the inkblot features, the comparison of the features of the objects associated with those of the inkblot, and the concomitant restructuring of the inkblot features, and the critical evaluation of the degree of likeness. Not all form responses are based on all of these steps. For example, some testees respond with everything that comes to their mind, without critical evaluation of likeness. In very young children a global perception of the inkblot is usually followed by one "association" only, which often has more the character of "naming" this curious object, the inkblot, than of interpreting what it could be; in these cases no critical evaluation takes place and probably often no restructuring of the inkblot in line with the "name" given it, i.e., no trying on of the association for fit, for congruence with the inkblot. Their form perception is not yet sufficiently developed and differentiated.[17] While, thus, the degree and the quality of the active attitude vary, it is not possible to give a response determined by form without at least a minimum of active attention to the form of the inkblot and of the object associated, even though such minimal attention may be insufficient for the production of an F+ response, i.e., of an acceptable likeness.

The *typical attitude* in which the majority of form responses are given by most people, especially in the nonclinical, normal population, shows, in addition to the active attitude inherent in form perception, a

---

*cit.,* p. 190. The described phases or steps in the genesis of a response are not so neatly separated in reality as in the above account. Probably, there usually is a back-and-forth movement among them in which their basic sequence may be changed.

[17] Pathology, too, often leads to the omission, or cutting short, of one or more of the described steps.

*neutral, impersonal, matter-of-fact, objective, detached* quality in relation to the percept. Indeed, this attitude usually characterizes their predominant approach to the test task. Rorschach's question in posing the test task, "What might this be?," is understood by most people, normal or abnormal, as meaning that they should find an object the form of which resembles that of the inkblot or of part of it. This does not preclude, of course, that it may also resemble the blot in other respects, e.g., in its color. But since man perceives objects mainly in terms of their form, he also judges likeness mainly according to form likeness. However, while this fact accounts for the prominent role of form in Rorschach responses, it does not necessarily imply the described neutral, impersonal, detached attitude. Man can get very interested in forms and they may have considerable experiential significance for him. But I am inclined to assume that a large proportion of the clinically normal population does not approach the test with such an interest but more as one might approach a puzzle or some such task: that they try to find a fitting likeness to the form perceived without becoming particularly interested in the inkblot and without being particularly impressed or stimulated by it. Most people can produce form responses and achieve a good form likeness (F+) by conscious, voluntary effort.[18] Thus, many people tend to solve the test task by matter-of-factly—often rather laboriously—finding a form likeness that will do. Some testees may have a quite critical attitude toward their achievements, often painfully so. With much ambition and little imagination they may try in vain to find something so closely similar in shape to the inkblot that they cannot satisfy their high aspirations. Their efforts may be accompanied by such strong emotions as wavering self-evaluation, great ambition, fear of failure. But it is not the specific form perceived that causes these feelings; it is the rigid, strained, and narrow attitude to the test situation. Whether the neutral, matter-of-fact attitude is accompanied by such strain or by relative indifference, it is the impersonal, detached attitude, the lack of openness toward and interest in the inkblots that are likely to lead to a high percentage of form responses. Most of these tend to have an adequate form level and are personally of little or no significance to the testee, aside from being the solution to the test task.

If the described attitude prevails throughout the test, it leads to a

---

[18] Compare Rorschach, *op. cit.*, pp. 67–69; he also points out that such effort tends to decrease the number of M and C responses, i.e., to impoverish perception.

coartated or coartative (constricted or tending toward constriction) experience type. There are some indications that this can indeed be expected to be the predominant type of Rorschach performance in the total population.[19] This would correspond to Deri's findings with Szondi's test, according to which the most common reaction in the unselected adult population is the "broken ego" reaction ($-k$, $-p$) which, in her interpretation, indicates a fixation to the latency period and is found in people "who are extremely realistic, down to earth, [and] by whom the world is perceived and accepted at face value. They are overwhelmed by concrete objects and by reality to such an extent that there is no psychic energy left for introspection." She found this reaction most frequently in the nonintellectual occupational groups.[20] It is in these groups, too, that I would expect to find a greater frequency of coartated and coartative Rorschach records, that is to say, a higher percentage of form responses, than in the intellectual occupations.

However, the prevalence of this uninterested, impersonal, matter-of-fact attitude is not only due to a lack of energy for introspection, but just as much to a lack of education, capacity, and energy for sensibility, critical thought, and for that play of imagination, thought, and perceptiveness which are the prerequisites for penetrating and going beyond the conventionally accepted "face value" of the world as it is commonly presented in a given culture. As the reality and the possibilities of the world go far beyond and are different from the world seen through the culturally current clichés, so the reality and the possibilities of the inkblots go beyond and are different from those seen in the average, impersonal form responses.

The wide prevalence of this "realistic," neutral, impersonal, matter-of-fact perspective in our society and in the just-described attitude to the test situation is probably the reason why the form response, a frequent product of this attitude, is often considered a limited, impoverished

---

[19] Compare the relatively high F per cent of Rapaport's well-adjusted control group (average 65 per cent), *op. cit.*, II, 115. Compare also the striking coartation found in a group of 1000 adolescent boys from a low socioeconomic level. E. G. Schachtel, "Notes on Rorschach Tests of 500 Juvenile Delinquents and a Control Group of 500 Non-Delinquent Adolescents," *Journal of Projective Techniques*, 15 (1951), 144–172, p. 170. That this coartation is not characteristic of all adolescents is shown by Hertz's findings in a group of adolescents from a high socioeconomic background and with high average intelligence who tend to have a dilated experience type. Marguerite R. Hertz, "Personality Patterns in Adolescence as Portrayed by the Rorschach Ink Blot Method. I–IV," *Journal of Genetic Psychology*, 27 (1942), 119–188; 28 (1943), 3–16, 225–276; 29 (1944), 3–45.

[20] Deri, *op. cit.*, pp. 227–228. See also page 67, footnote 26.

type of perception.[21] But this is true only of the form responses given with the described attitude. It is also true that, in order to deal effectively with everyday reality, this attitude is indispensable for many situations. However, while it is prevalent it is not ubiquitous or indispensable in the giving of form responses, including F+ responses. Indeed, as we shall see later, it conflicts with, and usually prevents, the giving of especially well-perceived, original, or otherwise highly articulated and convincing F+. Actually, a good form response does not require an impersonal attitude throughout its genesis. It may have considerable personal, emotional significance; it may partly be determined by conscious or unconscious personal needs, drives, or feelings. But it does require that the testee be able to perceive objectively, consciously, and critically whether or not the object named in his response has a good form-likeness to the inkblot. In other words, it requires realistic, critical judgment. But whether this judgment is applied to an impersonal or to a personally meaningful form, whether it is applied to a "neutral" percept or to one that originated in a high degree of personal interest in and emotional openness to the form perceived, does not change the fact that we are dealing with a form response. That this is overlooked in most of the literature probably results from the fact that the personally meaningful F+ are relatively rare. It is also the result of a lack of clarity in the concepts of reality and of conscious intellectual control. It is said, rightly, that form responses are related to reality-testing, adaptation to reality, and conscious intellectual control. However, we have to distinguish conventional everyday reality and reality transcending the conventional, routine perception. As a matter of fact, true perception of reality presupposes intense interest in it and a fresh, unbiased eye and mind, not blinded by what is conventionally agreed upon as reality and usually veils rather than reveals true reality. Freud's concept of cathexis embodies the truth that only that in which we are deeply interested will become really accessible to our mind and our attention, even though such interest need not stem from libidinal, in the sense of sexual, needs. We also have to distinguish the type of conscious control which tends to be repressive of what does not conform to the demands of conventional reality from a control which is not thus repressive but permits objective, critical perception of those aspects of reality which may not fit in with the most widely socially, conventionally agreed-upon, and ac-

---

[21] Klopfer *et al.*, *op. cit.*, I, 270.

cessible reality. What the maintenance of an adequate or high form level ($F + \%$) does require is that the testee's critical judgment not be invaded, overpowered, or otherwise impaired by conflicts, need pressures, or other emotional factors. It does not require that the forms perceived and the form-likeness determining the response be personally or emotionally neutral or insignificant to the testee.

The meaning and the implications of the described differences in the genesis, perceptual attitude, and quality of most F responses and of those that are not so neutral and impersonal as the majority of F are will become clearer when we consider the function of form perception insofar as it serves to *grasp,* to *take hold* of reality, of the distinguishing features of the objects in man's environment.

### The Form Response and the Concept of Perceptual Hold

Mainly by means of form perception man's world becomes one of a great variety of definite, recognizable objects. I shall designate his taking hold, perceptually, of the object world as his "perceptual hold." By this I mean an experiential dimension of perception which extends from a firm to a weak or tenuous perceptual hold of the object perceived. This aspect of perception is a part and function of the quality of the person's relatedness to the world. It has not yet been sufficiently noticed and studied. Therefore, I shall discuss the concept of perceptual hold first with regard to some of its general implications for perception and then describe some ways in which this aspect of perception becomes apparent in and affects the form responses in Rorschach's test.

Like all individual differences in perception, the habitual quality as well as the fluctuations of a person's perceptual hold are usually obscured by the common currency of the linguistic labels by which we communicate what we see, hear, or feel to others and which reveal only in rather exceptional cases that we perceive the same object in some respects differently from the way in which the person with whom we talk perceives it. Moreover, the elusive quality of perceptual hold usually does not come, or comes only dimly, to the awareness of the perceiver and is hard to describe accurately.

In spite of its elusiveness, the phenomenon of perceptual hold is familiar to *language,* and the consequences of a firm or weak perceptual hold occur in everybody's life, even though not everybody pays attention to them. The word "perceive" derives from the Latin *percipere,* which means both to take hold or possession of something and to notice, sense, perceive or learn—i.e., to take hold of something with one's senses and mind.[22] Similarly, the German *wahrnehmen* ( = perceive) is composed of *nehmen* = to take and *wahr* (from the Indogermanic root >*wer*< from which the English be*ware* derives) and means originally to take into careful, watchful attention.[23] Thus, language tells us that perceiving has to do with taking hold, taking possession by means of our senses and our attention. The capacity to do this develops only gradually as the newborn, on whom the outer world impinges in unpleasant or pleasant sensations, grows through infancy into early childhood and increasingly enjoys and learns to focus his glance, to listen *to* something, to explore by touch; in brief, to turn to the world and to take hold of it.

Fluctuations in the firmness of perceptual hold are part of everybody's experience. The two main factors on which such fluctuations seem to depend are the presence and strength or absence of a *framework of familiarity and orientation* and the *degree and quality of interest* with which a person turns to the object perceived. A striking example of the effect of the first of these two factors is the experience of waking up in a strange room when there is not much light, so that visibility is poor, or when one is dependent entirely on tactile cues for orientation. Although in these circumstances no more sensory cues are available in a familiar than in a strange room, the framework of familiarity in the former suffices to give the perceiver the feeling of a firm grasp of the objects dimly perceived and a sense of reliable orientation, while in the latter he may experience a most tenuous hold on what he touches or sees and a temporary sense of disorientation.

The *effect of interest on perceptual hold* becomes apparent when one compares the vivid and clear impression of an object to which one has turned with full interest and receptiveness with the shallow and vague or one-sided impression made by an object at which one has looked without any interest or merely to use it for some routine purpose, as in looking at a clock to know what the time is, at a bench or chair to sit on it, or at a man to ask directions. This does not mean that, whenever one uses an object, this excludes a fuller turning to the object. One may be

---

[22] Compare also "to behold," which in current usage connotes an emphatic taking hold of in sight or with the mind, and in which the root "hold" is obvious.

[23] Friedrich Kluge, *Etymologisches Wörterbuch der deutschen Sprache* (Berlin: Walter de Gruyter & Co., 1957), p. 834.

quite interested in the person from whom one asks directions in a strange city, or one may take in the functional or aesthetic qualities of the chair on which one intends to sit. I am speaking here of those cases only where one is *merely* interested in the use to be made of an object or a person and in nothing else.[24]

However, firmness of perceptual hold is not identical with perceptual openness and receptiveness. While it can be a consequence of such openness, it also can be a barrier preventing it. The subjective experience of a firm perceptual hold can stem from a rigid framework furnishing the perspective from which the object is viewed and which limits or prevents open receptiveness, or from a flexible, relaxed, yet concentrated openness toward the object. While there are significant phenomenological and dynamic differences between the perceptual hold resulting from a stable, familiar perspective and that from flexible openness toward the object, both kinds can give the perceiver a subjective feeling of security and of knowing what he sees and where he is, that is to say, a secure feeling of orientation in the world and of himself in relation to the world.

The human tendency to cling to a familiar and often rigid framework that furnishes a perspective on the phenomena perceived by the senses and the mind and at the same time bars other, possibly more adequate perspectives, pervades all spheres of man's life. Thus, the human need for a secure and stable framework of orientation often leads to a preference for closed systems of thought, belief, and ways of life which are more tolerable to man than his actual condition of living in an open and infinite world where there is no certainty. Such systems, often largely and always to some extent unconscious, are the basis of particular perceptual perspectives. These supply a firmness of perceptual hold which can be so rigid as to exclude openness toward the world, or they can be sufficiently flexible to allow a certain degree of such openness. The barriers protecting a rigid perceptual hold supplied by the perspective of the familiar may quite literally prevent people from moving outside the home, the family, the home town, the country; by avoiding such moves many people never become aware of these barriers, and others may feel mild or severe anxiety when they attempt or are forced by circumstances to leave the familiar environment. Such anxiety may take the crippling form of, for example, agoraphobia or the milder form

---

24 Compare Schachtel, *op. cit.*, pp. 166–248.

of fearing traveling or being anxious about one thing or another while traveling. But the barriers protecting the familiar perspective may also take the more subtle form of selective inattention, of not allowing the person to see the familiar from a new perspective, or, in the example of travel, they may be maintained by one's not being open to the new but trying, in one way or another, to stay at home as it were even while traveling. This can be achieved, for example, by automatically comparing the new and different unfavorably with the familiar, thus rejecting rather than receiving it and relating to it.[25]

Genetically, frames of reference leading to a certain perspective derive from several sources. A major source is that provided by the society, culture, language which have formed the perceiver's personality and mind. Within this larger framework, the more specific influences of a particular social group and, for example in the cases of an artist, writer, scientist, the influence of a particular style or school of thought or of a significant teacher or admired model, may lead to a particular perspective. The viewpoint of the scientist, too, is an example of a particular perspective which tends to focus on certain aspects of the world while excluding others. And among different types of scientists there will be found, as among different painters and writers, a variety of such perspectives. They also vary individually in their rigidity or flexibility, thus leading to more or less blindness or openness to other aspects of the world.

Finally, the personal history of each individual man will lead to a personal perspective, a personal view of the world and of himself of which, more often than not, he is not aware at all or not aware as something peculiar to himself, and which others may also not become aware of in him, but which can be discovered by psychological analysis. Furthermore, the degree to which a person is caught, usually unwittingly, in the perspective of a particular culture or social group depends, in turn, on his individual personality structure and the individual circumstances and opportunities of his life. Awareness of the particular perspective of a culture can usually be gained only by transcending the confines of this culture in some way.

A pathological example of the reassuring function of a rigid framework of perception which supplies a firm, if distorting, perceptual hold can be observed in the paranoid development of schizophrenia, espe-

---

[25] Compare the discussion of the impact of the unknown in Chapter 3, pp. 21–23.

cially if such a development follows catatonic stupor or excitement. The terrifying, awesome and incomprehensible events, the cosmic struggles between good and evil in the midst of which the catatonic patient lives are replaced by a new "understanding" in which unfortunate aspects of his life are seen as the work of particular persons, his "enemies." In this transformation his confusion and panic are supplanted by a stable frame of reference. The narrow and distorting perspective of this newly found frame of reference is rarely given up by him, because, as long as he remains in it, he gains not only the great relief of being able to ascribe to others what has previously burdened him as blameworthy in himself, but also he wins the relative security of what is to him a clear and stable, henceforth familiar, orientation in and perspective on his environment and his relation to it. Sullivan makes the interesting observation that, in some cases, "the beginning phase of the paranoid state has a curiously relationship with . . . 'moments of illumination.' These occur when, by extremely fortunate circumstance, one actually sees . . . a real situation that he has been selectively inattending to previously, so that he is really better oriented." [26]

This touches on a point that is significant for both normal and emotionally disturbed people. It thus has a much wider bearing than merely on the understanding of paranoid development, in which the peculiar tenacity of a rigid and distorting perspective stems in large part from the urgency of the defensive need to keep from awareness the real or imagined liabilities and shortcomings of the patient's personality. The illumination which occurs when one suddenly sees a situation or a person as they really are will henceforth provide a new frame of orientation that in turn has the tendency to become rigid because man cannot, at every moment, perceive the world afresh but, in order to be able to orient himself, has to hold on to a frame of orientation that he has taken over from others or developed for himself from what he has learned, perceived, and experienced. Hence the need to hold on to a newly found or to a long-familiar "point of view." The similarity of the paranoid transformation and the illuminating experience of seeing something afresh, in a new light, from a new angle lies in the fact that they are both usually the outcome of a crisis, of doubt, struggle, anxiety,

---

[26] This account is based on Sullivan's vivid and detailed description of the paranoid transformation. Harry Stack Sullivan, *Conceptions of Modern Psychiatry* (New York: W. W. Norton and Co., 1953), pp. 151–157; *The Interpersonal Theory of Psychiatry* (New York: W. W. Norton and Co., 1953), pp. 361–362.

and confusion, and that they both lead to a relatively stable new perspective. Their differences lie in the nature of the crisis and in the greater rigidity and the distortion of the newly established paranoid perspective as compared with the more flexible, newly won realistic perspective on some aspect of the world.

The illumination of a newly found perspective takes place not only in the example of suddenly seeing a person or a situation in a new and truer light, but also in the work and life of the great artists, poets, writers, scientists, philosophers, and founders of religion and in our own lives when we suddenly see a tree or a landscape in a new and fresh light or when we gain a new and enriching understanding of something. In the area of visual perception, which is our primary concern in thinking about the problem of perceptual hold in connection with Rorschach's test, the foregoing is best illustrated by an example from the sphere of art, brought to life in Proust's description of the effect of Renoir's paintings. In the artist's work "the world, which, far from having been created once and for all, is created afresh each time that a new artist comes on the scene, is shown to us in perfect clarity—but looking very different from the one we knew before. The women walking in the street are different from those we saw formerly, because they are Renoir's, those women of Renoir whom once we refused to recognize as women at all. The carriages, too, are Renoir's, the water, the sky. We are seized with a longing to walk in the forest which, when we first looked at it, seemed anything *but* a forest, seemed, for instance, like a tapestry, showing every shade of color, every nuance of form, *except* the colors and the forms peculiar to forests. Such is the new and perishable universe freshly created. It will remain convincing until the next geological catastrophe precipitated by a new painter or a new writer of originality. . . ." [27] The new perspective, opened up in the work of the artist, is based on the openness of his sensibility toward the world that permits "a true vision; that is to say, a vision felt rather than imagined and wholly distinct from the ordinary, collective vision which is what lies at the basis of realism." [28]

The examples of the paranoid shift of perceptual perspective, which

[27] From *Marcel Proust, Selections from His Miscellaneous Writings*, translated by Gerard Hopkins, quoted by André Maurois, *Proust* (New York: Meridian Books, 1958), p. 189.

[28] *Ibid.*, p. 188, quoted from René Huyghe, *"Affinités électives: Vermeer et Proust," Amour de l'Art*, XVII (1936), 7–15.

henceforth will imprison the sufferer in a rigid and distorting frame of reference, and of the illuminating breakthrough to a new perspective in creative work, which subsequently may become rigid and an obstacle to openness toward the world, are particularly telling illustrations of a phenomenon that is part of everybody's life—although it usually takes less striking forms. Significant examples of this can be seen in childhood development, on a consciously manipulated mass scale in modern advertising, and in man's attitudes toward other people, especially toward the stranger and toward the enemy in war.[29]

---

[29] In the development from earliest infancy to later childhood, there is in all not severely disturbed children a constant opening up of new perspectives on the world in the child's exploration and learning. Education and the child's own need for a stable framework of orientation tend to solidify these perspectives in the direction of the prevailing culture and of the social group into which the child is born and in which he grows up. The degree to which these developing perspectives exclude or make difficult access to other perspectives depends on the attitudes of parents and other significant people in the child's life and also on the constitutionally given strength of the child's desire to explore, to use his own senses and mind, versus his anxiety in the face of the unknown and his needs to depend on, be in agreement with, and accepted by others.

In modern mass-media advertising and brand packaging, a conscious attempt is made to establish in the consumer's mind a perspective that will make a brand of merchandise stand out visually and appear particularly familiar and desirable to him and will prevent him from using his senses and his reason to explore what his real needs are and what kind of merchandise is best suited to satisfy them. The possible rational function of advertising, namely, to make known the objectively relevant kinds and qualities of available goods so that the consumer may make a reasonable choice, plays a minor role.

In war a deliberate effort is made to depict the enemy as inhuman or, at least, as less human than one's own people. This is done by creating a negative cliché of the enemy which is intended to prevent, and to a large extent succeeds in preventing, that open receptiveness and active interest which lead to a full and clear perception of another human being. The enemy must not be seen as being as human as oneself. A similarly limiting perspective, although sometimes not so deliberately planned and manipulated as in wartime, can be found in man's attitude to the stranger. In the case of the stranger and the enemy, the visual distortion of a rigid, preconceived, schematic perspective becomes especially palpable. In its milder form it is apparent in the fact that to many people persons belonging to a race that is markedly physically different from the perceiver's own seem to look alike, lacking in individual characteristics. Many Westerners fail to see the individual features of a Japanese or Chinese and find it hard or impossible to tell one Chinese from another, unless they develop a personal relationship with them. The gross concept and rigid visual schema of "the Chinese" replaces and effectively obliterates the more differentiated, flexible openness toward the individual features of this particular Chinese person. Only by entering a personal relationship with the other person, which means by becoming open, receptive, interested in him, do the individual features become part of how the other person is seen. Without such a personal relationship a mask is seen instead of a unique living face.

In its more hateful form, e.g., in relation to hated minority groups or to the hated enemy, this mask becomes a caricature which makes the real human face of the other peson not only invisible but distorts it into monstrosity or grotesqueness. The

The psychoanalyst is in a particularly favorable position for the observation of individual, rigid perspectives, their development in a particular person's life, and their limiting effect which bars a fuller, more realistic view by the analysand of other people. A striking example is the tenacious hold with which many patients cling to a one-sided, hence distorted, view of their parents, marriage partner, and other significant people in their lives. While often these perceptions are based on some realistically present quality of the other person, this quality becomes so overemphasized, because of a particular fear, vulnerability, need, or wish of the patient, that everything else about the other person is blotted out, thus giving rise to a distorted image which, in actual perception, covers the other person like a caricaturing mask behind which all other human qualities disappear. The person thus becomes hero or villain, as the case may be, while actually he is neither a hero nor a villain but simply human like the perceiver himself. Even though such a one-sided view may be painful, irritating, or aggravating to the patient and may perpetuate unnecessary suffering, he nevertheless often derives a certain security from such a framework of (mis)orientation. The prospect of renouncing it may arouse anxiety or panic, connected with the prospect of encountering something different from the familiar person and therefore of no longer being able to respond in the accustomed way and of having to give up a long-ingrained attitude without yet knowing where this will leave him. Similar perspectives in which people appear as black or white are also found in many normal people.

Seeing people as black and white is a particularly striking and obvious example of a rigid, distorting perspective. More subtle yet pervasive perspectives derive from the basic dynamics of character structure and from the resulting total attitude toward the world. This attitude comprises the individual experiential structure of time, space, and of

---

*Stürmer*, periodical of the rabid Nazi anti-Semite Streicher, was largely devoted to contriving a hateful stereotype of the "Jew" by means of vicious caricatures. The "slit eyes" attributed to Far Eastern people have similarly sinister implications; those who have succumbed to this mask-stereotype are unable to perceive fully the eyes, one of the most expressive features of the face, of the stranger.

These examples illustrate that perception, as an ongoing process, cannot be separated neatly from the concepts, ideas, images, anticipations, feelings, interests, preoccupations, and general perspectives with which the perceiver approaches the world, but that these become intrinsic parts of the actual scope and clarity of perception. The cliché perception of the stranger as somewhat less human than oneself and, at worst, as an object of suspicion and hatred may be termed a normal (in the statistical sense of normality) paranoia which shares some dynamic features with the perceptual distortions occurring in pathological paranoid states.

the meaning of self and world, hence also has a decisive impact on the structure of perception.[30]

While all perspectives originating in a (conscious or unconscious) familiar framework of orientation give to the perceiver the experience of a firm perceptual hold, the quality of this hold differs from that based on the perceiver's turning to the object with openness and interest in a direct encounter with the object. The general perspective applies to a wide range of things, often to the whole world-view of the perceiver, and in that sense is less limited than the single encounter with a particular object. On the other hand, it is more limited than the perceptual hold based on the open, immediate encounter in that it is less rich, less full, less alive. This paradox is familiar to those who are able to see all of life in the face of a person or the leaf of a tree and also know, at the same time, the value and significance of general laws, a general frame of orientation. It reminds us of the fact that the firmness of perceptual hold depends on both the framework of orientation *and* the quality of interest. While these two factors can be in harmony with each other, they can also be in conflict. Rigidity of (holding on to) a general perspective may block the capacity for spontaneous interest and open receptiveness. The illuminating impact of a sudden new vision may shake the foundations of one's accustomed general perspective and arouse anxiety and doubt. Only careful analysis can reveal the role of these two factors in the quality of the perceptual hold in any concrete act of perception. This has to be kept in mind in the following consideration of various conditions which lead to a weakening of perceptual hold.

*Anxiety* is one such condition. Overt, diffuse anxiety weakens perceptual hold. It interferes with the firmness of the general framework of orientation as well as with the capacity to turn with interest and openness fully to any particular object. The interference of anxiety with perceptual hold is consistent with its generally disruptive effect. It is an expression, in the particular area of perception, of the disruption of relatedness by anxiety. The disturbance of perceptual hold by anxiety varies in degree from a slight uneasiness in which everything seems to be not quite so fully or firmly there as it is in a confident, anxiety-free state of mind to actual states of disorientation, dizziness, or nausea in

---

[30] For detailed phenomenological analyses of pathological changes in the structure of experience and perception compare the work of E. Minkowski, von Gebsattel, E. Straus, and L. Binswanger.

which reality recedes or seems to become slightly confused and unreliable and in which the person no longer feels able to turn with interest to anything at all.

This disruptive effect of overt, diffuse anxiety differs from the effects of *fear* and from the effects of *defenses* against anxiety, i.e., from the effects of covert anxiety. Fear usually leads to the formation of a rigid perspective in which a heightened, vigilant alertness is focused on the fear-arousing object or is waiting for its appearance, and where at the same time possibilities of eliminating the object, by fight or by escape, are sought. Thus, a one-sided but often sharpened, limited view of the fear-arousing object and of the environmental possibilities of dealing with it results. Defense against (covert) anxiety often increases the rigidity of the general perspective and frame of reference, or it seeks to distract by means of some preoccupation. Thus, both fear and defense against anxiety interfere with the possibility of flexible and full openness of perception toward the world, but they do not lead to an over-all weakening of perceptual hold. In fact, the strength of a quite limited and one-sided perceptual hold may be increased by fear and by defense against anxiety.

*Depression* and *boredom* also interfere with the firmness of perceptual hold. In both conditions the person feels unable to become interested in anything. The lack of interest prevents the type of perceptual hold which derives from turning to the object fully and with receptive openness. Thus, the richness, vividness, and full presence of the objects are lost. Depression and boredom usually do not interfere drastically with the general framework of orientation. The depressed or bored person does not feel disoriented; yet the objects among which he is able to orient himself acquire a peculiar quality of emptiness and a loss of meaning. As in anxiety, they do not seem fully present because the perceptual hold and the general relatedness to the world have weakened. The reason for this is that, without the emotional charge (cathexis) which activates man's pursuits, the interest in these pursuits is weakened or lacking altogether. This lack of zest and interest weakens also that perceptual hold which is based on a one-sided perspective or frame of reference, for example the perspective characteristic of perception in most human activities in which objects are perceived primarily as serving a particular purpose, use, appetite, or need.[31] Interest alto-

---

[31] For a fuller discussion of this perspective, see Schachtel, *op. cit.*, pp. 166–212.

gether, one-sided or total, is lost or weakened and this leads to a more tenuous perceptual hold. Sensory communication with the world palls in states of boredom and depression.[32]

Perceptual hold also becomes more tenuous in the polar opposite of depression and depressive mood, in *manic* or *hypomanic excitement*, and in the restlessness which sometimes replaces, sometimes goes with, boredom. In these states the person makes a frantic effort to escape from the emptiness of world and self that he experiences in depression and boredom. But the frantic nature of these efforts results in flighty pseudo-contacts which are based not on interest but usually on impatient and angry demands.[33] In the sphere of perception this leads to an erratic, short-lived, and flimsy perceptual hold in which nothing is allowed to have a full impact on the perceiver and in which the perceiver grasps nothing fully.

In the pathological phenomenon of *derealization*, which usually goes together with depersonalization, the weakening of perceptual hold becomes conscious in the feeling of estrangement from the object world. The usual bond between perceiver and object perceived is curiously disrupted and the perceiver is painfully aware of this fact. Actually, the estrangement from the object world in derealization feelings is a close relative of the unaliveness and dullness of the world in depression[34] and boredom.

The strength of perceptual hold may also be impaired by a *general, basic inhibitedness of the capacity to approach and turn to the world and its objects*. Such inhibitedness has been described by Schultz-Henke as inhibition of intentionality (*"intentionale Gehemmtheit"*).[35]

The degree and quality of perceptual hold are closely linked to subsequent *memory* and *recall*. In general, a firm perceptual hold makes it more likely that something which has been perceived will be remembered and will be accessible to recall. If perceptual hold is impaired, as in anxiety, depression, and boredom, nothing much is remembered later. And while during these states time seems to stretch out unbearably, in retrospect it shrinks because it has been empty, due to the disruption or

---

[32] See *ibid.*, pp. 231–233.

[33] *Ibid.*, pp. 233–234.

[34] The affinity between depression, depersonalization, and derealization has been pointed out by von Gebsattel, *"Zur Frage der Depersonalisation"* in *Prolegomena einer medizinischen Anthropologie* (Berlin: Springer-Verlag, 1954), pp. 18–46.

[35] Harald Schultz-Henke, *Lehrbuch der analytischen Psychotherapie* (Stuttgart: Georg Thieme Verlag, 1951), pp. 24–25, 56–58, 104–105.

impairment of relatedness and perceptual hold. Where perceptual hold is based primarily on a familiar and rather rigid perspective, recall is likely to function well but schematically, that is, the familiar schema of things will be available to recall rather than the always more elusive richness of a fully experienced object. But when the perceiver has turned fully to an object with all his sensibilities open and receptive, he is likely to remember it more fully than an object seen merely from a long-familiar perspective, even though the richness of such memory will eventually fade with time and no longer be readily available to vivid recall.[36]

The way in which a testee perceives and responds to Rorschach's inkblots is affected by and expressive of his perceptual hold on them. In fact, Rorschach's test is more sensitive to, and more readily permits observation of, the degree and quality of perceptual hold than does everyday perception. The main reason for this lies in the unfamiliar and ambiguous structure of the inkblots, which has the effect of making it more difficult to see them from the same perspective as that from which the familiar environment is viewed, and which renders observable differences in perceptual hold that, in ordinary communication, would be hidden under the shared, common language labels.

The most significant clue to the degree and quality of perceptual hold lies in the *form* responses. The function of form perception in man is to take hold of the salient features of objects. It does so by focusing on an object, thereby lifting it out of the total impinging field, as it were. In abstracting the salient features from the global visual impression of the object, in following its basic structure and Gestalt with the eye, we recognize, fixate, identify it.

Form perception can fulfill its abstractive, objectifying, identifying, orienting functions well only if the forms perceived are adequate; that is, if they correspond to the actual object seen and if the abstraction from the total object in the form perceived is valid and grasps the essential qualities of the object. Only if these requirements are fulfilled does the perceiver have a firm perceptual hold. In everyday life this firm grasp is usually supplied by our familiarity with the objects around us and, on much less frequent occasions, by a convincing, fresh view of an object to which we have turned with deep interest and receptive openness. Thus, perceptual hold rests on the firm perspective of familiarity or on active interest, receptive openness, and decisive grasp. These

---

[36] For a more detailed discussion of these relations between perception, experience, and memory see Schachtel, *op. cit.*, pp. 279–322.

are not mutually exclusive alternatives. Concrete acts of perception probably never take place entirely outside a framework of familiarity. The degree to which they transcend this framework or offer the possibility of transcending it varies a great deal and depends partly on the degree and quality of interest, openness, and decisiveness or daring. But nobody would be able to live and to function effectively if he saw everything from a new perspective all the time. Even the most spontaneous person is dependent on the kind of automatic routine perception that is based on a relatively stable frame of reference and orientation.

In Rorschach's test the perspective of familiarity is lacking or is at least much less readily available; hence it is more difficult to gain a firm perceptual hold of the blot. As a rule, this implies the task of selecting out of the unfamiliar and ambiguous structure of the blot such features as will lead to a convincing, or at least acceptable, likeness. The main yardstick by which Rorschach measured success in solving this task is the F+ response and, especially, the F + %, the percentage of acceptable likenesses (F+) in relation to all form responses given. However, his concept of the form response and especially of the F+ response obscures significant qualitative differences. I shall discuss these differences here mainly insofar as they have a bearing on the problem of perceptual hold and shall consider first two different types of F+ responses which are particularly significant for this problem.

The perceptual hold is based in one of these two types of F+, either on the closed and often rather stereotyped or even rigid perspective of familiarity or on other, similarly stereotyped frames of reference. In the other type, perceptual hold is based on a more alive and fuller encounter with and flexible openness toward the inkblot and on a fresh, decisive, usually more personally meaningful grasp of its essential features. I believe that these two types of F+ are based on and expressive of two different perceptual attitudes and modes of relatedness. Hence, they are likely to be distributed differently among different clinical groups. We can expect to find records which will show F+ based on the perspective of familiarity or other rather stereotyped or schematic F+ and other records which, in addition, will show a number of freshly and convincingly seen, possibly original F+. I shall call the two types of F+ the ordinary F+ and the special F+.[37]

---

[37] The term "special F+" is taken from Rapaport, *op. cit.*, pp. 187–193. I have the impression that his special F+ are largely identical with the more alive and keenly grasped forms I have in mind. His score Fo, by which he designates the "mediocre, but acceptable form response" (p. 187), seems to be identical with Rorschach's sta-

I believe that the special F+ are not indicative of a number of traits, tendencies, and qualities that in the literature on Rorschach are quite generally attributed to all F, including the F+ responses, namely, inhibition, repression, constriction, impersonal objectivity; that they are not always free from personal "complexes" and that they do not represent "a limited or impoverished type of perception" or indicate the "capacity of handling situations in an impersonal . . . way." [38] This belief is based on my clinical experience as well as on a number of findings mentioned by Rorschach and others which seem incompatible with these generally accepted meanings of F responses. On the other hand, these meanings do usually apply to the ordinary F+.[39]

One of the requirements for the special F+ is the availability of a wide variety of clearly remembered form images.[40] This, in turn, implies (1) that many forms have been clearly grasped in the past experience of the testee and (2) that they are available for recall. This accessibility of memory images and of memory in general, i.e., the capacity for recall at the right moment, is a highly sensitive function that can be easily disturbed. It requires a freedom and flexibility of association not present, for instance, in the depressed and in the anxious. In most people, freedom of association and recall is also disrupted by excessive straining for a narrowly defined goal. This is the case in the habitually exaggerated concern of the pedant with accuracy and order. A temporary impairment of freedom of association often occurs in people who experience pressure toward top performance in an examination situation.[41]

---

tistically arrived-at F+, namely, those forms which are seen most frequently by a large number of normal testees (Rorschach, *op. cit.*, p. 23) and thus with the concept of ordinary F+. While I shall use Rapaport's term special F+, I shall discuss the two types of F+ here primarily from a different viewpoint, namely, in the context of the dynamics of perceptual hold rather than as indicators of the capacity for formal reasoning, of a component of intelligence, of intellectual control, all of which they are, too, according to Rorschach and the general consensus of the Rorschach literature.

[38] Klopfer *et al., op. cit.*, I, 270.

[39] Not always. Both ordinary F+ and F− responses can be dynamic form responses codetermined by personal "complexes" (see below, pp. 123–144). Compare also Rorschach's remark that in people in good humor (i.e., a nonrepressive, non-inhibiting frame of mind) "material otherwise repressed . . . [may] get smuggled into consciousness" and may appear in their form responses. Rorschach, *op. cit.*, p. 214. This important observation of Rorschach shows that form perception *per se* is not repressive, but that the mood or attitude in which form is perceived has a significant bearing on this.

[40] Compare Rorschach, *op. cit.*, pp. 56–57; Rapaport, *op. cit.*, p. 192.

[41] Many people experience the Rorschach-test situation and, for that matter, a great many situations in life as though they were an examination in which they

Another requirement, closely related to freedom of association, is an openness and receptiveness which permits the inkblot to be taken in by the perceiver. This contrasts with premature closure as it occurs when the blot is quickly disposed of by labeling it with a familiar cliché or when, in a Procrustean way, some empty or even misjudged likeness is imposed on it. There is a significant difference between form responses which resemble the forms perceived in quick, abstractive, labeling, everyday recognition and those which resemble the felt contemplation of, say, the forms in a drawing, a sculpture, the line of a mountain or a tree. The latter kind of form perception is not a quick, active fixating but takes place in the oscillation between attentive following of the form and permitting oneself to experience how the form feels. The perceiver reacts to the rhythm and melody of the form, to its smooth or abrupt, flexible or rigid, gentle or hard, flowing or staccato, curving or angular qualities. Probably in such experiential openness to form empathic processes play a role related to the capacity for kinesthetic experience. Eventually, such perception fixates the experience in an image which to the perceiver and—if it is a telling image—also to those to whom it is communicated bears the traces of this perceptual process: it *captures* the life of the form, it is form pregnant with meaning. The capacity to see form in this way, again, is missing in the depressed who is closed off from the world and in the pedantic who tries rigidly to find a highly accurate fit without being able to respond fully to the objects around him.

Finally, the special F+ require a certain decisiveness and daring in the perceptual structuring of the inkblot.[42] These, too, are lacking in depression, anxiety, and in the pedant.[43]

In spite of this, Rorschach writes that the highest F + % is found in pedants and in depressed people.[44] However, an examination of records

---

will receive good or poor marks. Also, most readers will be familiar with the experience that, when one urgently wants to recall a name, a telephone number, a line from a poem, he often is unable to do so; but at a later moment, when the urgency has passed, what was previously inaccessible suddenly comes to mind seemingly of its own accord.

[42] Compare Rapaport, *op. cit.*, p. 192.

[43] This enumeration of requirements for the special F+ is not complete but considers only factors in which the special F+ differs from the ordinary F+ which can be achieved without these factors. The main other requirements are attention and critical judgment regarding the likeness of image or concept and inkblot.

[44] Rorschach, *op. cit.*, p. 57. In severe, especially psychotic depression the F + % is not as high, in my experience, as Rorschach found it and as it usually is in milder, neurotic depression and in the depressed mood of clinically normal people. This is also the finding of Rapaport, *op. cit.*, p. 199, and others.

of these groups will show that their high F + % is based on ordinary F+ and that they usually produce no special F+.[45]

While neither the depressed nor the pedant has the freedom and flexibility of association, the openness toward the inkblot, and the decisiveness and daring necessary for a high special F + %, these capacities are lacking for different reasons. Rorschach expressed the difference between the depressed and the pedant by saying that the former is passively the latter actively stereotyped.[46] They both screen out with "exaggerated conscientiousness" [47] poorly seen forms rather than taking hold, actively, of penetratingly grasped forms. Nevertheless, the pedant takes hold of the inkblots more actively than does the depressed. But his taking hold is a cramped attitude and consists of imposing his narrow and rigid perspective on the inkblot, often with a tyrannical yet petty insistence on unessential detail and order. This prevents him from gaining a more sweeping and penetrating view of essential form. He clings to this perspective both for safety and because it satisfies his aggressive-sadistic impluses, whereas the depressed experiences consciously a lack of meaning and interest in the world, a guilty and critical attitude toward himself and his achievements, and—usually unconsciously—by means of this experience expresses his reproach and anger against the world.

The overconscientious elimination of F— responses and the increased effort to find accurate likenesses are subject to voluntary control. Rorschach found that if he asked his subjects to find forms as clear as possible the F + % was raised, but at the same time the over-all results of the test approached those seen in the pedantic and the depressed, showing a decrease of whole, kinesthetic, color, and original responses and an increase of stereotyped responses (A%).[48] The pedantic and the depressed are those who, according to Rorschach,[49] take the test very seriously, that is, make a strong voluntary effort and exercise particularly stringent control. I believe that such voluntary effort probably leads to a more careful screening out of responses that do not meet the testee's F+ standard, and possibly to the finding of a few more ordinary F+ responses, but that it is unlikely to lead to a significant

---

[45] Compare Rapaport, *op. cit.*, p. 201, who found that the depressives who have a high form level in general show a strikingly low special F + %.

[46] *Op. cit.*, p. 83.

[47] *"überspitzte Gewissenhaftigkeit"* Rorschach [German edition], p. 52.

[48] *Op. cit.*, p. 67.

[49] *Ibid.*, p. 43.

increase in the special F+ responses. Introspection will show the reader that if he attempts the consciously increased focusing on the goal of clear form responses required by the demand to find especially good form-likenesses, he is likely to experience a narrowing of his whole perspective, often even a muscularly more tense and cramped attitude, and a relative loss of the freedom of association and of that relaxed openness toward the inkblot which is conducive to taking it in fully. He is also likely to become less daring and more cautious and critical in his attitude to the task of interpreting the inkblot. Rorschach's experiment of the artificial increase of the F+ % offers a good opportunity to those who participate in it to become aware of this change in attitude and its constricting consequences for the capacity for experiencing and responding to the inkblots.

There is a contradiction between Rorschach's statement that the highest F+ % is found in pedants and depressed persons and the tabulation in which he summarizes his findings. According to the latter, he found the highest F+ % in artists (90–100 per cent), followed by the "Intelligent, Pedantic, Depressive" with an F+ % of 80–100.[50] In the artists, in contrast to the pedants and depressives, this high F+ % goes together with a dilated experience type and many W responses. Perhaps Rorschach was led to overlook this contradiction by his emphasis, shared by most of the later literature, on the factors of conscious effort, concentration, and control in the genesis of clearly seen form. The high F+ % of the artist fits such a concept less well than does that of the pedant and the mildly depressed. In contrast to the pedantic and the depressed, artists tend to give a rather high number of special F+, as do some other mentally gifted people who do not suffer from depression or from the personality difficulties found in the pedantic character. This bears out the qualitative difference between the special and the ordinary F+ which is to be found not only in a better form level but in a different experiential attitude. To grasp essential forms in a penetrating, true, and daring way is indeed a major task of the artist. But he cannot succeed in this task if he pursues it in a cramped, narrowly goal-directed attitude. The forms reveal themselves to his attentive glance only if he is open and receptive to the objects and free to respond to them with all his sensory, emotional, and intellectual sensibilities which cannot really be separated from each other except by artifi-

---

[50] *Ibid.*, Tables VIII and I, pp. 50 and 24.

cial abstraction. The openness and sensibility which are prerequisites of the special F+ also have the effect that ordinary F+ as well as other determinants are likely to be present, as well. But the ordinary F+ in the creative person's performance do not result from the rigid need for and preoccupation with the achievement of a narrowly defined goal, as they do in the pedantic and the mildly depressed.

The special F+ tend to have a more dynamic and often a more personal quality than the ordinary F+. The person who is sensitive to form experiences dynamic relations of balance and imbalance and other dynamic factors in seeing form.

The dynamic quality of the special F+ need not, but can, find expression in kinesthetic responses proper in which the excellent grasp of form is combined with kinesthetically felt movement or posture. In fact, this combination is rather frequent, and while the special F+ are also found in combination with color they tend to be combined in my experience, more frequently with kinesthetic factors. This also seems to have been Rorschach's finding; he defined his M as "form perceptions plus kinesthetic factors" and found that in the capacity for keen observation the introversive features (M) are more important than the extratensive ones (color) although the latter have to be present, too.[51] Consistent with these observations is Rapaport's finding that in his normal control group those showing a higher F+ also showed a greater number of M.[52]

While the firmness of the perceptual hold in the special F+ is based on the convincing and often dynamic grasp of clearly perceived, essential, and personally meaningful features, this is not the case in the ordinary F+. The perceptual hold on the blot that they indicate is at its firmest where the blot offers an obvious, compelling likeness or where the likeness corresponds to a familiar schema rather than being a concrete, factual likeness. This is the case in the popular responses.[53] Exam-

---

[51] Rorschach, *op. cit.*, pp. 25 and 110.

[52] *Ibid.*, p. 117, special Table 2A. I am indebted to Rapaport for a list of examples of his *special* F+. They tend to confirm the intrinsic relation between the dynamic nature of convincingly seen form and the kinesthetic responses. Out of twelve examples, eight are kinesthetically co-determined human or animal movements or posture. (David Rapaport, personal communication, 1960.) In his book (1946) he uses the score special F+ only for pure form responses.

[53] Firmness of perceptual hold based on compelling, concrete likeness or on convincing, alive grasp of essential features are not mutually exclusive and may be combined in one response, for example in a popular response which is perceived

ples of obviously compelling, concrete likenesses are the dogs, puppies, calves, or bear cubs in the gray and black areas of card II, the animals in the lateral details of card VIII, the head of a rabbit in the pale-green detail of the center bottom of card X. Examples of more schematic likenesses are the bat or butterfly of card I and the butterfly in the center red detail of card III. Somewhere in between these two is the bat, bird, or butterfly of card V. The people in card III are particularly interesting: they become compelling only when seen kinesthetically. When seen as pure form, they are less likely to be seen as people because then the emphasis often shifts from the convincing dynamics of the movement to the lack of good likeness in the shape of the head and other features which may altogether prevent the perception of people or make the testee reject this concept if it occurs to him. In all the popular responses the perceptual hold derives from the framework of familiarity, either concrete and compelling or based on a highly familiar schema such as central body and lateral wings in the popular bat and butterfly responses. I have the impression, which requires further substantiation, that the perceptual hold based on such a familiar schema is perhaps less firm than that based on a more concrete likeness and therefore more readily subject to subsequent doubt or forgetting.

The special F+, thus, tend to be based on an attitude of flexible openness toward and interest in the inkblot, freedom of association, decisiveness of perceptual grasp and organization. Hence, they do not point to inhibition, repression, and impersonal objectivity and do not constitute an impoverished type of perception. They tend to correlate positively with a dilated experience type, and form perception of a convincingness equal to the special F+ is also likely to occur in responses where form is combined with shading, color, and particularly with kinesthetic factors. The ordinary F+, on the other hand, tend to represent the attitudes and traits traditionally ascribed to all form responses, and they may go together with a coartated as well as a dilated experience type.

The contrast described so far between the ordinary and the special F+ has to be qualified and extended. It is not an absolute contrast but rather one between the two extreme ends of a continuum. The continuum refers to the quality of relatedness between perceiver and per-

---

with particular vividness or convincing, specific detail. On the other hand, a popular response may lack convincing familiarity for the testee and may be seen with doubt and with a rather weak perceptual hold.

cept underlying the quality of the form response. The range of this continuum extends from alive interest to impersonal, schematic conventionality, from dynamic and personally meaningful to detached, impoverished, and personally meaningless perception. Where on this continuum any specific form response is located is not always readily apparent and sometimes may not be discernible at all, even with the help of inquiry. In the case of the special F+, the rich and complex achievement of the communicated response reveals directly the interestedness and aliveness of the perceptual attitude leading to it. But quite often these qualities are more submerged, either because the response is less complex, perhaps even a popular response, or because the style of the testee's communication is less articulate and explicit. In such cases more subtle cues have to be considered to discern the quality of perceptual relatedness. Content alone does not help in such discernment, especially not content as traditionally scored. Just as a tree or a dog may be seen in a rich, vivid, alive, or a dull, schematic, impersonal way, so the popular "dogs" on card II may be seen in either of these ways, without necessarily involving movement: they may be seen as a neutral, schematic likeness or with alive interest and vividly. The tester has to be alert to the total attitude of the testee and its changing nuances in order to be able to locate the quality of the form perceived on the continuum of the type of relatedness, which is different from the continuum from F+ to F−.

While the fresh, convincing grasp of clearly perceived form in the special F+ and the compelling, familiar likeness of some popular responses are the two main types in which form perception in Rorschach's test tends to go together with a firm perceptual hold, there are many form responses, both F+ and F− as well as the intermediate F±, in which the quality of the perceptual hold is different and usually less firm. The weakening of perceptual hold, however, may take qualitatively different forms some of which are more obvious while others are more subtle and not as readily observable, except by means of a detailed and searching analysis to which not every Rorschach record lends itself.

Overt, diffuse *anxiety* interferes with a firm perceptual hold even more in Rorschach's test than it does in everyday life. While the familiarity of the environment in everyday life makes the weakening of perceptual hold by anxiety less apparent, the unfamiliarity of the inkblots tends to increase and accentuate it. The greater the anxiety, the less capable is the person of turning with interest and attention to anything. Anxiety interferes with perceptual openness toward the inkblot—the anxious person cannot really stay for any length of time with anything and cannot look fully and with interested attention at anything. Anxiety also interferes with freedom of association and with taking hold of and pursuing an idea. Hence, overt anxiety tends to result in an increase of vague form responses, sometimes vague anatomical responses which may be based on not much more than the symmetry of the inkblots and/or their vertical axes.[54]

The effect on perceptual hold of *defenses against anxiety* is different from that of overt anxiety.[55] The type of defense will determine the specific quality of perceptual hold. Some defenses will result in a rigid perceptual hold which tends to prevent the giving of special F+ responses but does not lead to the weakening of perceptual hold in vague form responses. This may happen, for example, when intolerance of ambiguity leads to a premature "closure" in a response and does not allow the testee to take in the blot fully, or when repressiveness prevents him from responding with more than a highly controlled, superficial, intellectual level of his mind, or when both these factors are present together.

In the milder forms of *depression* the high F+ % usually does not go together with the experience of a firm perceptual hold. As Rorschach pointed out, the depressed tend to feel painfully uncertain about their responses[56] at which they have arrived laboriously and with strained effort and often with a self-destructive, overcritical attitude. Also, they experience their responses as lacking in meaning and as dead and empty. The *bored* also do not have the experience of a firm perceptual hold. They feel a lack of meaning similar to that of the depressed, but the painful uncertainty of the latter in them is replaced by indifference, which in some also tends to lower the F+ % as compared with that of the mildly depressed.[57]

---

[54] Compare the similar findings of Rapaport, *op. cit.*, pp. 191–192.

[55] In part of the literature on Rorschach the "signs" of anxiety are not distinguished from those of the defenses against anxiety. The failure to make this distinction makes it difficult to differentiate overt from potential (covert) anxiety.

[56] *Op. cit.*, p. 57.

[57] Compare also Rorschach's remarks about the indolence and dulling of affect in simple dementia, *op. cit.*, p. 93. Not all of the many people in our time who are bored show a lowered F+ %. Boredom often goes together with egocentric self-preoccupation, and this, in turn, may lead to a quite "ambitious" Rorschach performance with a high F+ %.

Of special interest is the quality of perceptual hold in those people who are not aware of the assimilative effort in the attempt to achieve an acceptable likeness between inkblot and memory image and who therefore, in Rorschach's words, do not interpret, but name the inkblots, and who may be astonished or may not even comprehend that someone else is able to see something different in them.[58] According to Rorschach, they "perceive" the inkblots in the same way a normal person perceives and recognizes a familiar face or a tree, and they name them accordingly.[59]

At first glance it would seem that the perceptual hold of a testee who perceives and names an inkblot rather than interprets it must be particularly firm. He seems convinced that this and only this is what the inkblot means. The group in which Rorschach found this attitude most pervasive is that of the feeble-minded. If one analyzes their attitude in the Rorschach-test situation two tendencies stand out.[60]

The *feeble-minded* usually assume that there is only one "right" response because they feel that the inkblots are intended to represent one particular thing. They tend to give only one response to each blot and they may be unable to find out what a particular blot "means." They may express this by saying something like "I don't know it." Occasionally they will give more than one response to a blot, but in these instances the responses almost always refer to different areas of the blot. They seem unable to conceive the idea that any one area might be interpreted in different ways. When it is explained to them explicitly that there are no right or wrong answers, that the blots may be seen in more than one way and that they are not supposed to represent anything, they may very well nod assent or profess verbally that they understand this, but from their behavior it is clear that they do not really understand and believe it. This incapacity may well be due to an inabil-

---

[58] Rorschach, *op. cit.*, p. 17, found this in most organic cases, epileptics, many schizophrenics, most manics, almost all feeble-minded, and even in many normal subjects.

[59] Rapaport's concept of "loss of distance" to the inkblot, so far as I can see, is identical with Rorschach's concept of lack of awareness of assimilative effort. They both refer to an attitude in which the inkblot is taken as representation of something real, they both attribute considerable diagnostic significance to this, and they both assume that there are various degrees of "loss of distance" or loss of awareness of assimilative effort. Rapaport, *op. cit.*, pp. 329–349. In my experience, these differences are not only differences of degree but also significant differences of the quality of the attitude to the test task and the inkblot.

[60] I am indebted to my wife, Zeborah Schachtel, for the data on which the following description is based.

ity to think in terms of the "possible," to an incapacity for abstract behavior in Goldstein's sense, and to a need to live in a quite concrete, definite world where everything has one and only one meaning.

The second outstanding feature in the feeble-minded is that when they are questioned about a response, or when they are asked "What else could the blot be?" they seem to experience this as a rejection of their response as "wrong" or as a doubt on the tester's part in the "correctness" of their response. They react by defending stoutly that the blot does represent a butterfly or whatever they felt it represented. This sounds as if they felt a good deal of conviction about their responses and as if they experienced a firm perceptual hold. However, it is defensive rigidity rather than conviction based on real exploration of the blot and on reflective consideration and judgment of the fittingness of the response. They do not want to raise any question, in their own mind, about the fitness of their response, and they react defensively if somebody else raises one. They show a very marked intolerance of ambiguity. This intolerance does not allow reflectiveness, exploratory behavior, the entertaining of multiple possibilities. Their feeling of perceptual hold does not derive from the firmness of the conviction of having achieved a good likeness by their own imaginative efforts. It derives from the assumption that the blot can and does mean only one thing and that, if they have guessed right, their response *must* be what the blot "represents." Thus, their conviction is based on the imagined or hoped-for validation of their response by the person who designed the blot to represent what it is "intended" to be or by the person who "knows" what it is intended to be.[61] In a test situation they feel vulnerable, if they have not become indolent; it is important to them to find the *right* answer. The resulting defensiveness reinforces the rigidity, which is strong to begin with because of their intolerance for ambiguity. Their rigid perceptual hold is based on a narrow frame of reference and on the closed perspective of their expectation that the blot must represent some object with which they are supposed to be familiar.

This rigid hold stabilizes the perceptual field in relation to the Rorschach blot and the test situation for the moment in which the response is given, but it is apt not to survive for very long, especially if the response was an F−, but sometimes also if it was one of the more schematic popular responses, like "bat" or "butterfly" for card I. Thus it happens quite often that the feeble-minded (as well as quite a few

---

[61] I do not mean that these thoughts are explicit in the mind of the feeble-minded testee, but that they describe his implicit attitude.

people of normal intelligence) will deny in the inquiry that they have
given such a response, or will maintain that they saw it in some other
blot. Since the feeble-minded have little or no autonomous motivation
to become interested in the test or in the kind of mental activity involved in it, the stabilizing function of their perceptual hold probably
tends to be limited to a short time in which they "dispose" of a particular inkblot. During that time it serves to eliminate any doubt and ambiguity. After that they return at once to their concrete, immediate world
in which there is no further need for orientation with regard to such an
ambiguous and unfamiliar object. And there is no other reason to remember their response since, in contrast to many other testees, finding
the response is not a personally meaningful experience for them and
their relatedness to the inkblot tends to be fleeting and superficial.

The problem of the perceptual hold of various types of *schizophrenic*
patients would require a monograph of its own. I want to discuss here
only two points. As pointed out by Rorschach,[62] some schizophrenics
seem to name rather than interpret the inkblots. However, in my experience the "naming" of an inkblot by schizophrenic patients has a very
different quality from the "naming" by feeble-minded testees; the perceptual hold in these "naming" responses is different from that of the
feeble-minded, and the attitude to the test situation is different, too.
Many schizophrenic patients give some of their responses with a feeling
that it is quite evident to them that this is what the inkblot means. Such
responses may or may not be F−. The patient seems to be *struck* by
the to-him evident significance of the blot rather than actively interpreting it. In contrast to the feeble-minded, these patients do not seem concerned at all with what the blot is *supposed* to mean or with whether
somebody else might or might not see something else in the blot. The
self-evident quality the response has for them seems to derive not from
the thought that the blot was intended by someone to mean such-and-
such, but rather from the power of the patient's associations, especially
those associations that are largely determined by primary process
thought. Hence the perceptual hold in these responses is usually based
on a highly individual, usually personally meaningful perspective which
may result in a special F+ or in an F− response, either of which is
likely to be original or even unique. Unlike the feeble-minded, many of
these patients will give more than one response to the same blot or the
same area, often within a few seconds after the "evident" response, and

---

[62] *Op. cit.*, p. 17. Compare also Rapaport's emphasis on the loss of distance in
schizophrenics, *op. cit.*, pp. 329–350.

this new response may or may not be given with a similar feeling of self-evidence.

The perceptual hold in these responses is momentarily convincing to the patient, but it is usually not *lasting*. This leads to the second point that is striking about the perceptual hold of many schizophrenic patients, namely, the often-observed *fluidity* of their percepts in Rorschach's test and of their thoughts in general. This is most striking in those patients who may forget very quickly a response which, just a moment before, may have been given by them with all signs of being quite evident to them. This fluidity of percepts probably is due both to rapid shifts in levels of consciousness (from primary to secondary process thought and vice-versa) and to shifts within largely primary process associations which lead rapidly from one preoccupation to another and, thus, to a quick succession of responses.[63]

Lack of interest is likely to lead to a weakening of perceptual hold and so is a one-sided, forced interest in finding the most accurate likenesses. The quality and degree of interest largely determine the quality of attention, openness to or avoidance of the inkblot. All of these play decisive roles in the quality of perceptual hold. Thus the analysis of the type and degree of perceptual hold, in turn, furnishes clues to a better understanding of the testee's attitude to the inkblots, the test task, and the test situation.

In addition to the qualitative analysis of responses, the *recall* and *forgetting* of responses probably offer significant clues to the quality of perceptual hold. Many normal and many neurotic testees, for example, are more likely to recall personally meaningful responses for a longer period of time than responses of a more neutral or stereotyped quality. Such personal meaning may be based on the mere experience of discovery, for example, of a special $F+$, or/and on the relation of the percept to some need, fear, or otherwise significant personal interest or preoccupation. The relation of recall and forgetting of Rorschach responses to perceptual hold, to personality dynamics, to different clinical groups, and to their experience of the test situation and the various inkblots offers a field for research that might prove quite illuminating.[64]

---

[63] The two points discussed do not apply to all schizophrenic patients. They are especially striking in some acutely disturbed patients and, to a lesser extent, in some patients of the group called by Rapaport the overideational pre-schizophrenics. They apply not only to form responses but to other determinants as well.

[64] In such research it would be important to distinguish between recall over different periods of time, such as recall during inquiry, after a month, after several

## Dynamic Form Responses

As we have seen, not all form responses derive from a completely matter-of-fact, neutral, impersonal, detached, objective attitude and represent a limited, impoverished type of perception. While objectivity and realistic, critical judgment of form likeness are necessary conditions for a high F + %, this does not exclude that in the genesis as well as in the final form of an F+ response considerable interest in what is seen, a vivid or dynamic way of seeing, and personal, emotional significance of the percept, or any one of these, may play a significant role. Thus, while it is true that most form responses are the results of an impersonal, detached attitude and that in many people all form responses have this quality, there also occur form responses that are perceived in a different way.

Form as well as other responses are given by some people not with a neutral, matter-of-fact attitude, but with vivid, keen interest and often with satisfaction in what they see. They are often people who enjoy the test task, and some of them are in good humor when taking the test. As Rorschach observed, good humor dilates the experience type, i.e., increases the capacity for rich and varied experience. This also affects the form responses. It leads to greater receptiveness toward the inkblot and freer play of associations, hence also to richer, more alive form responses and to an attitude of interest and pleasure in what is seen. One of the consequences of this can be, as Rorschach put it, that "complexes" appear in the form responses and otherwise repressed material gets "smuggled into consciousness." [65]

Good humor is only one instance in which repressiveness is loosened. As we have seen, there are people with habitually little, or loose, repressiveness, and there are types of pathology in which formerly repressed attitudes, feelings, material become conscious and may affect

---

years, etc. Also, recall without renewed exposure to the inkblots has different implications from recall upon being shown the inkblots again. The latter is likely to lead, for example, to the recall or the renewed finding of popular responses, whereas the former might not always have this effect. Also, the recall of a percept after the response has been repeated to the testee is different from spontaneous recall and from recall upon being asked to show or to repeat what one has seen in the blot without being read or told one's responses by the tester. Any leading questions should be avoided in an inquiry, both in general, but particularly if it is aimed at finding out something about perceptual hold, recall, and forgetting of responses.

[65] Rorschach, *op. cit.*, p. 214.

the form responses. Actually, dynamic form perception in general, and the appearance in Rorschach tests of *dynamic form responses*,[66] as I shall designate them, is a phenomenon that occurs not only in the types and conditions mentioned in the text, but is relatively widespread in all conditions in which repressiveness is not too stringent.

The dynamic factors in these responses escape the usual scoring procedures because they are neither kinesthetic in the sense of Rorschach's M nor movement responses in the expanded sense of Klopfer's FM or m. Some of them are not form in the strict sense of outline or contour. Some are in part determined by structural factors which have to do with the dynamic relationships between the parts of the inkblot.[67] Others concern not the perception of dynamic relations between different structural parts of the blot but dynamic qualities of a detail or of the whole blot as perceived by the testee; they correspond to what Werner described as physiognomic perception.[68]

I suspect that these structural as well as other dynamic factors play a role in many more form responses than we are able to identify and than testees are aware of. This probably is particularly true of the theme of balance (the significance of the vertical axis, the symmetry and distribution of mass in the blots) that plays a ubiquitous role in human perception and comes to awareness more readily where an absence or disturbance of balance is perceived than where its presence is taken for granted as a background of all visual perception. When Rorschach writes that the distribution of the blots on the plate has to meet certain requirements of spatial rhythm,[69] he is speaking of these factors of balance. His observation that, if the blots do not meet the requirements

[66] The dynamic form responses have in common with the "special F+" (pp. 110–117) that they do not have a neutral, detached quality. The special F+ usually are based on a conscious, lively interest in the particular form perceived which, in turn, may or may not be related to a personal "complex" in Rorschach's and Jung's sense. The dynamic form response is always related to such a complex which may or may not be conscious, and the response may or may not be accompanied by heightened conscious interest or emotion. While by definition the special F+ has a high form level, the dynamic form response can be F+ as well as F−.

[67] For a detailed discussion of various themes occurring in responses based on the dynamic perception of these structural factors, see above, Chapter 3. Rorschach touched on one such theme, the significance of the relation of the central axis to the lateral details of the blot, in his discussion of some "abstract interpretations"; Rorschach, *op. cit.*, pp. 209–213.

[68] Werner, *op. cit.*, pp. 67–82.

[69] Rorschach, *op. cit.*, p. 15. Spatial rhythm translates the German *Raumrhythmik*, which is not the same as the word "composition" used in the English translation of his book.

of spatial rhythm, many testees reject them as "simply an inkblot," shows their importance. The human sense of balance and proportion is present in our perception of all we see around us even though we may not be aware of it. It is absent probably only in certain "narrow-focus" ways of seeing such as occur in Rorschach's test in many Dd and, less, in D responses.[70]

Dynamic form perception differs from detached form perception in that the perception of the specific form is coupled with and partly determined by emotions—conscious or unconscious—related on the one hand to the specific quality of the form perceived and, on the other, to specific drives, needs, and former emotional experiences of the perceiver.

The emergence of such feelings or ideas in the perception of certain forms, the fact that these forms assume such significance for certain individuals is based on a peculiar relationship of the perceiving subject to the form perceived. While in detached form perception the form remains something at which the person can look without any personal interest and without reference to his own self, in dynamic form perception there seems to be always the implication, however slight and tentative, that the subject "lives" in a certain dynamic relationship to the form perceived. This relationship is in many cases a purely phantastic one, for instance when somebody looking at the baylike incisions and inlets of card I has a feeling that these might be havens in which he could find security. Nevertheless, it requires that the subject, for however short a moment, imagine himself, at least potentially and often without being aware of it, in this haven of security.

Common to all examples of dynamic perception of objects is the fact that the objects are not eyed detachedly, but as in a dynamic relation to the subject. This relation may be of widely different quality: it may be one of potential protection or danger, of competitive comparison with or without the implication of possible aggression or submission, of identification or opposition, of antipathy or sympathy. The object is thought of and is perceived as something with an actual or potential living significance for the perceiving subject, a significance which may be en-

---

[70] Kuhn's and Booth's observations on the distribution ratio in different people of the responses given to the central as compared to the lateral details are good examples of the unconscious reaction to structural factors; see above, p. 28, note 15. Compare also Witkin's work on the perception of the vertical and its relation to proprioception and to field-oriented perception. H. A. Witkin *et al., Personality through Perception* (New York: Harper & Brothers, 1954).

tirely imaginary, as in looking at the Rorschach-test plates, or real, as in the mutual estimate of size and strength of two people who are going to fight each other, or somewhere vaguely in between, as in some persons who have a preference for corner seats because they feel more sheltered in them.

The described relationship in dynamic form perception between perceiving subject and object perceived shows various specific qualities according to the personality of the perceiving person and to the particular object or form perceived. While the undetached, emotional relationship is the general condition for, and a quality of, dynamic form perception, only the specific content of this relationship, the specific way in which a concrete form is experienced emotionally, will provide insight into the psychic mechanisms characteristic of the individual dynamic form perception and the individual personality structure.[71] I intend in the following, therefore, to examine more closely different types of dynamic form perceptions with a view to their psychological implications for the perceiving individual. The variety of such dynamic perceptions, especially in their finer nuances, is endless. I shall present some recurrent patterns which are taken, chiefly, from experience with a great number of subjects and their form perceptions in the Rorschach test.[72] These examples will serve to clarify the concept and process of dynamic form perception.

A frequent and psychologically important example of dynamic form perception concerns the attitude to and perception of *size*. Size, in this connection, is closely related to strength. Whether a person, an animal, or a thing is seen as tall, large, big—strong, powerful—or as short, little, insignificant—weak, helpless—while seemingly an objective, visual estimate, depends actually, in many persons and to an astonishing degree, on the self-evaluation of the perceiving subject. This is true, of course, only of dynamic and not of detached form perception. The physicist measuring the length of a beam, the anthropometrist measuring the size of a human body, the salesgirl measuring yards of fabric are typical examples of detached, critical perception of length and size. Their self-feeling does not as a rule enter into their attitude toward the object

---

[71] The degree to which detached and dynamic form perceptions are actually and potentially present in an individual is an important factor, too, regardless of specific content of dynamic form perception.

[72] In the majority of these cases the psychological interpretations of the dynamic from perception have been checked with therapists who had an intimate knowledge of, and prolonged acquaintance with, the persons.

they measure. Size takes on an entirely different meaning, however, if two men who are going to fight each other "size up" the physique of their adversary. They perceive size dynamically, in relation to the coming fight, to victory or defeat, to strength or weakness, to their *own feeling of strength or weakness*. The two men intending to fight have good reason to perceive their mutual size in dynamic terms because size, together with other factors, may become decisive for the outcome of the battle. It is the possible decisiveness of the size factor, however, which often makes perception in such a situation less detached, less objective, less critical than it might have been in a situation where less personal concern—about the outcome of the battle—is involved. The lack of detachment might lead to an "intuitively" sharpened, correct estimate as well as to a wrong estimate detrimental to the chances of victory. The latter would be the case, for instance, if one of the two men in our example, A, although physically as tall and strong as his adversary B, suffered from inferiority feelings originating in his personality structure and under the effect of these feelings perceived B as of a more powerful, taller physique than A imagines himself to be.

In this example there is ample subjective reason to perceive size emotionally, dynamically instead of detachedly, objectively, and critically. The situation of an impending fight provides the reason. But at the same time, the inferiority feelings of A influence his perception in an irrational way. In a great number of persons the influence of self-feeling on perception of size becomes habitual and thereby relatively independent of the acute situation in which they perceive. In this case, even without an impending fight, in a "neutral" or even "friendly" situation, inferiority feelings may lead to exaggerated perception of size, power, strength, and the like. The inferiority feeling, though, cannot be separated from its function and place in the personality structure. It may be allied with a strongly competitive, hostile attitude. This attitude may lead the subject to experience unconsciously the "neutral" or "friendly" situation as an equivalent of the "fight" situation, and this entire mechanism may lead to the dynamic form perception of exaggerated size. The feeling of smallness, weakness, helplessness, and the resulting tendency to perceive others, persons as well as animals and things, as big and tall, may have just as many and varied sources as any kind of inferiority feeling. Actual physical smallness may play a role. This is especially the case in the relationship between child and adult in which insecurity, whatever its origin, most easily is consciously as well as unconsciously focused on and rationalized by the actual fact that the child is small and weak among big and powerful adults. The perceptual mechanisms are influenced by the actual size of the child but also by his self-evaluation as it results from the entire structure of his personality and from the quality of his relations to the parents and other significant adults. Size, psychologically, is a relative concept varying according to the scale of comparison used, and this scale of comparison often is a function of the size of the person perceiving and estimating size. It is also a function of self-evaluation as conditioned by the entire structure of the personality. Such self-evaluation frequently takes the dominant role over the actual size of the perceiving person in determining the quality of his size perceptions. This implies that wavering self-evaluation or a change in self-evaluation may lead to differences in size perception in one and the same individual at different times. Thus, one of the subjects whose Rorschach responses contained instances of a dynamic perception of size had, according to subsequent information, in his mid-twenties always felt that another man on whom he looked as an authority, and in the presence of whom he used to feel much insecurity, was considerably taller and larger than he. When the two men met again, about ten years later, he was astonished to notice that the other man, whom he now felt to be his equal, was neither taller nor larger than he, although actually not only their size but also their figures had remained about the same.

Just as frequent as perception of exaggerated size on the basis of insecurity and low self-feeling, one can observe perception of minimized, belittled, underestimated size due to increased, exaggerated self-feeling. This is especially noticeable in persons in whom a repressed basic insecurity leads to a compensatory stress on power, dominance, superiority, and who, for this reason, are compelled to think of themselves as big and strong and of others as small and weak. Depreciating, belittling tendencies in general may influence the perception in the same direction. But seeing things and persons as "little" may also serve other purposes. In one case a subject saw as "little," "cute," and "small," many of the Rorschach inkblots or parts of them that are otherwise seen either without any reference to size or as large. Perceiving them as small, in this case, served to make them harmless, peaceful, friendly. The subject, to whom the world, and especially his environment, unconsciously seemed menacing, hostile, and confusing, felt quite generally a strong need to act as a kind of peaceful intermediary hushing up threatening conflicts, having the surface, at least, of his relations to others appear smooth and friendly, and covering up difficulties rather than facing and trying to solve them.[73]

In the examples given so far, the dynamic perception of size is based on an attitude in which the perceiving subject compares a usually unconscious idea of his own "size"—self-feeling—with the size of the person or object—inkblot—perceived. The object perceived does not remain detached but is brought into an emotional relationship with the subject, and the quality of this relationship together with the structure of the perceiving personality—especially self-evaluation—are factors determining whether the object is seen as large or small. The dynamic perception of size, however, can also be based on a different mechanism, namely, *identification* of the perceiving subject with the object perceived—or participation of the subject in the object.

A case in point is that of a subject who suffered from strong inferiority feelings that were partly concentrated on and rationalized by a number of beliefs he held with regard to his own bodily physique and which, to a great extent, had no basis in fact. One of these beliefs, symbolic of his general feeling of nothingness, powerlessness, and weakness, was the idea that his arms were exceptionally thin and weak. He saw in the upper lateral details of card IV "little, puny arms, small and skinny, they make me think of my own arms. . . ." The arms seen in the inkblot were not detachedly compared and recognized as similar in shape to his arms—which they were not at all—but their thinness and smallness, in a momentary process of identification, was felt as the presumed thinness and smallness of his own arms.[74] The identification of the subject with these "arms" makes his perception of them a dynamic, undetached form perception; he lives, for a moment, in the arms he perceives, and he perceives them in this way because he identifies with them.

The dynamism of identification with an object, a form seen, and the influence of this dynamism on the resulting perception and on the total experience in which this perception is embedded can be observed fre-

---

[73] Correspondingly, seeing things large and feeling oneself small can express also the need for protection—instead of fear—by others who, consequently, are looked upon as stronger, larger, more powerful, and therefore more capable of offering protection.

[74] His experience with his interpretation of the "arms" on card IV made such an impression on him that he mentioned it, several weeks later, in a psychoanalytic session.

quently in Rorschach's test,[75] as it can in everyday life. This process of identification with size, which in turn is associated with importance and power, plays a role in such well-known phenomena as the pride in having built the highest house or the longest bridge, the tallest tower. In comparison with the frequency of these feelings the people are rare indeed who are proud to have built or to have in their town the most beautiful, or the architecturally most interesting, house or bridge. Identification with the size symbol is also a factor in the desire to surround oneself with objects—rooms, furniture, and the like—on a grandiose scale. In the 1920s the press published a striking example of this in pictures and accounts of the enormous dimensions of Mussolini's working room.[76] Today, corporate practice assigns to the various executives rooms the size and the quality of furniture of which are in exact proportion to the executive's status in the corporate hierarchy.

In the perception of landscapes, too, different personal experiences of size may be observed. Standing on the top of a mountain and looking over a vast expanse of mountains and valleys, one person feels primarily the elevation of his position, that he is high, higher than everything else; his self participates in the grandeur of the mountain on which he stands. Another person feels dwarfed by the grandeur of the same view, he feels lost in the vast expanse, he experiences not identification but opposition or comparison of his small self and the gigantic world around him. These two kinds of experience profoundly affect what those two persons actually see, what is accentuated and what is lost among the variety of objects before their eyes.[77]

While the dynamic perception of size is mostly related to the various processes of self-evaluation and self-feeling, another series of phenom-

---

[75] Compare Kuhn's concept of magical identification or interchangeability in certain mask interpretations. Kuhn, *op. cit.*, pp. 20–21 and 42. Empathic identification with the object perceived plays also a role in kinesthetic responses; in these the subject in an act of empathy identifies often with the *movement* he believes he perceives. But, as our example shows, it occurs also in dynamic form perception; not, however, in detached critical form perception.

[76] This example is psychologically of special interest since the same trait of need for self-aggrandizement impresses one in Mussolini's gestures and even his physiognomic features and since this trait seems to have a compensatory function for a pronounced feeling of insecurity, fear, and weakness mentioned repeatedly in the memoirs of Angelica Balabanoff, *My Life as a Rebel* (New York and London, Harper & Brothers, 1938), pp. 44–49, 100–112. Charles Chaplin makes delightful use of such identification with superior size in the barbershop scene of his movie *The Great Dictator,* in which Hitler and Mussolini try to outdo each other.

[77] Compare also Kuhn, *op. cit.*, pp. 41–42.

ena in dynamic perception is related to a psychic complex which can be designated as the need for shelter versus fear of enclosure and imprisonment. The need for "shelter" may comprise such trends as need for protection, fear of being exposed, fear of freedom and spontaneity, fear of free contact with the outer world, fear of "openness"; it may appear also in the extreme form of agoraphobia. The "fear of enclosure," which is the opposite pole of this complex, comprises fears of being oppressed, tied down, imprisoned, hemmed in, becoming dependent. In some cases, these fears may lead to claustrophobia.

The form symbols which seem most specifically related to these psychic trends are V- or U-shaped, like a vase or the cross section of a valley, or actual enclosures such as circles, ellipses, or similar forms.

In the Rorschach plates the V or U form is to be found most prominently in Plate VII and is not quite so pronounced in Plates III and IX, all of which are designed open at the top while closed at the sides and the bottom. It is also to be found in numerous incisions, bays, etc., in almost every plate, especially I, V, VI, and X (reversed).

The way in which the opposing tendencies—need for shelter and protection versus fear of enclosure, imprisonment—involve the perception of the V or U form is of special interest not only because of the rather frequent occurrence of this form symbolism in Rorschach's test and in everyday life but also because the same configuration is perceived in diametrically opposed ways by many persons subject to one or the other of the described psychic tendencies. To one person the V shape seems to promise some sort of protection against a dangerous or cold outside world, like the walls of the cradle or the cavity formed by the mother's arms once did for the infant, or the mother's womb for the embryo.[78] There he may feel safe from the intrusion of others. Very

---

[78] The deeply rooted significance that certain forms, like the V or U shape, have for some persons cannot be explained, probably, by merely saying that they are symbolic expressions or symbolic satisfactions of certain needs of the individual. I would be inclined rather to suppose that these forms belong to what one might call the "memory of the body" as contrasted to the conscious or subconscious memory of the mind. Bodily and psychic experiences are so closely interwoven, especially in the earliest stages of infancy and perhaps already in the prenatal life of the embryo, that a separation of these two spheres often seems artificial. In this connection Marcel Proust's distinction between voluntary and involuntary memory and his frequent references to what he calls the involuntary memory of the body, of the limbs—in contrast to the voluntary memory of the conscious mind —are very interesting. For him the essential memory, the memory that brings back to life the realities of his childhood and youth, is involuntary memory. Marcel Proust, *À la recherche temps perdu.* I: *Du côté de chez Swann* and VIII: *Le temps retrouvé.* A similar concept of memory is developed in Freud's theory

often the type of person who tends to experience the V shape in this way is also the type who finds security chiefly in being protected by somebody else, or in the "home" rather than the world at large, in "privacy," in all sorts of actual physical or psychic enclosures which set his own sphere apart from others, the world. He is often the person to whom a house cannot be cozy enough, who regards others, perhaps with the exception of the closest relations, as strangers rather than fellow human beings. He feels protected in the valley by which another person may feel oppressed.

Rorschach records offer many examples of this kind of dynamic perception. Some typical responses of this type—with more or less outspoken comment on the feeling those forms arouse—are: to Plate V, top center, "a yoke upside down; no, rather a saddle, I prefer that, it pleases me"; to Plate VII, whole: "a deep valley, restful, with a stream at the bottom"; to Plate VI, reversed, the two little round protrusions in the baylike indentation on top: "two little men with bald heads in a hideout"; to the baylike indentations on the outside edges of Plate I: "feeling that I could find many havens, shelters in the drawing which might provide some sort of safety, hiding, perhaps." The same subject remarked to the pink portion of Plate IX: "one of my phantasies in sexual intercourse: penis in between the two breasts." This seemed to be for him the symbol of motherly protection, whereas there was at the same time, with regard to the vagina, a strong fear of castration appearing in some of his Rorschach responses. He had a marked fear of genital sexuality and a deep feeling of being weak, not being taken care of, being exposed to all sorts of dangers.[79]

The same psychic trends are often involved in the preference for corners, whether the corner of a room, the corner of a couch or sofa, the corner seat in a train. They are perceived by some persons as offering shelter and protection to a higher degree than the middle of a room or a seat in the middle of a row would offer.

---

of memory when he says that memory traces "are often most powerful and most enduring when the process which left them behind was one which never entered consciousness." Sigmund Freud, *Beyond the Pleasure Principle* (1920) [Standard Edition], XVIII, 25. Compare also the concepts of re-sensation and déja vécu and their relation to memory and recall in Schachtel, *op. cit.*, pp. 158–164, 299–302.

[79] It is relatively rare that such outspoken comments and descriptions pointing to the security offered by the V shape are presented. Much more frequently the persons are unaware or less conscious of their feelings and their pleasure in these forms, or they are reluctant to be so "subjective" in their interpretations. An experienced observer, nevertheless, will be able to discover the dynamic form perceptions.

In other cases of dynamic perception of the V or U form, the emphasis may be on the opening rather than the protected bottom of the V, especially if this opening is wide—as it is in Plate VII, for instance. In this case the person with the "need for shelter" will often react with uneasiness and fear—mostly unconscious—to the form, will perceive primarily the insecurity, the lack of a roof, the openness to the dangerous outside, the danger of intrusion, the danger of reaching out into open spaces, into the strange outside world. According to individual proclivities the fear may consist in a feeling that he is exposed to the outside world, that he cannot effectively bar the intrusion of "the outside," or the stress may be more on the fear of and inability to reach out toward others, the fear to feel and act spontaneously. Usually both fears are present in some mixture.

Examples of this type of dynamic form perception in Rorschach tests are especially frequent in Plate VII. Thus, one subject saw in Plate VII "some sort of pagoda, but the roof is missing," and "a valley; if it were flooded by a cloudburst you would be unable to get out," thus expressing both the impossibility of protecting himself from the danger from above, the rain, and the impossibility of escaping because of the high, precipitous mountains on either side of the valley. Another subject saw in VII "a harbor, not too well protected," whereas in III he had seen a well-protected harbor, explaining that, in addition to breakwaters on both sides, the central red spot afforded "good protection."

The same V or U shape perceived by some persons as sheltering—the stress of the perceived Gestalt being on the protecting side walls and the sheltered bottom—or as exposed—stress on the opening—is perceived by other persons as oppressive, imprisoning, hemming-in—stress on the side walls, which in this type of dynamic perception assume the quality of prison walls. One might speak in these cases of the claustrophobic quality of the dynamic perception—although, of course, the presence of this type of perception need not indicate actual claustrophobia symptoms. Fears of being overpowered, helpless, unable to move and breathe freely, of being tied down, unable to escape, may lead to this type of dynamic perception. When persons feel oppressed living in a valley, which another person may experience as particularly sheltered and friendly, when they feel uneasy in a room with closed doors, they experience the walls of the valley or the room as a kind of prison wall, that is, in a dynamic relation to their own person, preventing them from freedom of movement. One can find the same phenomenon on a still more imaginary basis in Rorschach responses, often also in connection with fears of castration—the idea that the penis will not be able to get out of the vagina.

Examples of such responses to Plate IX, center line and upper part of card, are: "This is the phallic thing, very little obstruction to its getting out"; and although the subject says that there is *little* obstruction to the phallus getting out, he must have perceived the figure as potentially obstructing an "escape," otherwise there would be no good reason for such a statement; this is corroborated by the immediately following response, which refers to the two top orange figures at the two sides of the enclosure of the phallus as "The two figures laughing at it trying to get out." Another subject said of the whole Plate VII: "There seems an outlet in this picture, escape from center." Another subject responded to the whole Plate III by saying: "I do not see how the butterfly—center—might get out so easily"—the surrounding part is experienced as barring the butterfly's escape, although actually there is a sufficiently large opening to permit it. To the same type of dynamic perception belong the not-infrequent responses in which the center is perceived as hemmed in by the sides.

Very often the O or "cave" form is perceived with the involvement of the same psychic trends—either "need for shelter" or "fear of enclosure" —that have been discussed with regard to the V form. In these cases perception differs individually, especially with regard to the function of the "walls" of the "cave"; the encircling figure may be viewed either as oppressive, imprisoning, or as fortifying, defending the enclosure against the outside world.

In Rorschach tests these dynamic "enclosure" responses are mostly to be found in Plate II, where a dark figure encircles a blank, white space; sometimes in Plate X; and also in Plate I.[80] The question whether the surrounding walls are strong and solid enough for their separating, defending purpose sometimes plays a role in these responses.

Perceptual emphasis on oppressive, paralyzing, or suffocating enclosure is often related to fears originating in the child's relation to a possessive mother or mother-substitute and to later similar experiences. In such cases also often occur dynamic form percepts (and also kinesthetic percepts) of claws, pincers, spiders, or crabs and the like, especially if the spider or crab is seen in areas or cards other than the blue lateral D

---

[80] The "tunnel" response, to be found also in some other plates, often also belongs to this category.

on card X, where they are a popular percept,[81] for example a spider in I
(W) or a crab in III or VII (reversed).

An important and frequent complex of dynamic perception of many
different forms is related to aggressive-sadistic tendencies and their
counterpart—the fear of being hurt, tormented, injured. Perception
may concern either an object[82] thought of as capable of injuring a living being or a living being[83] as the object of aggression. The emotional
involvement in perceiving an object as potentially injurious takes the
form of either a conscious or unconscious identification ("I am the person who is using, may be using, this object to hurt somebody else") or
of opposition ("I am the person who is hurt, or may be hurt, by this
object"). In cases in which the damaged, hurt person or animal is seen,
perception may become involved through both: identification ("I am
the suffering and threatened being; I fear being hurt in this way") and
opposition ("I am injuring, tormenting this being").

Examples of all these types of dynamic perception are as frequent in
everyday life as they are in the perception of the Rorschach plates. The
fear of sharp objects, for instance—knives, needles, protruding edges—
often leads to a particularly heightened awareness of any potentially
"dangerous" object of this type, which other persons do not perceive at
all, or not with emphasis on its dangerous qualities. It does not seem to
make any difference whether the fear concerns primarily the phantasy
of one's self making aggressive use of the object, wishing that somebody be hurt by it, or the idea that one himself could be hurt by it.
Usually both phantasies are present in different degrees of repression or
consciousness. In Rorschach responses these perceptions range all the
way from the schizophrenic patient who refuses to go on with the test
because he believes that the sharply pointed ends of the figure in Plate
V are going to pierce or cut him if he handles the plate to the "normal"
person who, without being aware of it, rather persistently singles out
the pointed edges or knife or sticklike center lines of the plates for interpretation. The objects seen range all the way from weapons such as
swords, arrows, knives, guns, revolvers, needles, pincers, and claws—the

---

[81] This popular response may or may not be a dynamic form response. Its
mere occurrence is not sufficient to warrant the assumption that it is.

[82] Such an "object" may be anything: a weapon, anything that may cause
injury without being intended for such a purpose, or an aggressive person or a
part of his body.

[83] Lifeless objects may, of course, be substituted for a living object of aggression.

latter two often also having the connotation of the fear of enclosure—to lesions such as cuts, gashes, and sores, which may be seen in some part of a plate with small and sharp incisions. Things bound together often belong in the same category—the implication being either one of wanting to fetter or of fearing to be bound. The center line of the plates sometimes plays a role in this type of dynamic perception, especially when it is perceived as something forcibly injected into another object, as some foreign and dangerous substance or thing in a body or as something separating the two halves. Responses of this type are: "a hypodermic syringe inserted in the body"—orange center line between pink, or gray between blue[84] in Plate VIII; "a sword sticking in the body of an animal"—center line and surrounding parts, especially in the upper half of Plate VI; "a piece of bone in the alimentary canal"—the deviation to the left of the center line in the upper part of the pink portion of Plate IX. Also, when the center line or some part of it is seen as a cleft, or a tear,[85] separating the two halves of the figure, we often have to deal with dynamic perception in which either identification—self-destructive tendencies ("I am torn in two halves")[86] —or opposition—object-destructive tendencies ("I want to tear in halves, to force apart") may prevail.

In many if not in all cases, the sadistic—and masochistic—components of perception are closely amalgamated with sexual impulses and sexual symbolism. This is not surprising, since sadistic and masochistic tendencies often find their strongest expression in sexual intercourse or masturbation and in accompanying phantasies unless they are repressed in this area.[87] Most of the examples given can be understood also as sado-masochistic sexual symbols—the pointed instruments of aggression as phallic; the forcibly invaded or dissected objects as vaginal symbols in which the vagina is threatened; the deep and threaten-

---

[84] One subject who suffered from several hypochondriacal fears and phobias saw in this part "a worm in the spine," an unusual interpretation that is, however, quite characteristic of the type of dynamic perception in which identification with a body suffering from the intrusion of some alien object or being plays a role.

[85] For instance, "woman sawed through" to Plate V, whole, or "nut, cracked open" to Plate II, black parts including the "crack" in center of lower red; "broken hip bone" to Plate III, the section where the leg is severed from the "body" of the two men by a small white space.

[86] This feeling of identification is expressed in the second part of a response to Plate IV: "a monster—the top a cleft in the head—which makes me feel woozy."

[87] I do not refer, here, to the sadistic and masochistic perversions but to "normal" sexual activity.

ing cleft, the encircling claws or hooks as vaginal symbols in which the phallus is threatened—the fear of castration.

Another complex of dynamic perception concerns stable, solid, massive, compact versus unstable, fragile, delicate, collapsible forms. The former are rather closely related to the phenomena encountered in the dynamic perception of tall or large size. By way of identification some subjects perceive primarily the power, strength, and security a solid, compact form seems to possess, while by way of opposition others perceive them as menacing, frightening, or dwarfing them. Of greater variety are the dynamic perceptions of the fragile, delicate, collapsible qualities of certain forms. In these cases the perceptual emphasis may be on the weakness or fragility of the links between the various details of a blot. Thus, one subject said to card X: "Sense of disorder, fragility, like those glass things that hang together with just a bit of glass," and to Plate VIII: "If anything goes out, everything would collapse." Or the emphasis may be on the precariousness of the balance or the support or the connectedness between various details, a theme often stimulated by card VII.

A sense of insecurity is often present in responses in which the white space is seen as a hole in the figure. In these cases the subject leaves, so to speak, the usual, naïve, natural, solid, and safe habit of seeing figure as figure and being aware of the white space either not at all or merely as background; the figure assumes a more questionable quality, is no longer a solid drawing precisely limited within its contours but an object that has lost its solidity by being pierced or by having cavities that interrupt its surface. It is possible that in all cases where the white spaces within a figure are perceived as such an interruption of the otherwise solid picture surface we are dealing with dynamic perception. A sense of hollowness, emptiness, or of wanting to destroy or of having been destroyed may also be expressed by the perceptual emphasis on the space as a hole or a hollow.

Some testees accentuate in some of their responses, probably usually without being aware of it, the few details which approximate geometric forms and thus contrast with the general accidental and ambiguous quality of the blots. The most prominent ones are to be found in the top-central gray and the upper-central orange areas of card X, in the center line of card I, and—somewhat less precise—in the center axis of the large lower D of card VI. Such emphasis occurs especially in card X, where it may be expressed by responding first to the top "geometric" detail or by giving a disproportionately large number of responses to the "geometric" as compared with the number of responses given to the many—to most people more striking—other details of the blot. It is usually a flight from the "chaos," the profusion, the disorder, the ambiguity these people experience in the blots, especially in X, where the many details and—often—the added impact of the color are felt as overwhelming and/or disturbing. By concentrating on the "geometric" detail these people attempt to impose, or cling to, order, accuracy, and definiteness and thus find security in the disquieting ambiguity and variety of the blots. The geometric shape promises them certainty in the uncertain world of the inkblots.

One relatively rare phenomenon in Rorschach records is not mentioned, so far as I am aware, in the Rorschach literature, but in a pronounced way shows the element so characteristic of all dynamic form perception, namely, the dynamic—instead of the detached, intellectual—relationship between perceiving subject and form perceived. Some subjects occasionally give a response in which they express the urge to do something with the figure perceived on the Rorschach plate, either to change that figure in some way or to perform some movement or assume some posture which will bring them into a definite bodily relationship with that figure. Sometimes, also, a fear or aversion is expressed against coming into some such contact with the figure, a contact which would again require a specific movement or the assumption of a specific posture by the subject with regard to the plate. These responses are not kinesthetic in the sense that the figure on the plate is perceived as moving. They express a desire, or fear, of the subject to move with regard to the figure perceived;[88] one might therefore call them "motor responses."

One subject reacted to the two little upper central protrusions on Plate I by saying: "Breasts of a woman, urge of tearing the thing up between them, perhaps I don't want to look at it any more, I would like to cut through the center line [of the whole figure] and fold these pieces [the two halves] together."

The same subject responded to Plate II with the remark that this is "again a figure that could be spliced in the middle."

To Plate III he said: "I have a desire to straighten out these figures, push their buttocks in, make them stand erect." He had seen the figures as "two comedians on stage, buttocks sticking out."

---

[88] I have found them, so far, only in some subjects suffering from rather severe neuroses and in some schizophrenic patients.

The same subject responded to Plate IV: "Again desire to cut this in the middle."

Another subject expressed a feeling of dizziness and of being tempted to jump into the white hole in Plate II after having looked at it for a long time.

To Plate VII, another subject remarked: "I would like to push it together, make it more solid."

Another subject responded to the two oval white spaces in the center of Plate IX by saying: "I would like to put my arms through these holes, lift the whole thing up."

These responses are the logical consequence, one might say, of experiencing the forms perceived as in a dynamic relation to the subject's personal situation. They represent the irrational action—provoked by desire or fear or both—by which the subject feels urged to meet the situation as represented in the forms perceived. The impulses which are only implicitly contained in all the earlier examples of dynamic form perception—flight from menacing bigness, hiding in a secure corner, sadistic destruction by breaking apart or tearing up something, for example—become explicit in these responses. The examples mentioned here are all taken from records of neurotic patients who are aware of the phantastic quality of their responses. This awareness is sometimes not present in psychotics, for whom the artificial blots may assume the character of reality. The psychological interpretation of these responses is not different from the interpretation of other dynamic form perceptions. For example, the sadistic wish to destroy another person by tearing him up along the center of his body which is so drastically expressed in the first group of responses to Plates I, II, and IV just quoted is the same that can be found in the examples quoted above (pp. 135–136). The subject who gave those motor responses was suffering from severe inferiority feelings, especially regarding physical weakness and potency. There were strong fears of being humiliated in sexual intercourse and phantasies of sadistic revenge by tearing up the women who humiliated him. On the other hand, the desire to "push erect" the figures in Plate III represented the sadistically tainted desire to be sexually potent. Intercourse was thought of chiefly as a sadistic penetration of and "sawing through" the woman. The same subject had given the response quoted above, "woman sawed through" to Plate V.

The degree of consciousness of the needs, trends, and complexes determining dynamic form perceptions varies a great deal in different people. So does the degree of consciousness of the emotional significance of a specific form for a particular person. Some people are not aware of the fact that they single out or avoid certain objects in their perceptions and are still less aware of the reasons why they do this. In other cases, perception of these forms is accompanied by feelings of fear, attraction, pleasure, and aversion.[89] This is especially true in some pathological cases, for instance, in phobias or in psychotics, who sometimes do not seem to differentiate between the illusory threat of a form on the Rorschach plate, a pointed arrow, for example, the somewhat less illusory threat of the real object—a real arrow[90]—and the realistic threat of an arrow or other weapon actually used against them. It is also sometimes true in people with considerable awareness of their own psychic problems and tendencies, often during and after analysis, for example, and in persons with a wide and subtle capacity for experience and empathy.

Another difference in the way in which dynamic perceptions are experienced concerns the degree of reality the perceiving subject attributes to the emotionally significant perceptions. If we call the degree of reality attributed by the subject to the dynamic percept "subjective reality" and the rationally determined reality of the object perceived and its qualities "objective reality," we can say that in dynamic perception we may encounter coincidence of subjective and objective reality as well as all degrees of disparity between them. An example of extreme disparity between subjective and objective reality is the schizophrenic patient who fears to be hurt by the pointed protrusion of one of the Rorschach blots. An example of coincidence of subjective and objective reality can be seen in two adversaries, the smaller and weaker of whom perceives his opponent as big. Between these two extremes there are innumerable transitions. For example, among the many persons who show a marked preference for corner seats in streetcars, in subways, on sofas and benches, there are quite a few whose preference is based on the mostly unconscious belief that a corner seat affords more protection

---

[89] Most of the examples of dynamic perception quoted above belong more or less to this latter category. They have been selected purposely to show in a more articulate way how form perception may be determined by certain psychic trends and emotions.

[90] Rorschach gives a good example of this type in a paper published many years before *Psychodiagnostics*: A schizophrenic patient of his sees a pen lying on the desk and has the sensation of being stabbed in the abdomen by the point of this pen. Hermann Rorschach, *"Reflexhalluzination und Symbolik," Zentralblatt für Psychoanalyse und Psychotherapie*, 3 (1912–1913), 121–128, in particular p. 122.

against a dangerous and unfriendly outside world, that it is more sheltered; that is, they have a dynamic perception of corners. Corners would be an example of the basic V or U shape. The protective quality of the corner seat is certainly not realistic, yet it is also not quite so phantastic as the protective quality of a drawn or printed V shape.

The dynamic form responses often add significant data for the evaluation of Rorschach records. Their use for diagnostic purposes raises two questions: first, how to distinguish dynamic from detached form responses; second, how to interpret them. Both these questions are in some respects similar to some problems of dream interpretation. There, too, the problem arises of sifting the relevant from the irrelevant and of interpreting the more relevant parts in placing them in a meaningful and correct way within the total texture of the individual's life situation and the structure of his personality. The interpretation of form "symbols," as we might call dynamic form percepts, shares with dream interpretation the difficult and delicate quality of the task that requires experience, skill, and psychological insight.

The first and most important rule for the *recognition of dynamic form perceptions*—and, one must add, for the analysis of Rorschach tests in general—is never to rely merely on the words used by a subject but always to go back to the things he has seen and to try to revisualize them in the entire context and sequence in which they have been seen. The closer one gets to the original perception of the subject, the more successful one is in this process of empathy in his experiences and perceptions during the test, the more accurate the diagnostic material grasped. Neither the words of the responses nor their technical scoring alone can be substituted for the concrete visualization of what and how the subject has perceived. Unfortunately, such visualization of another person's perceptions is possible only approximately, and the degrees of approximation to the original perception vary in accordance with the astuteness as well as the individuality of the observer. This situation is similar to that prevailing between any psychological or clinical observer and the behavior, feelings, and thoughts of the subject he studies. But there are some rules of thumb which may sometimes facilitate discernment of dynamic perception. They are essentially those which have already been discussed with regard to the interpretation of perceptual themes: originality, especially if it runs counter to the objective structural qualities of the blot or singles out a rarely used part of the blot, and recurrence of the same perceptual theme. Again, it must be emphasized that originality and repetition refer not to the words used but to the percept seen by the testee. Often it is helpful to inquire about the testee's preferences and dislikes among the ten Rorschach blots and into his reasons for them. These may furnish data for the recognition of dynamic form responses as well as show feelings about the inkblots revealing dynamic factors that have not led to actual responses and, of course, may yield other significant data.

In the *diagnostic interpretation* of dynamic form responses a major difficulty lies in their frequent ambiguity. Does a form represent something feared, desired, or both feared and desired? Is identification with or opposition to the perceived form the process in which this form obtains its emotional significance for the subject? While in some cases the subject seems to leave no doubt about this question, in others the form-symbol appears "pure," so to speak, without any immediate indications about its role and function in the individual's life. Often, not only the positive or negative quality of the attraction, the desire and need, or the fear and repulsion that the specific form holds for the individual is not immediately visible, but also the emphasis on some specific quality of the form is not apparent—the opening, or the bottom, of the V or U shape, for example. In all these cases only a careful scrutiny of the dynamic perception within the framework of all the other data available on the subject, whether offered by the Rorschach or by other sources of observation, can lead to a correct interpretation, just as a symbol in a dream lends itself only to an interpretation which takes into account the context of the dream as well as the personality and history of the dreamer. Dynamic form perceptions do not have an absolute meaning regardless of where, in whom, and how they occur; their meaning may vary, as we have tried to show in the discussion of some typical form perceptions.

Aside from the diagnostic meaning of the specific themes appearing in or underlying dynamic form responses, their mere presence, regardless of their specific theme, has diagnostic implications different from those of other form responses and similar, in some respects, to those of the special F+.[91] The similarity lies in their greater aliveness and the relative lack of detachment. This implies that, if they are included in the F%, its usefulness as an indicator of the degree of coartation and of

---

[91] Of course, in contrast to the special F+, dynamic form responses can also be F−, ordinary F+, or of vague form level.

an impoverished way of perceiving will be diminished, since neither the special F+ nor the dynamic form responses have this diagnostic signifi-cance to the extent that other form responses do.

As is the case with physiognomic perception in general, dynamic form perception cannot be interpreted as indicating necessarily a path-ological, more primitive, or regressive form of perception, compared with detached form perception. Dynamic is older than detached form perception; the infant and young child see everything in a dynamic or physiognomic way, as Werner and others have shown. Detached form perception is a late phenomenon. Phylogenetically, it appears in man only; ontogenetically, too, it is a late achievement of the growing child and requires a relatively high degree of intellectual development. Only with the gradual freeing of perception from its immediate reference to the psychobiological needs of man does his ability for allocentric per-ception, his capacity to "observe," to perceive with detachment arise. This capacity brings with it an enrichment but can also lead to an im-poverishment of human perception. The enrichment is brought about by the new ability to look at things without and beyond the limitations of a perception tied to immediate instinctive and psychic needs and interests. This makes possible scientific observation, for example. It en-ables man to make the discoveries that have made possible his mastery of nature, that are indispensable for the development of a technical civilization. It enlarges the variety of the objects he perceives beyond those relevant to his needs and fears. The impoverishment to which detached perception can and often does lead is less well and less widely known than its advantages, although our whole civilization bears wit-ness to it and, in Rorschach tests, the large number of coartated and coartative Rorschach records. A few hints must suffice to indicate the kinds of impoverishment that occur when detached perception leads to an atrophy of dynamic perception.[92]

The immediate relation between instinctive needs and perception is responsible for the greater keenness of the sensory perceptions so many animals have, compared with human perception. For similar reasons, members of primitive tribes generally have keener senses in many re-spects than the members of a modern industrial community. In the field

---

[92] Much of what has been described here as detached form perception as apparent in Rorschach form responses is closely related to what I have called elsewhere the development of secondary autocentricity of perception in contrast to the primary autocentricity of the infant and young child. Compare Schachtel, *op. cit.*, pp. 166–212.

of interpersonal relations, it has often been observed that small children have a much better "physiognomic" understanding of other persons, that they are much more sensitive toward the attitudes other people have toward them, than the average adult person. The "intuitive," largely physiognomic[93] understanding of others is a faculty based on dynamic perception, on a perception that is part and parcel of the entire interpersonal relation between the perceiving and the perceived person. For obvious reasons, such dynamic perception can never be entirely objective since it always involves the total relation between the perceiver and the perceived and, in addition, other, earlier relations to other people which influence the present one. Nevertheless, dynamic (or physiognomic) perceptions are one of our chief sources of information—and misinformation—about other people, and often such information is richer and more correct than what the other person could tell us in a short period about himself and what we would be able to perceive without our physiognomic understanding.

The fact that dynamic is older than detached form perception and that, early in life, it is a primitive and not yet very differentiated mode of predominantly autocentric perception does not mean that it has to remain at this stage, nor does it imply that its occurrence always involves a regression, albeit in the service of the ego. Dynamic form perception is capable of development to a high degree of differentiation and can take place with full awareness of its significance. Always to see in it a primitive or regressed form of experience makes no more sense than to see in art and poetry a more primitive or regressed form of human experience and its expression than, say, in what is commonly called a "realistic" view of life, or in science, merely because poetry and art are older than science.[94] In fact, dynamic form perception is essential for that richness of human perception which allows man to experience fully the world around him and which finds its highest and most precise expression in art and poetry.

---

[93] The term "physiognomic" is used here in its widest sense. It implies the understanding of another person on the basis of immediate sensory perceptions. Usually visual and auditory perceptions play the major role. For these the gestural, the mimic, expressive behavior, and the voice and intonation are the major objects.

[94] Compare Schachtel, *op. cit.*, pp. 237–248.

### The Problem of Delay

The active attention, taking hold, comparison, and critical judgment inherent in the genesis of most form or form-dominated responses constitute an amount of mental activity considerably greater than that present in the immediate, impulsive reaction to a striking stimulus such as color, the response to which does not require the kind of active organization underlying the typical F+ response.[95] Rapaport has some of these factors in mind when he postulates that "the coming about of form responses represents a capacity for delay of discharge of impulses —or, as it could be phrased in psychoanalytic terminology, for a delay of instinctual gratifications and their derivatives." He believes that the "occurrence of any form response implies some delay" (in contrast to a pure color response) and that, in order to give a satisfactory form response (F+), "the subject's mode of functioning should allow for the delay necessary for a perceptual articulation of the inkblot, for an initiation of associative processes on the basis of the initial perceptual impression, for a consequent reorganization of the perceptual material to obtain a congruence with the possibilities offered by the associative processes, and finally for a critical appraisal of the response which came forth." [96] He thus links the amount and quality of the mental activity inherent in the genesis of form responses with the important psychoanalytic concept of delay. This concept cannot be separated from the question of *what* is being delayed. In Freud's theory it is the discharge of need tensions that is delayed, for example during thought, which is conceptualized as a detour to such discharge. His concept of delay can be understood only in connection with his theory of the pleasure principle according to which the basic striving of man is to reduce or abolish tension and excitation and to return to a tensionless state. Since reality conflicts with the prompt satisfaction of this need, detours and delay are instituted with the aim of permitting satisfaction by finding the need object in reality, with the help of consciousness, attention, realistic perception, and thought. Detour and delay are compromises in the basic conflict between need, fulfillment of which is delayed, and reality. Rapaport's formulation leaves the reader in doubt as to what is being delayed. On the one hand he speaks of impulse discharge, instinctual

---

[95] This is true especially of the pure C and the Cn (Color-naming) responses. It does not apply to the FC, in which form perception plays a decisive role.

[96] Rapaport, *op. cit.*, II, 189, 190.

gratification and its derivatives. On the other hand, he seems to imply that what is being delayed is the giving of the response in order to allow for the complicated mental processes necessary for the achievement of a satisfactory form response (F+). This would imply that the giving of the response constitutes the desired discharge and gratification of an instinct-derivative.

It would lead too far to discuss in detail whether in what sense and under what conditions the giving of a Rorschach response could be justifiably described as a derivative of instinctual gratification.[97] However, in a mental task, as in any attempt to solve a problem—whether posed by others, e.g., by a test, or by oneself—there is a wish to find the solution, and energy is mobilized to this end, unless the task is rejected to begin with.[98] The Rorschach task has qualities which make it for many people more difficult than the kind of tasks to which they are accustomed from school and from their work. The most important of these qualities are the relative lack of directions as to how to go about the task and what, if any, standards to apply to its solution; the ambiguity, strangeness, and unfamiliarity of the inkblots; and the lasting "openness" of the question posed by the test. These qualities are particularly difficult and anxiety- or uneasiness-arousing for people who find it hard to tolerate ambiguity and an "open" world to which there are no final, definite solutions or answers. For many of these people Rorschach's test increases the tension inherent in problem-solving to a degree they cannot tolerate and they cannot delay their responses long enough to make adequate use of the possibilities offered by the blot. Their need for closure is so great that they have to push the problem aside by finding an "answer" quickly. Thereby they transform the unfamiliar and "open" into the closed and familiar, at the expense of further exploration and richer experience. In them, the response satisfies an urgent wish for closure, for a return to embeddedness in the familiar. At the

---

[97] What Rapaport probably had in mind was his notion of a new distribution of cathectic energies, derived from the drive cathexes and superimposed on them, in a hierarchy of progressively more and more "bound" energy distributions. Rapaport, *Organization and Pathology of Thought* (New York: Columbia University Press, 1951), p. 405, footnote 17.

[98] The intention of fulfilling the task creates a quasi-need in Lewin's sense. See Kurt Lewin, "Intention, Will and Need" in Rapaport, *Organization and Pathology of Thought*, pp. 95–153, especially 113–144. However, this quasi-need arises in the context of the interpersonal test situation and of a wide variety of attitudes that different testees are bound to have toward the test situation and the test task. Thus, the quality of the intention and of the quasi-need created by it show a great variety of nuances and of determining factors.

same time, some people may be motivated by an imagined pressure of the tester for quick or many responses, which does not leave them free to perceive the blot fully and to play with the possibilities it offers. They want to get rid, to dispose of a task, a situation which makes them uneasy because it threatens the closed world in which they prefer to live. This wish can be so strong that its satisfaction cannot be delayed till a more adequate response is found.[99]

While the test task always creates tension and mobilizes energy directed toward its solution, such tension need not lead to the wish to abolish it as quickly as possible. The activity and effort of thought and of perception of the unfamiliar, and the fluctuating tensions of such activity, can be satisfying in themselves. Need is not the only ancestor of thought and of the perception of reality, and the latter are not mere detours and delays on the path to tension reduction. Perception and thought originate also in play, when the infant is not under the pressure of urgent needs but looks at, touches, handles, gazes with intent interest at the objects of his environment in exploratory play. Man's creative activity, whether in solving a problem in living, in art, in science or philosophy, or in seeking a solution of the Rorschach task, involves play with the various aspects and possibilities of the task and of tentative solutions. Only if he does not press toward premature closure, premature answers, but allows the problem, the object contemplated to be what it is and to reveal many of its aspects to him, only if he plays with it as well as critically examines what such play lets him see, will his findings be rich and satisfying.[100] In this approach the search itself is its own reward. Lessing once expressed this by saying that if God offered him the choice between the truth and the search for truth, he would choose the search for truth. This does not mean that such search is entirely free from tensions and conflict; nor does it mean that, e.g., in the Rorschach situation, the testee who engages in such play with an open eye and an open mind will continue in it indefinitely. It does mean that the exploratory play itself is, for the time being, fully accepted and engaged in. It is the exaggerated pressure for an answer, or for a particularly "good" answer, which gets in the way of the desirable time and

---

[99] Of course this does not mean that they give only one quick response to each blot. There are many ways in which the defense against the described uneasiness can take place in the test responses.

[100] Gustav Bally, *Vom Ursprung und von den Grenzen der Freiheit. Eine Deutung des Spiels bei Tier und Mensch* (Basel: Benno Schwabe, 1945). Schachtel, *op. cit.*, pp. 63–64, 271–274.

freedom for play in the search for an answer. This pressure and the motivations generating it lead to impatience, more pressure, hence to a premature narrowing of the path to the answer. The searching play with the inkblot is a rich and varied mental activity. It is this activity and the concomitant receptivity and openness which are likely to yield the richest responses to Rorschach's test, including the optimal F+.

The form responses, as we have seen, presuppose and represent intellectual activity necessary for allocentric, objectifying perception and judgment. This is especially true of the F+. Only if one assumes with Freud that *all* thought is ultimately *delay* of instinctual gratification through discharge of tension would it follow that the form responses, since they represent thought and reality judgment, also must represent delay of discharge. But if one assumes, as I do, that thought and reality-perception derive to a large extent from the infant's and child's exploratory play, from his enjoyment in expanding his relation to the environing world of objects, then the form responses need not always represent delay of gratification; they can also represent the enjoyable and fluctuating tension of exploratory play in contact with the world of the inkblots. This implies that the exploration of the inkblot and the finding of responses to it (form as well as other responses) can be satisfying in itself and that the amount of mental activity involved in the form responses (necessary especially for the F+) does not always have the quality of delay in Freud's sense.[101]

The delay inherent in the mental activity necessary for adequate form perception as contrasted with the typically more passive attitude char-

---

[101] Hartmann's view of partially conflict-free development of perception, thinking, and productivity seems to take into account the fact that much of this development does not imply detours and delays of ultimate gratification, although he does not explicitly say so. However, he assumes that the functioning of the ego "may secondarily yield pleasure," namely, through discharge of tension. Heinz Hartmann, *Ego Psychology and the Problem of Adaptation* (New York: International Universities Press, 1961), p. 43. In my opinion the *fluctuating* tension rather than its discharge alone is enjoyed, but mainly the *contact* with reality, the *relation to reality* in thought, perception, and feeling. Rapaport assumes that drive tension is never fully discharged and that tolerance of tension varies individually, partly due to innate structural differences in thresholds of tension tolerance. (Rapaport, *Origin and Pathology of Thought*, pp. 692–693.) I agree with this assumption, but feel that it involves a significant change in the concept of delay. When tension is accepted, tolerated, and—as I believe—often enjoyed by the healthy organism, then "delay" of discharge, to that extent, no longer has the meaning it has in Freud's concept. Compare also Schachtel, *op. cit.*, pp. 3–77, especially 55–68. A fuller discussion of the concept of delay and of the change in its meaning necessitated by a critical review of Freud's theory of the pleasure and reality principle would go beyond the scope of this book and must be left for another occasion.

acteristic of color perception (see Chapter 8) could give rise to the question whether there is a *conflict* or an *alternative* between form perception, especially accurate form perception (high F+ %), and the perception of color. Some of Rorschach's findings might be taken to support such a view. The most relevant of these findings are: (1) The more C and CF (the more labile the emotions), the lower the level of form accuracy, except in artists and in the neuroses; (2) The pedantic personality and the depressed have a high F+ % but no or few color and M responses; (3) When a conscious effort is made to reach a high level of form accuracy, the number of color and movement responses decreases, i.e., the test results approach those of the pedantic and depressed personality.[102] Shapiro assumes that "color originally is probably antagonistic to form perception." [103] It seems to me more likely that the conflict does not exist between form and color perception *per se*, but between a strained, rigid, effortful, inhibiting, and a more relaxed, open, receptive, flexible, freely playing attitude. Where form responses result from the former, the defensive and warding-off aspects of concentration contribute to a high F+ %, at the same time excluding the possibility of rich experience and of openness to the inkblot. Where they are given with a more relaxed, open, flexible attitude they do not conflict with the giving of M and C responses. This would be consistent with Rorschach's finding that artists tend to show a high F+ % and a dilated experience type.[104]

The significance of the receptive, flexible versus rigid, coartated, inhibiting attitude can be studied not only in the total sequence of the responses but also plays an important role in the microgenesis of a single response. Rorschach touches on this point when he discusses the intuitive response. A good intuitive response requires, according to him, the capacity for dilation as well as for coartation. He writes: "Intuitions can be of value only when the subject has the ability to grasp and hold the intuition achieved in the dilated experience as a whole form; that is to say, he must be able to shift from dilated to coartated type quickly, and only if this is possible will the intuitions be of value." [105] This parallels, in a short time span, the often-observed distinction between the "inspirational" and the "elaborative" phase in the creative process. In

---

[102] Rorschach, *op. cit.*, pp. 31, 83, 67, respectively.

[103] David Shapiro, "A Perceptual Understanding of Color Response" in Maria A. Rickers-Ovsiankina (ed.), *op. cit.*, p. 188.

[104] Rorschach, *op. cit.*, p. 31 and Table VIII, p. 50. See also above, pp. 111–117.

[105] Rorschach, *op. cit.*, p. 203.

the receptive, open attitude there occurs an oscillation in which at one moment the receptiveness toward what one is looking at predominates, at another the more definite, fixating attitude in which an active grasp of the object takes place and fixes it in one's mind, and in which form elements predominate. Where such oscillation does not occur, form becomes indeed antagonistic to color and movement.

### The Development of Form Perception and the Form Responses

The complexity of the perceptual attitude in form perception and recognition—accentuated and even more complex in the genesis of form responses to Rorchach's test—would lead one to expect that form perception is a relatively late development in the life of the infant and child. This is borne out by the relevant developmental facts which show that the perception of distinct, differentiated form is a late achievement compared with the perception of light and dark, of contrast, of color, and with undifferentiated, global perception. It requires maturation[106] and a great deal of learning by means of ever-repeated exploration and experience. The main motivating forces in this development are the attraction by, interest in, and curiosity about the environment. These are innate Anlages; not, as Freud assumed, exclusively either sublimations of more basic drives, or a reluctantly accepted necessity, imposed by reality as a detour to the fulfillment of the wish for an excitationless state.[107] Their first, brief, slight manifestations sometimes can be observed on the first day of the neonate's life.[108] They show a rapid growth throughout infancy and early childhood; in cases of fortunate development, they may continue to grow, usually at a slower rate, throughout life. This development is part of the change from be-

---

[106] Both physiological and psychological maturation. At birth the infant is physiologically incapable of exact vision because, among other factors, the fovea centralis is not fully developed. Compare F. Stirnimann, *Psychologie des neugeborenen Kindes* (Zürich and Leipzig: Rascher Verlag, 1940), p. 55.

In the following discussion psychological factors of development only will be discussed, even though some of them depend partly on physiological maturation, for instance the finer muscular control and coordination of the eyes.

[107] These latter dynamics are highly significant, but Freud's "nothing but" formulation overlooks that they are not characteristic of the healthy child's or adult's waking life and that even in the neonate and infant, where they play an impressive role, the Anlages and interests mentioned in the text are already present in the first days of life. For a detailed discussion of this whole problem, see Schachtel, *op. cit.*, pp. 55–68, 116–165, 251–278.

[108] Stirnimann, *op. cit.*, Schachtel, *op. cit.*, pp. 114–146, with further references.

ing passively and helplessly exposed to the impinging stimuli to a state in which the child becomes able to control, to some extent, the impact of the environment and of internal needs. One significant factor in this developing control is the capacity for active, selective focusing of attention. This capacity is crucial for the development of form perception. Its increasing significance can be observed in those periods of wakefulness of the infant which are not taken up by nursing or by the alleviation of discomfort. They become increasingly differentiated from the prevailing periods of sleep[109] and rapidly expand in time during the first years of life.

The growing interest in the environment and the growing capacity for active focal attention become most apparent in certain changes in the infant's and young child's behavior. The most significant changes in the area of visual perception can be described summarily as shifts from passivity (being impinged upon) to an increasing amount of increasingly differentiated activity (actively attending to). During the first days of life the infant's organism has to cope with the sudden shift from intrauterine to extrauterine existence with its massive physiological changes.[110] To accomplish this work, the organism tries to protect itself by reproducing the conditions of intrauterine life as much as possible outside of the womb. It does this mainly by sleep and by a state of consciousness which, during the relatively brief periods of wakefulness, is not so much of a contrast to sleep as it will be later in life. Thus the newborn is receptive to considerably fewer stimuli from the environment than he will be a few months later. In the area of vision, these are usually striking stimuli—this implies that they are usually not very small unless, like a narrow but strong beam of light, they can be striking in spite of covering only a small area.

Some stimuli attract and hold the neonate's gaze; from others he turns away. Stirnimann observed that in the first week newborns looked at certain colors up to twenty-two seconds (seeming to show a preference for blue and green and an aversion to yellow) and at a contrast pattern of a post-card-size red paper with a black spot of one cm diameter in its center, fifty seconds.[111] Valentine, observing a three-month-old,

---

[109] For the significance of the developing differentiation between sleep and wakefulness see Schachtel, *op. cit.*, pp. 64–65.

[110] For a brief enumeration of the amount of changes involved, see A. Gesell and C. G. Amatruda, *Developmental Diagnosis* (New York: Paul B. Hoeber, 1959), p. 218.

[111] Stirnimann, *op. cit.*, pp. 57–58.

kept a record of the time the child looked at a series of colored skeins two of which were held before his eyes at the same time for two minutes. He computed times of preference and nonpreference, as inferred from the length of time the child looked at each of the two skeins and obtained the following rank order from longest to shortest periods of looking: yellow, white, pink, then considerably less long red, brown, black, green, blue, violet.[112] This is the reverse of what Stirnimann observed in the newborn who seemed to prefer blue and green and to avoid yellow. Perhaps at first the bright colors are avoided while somewhat later, after the shock of the impact of light and color has worn off, they become the most arresting. More research is needed to clarify these questions.[113] In any case, the staying with a particular stimulus, being attracted by it rather than wanting to abolish it, is the first manifestation of what later develops into interest, of stimulus appetite rather than stimulus avoidance,[114] and it is, perhaps, also the first trace of a transition to activity, in the sense of choosing one stimulus to stay with rather than another. It seems likely that in the newborn's experience of such attractive stimuli there is a fusion of sensory quality and pleasure or unpleasure;[115] they have no "object" quality; they are seen in the autocentric perceptual mode. Speculating about the kinds of pleasure experienced in the perception of such attractive stimuli, I am inclined to the hypothesis that, depending on the stimulus and on the state of consciousness of the infant, it may lean more toward sensory pleasure or more toward activity-pleasure—i.e., the kind of pleasure felt in the exercise of an activity.[116] The stimuli which thus attract and hold the

---

[112] C. W. Valentine, "Color Perception of an Infant," *British Journal of Psychology*, 6 (1913–14), quoted by Werner, *op. cit.*, p. 99.

[113] In such research it would be important to compare at different age levels the reaction to uniformly colored with contrastingly colored stimuli. I would anticipate that contrasting color (multicolored, or color against white or black-and-white stimuli) would attract more attention than uniform color. Specific color attraction or aversion would have to be tested by the exposure of uniformly colored objects.

[114] In sensory deprivation experiments a lack of contrast, a uniformly neutral, dull sensory field is artificially created so as not to cater to the native stimulus appetite of man.

[115] Schachtel, *op. cit.*, pp. 119–130, with further references.

[116] Piaget speaks of light as an aliment for the neonate's visual activity. Jean Piaget, *The Origins of Intelligence in Children* (New York: International Universities Press, 1952), pp. 62–63. My guess would be that the perception of soft light and of certain colors leans more to the sensory type, while the perception of contrast leans more to the (mental) activity type of pleasure. Of course, the two are not mutually exclusive.

newborn's gaze are mainly soft light, luminous objects, certain colors, especially multicolored objects and particularly patterns of sharp contrast, such as black and white, or black and red, or white and red, all of which, at this point and for some time to come, are perceived not as differentiated, definite forms but as global impressions of something striking.[117]

Fantz believes that form perception is present as early as the perception of color and light.[118] He worked in one series of experiments with one- to fifteen-week-old infants, in another with four-day- to six-month-olds. However, what he considers early instances of form perception seem to me not different from the infant's reaction to light, contrast, and color; namely, a reaction to a striking, impinging stimulus and the staying with this (attractive) stimulus, in this case, the *striking impact of contrast* rather than the distinct and differentiated perception of form, which is a later development. Thus it is significant that in his experiments the infants' attention stayed considerably longer with striking black-and-white patterns than with the line drawing of a circle. Even at a later age children low in the developmental scale tend to base their choices of similarity between a variety of geometric figures not on the *form* of the figure but on such qualities as blackness and solidity, i.e., *on the striking impact of a solidly black figure* rather than on the geometric form (e.g., the circular outline of the figure), whereas adults or children with a more advanced, more actively discriminating perceptual organization base their choices on the circular form. This has been shown in experiments by D. Knoblauch, which Werner reports and summarizes by saying: "We must conclude that the development of optical percepts occurs through an increase of articulation" (i.e., a more actively structuring perceptual activity), whereas lower in the developmental scale choices are based "on the vague qualities of blackness, solidity, etc., rather than on real figural qualities" [119]—i.e., on qualities that have a striking impact.

Probably, as perceptual organization advances, the attention of the young child will still be caught by striking contrast of (chromatic or

---

[117] Stirnimann, *op. cit.*, pp. 56–59; Schachtel, *op. cit.*, pp. 121 and 144–145, with further references.

[118] Robert L. Fantz, "Pattern Vision in Young Infants," *The Psychological Record*, 8 (1958), 43–47; "The Origin of Form Perception," *Scientific American*, 204 (1961), 66–72.

[119] Werner, *op. cit.*, pp. 115–116.

achromatic) color against a different background, but will then begin
to explore more actively what has arrested his attention by impinging
on his receptors. And since form, too, can only be perceived when it is
in some, though not necessarily striking, contrast to its background it is
quite likely that the attention paid by infants to striking contrasts, while
originally not different from staying with any other striking, impinging
stimulus, becomes the aliment which, with the changing quality of attention toward more active exploration, nurtures and eventually produces at first global and later more differentiated form perception.
Fantz reports that, among his subjects, the two- to three-month-old infants' attention was held longest by the pattern of a face drawn either
in broad, striking black-and-white strokes or in a black-and-reddish pattern. At that age, global "form" perception of the face is sufficiently
advanced to start evoking the smiling response to the human face. As
Spitz has suggested, "smiling in reaction to the human face and to
the human only is the first step in the development of diacritic perception." [120] He demonstrated that this reaction is shown generally by infants three to six months old, that in cases of very advanced development it may occur at one month, that it occurs in response to a mask as
well as in response to a face, and that the infant cannot distinguish
between different expressions (smiling versus terrifying expressions) of
the face. The response disappears generally after the sixth month. At
this time perception gradually becomes sufficiently differentiated to dis-
criminate between familiar faces (parents, nurse) and strange faces.

The most important steps in the change from being passively struck
by, and staying for a while with, the impinging stimulus to active perceptual exploration consist in the development from diffuse, vague star-
ing to the capacity to focus both eyes on the object, to follow a moving
object with focused eyes, and later to move the head, thus keeping
visual hold of it; looking at the same object for prolonged periods of
time; from approximately the seventh or eighth month on, becoming
interested in and focusing on very small objects,[121] and finally, over a
period of several years, the continuing shift from the predominance of
global form perception to the perception of clearly structured and articulated objects in which the distinct perception of the object's form
plays an increasingly important role.

---

[120] René A. Spitz, "The Smiling Response: A Contribution to the Ontogenesis
of Social Relations," *Genetic Psychology Monographs* 34 (1946), 57–125.

[121] For a more detailed description, see Schachtel, *op. cit.*, pp. 147, 256–257,
with further references.

The shift from being passively struck by a vivid visual stimulus to actively looking at it is familiar to everybody. Traffic signs and many advertisements purposely make use of it by providing a striking contrast, such as black-on-yellow signs, strong neon lights, large black lettering, a mostly empty white page with a relatively small printed area, etc. Such contrast is intended to and does catch our eye—i.e., impinges on it so strikingly that we cannot help noticing it. Thus struck by it, we look at the sign and recognize the symbol on it (a sequence which may take a second or less) or—the advertiser hopes—look at and read his message. We retain the capacity to be struck passively by an impinging stimulus, and we take for granted that we then can pay attention to the details of its form and thus recognize it; it is this second part of the sequence that takes approximately a year to develop in a rudimentary form in the infant and several years to reach the stage of fully developed, finely differentiating form perception.[122]

The perception of light, dark, color, and contrast does not develop as much beyond what it is in the young infant as does that of form; the latter continues until a finely differentiated, rich form perception is achieved in the child which, of course, can be further cultivated, refined, and expanded throughout life by those who are interested in the world of forms. Human perception of form could not undergo such a prolonged and high development if the forms perceived were not significant for man's orientation in his varied natural and cultural environment. The infant's and child's great curiosity about and interest in what he sees serves man's need to learn about the meaning of the environmental objects. The first of these "objects," [123] a global perception of which becomes familiar to the infant, is the human face as seen in the mother at whom the infant gazes steadily when nursing. The infant and child would not develop a richly differentiated form perception if the objects perceived by means of such perception were not meaningful. Thus, language and concept formation come to be inseparably linked with per-

---

[122] The above description does not imply, of course, that the adult's and the infant's passive perceptual experiences are the same; it only wants to point up similarities. A major difference is that the adult sees a world of objects, while the young infant does not yet differentiate between self and object nor does he recognize, hence also not expect to see, distinct objects.

[123] I put "objects" in quotes because this early familiarity with the face does not require or imply that the infant see the mother as separate and distinct from himself. It just requires a feeling of familiarity when seeing the face. About this feeling, its difference from object recognition proper, and the important problem of the perception of the familiar versus that of the unknown, see Schachtel, *op. cit.*, pp. 147–165, 44–55.

ception, particularly with form perception, which is basic for man's recognition of objects.

An interesting confirmation of the amount of learning and experience necessary for differentiated form perception and its consequently late development compared with the perception of light, color, and contrast, comes from von Senden's observations of the congenitally blind who, in adulthood, acquired sight through successful operations.[124] Their vision has at first an amorphous quality in which distinct forms are not recognized, while light and color are. Von Senden describes the overwhelming quality of the impact of the diffuse, amorphous visual field, the plethora of impressions that characterizes the experience of these patients before they have gone through the long and difficult process of learning to see and differentiate distinct forms. Even conceptual recognition (correct naming) of colors occurs long before form recognition. One of his subjects learned to identify and name the different colors very quickly but even eleven months after the operation still could not recognize the simplest forms. Apparently the formerly blind share with the newborn the fact of being exposed passively to the impinging stimuli and of needing a long period in which to learn the active, differentiated perception of form. They differ from the newborn in that the latter does not seem to be so overwhelmed by what he sees as are these patients who, according to von Senden, sometimes go through a personal crisis in their attempt to master the difficult task of learning to see and recognize definite objects clearly distinguished by means of differentiated form perception. I think that this difference is in part due to the fact the newborn has a natural "stimulus barrier," [125] and that his state of consciousness during wakefulness is altogether not so sharply differentiated from sleep as is that of the adult; thus, the newborn is protected against a too sudden transition from intra- to extrauterine life by the temporary maintenance of quasi-uterine conditions in extrauterine life. In contrast to this, the adult patients of von Senden are exposed to the total impact of the visual world on a fully awake and highly developed mind including a sensorium that does not have a stimulus barrier comparable to the

---

[124] M. von Senden, *Raum- und Gestaltauffassung bei operierten Blindgeborenen* (Leipzig: I. A. Barth, 1932). English translation: *Space and Sight: The Perception of Space and Shape in the Congenitally Blind before and after Operation* (New York: Free Press of Glencoe, 1960).

[125] S. Freud, *Beyond the Pleasure Principle* (1920) [Standard Edition], XVIII, 27–28. P. Bergman and Sibylle Escalona, "Unusual Sensitivities in Very Young Children," *The Psychoanalytic Study of the Child*, 3/4 (1949), 333–352.

infant's without having acquired as yet the capacity to master this enormously vivid and powerful visual impact by active differentiation of forms, thus selectively reducing its force.[126]

This situation may well produce a conflict between the passive, overwhelming impact of light, color, and contrast and the perception of form, as Shapiro suggests.[127] But it seems questionable to me also to assume such a conflict for the child in which neither the suddenness, the power of the visual impact, nor the pressure to incorporate it into an already fully developed kosmos of experience are present and comparable to the situation of the patients on whom von Senden reports.

How do the *Rorschach responses of young children* fit into what we know and have briefly discussed about the complex and late development of form perception? Most observers have found that in the youngest group from which it is possible to obtain Rorschach responses, the two-year-olds, the percentage of form responses (F%) is very high, in fact higher than in most adults. Thus, Ames *et al.* report that the F% is highest (90%) at two years, then declines steadily to 52% at seven, then increases slightly (to 63%) at ten.[128] At first glance, this seems to contradict the assumption that the youngest children react more to color and contrast then to form and that form perception takes a long time to develop. However, at the ages of two to three, form perception is already considerably advanced and plays an important role in the child's ability to recognize a great variety of objects, animals, and people. In such recognition we deal mostly with *global* form perception, and in analyzing the youngest children's form responses we find that they, too, are usually global, poorly articulated forms, and that

---

[126] There are other difficulties for these people less relevant in the present context. One of them is the situation of the adult, with a fully developed mind and conceptualization of his world and his experiences, suddenly confronted with a completely new aspect of the world of which hitherto he had no direct experience but knew only from hearsay, and which he has to assimilate and incorporate in his experience of the world. While the infant feels no strong pressure and can take his time to explore the visible world, the adult who suddenly gains sight feels the pressure of having to assimilate this all at once, a pressure that comes from his own desire to integrate what he suddenly sees with his already highly developed concept of the world.

[127] Shapiro, in Rickers-Ovsiankina, ed., *op. cit.*, p. 168.

[128] Louise Bates Ames, Janet Learned, Ruth W. Métraux, and Richard N. Walther, *Child Rorschach Responses* (New York: Paul B. Hoeber, Inc., 1952), p. 286. Compare also Mary Ford, *The Application of the Rorschach Test to Young Children* (Minneapolis: University of Minnesota Press, 1946), pp. 40, 45, 86, and 95.

therefore the form level (F + %) is low. Often the young child's form response will be based on one impressive part of the inkblot that fits the child's concept or part of it, and the rest of the blot will be used regardless of its fit, thus leading to a confabulated, DW, response. This *pars pro toto* is typical in general of the global perception of two- to four-year-olds.[129]

Not only do global and *pars pro toto* qualities distinguish the young child's typical form responses from those of older children and adults, but also the fact that these form responses are usually not given with a detached attitude, of which the child is incapable, but with considerable affective meaning. As Werner has pointed out, perceptual discrimination has a very different quality depending on whether the discrimination is made on the basis of objective, perceptual factors or on the basis of a syncretic activity of the sensory-motor-affective type.[130] Young children's form responses, thus, do not usually represent an impersonal, impoverished, detached perception but a primitive, syncretic global one in which sensory and cognitive as well as affective and motor activities or impulses may merge and partake. The importance and frequency of this type of form response decreases and is replaced by more clearly articulated and objectifying form perception and, to some extent, by FC, M, and form-dominated shading responses as the child grows older and advances in his development.

---

129 Compare Werner, *op. cit.*, pp. 112–113. See also Jack Fox and Gertrude Meili Dworetzki in Klopfer *et al.*, *op. cit.*, II, 93–95 and 129, respectively.

130 Werner, *op. cit.*, pp. 100–101, 482.

# 8 / COLOR

*Welch Getöse bringt das Licht!* . . .
*Trifft es euch, so seid ihr taub.*

**Ein Feuermeer umschlingt uns, welch ein Feuer!**
*Ist's Lieb? Ist's Hass? die glühend uns umwinden,*
*Mit Schmerz und Freuden wechselnd ungeheuer.* . . .

[With a crash the light draws near! . . .
If it strikes you, you are deaf.

And seas of fire—and what a fire!—surprise us.
Is't Love? Is't Hate? that burningly embraces,
And that with pain and joy alternate tries us?]
—Goethe, *Faust II*, Act I [Sunrise] (Bayard Taylor's translation)[1]

The predominantly allocentric mode of perception of adult man's sense of sight does not exclude the survival and development of its autocentric functioning which prevailed in the newborn and the infant. This is particularly apparent in the perception of color and light. In contrast to the actively structuring and objectifying allocentric perceptual attitude characteristic of the perception of form and structure, the perception of color and light does not require such an attitude. Nor does color perception, by itself, permit objectification, while perception of form does. The visual recognition of a particular object is not possible without form perception. The perception of color, if it is not accompanied by and integrated with form perception, typically occurs with a passive, more autocentric perceptual attitude. Color and light "impinge on the eye which does not have to seek them out attentively but *reacts* to their impact." [2] Goethe speaks of the "sensual-moral" effect of color and de-

---

[1] Goethe, *Faust II* (New York: Random House, The Modern Library, 1950), pp. 3–4.

[2] Schachtel, *op. cit.*, p. 107.

scribes how one is "affected pathologically" by it. He does not mean pathological in today's meaning of the word but refers to the pathic, passive, reactive quality of the color experience.[3]

The perceptual attitude characteristic of color perception can be seen most clearly by analyzing the experience of seeing a color that has a strong impact. Imagine a large pencil drawing on white or light-gray paper, perhaps three by four feet square, on the wall of a room. Let the drawing consist only of the outlines, without any shading, of some figures or objects. Toward one corner of the drawing there is a bright red [4] splotch. On the wall opposite the entrance to the room there is nothing but this drawing. What happens to a person entering the room and looking at the drawing? His eye is "caught" by the bright red splotch. This red splotch thrusts itself on the observer, even on the quite casual glance; he cannot help noticing it at once, whereas he has to look at the drawing much more carefully, has to follow the lines drawn by the pencil much more closely, to recognize the figures in the drawing. Also, the red splotch will tend to unbalance the entire picture and to distract the attention of the observer from the penciled outlines. The red "strikes" the eye, but the eye observes, studies, follows, seeks out the lines of the pencil. The red "cries out," [5] the forms are "silent." The color seems to take possession of the eye, the forms demand more active observation. The color at once affects the eye of the person looking at this imaginary drawing, the forms await his attention. He is aware at once of "something red"—the red impresses him—but he has to look and "recognize" or understand the forms outlined by pencil. Color seizes the eye, but the eye grasps form.

---

[3] J. W. von Goethe, "Zur Farbenlehre," *Sämtliche Werke* (Tübingen: J. G. Cotta, 1850–51), XXVIII, paragraphs 758–920, 812.

[4] Red is chosen because it is the most vivid color, particularly in all its transitions to yellow, not to violet and blue. Red, thus, may be said to be the color par excellence if one wants to study the attitude in color perception where it is most outspoken. However, a similar effect will be obtained by substituting any other color in the experiment, provided the color is not too faint and subdued. Red provides merely the most striking example of an effect that any color in a neutral—gray or white—field will produce, although in different strength and quality.

[5] Rimbaud, in his famous *"Sonnet de Voyelles"* (Sonnet of Vowels), compares the colors to the sound of the vowels, red to the vowel *i* which, in French, is the shrillest, highest, sharpest vowel. The consonants may be said to give structure and outline to a word, the vowels color. Compare also Werner's remarks on synesthesia of different senses, especially of tone and color (chromesthesia), as a normal, primitive form in the development of perception which in some people persists after perception has become fully matured and differentiated. Werner, *op. cit.*, pp. 89–97.

Several factors can be distinguished by an analysis of such an experience of seeing the bright red splotch. First, the *passivity* of the perceiver: he is passively struck by the impact of the color which catches his eye. Second, the *immediacy* of this experience, which may occur without an act of directed attention and without any thought or attempt at recognition.[6] The use of colored neon light to call attention to a café, restaurant, dance hall, advertising sign exploits these qualities of color and bright light: they *assail* the eye whether one wants it or not. If there is only one of these signs visible on a dark street, the eye will inevitably be caught by it. If there are many, they will have a massive and confusing impact on the eye, each trying to outdo the other, only to drown in the over-all "noise" with which they assault the eyes of the passer-by. The passivity in being struck by color or light is present whether or not the perceiver consciously feels it. In fact, usually he does not feel it. It becomes apparent only when we pay attention to the quality of our experience, which requires a special, introspective effort.

Returning to our red splotch on the pencil drawing, we may note a third factor: the *exciting, fiery,* hot quality of this particular color, as contrasted, for example, with the cool quality of a pale blue. A particular *feeling tone* or *mood quality* is often immediately connected with various colors. Thus, colors are not merely recognized, they are *felt* to be exciting or soothing, dissonant or harmonious, clamorous and shrill or tranquil, vivid or calm, joyous or somber, warm or cool, cheerful or drab, disturbing and distracting or conducive to tranquility and concentration. Every decorator knows how much the color of the room influences its mood, how it is bound to affect the state of feeling of the people in the room. Thus, the pleasure-unpleasure and comfort–discomfort-boundedness characteristic of the autocentric senses such as smell, taste, and the thermal sense is also found in color perception. Even if people are not consciously aware of it, they may be affected by the color of their environment. This has been shown by Goldstein's work on the influence of color on brain-damaged patients,[7] can be observed in many normal people, and is probably true of all people. How-

---

[6] The immediacy of the color experience and the absence of organizing, reflecting thought processes in it have also been emphasized by Rickers-Ovsiankina, *op. cit.*, p. 10.

[7] Kurt Goldstein, *The Organism* (New York: American Book Company, 1939), pp. 263–266; K. Goldstein and O. Rosenthal, "Zum Problem der Wirkung der Farben auf den Organismus," *Schweizer Archiv für Neurologie und Psychiatrie,* 26 (1930), 3–26.

ever, the pleasure–unpleasure-boundedness of color vision is neither so strong nor is it in awareness of as many people so frequently as is the pleasure–unpleasure-boundedness of the autocentric senses. This is related to the absence of the *physical quality* and of the *felt organ localization* which characterize the sensations conveyed by the autocentric receptors.[8] Furthermore, our efficiency- and performance-oriented civilization tends to be on the whole inimical to the development and refinement of the autocentric senses; also, the very exploitation of the loudest and shrillest color qualities, for example in neon signs, tends to blunt sensitivity to the finer nuances of color's effect on man.

The affinity of color perception to the autocentric mode of sensory functioning is confirmed by the *ontogenetic* development of color as compared to form perception. The young infant reacts to light, color, and contrast which impinge on his eyes long before his capacity for the active grasp and articulation of form develops. This is consistent with the fact that in the neonate and infant the autocentric mode of sensory perception is the predominant one in all his senses.[9] In tasks which require the sorting of a variety of objects of different shapes and colors, the youngest children tend to sort according to color rather than to form; as they grow older, sorting according to the form of the object gradually becomes increasingly frequent while the frequency of sorting on the basis of color diminishes.[10] Also, the pleasure–unpleasure-boundedness of light, color, and contrast is more pervasive in infancy and early childhood than in later years, when the capacity for detached, neutral perception has developed. As Werner has pointed out, the young child perceives and discriminates color on the motor-sensory-affective level (i.e., color is pleasure–unpleasure-bound for the young child).[11]

While the charm as well as the disturbing qualities of color (shrillness, loudness, clashing color values, etc.) are felt by many adults, they can perceive color also in a detached, objective way; many, whose capacity for sensory experience has been dulled, no longer respond to color as much as does the child or do not respond at all.

---

[8] See above, Chapter 6, and Schachtel, *op. cit.*, pp. 94–97.

[9] Compare Schachtel, *op. cit.*, pp. 116–165, 144–145, where reference is made also to the similar development in people born blind who have gained sight as adults through operations. See also above pp. 150–157.

[10] David Shapiro, "A Perceptual Understanding of Color Response," in Maria Rickers-Ovsiankina (ed.), *op. cit.*, pp. 158–159, with further references.

[11] Werner, *op. cit.*, pp. 100–101.

According to Rorschach and the Rorschach literature, color responses "have proved to be the representatives of the affectivity," and their number provides "a good measure of affective lability." [12] While color responses are not identical with color perception, they cannot be given without color perception, without the color of the blots having had an impact on the testee and, furthermore, usually though not always they also presuppose that in his general visual experience color enters as a significant factor. For a color response it is not sufficient that color has been noticed—all testees, including most of the color-blind, notice the presence of color—the testee's susceptibility to the impact of color has to pass a certain threshold so that the color actually has a determining influence on his response and thus becomes a determinant.[13] In attempting to find a theoretical basis, a rationale for the demonstrable relation between the impact of color that leads to a color response and affectivity, it will be useful to examine the quality of the experience of affect. To this end we choose a strong, uncontrolled, impulsive *affect*, for example a fit of rage, interestingly referred to in idiomatic expression as "seeing red." A fit of rage blots out for a short time every other feeling, thought, consideration, and activity. It is an explosive discharge of affect. The very words "affect" and the often synonymously used "emotion" convey something of what happens in the subjective experience of affect. Affect, from the Latin *afficore*, means literally something "done to" a person. Something "affects" him. Similarly, emotion, from the Latin *emovere*, means literally a condition in which one has been "moved out of" a preceding state; omitting the prefix *e* ( = out of), it is also said that a person is "moved." Both words clearly imply the passivity of the subject so moved or affected. He does not move, he is moved or emoted; he does not do (*facere*), he is affected; something is done to him. Language is prolific in describing the *passive* state of the person who feels an affect. He is "touched" by pity; he is "seized" by rage or envy; he is "carried away" by enthusiasm or joy; he is "overwhelmed" by grief or "overcome" by anger. Different languages agree on this fact. Consider the German *gerührt* (touched), *bewegt* (moved), *ergriffen*

---

[12] Rorschach, *op. cit.*, pp. 76 and 98. Rorschach's concept of affective lability is quite comprehensive and includes normal emotional responsiveness. Stable affectivity, in his terminology, characterizes people who appear emotionally unresponsive.

[13] A strong impact of color on the testee, however, does not necessarily lead to a color response. It may also lead to blocking, color shock, to the exclusion of color from the response, and to other phenomena indicative of a *disturbing* effect of color on coping with the test task.

(seized), *überwältigt* (overwhelmed), *hingerissen* (carried away); and the French *touché, pris de,* and *ému.* Passion, in English, French, and Latin, and equally the German *Leidenschaft,* is originally something the person suffers and has the same root as "passive." The recurrence of the idea of passivity in the words describing the way in which man is affected by the various emotions and the agreement of different languages on this point cannot but derive from a common, basic experience of affects.

This experience is evident in the fit of rage chosen as an example of a strong, undiluted affect. The passivity of a person seized by rage—and similarly the passivity in the other affects—does not refer primarily to the adequate, or more often inadequate, "cause" of the rage; it does not refer to the person, animal, or object felt to have aroused the rage. Indeed, these "causes" of the rage may be very actively attacked by the infuriated one. The passivity is descriptive of the relation between the affect "rage" and the person seized by it, the "enraged." The enraged person "loses control" of himself; he is no longer his own master or master of his actions; rage has become his master. It comes over him like a wave and drowns part of his consciousness, particularly the faculty of thinking, deliberation, decision, judgment; he is "drunk" with rage.

This phenomenological description of the essential passivity of the affect experience can be understood dynamically on the basis of Freud's view of affect. According to him, the unconscious instincts are represented in consciousness by ideas and by a charge of affect. This affect-charge finds expression "in processes which are sensed as affect." [14] Affects are thus, together with ideas, the representatives of instincts in consciousness; they are furthermore a discharge of the instinctual energy. I would extend this view and say that affects are representatives and discharge processes of all drives, whether of instinctual or other origin. The element of passivity in the affect corresponds to the relation of the ego, the conscious control, to the totality of instinctual and other drives and is an expression of this relation. The drives are the motivating forces over which the conscious direction of the ego, with more or less success, tries to exercise some measure of control. The more the ego succeeds in channeling the powerful energies of the drives toward an adaptation to reality, the less noticeable will be the element of passivity

---

[14] *Repression* (1915) [Standard Edition], XIV, 152.

in the experience of the affect in which these drives are discharged. Yet even the experience of the most controlled drive and affect still retains something of this passivity. The subject is "driven" to do this or that; he is "affected" by this or that feeling in yielding to or resisting the drive. The degree to which he is entirely passive—swept away by the affect— or to which he succeeds in integrating the drive and its discharge in affect with his conscious, controlling functions resembles, in Rorschach's test, the relation between the sheer impact of color and the degree to which the testee succeeds in integrating the perception of color with actively structured form.

The affect reaction is characterized, furthermore, by the *directness,* the *immediacy* of the relation between the outer or inner cause—stimulus—of the affect and the person affected by this stimulus. When the affect is strong, there is no time for thought, detachment, objectivity, deliberation. All these may counteract or reinforce the affect-reaction, but the affect is there first; the thought is usually an "after"-thought. This directness of relation between affect-arousing object and affected subject is plainly visible even in such relatively controlled and mild affects as feelings of sympathy or antipathy upon meeting a stranger in civilized intercourse. The physiognomic and similar data on which such feelings are usually based, the identifications or similarities of the stranger with people significant for the subject's own life history and previous experiences, are often entirely, and usually to their greater part, not noticed consciously. Yet the affect, unless repressed, is there at once.

The analysis of the color and affect experiences has shown that they have in common the passivity (toward the impact of color, perceptually, and toward the drive-discharge in an overwhelming affect or impulsive action) and the immediacy, the directness with which the person is affected visually by the color, or emotionally by the affect-arousing—outer and inner—situation. Furthermore, all affect experience is inextricably bound up with pleasure-unpleasure feelings, and the perception of color often (though not always) shows the pleasure-unpleasure-boundedness characteristic of the autocentric mode of perception. These structural and attitudinal similarities between the perception of color and the experiencing of affect provide the clue for the understanding, the rationale of the correlation Rorschach and the later literature found between color responses and affectivity.

Rorschach's findings concern not the single act of seeing color or the single affective reaction but are based on the assumption that the perceptual and other events occurring in the course of his test are representative of more persistent tendencies in the testee. We have purposely confined our experiential analysis so far to perceptual attitudes only in the sense of an attitude that is typical for a paradigmatic act of pure color or pure form perception, respectively. We are able to study these attitudes because we can usually adopt them purposely and at will by making ourselves receptive, passively, to the impact of color or by trying to grasp, actively, a particular form or structure. Actually, shifts, voluntary and otherwise, occur in the same person from more active, allocentric to more passive, autocentric attitudes, or vice versa, in the course of a day, a life, and often even from one second to the next.[15] But there are also more lasting perceptual attitudes that can be described as an enduring inclination, or readiness to perceive; for example, in a more passive or a more active mode. In using a term proposed by Klein, I shall call those enduring perceptual attitudes characteristic of a particular person this person's *perceptual style*. Such basic attitudes as the inclination to be more active or more passive are pervasive in the structure of the personality. They find expression, in different ways, in all of a person's behavior and experience. In the sphere of affect discharge, extreme passivity takes the form of being overwhelmed by affect, unable to control it, flooded by it, helpless toward it. In the sphere of perception, it is conducive to a perceptual style in which there is a tendency to being passively struck by the impact of the sensory stimulus or the sensory field, relatively unable to organize and structure it adequately or to take hold of it. Since color has the perceptual quality of a striking, immediate stimulus, while form perception requires active organizing and taking hold, extreme passivity is likely to lead to a strong impact of color and relatively poor capacity for form perception.

While the excitability of affect or affective responsiveness probably offers the most frequent example of the relation between the susceptibility to the impact of color and other areas of behavior and experience, it is not the only one. As Shapiro has pointed out,[16] the C responses of certain chronic schizophrenics and of many organic patients are probably not related to affect which, in these patients, often is shallow and blunted; but they *are* related to their passivity, which is manifest in the

---

15 For a more detailed discussion of such shifts in mode of perception (perceptual attitude) compare Schachtel, *op. cit.*, pp. 213–220.

16 David Shapiro, *op. cit.*, pp. 172–173.

general impairment of their active, organizing capacity (indicated also by the low F+ % of their Rorschach tests) and to their helplessness in coping with the world. It is interesting that, usually, these patients do not seem to experience the pleasure or the unpleasure which many other people feel and often express when they react to the colored blots, whether they give color responses or not. The distress apparent in many organic patients does not seem related to any feeling that color is unpleasant but to the over-all feeling of helplessness in relation to the test task.

The passive attitude, represented in the perceptual sphere by color perception, can also be found in certain types of *motor behavior,* even though we are wont to consider most motor behavior as activity. Drive tension can be discharged not only in affect discharge but also in motor activity. The two may go together, as in expressive movements or in an affect-fraught action such as an angry physical assault, but they also occur separately. In the sphere of motor behavior, the parallel to being passively overwhelmed by an affect may be seen in such activities as physical restlessness resulting from drive tension, or impulsive acting out without any or with hardly noticeable affect. In both these cases the decisive factor is that the motor activity has a *driven* quality rather than resulting from a truly active, autonomous decision or intention. This driven quality, together with the lack of control and/or direction, points to the basic passivity underlying such behavior. Rorschach records of people who characteristically show such behavior are likely to contain CF and sometimes also C responses even though these people show little affect.[17]

The quality of passivity inherent in the typical perceptual attitude in color perception is, of course, usually very different in a C from what it is in an FC response, since by Rorschach's definition form is the predominant determinant in the FC response while color plays a significant but not equally important role[18] and the predominance of F points to an active, structuring attitude. What then is the "passive" quality in the FC response? Rorschach felt on the basis of his clinical and statistical data that the FC represent "that biologically necessary affective lability which is the basis of the capacity for emotional rapport and for

---

[17] Compare *ibid.,* p. 179.

[18] Rorschach, *op. cit.,* p. 30. I score FC also where form and color seem to play an equal part in determining the response, provided the level of form accuracy in the response is not below the testee's average level of form perception; if it is lower, I follow Rorschach (p. 30) in scoring CF.

meeting the environment emotionally halfway" [19] (rather than leaving it up to them to approach all the way). Rorschach thus describes what I would call sensitivity and appropriate responsiveness to the emotional cues of the environment. It is indeed a prerequisite of emotional rapport that one immediately senses, is struck by, these emotional cues; and the capacity for rapport presupposes that one's reaction to their impact will be not explosive or egocentric but appropriate—i.e., modulated in accordance with the total situation. It is the sensitivity to the cue emanating from the other person physiognomically, in gesture, intonation, etc., that corresponds to the "passive," in this case more appropriately called receptive, attitude toward the impact of color, while the form element in the FC response may be said to correspond to modulation of the affective response in accordance with the understanding and the requirements of reality.

As Rorschach points out, the relation between color and affectivity has long been realized.[20] While forms, unless seen dynamically or kinesthetically, are observed in an atmosphere of neutrality, colors give life, vividness, warmth, and many other "feeling"-qualities to the scene. Things are seen in a "rosy light" when people feel cheerful and optimistic; things seem gray and drab when they feel depressed.

Different colors differ in the quality and intensity of their affective tone; and different people will feel differently about these affective tones. The differences become even more pronounced when people from different cultures are considered. Despite these differences, some fairly general observations on the specific affective tone of various colors may be made, particularly if they are limited to the sphere of Western civilization.

*Red* has a unique position among colors. Red is striking, exciting, explosive. Passion and excitement are closely akin to red, and it may be connected with such varied affects and feelings as passionate love, blind rage, savage cruelty, hysterical excitement. It is the color of blood and is often thought of as the color of fire—both of which are, for the unconscious as well as in conscious symbolism, related to joy, sex, and love, but also to destruction, rage, battle, and murder. Because of its striking impact, red is used as a danger signal and as a stop light in traffic. Havelock Ellis writes that red is "the color that attracts our at-

---

[19] *Ibid.*, p. 33; translation changed to correspond more closely to the original German text.

[20] *Ibid.*, p. 99.

tention most readily and that gives us the greatest emotional shock. It by no means necessarily follows that it is the most pleasurable color. As a matter of fact, such evidence as is available shows that very often it is not." [21] According to Ellis, in every country the words for the colors at the red end of the spectrum appear earlier, are more numerous, and more definite than for those at the violet end. On the Niger there are only three words for color—red, white, and black. All that is not white or black is called red. It is known that in Greek painting and sculpture the colors used were red and yellow only, never blue and green, and, according to Pliny, in the earliest paintings only various reds. The same holds true for the entire ancient Mediterranean culture, including Egypt and Mycene. Goethe observed that a yellowish-red seems to bore into the eye.[22] Katz reports an experiment in which he drove a row of broad-headed nails into a dark-gray board so that all the nails stood out equally far from the board. On these nails he pasted alternate red and blue paper squares. Looking at them from a distance of 80 centimeters the reds appeared "to a surprising degree—approximately ½ to 1 cm. —nearer than the blues." [23]

While these experimental observations refer merely to the optical mode of appearance of red, the psychologically most significant qualities of red, undoubtedly related to the optical appearance, have been recognized and expressed by Ellis, namely, the "shocking" character of red and the fact that it is felt to be a pleasant color by some, an unpleasant one by others. To this I may add that in many people the affects aroused by red are *ambivalent*, as ambivalent as those aroused by thoughts of sex or of sadistic or destructive strivings or acts. A few clinical observations may illustrate these Janus-like qualities of red.

Hyperesthesia to color is nearly always an oversensitivity to red, very rarely to any other color; on the other hand, the morbid condition in

---

[21] Havelock Ellis, "The Psychology of Red," *Popular Science Monthly*, 57 (1900), 365–375 and 517–526; p. 372. This paper and "The Psychology of Yellow" (*Popular Science Monthly*, 68 [1906], 456–463) contain a wealth of anthropological, historical, and physiological data and should be read by anyone interested in the subject.

[22] Goethe, *op. cit.*, paragraph 776.

[23] David Katz, *The World of Colour* (London: Kegan Paul, Trench, and Trubner, 1935), p. 69. He reports that the same observation on the "advancing character of reds and yellows was made by Sophie Belajew-Exemplarski, *Zeitschrift für Psychologie*, 96 (1925), 424. Ellis mentions Muensterberg's experimental finding that red and yellow have considerably more power in stimulating the eye than the other colors. (Ellis, *op. cit.*, p. 375.)

which color is seen where it does not exist most usually produces red, and next to red yellow, while the other colors are rarely seen.[24] According to Charcot, in achromatopsia of hysterical patients, the order in which the colors usually disappear is violet, green, blue, and finally red. Ellis believes this persistence of red vision in the hysterical to be "only one instance of a predilection for red which has often been noted as very marked among the hysterical." In my experience, in Rorschach's test hysterical patients often react very strongly to red and give several red color responses. However, this reaction is usually of a very ambivalent character and they are at least as much shocked and repelled by red as they are attracted to it. Equally, the victims of the German medieval epidemic of "St. Vitus's dance," who imagined that they were immersed in a stream of blood which compelled them to leap up, also reacted strongly to the hallucinated red, but they hardly had a predilection for it.

In analyzing reactions to red color one has to distinguish two factors. One is the fact that red is the most striking, strong, vehement color and hence catches the attention readily and on primitive levels of perceptive and mental organization, as evidenced by the fact that some primitive tribes react only, or primarily, to red. The other is the fact that red is, particularly for the unconscious, at the same time a most attractive and a most dangerous color, but always a very fascinating one. The primitive quality of red accounts for the fact that, in Rorschach records of undifferentiated or feeble-minded people who react to color, such reaction is often limited to the reddish and pinkish color blotches.[25] The ambivalence of the red color, or rather of the affects and strivings related to it, is the more interesting and complex phenomenon which leads to a great variety of reactions in the Rorschach test.

I have dwelt on the significance of red because it is the most striking color with the strongest impact and thus tends to evoke stronger reactions than the other colors,[26] especially blue, which is experienced generally as a cool color and a distance color, the color of sky and sea. Blue

---

[24] Ellis, *op. cit.*, pp. 374–375.

[25] Ruesch and Finesinger, in an investigation of the frequency of responses to the various colors in the Rorschach cards, using a mixed group of 55 abnormal and 5 normal persons, also found that feeble-minded patients responded to red more frequently than others. Ruesch and Finesinger, "The Relation of the Rorschach Color Responses to the Use of Color in Drawings," *Psychosomatic Medicine*, 3 (1941), 370–388.

[26] For a discussion of yellow, orange, blue, and green, compare E. Schachtel, "On Color and Affect," *Psychiatry*, 6 (1943), 393–409, 401–403.

recedes, makes a room larger, in comparison with red, which advances and makes a room appear smaller. There seem to be physiological reactions to the relative impact of the different colors. Féré reports that muscular power, measured by dynamometer, and circulation, measured by plethysmographic tracings of the forearm, were increased by colored light in the sequence from blue (least) through green, yellow, orange, and red.[27]

Goldstein states that "a specific color stimulation is accompanied by a specific response pattern of the entire organism" and describes red as causing a stronger attraction and distraction from the outside and as "an impairment of performance in the direction of shock reaction," whereas green "favors performance in general." [28]

Rorschach was aware of the difference in the impact of different colors and of the *significance of the selective pattern* of a testee's responses to certain colors and his avoidance of others. He remarks that "'emotion-controllers' show a preference for the blue and green figures . . . and avoid the red in a striking way." [29] Most people who have a normal responsiveness to color react to the red as well as to the other colors. In fact, a predominance of responses to red [30] is quite frequent in Rorschach records, probably not only because it is the most striking and "colorful" color but simply because it covers a much larger area and appears in many more blots on the Rorschach plates than any other color, and because on two plates—II and III—it is the only chromatic color present.

Another rather typical color syndrome is a pronounced response to red in the form of one, or usually more, definite color responses, often of the CF type, and a paucity of response to the other colors. Depending on the total picture, this can be a primitive, undifferentiated reaction of

[27] Charles Féré, *Sensation et Mouvement*; 2nd ed. (Paris: Félix Alcan, 1900), pp. 43–47. Féré found these effects of color even more marked in "nervous" patients. He states that the color even need not to be perceived to produce similar effects (p. 57). This would seem to point to physiological processes as a substrate of the psychological ones discussed, and would probably have to be explained by the well-known general sensitivity of the skin to different light rays of which the eye is the highly specialized recipient.

[28] Goldstein, *op. cit.*, pp. 265, 484; compare also Goldstein and Rosenthal, *op. cit.*

[29] Rorschach, *op. cit.*, p. 35.

[30] By red color in the Rorschach plates reference is made to red, reddish, and pink areas: the three red areas on Plate II and the three red areas on Plate III, the pink blot at the base of Plate VIII, and the pink lateral blots on Plate VIII, the pink base of Plate IX, and the two large reddish areas on Plate X.

the "healthy, energetic, and crude people" described by Goethe in his observation that primitive people and children have an inclination for yellowish-red as the color of greatest energy.[31] More frequently, in my experience with Rorschach tests, it is the "excited" reaction to the ambivalent qualities of red. This excitement may have a panicky as well as an aggressive and impulsive quality. It is the response to the shocking quality of red, to its connotations of blood, fire, sex. The deeply rooted connection between the red color and sex; furthermore, the relation between red and the fearful as well as aggressive and destructive tendencies which are so often allied with sex consciously or unconsciously are the reason why the reaction to the second Rorschach card, where red appears for the first time with black, is often particularly indicative of the attitude to sex. This excited red reaction occurs especially in hysterical patients, often after an initial red-shock. But it also occurs in other people whose affectivity is excitable, explosive, responding to the sensational rather than having a warm quality and a more even and wider range. It tends to lead to CF and C rather than FC responses. Of course, not all responses to red have the same quality. As Rorschach remarked, there is a difference between a person who sees an open wound in a red blot and one who sees rose petals or a slice of ham.[32]

There is also a difference between *crude, undifferentiated* color perception or color responses and a *differentiated* color perception in which attention is paid to the specific finer nuances of color. There is a difference between the person who sees in the red blots fire or blood only and the person who responds to one of the blue areas with "This looks like a bit of sky, the pale blue you sometimes see early in spring." Even though this response is C, it is less of a short circuit, not crude, not necessarily indicative of impulsiveness or helpless passivity, and so forth, as are the crude, undifferentiated C. This type of response is possible only when color perception has not remained at a primitive level but has undergone a development requiring a considerable amount of attention to the nuances of color, and when this attention also is present and effective while responding to the Rorschach blots. It probably presupposes the development of aesthetic sensibility toward color, a late development in contrast to the primitive susceptibility to color of the neonate and young infant. Not only ontogenetically but also historically, the capacity for finer aesthetic discrimination of colors

---

[31] Goethe, *op. cit.*, paragraphs 775 and 835.
[32] Rorschach, *op. cit.*, pp. 208–209.

is a relatively late achievement. Rivers reports that colors which have primarily aesthetic value but are of no practical significance to primitive people leave them quite indifferent.[33] Similarly, words for colors that have no practical significance are absent in primitive languages while there is an abundance of words for colors describing differences of practical significance, such as the different markings of cattle.[34]

The difference between crude and differentiated color perception occurs not only in C but also in Cn responses. I define Cn responses as the naming of color with the intention of thereby meeting the test task. While most Cn responses are of the crude type, occasionally one finds such finely differentiated Cn as strawberry-red, lemon-yellow, or mouse-colored. C as well as Cn responses that are not crude but highly accurate in the sense of naming or implying the specific nuance of color as a determinant presuppose, on the cognitive level, an unusually differentiated awareness and knowledge with regard to color. They also presuppose special sensitivity to it, and a kind of quasi-tasting, receptive attitude, an attention which is not actively structuring but rather tuning in on the stimulus, a capacity which usually goes with increased pleasure–unpleasure-boundedness in the perception of colors, their nuances and combinations.[35] In some other color responses, there is a kind of conscious immersion in or surrender to the color, usually seen as film rather than surface color, as in the just-quoted "sky" response. These are always C or CF or Cn responses. They usually come from a conscious style of seeing which, in art, is represented by the Impressionists and which tends to dissolve the contours and to be sensitive to the atmospheric or quasi-atmospheric light and color values. If the person who

---

[33] W. H. R. Rivers in Alfred Cort Haddon (ed.), *Reports of the Cambridge Anthropological Expedition to Torres Straits* (Cambridge University Press, 1901), II, 06.

[34] Emil Reche, *Tangaloa, Ein Beitrag zur geistigen Kultur der Polynesier* (Oldenbourg, Munich, and Berlin, 1926), and Hugo Magnus, *Untersuchungen über den Farbensinn der Naturvölker* (Jena: Engelmann, 1880).

[35] For the concept of taste (in the figurative sense) and the relation between color and taste compare Schachtel, *Metamorphosis*, pp. 112–113. Rorschach wrote of people who give Cn responses with fine nuances of color as "watching their drives but nevertheless surrendering to them" and meant a conscious not impulsive surrender. On the same occasion, he remarked that the color responses of a particular record (characterized by unusually specific color discrimination) indicate that the testee "does not at all fight his affects, but affirms and enjoys them" and that he is a sensualist, a person giving in to his instincts (*Triebmensch*). E. Schneider, "Eine diagnostische Untersuchung Rorschach's auf Grund der Helldunkeldeutungen ergänzt," *Zeitschrift für die gesamte Neurologie und Psychiatrie*, 159 (1937), 1–10.

gives such responses also has a high form level and is capable of shifting at will from such conscious, passive surrender to coartation and vice versa, the usual interpretation of C and CF responses has to be modified. Both the "tasting" and the "immersing" types of color responses are relatively rare; I have never found them in organic conditions or in chronic schizophrenic patients. I have seen them occasionally in artists and in sensitive people with highly developed taste. Responses in which color and texture is combined, for example strawberry ice cream to the pink bottom D in card VIII or IX, while less sensitive, still show greater attention to the specific quality of the stimulus than do the crude color responses and therefore have fewer pathological implications.[36]

The analysis of form and color perception has shown that each tends to occur with a typical perceptual attitude. We have also seen that the active attitude characteristic of form perception tends to be enhanced by the Rorschach-test task more than in everyday perception. What is the *effect of the Rorschach-test situation on color perception and on whether and in what way color is or is not used as a determinant* in the genesis of the responses to the test? Probably all people, with the possible exception of some of the youngest children, understand Rorschach's question posing the test task ("What might this be?") as implying that they should find something which resembles the blot in its *shape*. I have not yet seen a record in which form plays no role at all; the overwhelming majority of responses are characterized by the presence of some form elements, whatever other determinants play a role in them, whereas responses without any form influence are quite the exception. The appearance of color on cards II, III, VIII, IX, and X, if it is not disregarded by the testee, poses the problem of finding a suitable combination of form and color. Hence the predominance, at least in the normal and most of the neurotic range, of FC and CF over C responses. The integration of color with form is easier for some of the colored areas than for others; some areas offer a close and readily seen resemblance to a familiar object—e.g., the popular response "green caterpillar" to the center bottom detail of card X—while in other areas it is difficult to find an object resembling them in both color and form (color-form incongruity).[37] Not every testee copes with the problem of integrating color with form in a fitting response. Those who do as well as those who

---

[36] Rapaport, *op. cit.*, p. 232, takes the same view of the color-texture response.

[37] This point has been stressed particularly by Elsa M. Siipola, "The Influence of Color on Reactions to Ink Blots," *Journal of Personality*, 18 (1950), 358–382.

do not may or may not experience it as a problem. The color may be included by the testee in the demand quality of the test task: he feels he should pay attention to it and take it into account in order to solve the test task properly. This may lead to an acute conflict between the "demands" of form- and of color-likeness that may temporarily stymie him until he either succeeds in finding a likeness which does justice to or at least accommodates both color and form, or until he gives up and decides to ignore either the color (the more frequent solution of this conflict) or the form. To others the color *distracts* from what they feel is the test task: to find accurate form-likenesses. To still others the impact of the color is so overriding that the form problem does not arise and there results a C or Cn response that may be an impulsive or a passive, flat, or consciously helpless reaction, the latter typical in organic damage (Piotrowski's "impotence").[38]

This brief and in no way exhaustive sketch of some reactions to the appearance of color in the Rorschach blots merely illustrates the fact that—in contrast to adult everyday perception—color poses a *task* in the context of the test situation, a task that can be tackled, solved in different ways, given up or—consciously or unconsciously, wittingly or unwittingly—avoided or ignored. In everyday perception color poses no problem, no task. It is all around us. It appears in familiar contexts; it partakes in our prompt recognition of the many familiar objects of our environment. But while it does not, as a rule, pose a problem, there is no question that the impact it has on different people varies a great deal individually, both quantitatively and qualitatively. Some people barely seem to notice it, prominent among them the clinically depressed, whose sensory experience is altogether dulled and blunted, but also the much vaster number of people who are quasi-depressed without even being aware of it. Others feel it consciously as enriching and enlivening or, on occasion, as unpleasant, shrill, or clashing. To most, I believe, it plays a quite significant role, although they may not enjoy it consciously. But if it were absent they would miss it sorely and the visible world would be very much impoverished to them. In Rorschach's test *both* factors—the person's *general reaction to color,* the quality of his perception of color *and* the specific problem posed by the *appearance of color in the Rorschach test situation*—are significant fac-

---

[38] Zygmunt Piotrowski, "On the Rorschach Method and Its Application in Organic Disturbances of the Central Nervous System," *Rorschach Research Exchange,* 1 (1936–1937), 23–40.

tors determining the number and quality of his color responses as well as his reactions to color other than those resulting in a color response. In some testees the color responses (usually FC and CF) or their absence will reflect more their general reaction to color (i.e., their perceptual style), in others more their reactions to the test situation and to the difficulties of solving the test task with regard to the colored blots. Usually both perceptual style *and* the problems posed by the test situation and by the testee's subjective definition of that situation and of the test task account for the quality of his reactions to the colored blots.[39]

These reactions are observable in two major ways: one, in the relative role form and color play as a determinant in the color responses and in the quality of the integration of form and color in these responses. Two, in reactions other than actual color responses—e.g., a change in the manner and sequence of responses; or in the quality of responses; or in expressed reactions to the color other than color responses, for instance exclamations, expressions of pleasure or displeasure about the color; or in hesitation, change of reaction time, change in number of responses per blot, etc. The first of these two ways has been the main concern of Rorschach and the literature. It led Rorschach to distinguish FC, CF, C, and the naming of color (Cn), thus differentiating mainly whether form or color was the predominating or exclusive determinant in the genesis of the response; the two main additions to this by the literature are the *forced* combinations of form and color, in which the integration of form and color is forced, and the *arbitrary* color response, in which the color is used in an arbitrary way—i.e., in a way in which it does not occur in reality.[40] Since the various types of color responses and their meaning have been discussed extensively in the literature,[41] I shall not discuss them systematically or in detail. In-

---

[39] Siipola believes that color shock and similar indications of disturbance or increased difficulties in the colored blots are not due to the presence of color as such but to the difficulties created by color-form incongruity, that is to say, by an increased difficulty of the test task. I believe that such an assumption, while true in some cases, does not hold for all. Both the test task as defined by the testee *and* the perceptual qualities of color, or either one of these may cause the difficulty. Siipola, *op. cit.*, p. 381.

[40] I omit individual differences between different authors in the use of these and similar categories, since it would go beyond the scope of this book to discuss the various types of color responses in detail.

[41] The most significant contribution, outside of Rorschach's book, is that by Shapiro, *op. cit.*, who gives an insightful rationale and discussion of the different types of color responses. Every student of Rorschach's test should read his article and note especially that each of the different color scores—just as every other

stead I shall deal, first, with the general problem of conditions facilitating or impeding the integration of color and form in one response; second, with some conditions leading to the absence of color responses; third, with some factors other than those just mentioned, pointing to conflict, difficulties, negative reactions caused by appearance of color in the blots ( color shock and related phenomena).

A satisfactory solution of the problem posed to the testee by the appearance of color on some of the Rorschach blots requires the integration of color with form. One of the factors involved in such integrating depends on the testee's *perceptual style,* specifically on his openness, receptivity toward color in general, on the extent to which and the intensity with which he experiences a colorful world, perceives the environment as enriched by color. The more color registers with him, the more likely he is to recall objects not only as having a particular form but also as having a color specific to them. The person whose experience of the world is colorful is likely, to use Rorschach's term, to have many colorful *engrams.* Whether these are available to recall in the test situation is another question. But without them the giving of responses in which form and color are integrated would be impossible, and it would be difficult if a great variety of colorful engrams were not present and available. Obviously, the existence of such engrams not only presupposes that the person notice color—everybody does; it presupposes that the color made a sufficient impression to become a memorable part of the person's experience. What makes it impressive and memorable? The significance of its function in the person's life. The integration of color with form enriches perception in two major ways. It can be a useful cognitive aid, making possible more rapid, effective, well-articulated recognition or grasp of an object. In this case it is typically a surface color, the color of this particular object. It may be perceived in a neutral, matter-of-fact way as an adjunct, as it were, to the structure of the object. Thus, to distinguish raspberries from blackberries color is almost indispensable since their form is very similar. But the soft red of the

---

score—does *not* always have the same symptomatic significance, but that a careful, individual analysis of each response is necessary in order to grasp its meaning correctly. Also relevant is Rapaport's contribution; he centers his discussion of the color as well as the form response around the psychoanalytic concept of *delay.* This contributes to their understanding, but has two limitations. The more important of these is that the basic significance of the different perceptual attitudes is overlooked by him; the other is due to what I believe is an overextension in psychoanalytic theory of the concept of delay. See above, pp. 145–150, and Rapaport, *op. cit.,* pp. 234–244.

raspberry and the shiny black of the blackberry and all the many colors of nature and of manmade objects also have for many, if not all, people an immediately enlivening, enjoyable sensory quality or, sometimes, a disagreeable, unpleasant one. To this quality—color's pleasure–unpleasure-boundedness—Goethe refers when he begins his first book on color theory by saying that "only a few people will remain insensitive to the charms of color spread over the entire, visible nature." [42] Both qualities, the usefulness for recognition with its adaptive function, and the enjoyable, stimulating quality with its life-enhancing function, adding to man's emotional tie to nature and to his pleasure in his own creations, can be present and effective at the same time for the perceiver.

In Rorschach records it is not infrequently apparent from the specific color response or from the over-all color reaction that one or the other quality, cognitive usefulness or sensory-affective tone (which may be positive or negative), predominates. The distinction may have diagnostic significance. My impressionistic clinical hunch is that FC responses with affective-sensory tone may point to a livelier, more responsive affectivity than the merely "cognitive" type of FC. These two types of FC are not easy to distinguish. An example of the affective-sensory FC is the response to the center green of card X, reversed: "a wreath of fresh, green leaves," whereas the same area seen, right side up, as the usual "two [green] caterpillars" is a frequent example of a cognitive FC. Another example of a cognitive FC is the W response to card VIII: "a coat of arms, with two animals rampant, and the different colors," whereas the response "a lovely butterfly" to the bottom D of the same card is likely to be an affective-sensory FC. In some FC responses it is impossible to decide whether they belong to one or the other type.

Where the color in all FC responses functions merely as a neutral, cognitive aid and where there are no CF responses, the FC usually represent an overcontrolled adaptation rather than emotional rapport. The presence of CF responses, in addition to FC, does not necessarily have implications of egocentricity but can represent spontaneity in the experience and expression of affect. This also seems to have been Rorschach's view; in the last two years of his life he expressed interest in the difference between people with general vitality and those who seem unalive. He speculated that the difference may lie in a shift toward the CF in the more vital persons; he expected them to produce numerically

---

[42] J. W. von Goethe, *Beiträge zur Optik* (Weimar: Verlag des Industrie-Comptoirs, 1791), I, section 1 (author's translation).

more as well as more outspoken M and CF than the "unalive" ones.[43] But even if a record has no or only one CF, but several FC of the sensory-affective type, I assume that this points to a capacity for emotional rapport.[44]

It is my impression that in the average normal Rorschach record of the majority of the population there would be few if any color responses and that they would more likely be of the cognitive than of the sensory-affective type. This is consistent with the average record's tendency toward coartation or coartativeness. The impact of color as a personally significant, enlivening, and pleasing element in the perception of the environment probably requires a certain development of the capacity for aesthetic experience. Where this is absent or is only minimally present, color responses are likely to be absent or scant except, of course, in certain pathological cases where the high number of color responses stems from the impairment of the active, structuring capacity and the prominence of passivity rather than from the significant, enriching sensory-affective impact of color. Cézanne has described the "blindness" of the common man which, I believe, is one of the causes of both the relative paucity of responses and the coartativeness, especially the scarcity of color responses, in the average Rorschach record of the majority of the population. He said in a conversation with J. Casquet: "Sometimes I have accompanied a farmer behind his cart driving to the market to sell his potatoes. He had never seen what we would call seeing; he had never seen Sainte Victoire. They know what has been planted here, along the road, how the weather is going to be tomorrow . . . ; they feel it like the animals do, like a dog who knows what this piece of bread is, only from their needs; but that the trees are green, and that this green is a tree, that this earth is red and that this red rubble and boulders are hills, I really do not believe that most of them feel that, that they know it, outside of their unconscious feeling for the useful." [45] In line with this, it will be remembered that certain primitive languages lack words for many colors beyond those that are of immediate practical usefulness to them.

---

[43] G. A. Roemer, "Hermann Rorschach und die Forschungsergebnisse seiner beiden letzten Lebensjahre," *Psyche, Jahrbuch für Tiefenpsychologie und Menschenkunde in Forschung und Praxis*, 1 (1948), 523–542, 541.

[44] Some authors assume that records in which the color responses are limited to a few FC indicate an overcontrolled adaptation and lack of emotional rapport. Compare Rapaport, *op. cit.*, p. 243; Klopfer *et al.*, *op. cit.*, I, 279, 296.

[45] Author's translation from Ernesto Grassi, *Kunst und Mythos* (Hamburg: Rowohlt, 1957), pp. 116–117, note 2.

A second condition facilitating integration of form and color is that the test situation be experienced as relatively nonthreatening, noncoercive, and noncompulsive. This permits being more fully receptive and open toward the inkblot and thus toward its color, and it also facilitates a freer and wider range of associations, a more flexible attitude so that a greater variety of remembered images, hence also of colorful engrams, are available for recall.

A *cheerful mood,* Rorschach observed, tends to increase the number of color responses and to shift the emphasis from the FC to the CF; it facilitates the integration of form and color for a number of reasons: it increases the openness toward the environment, the capacity for experience, hence also the capacity to be receptive toward the inkblots; it tends to go along with increased self-acceptance and with a reduction of the stringency of the standards and demands applied to one's productions. This in turn allows a freer play of associations and reduces the strictness of the subjective requirement for form accuracy. The whole definition of the test situation tends to become more liberal and lenient, making a greater variety of engrams available and acceptable, including more FC as well as CF. The shift to more CF is a result, probably, both of the greater openness toward the color stimulus and of the less stringent form (control) requirements.

The factors mentioned as facilitating the integration of form with color are, I believe, the most significant, but they are not the only ones. The list is not intended to be exhaustive, nor is the following consideration of some factors preventing or impeding the integration of color and form in Rorschach responses. Obviously, the absence of the just-discussed factors facilitating such integration will play a major role: the absence of colorful engrams; their unavailability, often due to the testee's subjective definition of the test situation, crystallized around the actual test situation but often, in turn, due to a habitual tendency to experience any task or even any interpersonal situation as a "test" situation of some sort. Since the reader can easily fill in the detailed implications of these general factors on the basis of the preceding discussion, I shall deal here only with some specific conditions.

Some types of subjective definition of the Rorschach-test task tend to impede the successful integration of form and color. An observation by Rorschach is relevant here: he found that when asked to produce as accurate and clear form-likenesses as possible (a high F + %), most people can do so because it is possible to increase attention, concentration, critical control of likeness by voluntary, goal-directed effort. However, this happens at the expense of other factors, including a decrease of color responses.[46] Some testees define the Rorschach-test task as demanding the most accurate form-likeness and they are very critical, in this respect, of the responses that occur to them. As Rorschach pointed out, this occurs especially in pedantic and in depressed persons who characteristically take the test "very seriously"—and not only the test but everything.[47] Their openness to the inkblots and their capacity to allow a free play of associations are drastically reduced by their effortful, consciously goal-directed, narrow, and self-critical attitude. Their habitual attitude thus has the same effect as does the temporarily increased focus on sharp form-likeness in people who are asked by the tester to concentrate on F+ responses: the narrowed attitude seems to conflict with the openness and freedom necessary for the giving of color responses. This conflict becomes even more apparent when these people are asked to give color responses. Rorschach noted that they *can* produce them,[48] usually FC, but that the pedant and the depressed do it awkwardly and that the "neurotic emotion-repressors" show remarkable tension in handling color.

Such tension is also apparent in many of the so-called forced combinations of form and color (F/C) in which no real or natural integration of form and color has been achieved, only an artificial one. They often give the impression that the testee had felt it incumbent on him to include the color in his response even though no natural combination occurred to him. This seems to happen especially in some compulsive personalities who feel that they *have to* or *ought to* account for the color. Because of their habitually rigid attitude and their rigid definition of the test situation, they cannot respond spontaneously to the color but make a demand on themselves to use the color and then search for a way in which to do this with a similarly cramped attitude as that of their search for accurate form. But while form accuracy can be improved by such an attitude, it obstructs that openness and flexibility which facilitates the integration of form and color. The color is added to, rather then integrated with, the form percept. These responses are not enriched by the color but have a labored quality. Also, the added color often retains some of the quality of a C response so that

---

[46] Rorschach, *op. cit.*, p. 67.

[47] *Ibid.*, pp. 43, 57.

[48] *Ibid.*, p. 68. In my experience, a considerable number of them cannot.

the F/C score really represents more an F+ plus C than an FC. I have the impression that in many of these responses the color is not experienced as particularly striking or stimulating, but that it is noticed and then endowed by the testee with the same exaggerated demand quality that he attributes to the whole test situation. The type of person who is apt to do this is very often also a person in whom control functions as a defense against giving in to emotions and who has therefore not developed much capacity for sensory enjoyment or for modulation of affect. The absence of sensory enjoyment is reflected in that color does not seem to act as an enjoyable, enriching stimulus to him, the lack of modulation in the C quality of the response, and the near-failure of the integrative effort.

Poor integration of color and form in C/F responses usually shows a genesis and quality rather different from that just described for the F/C responses. In the C/F the essential quality usually is the strong impact of the color together with the insufficient capacity to structure and integrate the form. The testee is passively struck by the vivid impact of the color and is unable to integrate it adequately with the form, which seems added after some groping or with the vagueness of a rather arbitrary afterthought. This quality is apparent even though the testee may not experience his attitude as passive or helpless, just as the impulse-ridden or the hypomanic do not experience their essential passivity in relation to their drives or to the press of their affects.[49]

A natural integration of form and color is also made more difficult where the capacity for actively structuring and grasping form is either not sufficiently developed or not sufficiently differentiated or where it has been impaired or where it is being temporarily disturbed by the impact of color.

One of the groups in whom empirically little or poor integration of form and color occurs is young children. In the youngest testable group, the two-year-olds, C and Cn responses predominate while FC responses are virtually absent; at later ages first CF and, still later, FC tend to predominate.[50] As we have seen, the youngest children give almost only F responses; the color responses they do give are almost only C and Cn. In other words, there is practically no integration of color and form.

---

[49] Compare Shapiro, *op. cit.*, pp. 182–188.

[50] Compare Ames *et al.*, *op. cit.*, pp. 50, 79, and 286. So far as I can see, the statistical data of other observers show the same trend with regard to the color responses. According to Ames, at two the average number of C is 0.37, of Cn 0.54.

While form perception plays a very important role in the two-year-old,
both in general and in his Rorschach reactions, it still has a global,
undifferentiated, unarticulated, and often a *pars pro toto* quality. This is
accentuated when the two-year-old is confronted with the strange and
unfamiliar Rorschach blots. To the extent that he responds to the particular quality of each blot at all, he is apt to do so by responding to one
global or otherwise outstanding aspect only. This is true of many of his
form responses and it is also true of his response to color. It will be
remembered that his form responses usually do not have the meaning
of detachment, of an impoverished perception, and of objectivity. I am
inclined to assume that in their genesis his at first briefly active attention is quickly *caught* by some striking aspect rather than that he follows the outline and penetrates and grasps the structure. Similarly,
when he does use color he is struck by this one aspect of the blot, and
yet is not able to integrate it with, or even pay much attention to, other
aspects of the blot. The meaning of color and of form responses is not
as different in the records of two-year-olds as it is later on. That this
should be so is not surprising if we consider that the young child's perception has much more the quality of "vital sensations" (Werner) in
which physiognomic, synesthetic, and global perceptions predominate
and in which experientially neither the differences between the different senses nor those between different sensory qualities conveyed by
one sense are as distinct and objectifying as they become at a later age.
The Cn responses of the youngest children have a different meaning
from those of older age groups. They are often apt to represent the
intellectual achievement—and the pleasure and pride in it—of having
learned the names of the colors and of wanting to share this with the
tester.[51]

In schizophrenic and organic conditions, the integration of form and
color is characteristically impeded by the impairment of the active,
structuring, and the integrative functions. In organic conditions C or Cn
are frequent, while FC are absent or quite rare. The impairment of
active, structuring, and abstractive functions usually leads to an acute
feeling of helplessness in relation to tasks requiring these functions, as
the Rorschach-test task does. The organic patient seems helplessly
bound to the impact of the concrete color stimulus, and often this feeling of helplessness is expressed in his reactions. This feeling is not pres-

---

[51] I am indebted to Florine Katz for having drawn my attention to this observation.

ent and not apparent in schizophrenic patients even though their being passively struck by color or, sometimes, by other qualities of the blot or by some idea occurring to them (probably in primary process thought) is apparent to the observer. Acutely disturbed schizophrenics may show FC as well as C responses, just as they often show original F+ side by side with F−. Perhaps these sharp, qualitative changes in their responses have something to do with rapid shifts in attitude and state of consciousness. In chronic schizophrenics, especially those hospitalized for long periods of time, the capacity for integration of form and color is rarely if ever preserved, and their bland responses, if they give color responses at all, tend to be C or CF. It is interesting that in Pfister's Color Pyramid Test schizophrenic and some other pathological groups, as compared with a normal group, also show a significantly greater predominance of color over structuring in the way in which they arrange the various colors in the pyramid.[52]

The *absence* of color responses or its near-absence can be due to very different attitudes. A rough distinction can be made among three types of records which show a complete or almost complete lack of color responses. One type consists of those on whom color does not have much impact; they notice it but it does not really register or impress them. Another type excludes it by a habitually rigid, compulsive attitude. The third type is passively open, though not welcoming and receptive, to the impact of color and may either helplessly give in to it or actively avoid it because he feels acutely disturbed by it.

The prototype of those on whom color makes little impression and does not register as a significant experience is to be found among the *depressed,* especially in severe neurotic and in many psychotic depressions. They tend to give only form responses, the form level of which— unless lowered by anxiety and sometimes in psychotic depression— tends to be high. The absence of color responses in them is due to several factors. Their over-all capacity for experience, including sensory experience, is dulled and blunted. They often are quite aware and sometimes can be quite articulate about the fact that everything seems to them gray, colorless, dull, literally and figuratively. Neither the colors of the Rorschach blots nor the colors in their environment register significantly with them; they are noticed but have no impact, are not felt to be stimulating, enjoyable, etc. Colorful engrams are not available to

---

[52] K. Warner Schaie, "The Color Pyramid Test," *Psychological Bulletin,* 60 (1963), 530–547, 539–540.

them. Even though before the onset of the depression they may have
experienced color vividly, this experience—like all others—in retrospect
has lost its vividness and become meaningless. Furthermore, they tend
to be self-rejecting and self-recriminating. Not only does every task become effortful to them, but they also tend to feel that nothing they do is
any good. Hence, their responses to the test tend to be the result of
active, though very labored, effort and they tend to be critical of them.
The result is a coartated record of usually few responses. The *indolent*
also do not react much to color and tend to give few or no color responses. Their condition dulls their capacity for experience, although
they usually do not show the laborious effortfulness or the self-rejecting
attitude of the depressed. *Indifference* toward the enriching quality of
color, because of the lack of opportunity or incentive for the development of the capacity for aesthetic enjoyment, tends to cut down or
prevent altogether the giving of color responses in a great many normal
people.

That the *pedantic* personality tends to ignore the color in the Rorschach blots has already been mentioned. His habitually compulsive
and rigid attitude, accentuated by a strained, excessively, and narrowly
goal-directed definition of the test situation, prevents an open and receptive attitude toward the inkblots and their colors. All effort consciously is directed toward achieving accurate form-likeness.

A very different situation prevails in some records which give the
impression that the testee felt as if he were skating on thin ice that at
any moment could break, so he has to be exceedingly careful. This attitude usually leads to a record with few responses and either no color
response at all or, perhaps, a C response. I have seen this attitude most
frequently in a group which Rapaport has termed the coartated pre-
schizophrenic.[53] I have the impression that this attitude is due to a feeling of being unable to cope actively with the situation and a fear that
the underlying chaotic and panicky state of mind may become manifest
both to the testee himself and to others. The testee feels that he is
walking a tightrope. His anxiety and his impaired capacity to cope actively with life and its tasks—including, in the test situation, the task of
active grasping and structuring of the inkblots—lead to a low F + %
and either a passive, helpless C reaction or to a brittle, tense avoidance

---

[53] He reports similar findings for this group: either no color response or a tendency toward C. Compare his Table 69, 70, *op. cit.*, pp. 252, 255, and the table
in Appendix I.

of the color. Similarly, many of these records have a vague, tense, impersonal quality which may or may not suddenly give way to a highly personal, idiosyncratic response. In most of these cases, the absence of color and the pure C responses have a similar meaning: the breakdown of the capacity for active coping, structuring, integration, and organization.[54]

The sudden and for most people *unexpected appearance of color* after the black and gray blots leads to a more or less pronounced *disturbance* in many testees. Some of these disturbances have been described by Rorschach as color shock. By this term he designates four different phenomena:

(1) "An emotional and associative stupor of varying length when the colored Plate VIII appears"; these testees "suddenly become helpless though previously they had been interpreting very well; they . . . react with astonishment or vexation." According to Rorschach, they "are always emotion-repressors, neurotics of varying grades of severity." (2) Fewer responses to the colored than to the achromatic plates. (3) A preference for the blue and green figures and a striking avoidance of the red ones. He considers 2 and 3 as symptomatic for the "emotion-controllers." (4) The responses to the colored plates become hastier and more phantastic, sometimes after an initial indication of helplessness. This group Rorschach considered to be on the border between the affect-repressors and the affect-controllers and designated them the "affect-shy." [55] The literature has added a number of other manifestations of color shock to these.[56] Most of these disturbances are found not only in neurotic but also in many clinically "normal" people. I shall deal here only with those disturbances most relevant to the problems discussed in this chapter.

The term *color shock* seems appropriate only to those cases where a momentary stupor and helplessness of varying length and intensity occurs. Such shock occurs not only in Plate VIII, but also in Plate II

---

[54] Shapiro has pointed out the similarity of records with C and with no color at all in the cases of chronic schizophrenics, severe schizoid character disorders, and severe narcissistic character disorders. Shapiro, *op. cit.*, pp. 176–178. I have not seen a large enough sample of these groups to form an impression about this point. But I do find it valid for the group discussed in the text.

[55] Rorschach, *op. cit.*, p. 35; translation slightly changed to render the original text more closely.

[56] Compare Hans Zulliger, "Erscheinungsformen und Bedeutung des Farbschocks beim Rorschach'schen Formdeutversuch," *Zeitschrift für Kinderpsychiatrie*, 4 (1938), 145–153; Klopfer *et al.*, *op. cit.*, I, 339–344.

where it may sometimes be a specific reaction to the already-discussed qualities and implications of the red color. It may or may not be followed by shock in Plate VIII. Whether shock appears in Plate VIII or in Plate II, it usually is primarily a result not of the testee's general reaction to color but of his reaction to and way of coping with the Rorschach-test situation. The perception of color in the environment after some time spent, say, in reading a book where only the black print on the white page was seen, poses no problem to people. But the appearance of color in the context of the task quality of the Rorschach test does pose a problem because the color now becomes part of this task. The testee is shown the ten inkblot plates, one after another, and asked to tell what they might be, what they seem like to him, what he sees in them, or other words to that effect. Obviously, it depends on him how he defines this situation, consciously or unconsciously. The interpretation of the inkblots is a task, and many people transfer to this situation their attitude to authority. The demanded activity is organized and approached in different ways. Once the initial strangeness of the task is overcome, most people tend to form a set of expectations of what is to come in the other cards and—with great individual differences—many establish a more or less pronounced routine of dealing with the expected situations. The more insecure they are, the greater importance such a routine may acquire for them in this as in other situations. With the appearance of the colors this routine may be upset. There is a marked change in the situation; an unexpected and striking new element, color, has entered. Even if the testee tries to maintain a by-now-established routine of handling the task, this new element may have such distracting and disturbing influence as to make it difficult for him to continue in the same way. This probably would also be true for other changes brought about by the introduction of a striking new factor other than color in the test task. How the testee meets such striking change has a significance similar to the reaction to sudden change in any life situation. Every rigidity in the adaptive dynamisms is likely to lead to increased importance of routine and to make changes in the life situation, particularly "surprise" changes, a difficult matter for the person. The more anxiety and insecurity prevail, the more a replacement of spontaneous, flexible behavior by rigid operations and defense mechanisms will take place, and the more dangerous every sudden demand for reorientation, every change in the situation, will become. Whether color shock is mostly a reaction to sudden change, to the challenge of integrating a new element in coping with the changed task, or whether the specific quality of the new element, the fact that it is *color*, contributes significantly to the difficulties of the testee who reacts with color shock, differs individually. Sometimes it is possible to gauge the relative significance of mere change and of the specific impact of perceiving color on the basis of the total evaluation of the test record; sometimes this question cannot be answered. The people who show color shock vary significantly in the ways in which they try to overcome the initial shock and deal with the changed situation. They may try to disregard the new element; they may become fixated to it in a rigid way; they may try to overcompensate the vaguely or distinctly felt disturbance in one way or another; they may not recover fully from their shock for the rest of the experiment; they may try to erect a sort of fence around the disturbing intrusion of color; they may become more cautious and may reinforce their rigid controls. The "stupor" and momentary helplessness in color shock is usually, at least marginally, experienced as such, although some testees who cover the uncomfortable gap preceding their first response to card VIII or II by exclamations, questions, descriptions, or other remarks may thereby avoid the discomfort of the conscious feeling of helplessness.

Whether preceded by color shock or not, one way of coping with the changed situation is by *limiting the impact* of the new, disturbing element, the color. One of the ways of doing this is the reduction of the number of responses to the first colored plate and, sometimes, if the difficulty persists, to all the colored plates. On the other hand, an increase of the number of responses to Plates VIII to X, after initial color shock, or if the responses do not include one or more successful integrations of color with form, does not necessarily indicate that the testee is particularly responsive to and his productivity stimulated by the emotional impact of the environment, as Klopfer and Ainsworth seem to assume.[57] Some testees are obviously disturbed by the appearance of color, experience color shock and a temporary feeling of inadequacy in relation to the problem posed by the appearance of color. But they then proceed to compensate for this with a more or less conscious effort to search for many responses, often resorting to Dd if they cannot find enough W or D. They feel, as many testees do, that a great number of responses is "better" than a smaller number, but thus show clearly that

[57] Klopfer *et al., op. cit.,* I, 297.

their increased "productivity" as measured by the number of responses is not the result of a stimulating or enlivening effect of color.

Other ways of limiting the impact of color are avoidance of red and sometimes of the other warm or bright colors in favor of the cooler or subdued ones; a tendency to give color responses only to small, sometimes only to Dd, areas and to avoid the large colored areas; a tendency either initially or (less frequently) throughout to favor the gray and white areas over the colored ones, and, of course, the absence or scarcity of color responses. The escape from color into form may occur very smoothly in card VIII, which has several clearly and simply structured D and in which the various colors are confined each within one or more of these D areas. In card IX such an escape into form is made more difficult, because the forms are more complex and the colors, especially the green and orange, merge without clear delineation. Many people find this card difficult; among them are especially those who tend to avoid color and who are generally not very flexible in their way of responding to the test. The various ways of limiting the impact of the color may be compared to a defensively erected rather than naturally existing stimulus barrier, created against the striking and potentially task-disrupting impact of the colors. The barrier is maintained by the way in which attention is focused, wittingly or unwittingly, away from the too-striking colors.

Exclamations or remarks expressing like or dislike of the colors, especially at their appearance in Plate VIII, may or may not be accompanied by color shock. Quite a number of people express pleasure at the appearance of colors, sometimes because they come as a welcome relief if the gray and black cards have been experienced as somber, dull or if the general feeling about the test situation has been one of tension and discomfort. But whether or not such relief plays a role, many feel and express enjoyment at the intrinsic, enriching sensory quality of color. However, in spite of this subjective experience of welcoming and enjoying the color, some of these people have considerable difficulty in using color as a determinant. They may not use it at all, or only after color shock, or they have to limit its impact in one of the already-described ways, or they have difficulty in integrating color with form, or their FC responses are of the "cognitive" rather than the "sensory-affective" type. The initial experience in which the pleasure–unpleasure-boundedness of color was felt gives way to an attitude in which it is no longer felt. This change is usually brought about primarily by the person's subjective definition of the test situation. The spontaneous exclamation of pleasure at the sight of color[58] gives way to a more labored and rigid attitude; the person seems to feel that the seriousness of the test task requires only work and excludes pleasure, almost as if the initial reaction had been out of place. The sphere touched upon by initial enjoyment of the color seems to them incompatible with the attitude they feel is required by the test. They usually are not explicitly aware of this, but they seem to act on it. The people in whom this shift of attitude from enjoyment of the color to the exclusion of its pleasurable qualities in a more rigid attitude occurs are a significant example of a conflict between clear form perception and free use of color as a determinant. We have encountered this problem from different angles in the discussions of repressiveness versus free play with and openness toward the inkblots and of the fact that form responses are not always indicative of inhibition, repression, and impersonal objectivity, but that optimal form perception (the special $F+$) requires openness and receptivity as well as firm taking hold of. I do not believe that there is an intrinsic "antagonism" between form and color perception but that where it exists it reflects a conflict within the person, and that the attitudes and rigidities leading to this conflict are fostered by a culture in which work and pleasure usually are mutually exclusive.[59]

One aspect of the reaction to color, implied in our analysis of color perception, deserves to be made more explicit: color perception is essentially a phenomenon of the impact on the person of the visible world around him. When the eyes are closed, colors are no longer seen and we are no longer affected by them. There are, of course, such subjective phenomena as colors in dreams, eidetic memory, afterimages, and colors produced by pressure on the eyeball. However, they do not compare in duration, intensity, and constancy of impact and often also not in variety, vividness, and richness of nuance with the perception of actual colors in external reality. We can distinguish in man's relation to the world two directions: one from the world to the person, the other

---

[58] Not all positive remarks about color are genuine and spontaneous expressions of enjoyment. Some, for example, have a conventional quality and may serve the primary purpose of covering momentary helplessness by marking time.

[59] This oversimplified formulation must suffice here, since a more adequate discussion of the social and cultural problems involved would go beyond the scope of this book. Compare Herbert Marcuse, *Eros and Civilization* (Boston: Beacon Press, 1955).

from the person to the world. The former is dominant in color perception where we deal with an experience in which the person is passively affected, impinged upon by the environment.

Forms, too, are part of the visible world, of course. However, as we have seen, the impact of color is a more immediate and striking one in which, in contrast to form perception, no active attention and grasp are required. The immediate impact, often pleasure–unpleasure-bound, of color and light as the most vivid and striking visual representatives of the world outside are the qualities which underly Rorschach's conclusion that color responses[60] represent, within the experience type, the extratensive tendencies, the appropriate as well as the egocentric, impulsive, quick reactivity, adaptive or otherwise, to the impact of the environment. The reader may wonder how the notion, frequent in textbooks, personality tests, and popular usage, that the extrovert[61] is an active type who does things, is enterprising, makes contacts and friends quickly and easily, is compatible with the *passivity,* the *being impinged on* that has been emphasized as essential in our analysis of the color as well as the affect experience. The solution of this seeming paradox lies in the fact that pronounced extroversion is not so much activity as *reactivity,* namely, reactivity to the emotional color, as it were, the emotional cues, the emotional impact of the environment. Rorschach emphasizes the passive quality of this reactivity when he says that "colors *tear* people into extratension," [62] and compares them to the irresistible force of music with a pronounced rhythm, as in marching music. He illustrates this point with the infectious quality of a colorful, gay festivity, a carnival, or a military parade with colorful uniforms. His observations about the C (or extratensive) type hold true mainly of the relatively normal (including much of the neurotic) range. He observed that the C type becomes indistinct where the prevalence of color over movement responses is very marked, and that where there are twice as many or more color than movement responses, provided the number of

---

[60] Rorschach included white, which may be said to represent light, in the color responses.

[61] Rorschach intentionally avoided the terms "extrovert" and "extroversion" in order to distinguish his concept of extratensive tendencies from Jung's concept of extroversion; while his concepts of introversiveness and extratensiveness also are not identical with the popular usage of the terms "introvert" and "extrovert," they are nevertheless closer to them. Rorschach, *op. cit.*, pp. 81–83.

[62] *Ibid.,* p. 99, italics mine; the German text's *reissen* emphasizes the irresistible impact and pull of the colors more than the English translation's "draw" does.

M exceeds 2, we deal almost always with a pathological case.[63] Why the extratensive type can no longer be discerned in these cases finds its explanation in the fact that in them we usually see C and CF responses, which represent passivity in forms other than affect discharge, whereas Rorschach's description of the extratensive person refers to a type of affective responsiveness to the environment.

---

[63] *Ibid.*, p. 79. The English translation does not render the German text. It should read: "Already in the middle between the center and the right outer columns [of Tables IX–XIII] (the C type) becomes indistinct"; Rorschach's text implies that this is even more so where there are twice as many or more C than M. Whether or not these figures are always applicable is not so important as the fact that they do represent a significant trend.

# 9 / MOVEMENT*

*Und so regt er sich gebärdend, sich als Knabe schon verkündend*
*Künftigen Meister alles Schönen, dem die ewigen Melodien*
*Durch die Glieder sich bewegen . . . .*

> [Thus he stirs and all his gestures, still a boy's and yet proclaiming
> Future master of all beauty, all the melodies eternal
> Moving through his limbs and body. . . .]

— Goethe, *Faust II*, Act III (author's translation)

The capacity for inner creation and the quality of basic character attitudes are linked to kinesthetic perception in Rorschach's concept of the movement response. This linkage makes the movement response a key concept in Rorschach's test. As I hope to show in this chapter, the implications of Rorschach's ideas about the movement response not only make it one of the most important tools for the analysis of character structure in the test; they also throw light on the nature of the mechanism of projection, on its relation to the process of empathy, and on problems of autistic thought and perception and of creative experience.

The origins of Rorschach's discovery establishing a relationship between three so seemingly divergent areas as kinesthetic perception, creativeness, and basic attitudes have deep roots in the personality of Hermann Rorschach. Like his father, who was a drawing teacher, he liked to draw and paint. He had a special gift of rendering characteristic human postures and movements. He would cut from cardboard silhouettes of a man playing the violin or of a patient working on something,

---

* This chapter is a reprint, with minor changes, of my article "Projection and Its Relation to Character Attitudes and Creativity in the Kinesthetic Responses," *Psychiatry*, 13 (1950), 69–100. Since the literature on M published since 1950 has not caused me to change the views expressed in that article in any significant respect, reference is made only to the literature up to 1950.

supply them with movable joints, and in this way produce a striking resemblance to the actual movements of the person portrayed.[1] This unusual gift must have provided a rich source of inner experience and intimate knowledge of the kinesthetic processes in perception and particularly of the kind of empathy necessary for such a keen understanding of the essential qualities of another person's posture and way of moving. He considered himself a kinesthetic type.[2] It is not surprising, then, that Rorschach's observations and ideas regarding the movement responses occupy a central place in his *Psychodiagnostics* and constitute the most original and thought-provoking part of the book.

The purpose of this chapter is not to answer all the numerous and difficult questions which the complex problem of the kinesthetic responses poses. Too little is yet known about them to permit definite answers. Instead I want to report some observations and to offer some hypotheses concerning their nature and diagnostic significance and the psychological processes underlying them.

I shall designate as kinesthetic (or movement) responses all responses in the perception of which kinesthetic factors play a co-determining role, together with form, color or shading, or a combination of these. For human or humanlike action or posture to which Rorschach restricted his observations I shall use Rorschach's symbol *M;* for all other kinesthetic responses the symbol *Mt* (movement tendency).[3]

Rorschach ascribes to the M responses a twofold significance and uses them, accordingly, in two quite different ways for diagnostic purposes: (1) They indicate a capacity for "inner creation" and, if they are significantly more numerous than the color responses, a tendency to live more within oneself than in the outer world. (2) The specific quality of the movement or posture perceived indicates certain basic attitudes of the person who sees these movements or postures. These two meanings of the M responses, which at first glance seem to be quite different and unconnected with each other, are presented by Rorschach as the results of empirical observations, as are all the symptomatic significances of his scoring categories. He does not give a theoretical explanation of *why* the M responses have the meanings he ascribes to them. The same

---

[1] M. Minkowski, "Hermann Rorschach," *Schweizer Archiv für Neurologie und Psychiatrie,* 11 (1922), 318–320.

[2] Ellenberger, *op. cit.,* p. 181.

[3] I use this symbol in addition to the traditional score, for example, the response to card VIII "two animals climbing up" receives the score D F̄ + A P Mt.

holds true of the Rorschach literature, with the exception of Furrer and Binder who, so far as I know, are the only authors who have tried to give a theory of the M responses.

Furrer[4] assumes that the M responses are substitutes in phantasy for actual, sometimes symbolic movements which, in turn, have taken the place of direct satisfactions of the person's drives. At first he speaks only of sexual drives. He believes that the M responses often contain sexual symbolism and that this symbolism is the end product of a sequence which led, phylogenetically, from direct sexual satisfaction via sublimation of sexual drives in motor activity in play, via symbolic motor activity to imagined motor activity. Later he states quite generally that the M responses are either symbolic actions or sublimations or attitudes toward the world and toward the person's own drives. These actions and attitudes take place in imagination. Binder[5] accepts Furrer's analysis and elaborates on it. According to him, the perception of the inkblot stimulates drive-conditioned psychomotor impulses. The resulting *"Antriebsgestalt"* [6] is a factor in determining the way in which the inkblot is perceived and interpreted by the subject. In this process the psychomotor impulses are "objectified," to a certain extent, and lead to the kinesthetically enlivened percept in which the motor experience of the subject is projected onto the object seen.

### Empathy, Projection, and M

To gain a better understanding of the movement responses it will be helpful to attempt an analysis of the experience and attitude characteristic of kinesthetic perception of the Rorschach inkblots. In order not to complicate this by the introduction of too many elements, I shall restrict the analysis, at first, to the significant factors typically present in the giving of M responses (human or humanlike movement or posture) and later extend it to the other kinesthetic responses.

---

[4] A. Furrer, "Ueber die Bedeutung der 'B' im Rorschachschen Versuch," *Imago* 11 (1925), 58–83.

[5] Binder, *op. cit.*; see particularly pp. 46–49.

[6] This concept is taken from Klages' theory of expressive movements. It is difficult to translate the term accurately. It refers to the Gestalt of a drive-determined movement in contrast to one which is consciously goal-directed. See Ludwig Klages, *Grundlegung der Wissenschaft vom Ausdruck* (Leipzig: Johann Ambrosius Barth, 1936).

Rorschach emphasizes as a requirement for a response to be scored M that the movement or posture described in the response must have been *felt* (*"erfuehlt"*), not merely named by the subject, that an actual kinesthetic sensation, however slight, must have been present.[7] The subject does not remain, as in the attitude typical of form perception, a detached observer critically comparing the shape of the inkblot with that of the object coming to his mind, with a view of determining whether they are sufficiently alike.[8] He *feels* the movement or posture which to him seems to animate the inkblot. He experiences it *as if* he knew, not merely from outside but from *inside,* how the human figure seen in the inkblot moves or holds its posture. It is as if he were, for a moment and to some extent, inside the figure seen. This is an experience similar to that which one has in the act of kinesthetic *empathy*. There, too, in looking at another person's movement or posture, one experiences in himself the kinesthetic sensation which he would have if he were in the other person's place. In empathic observation of the sprinter at the start of a race or the dancer holding an expressive pose, one experiences in himself bodily, kinesthetic sensations corresponding to the movement which the other person performs.

These kinesthetic experiences have a particularly intimate and deeply rooted connection with the core of the personality which has been demonstrated beautifully by W. Wolff's experiments. He showed motion

---

[7] The prerequisite of a kinesthetic experience for the assumption of a movement response distinguishes Rorschach's and my concept of the movement response from Rapaport's who feels that there is no evidence for the kinesthetic factor in movement responses. On the other hand, he states that he follows Rorschach closely in scoring M. This is contradictory because Rorschach scores *by definition* only those responses as M in which a kinesthetic experience is present. Rapaport's theory of the movement responses, very briefly stated, is that they come about because the subject feels that the inkblot perceived would become more balanced if the movement envisaged were performed. This assumption is open to two objections: (1) In many M responses neither a feeling of imbalance is present nor would the posture or movement seen lead to a better balance. Responses illustrating this point, taken from Rapaport's own examples of frequent M responses, are "Santa Claus" seen in the lateral details of card I; "Figure praying" seen in the center detail of I; "A man standing, or sitting" seen in IV, whole; "Two women with veils" seen in the upper lateral details of IV, reversed. On the other hand, if, e.g., the center detail of card I is seen as a person with hands raised, about to bend forward and strike somebody, the movement would be one from balance to unbalance and yet it would doubtless be an M response. (2) It seems to me at least open to question whether the feeling of imbalance itself, taken as the basis of M responses by Rapaport, does not necessarily contain a kinesthetic experience. I am inclined to think that it does. For Rapaport's viewpoint see Rapaport, *op. cit.*, II, 207–215.

[8] This attitude is typical of detached, not of dynamic form perception.

pictures of persons walking; their faces and all other marks of identification were obliterated in the photographs or had been removed before so that only the characteristic gait was visible. Of his subjects, 100 per cent recognized their own gait: significantly fewer people recognized, in parallel experiments, their own profiles, voices, or the movement of their hands. Only 70 per cent recognized the gait of their friends.[9] As Allport remarks, this indicates the "high importance of postural empathy in the process of self-recognition." [10] The reason for this is, I believe, that *in kinesthetic experience of his own body and its way of moving the person has the only direct, immediate, physical experience of himself from within.* The senses other than the kinesthetic provide, compared with this kind of experience, a less direct one, from outside, which is much in the same manner as other objects of the environment are perceived by the person.

In kinesthetic perception induced by visual perception of movement and leading to kinesthetic empathy, one ceases to remain a mere outside observer registering, like a camera, what goes on. Instead one experiences in himself the actual sensation of the movement, tension, or posture seen in the other person. While to the perceiver's mind the kinesthetic perception is part and parcel of the global experience of seeing the other person move, the empathic, kinesthetic element in this perception is, nevertheless, the feeling of movement or rather of initial motor impulses in his own body. Thus, the perception of his own body in the kinesthetic sensation is inextricably fused with the object perception through the visual data received by the eye. Because in this case the kinesthetic experience is *felt together with* another person actually performing the movement, one can speak of kinesthetic *empathy.* However, in those M responses in which the kinesthetic determinant is strong and in awareness, the subject, in spite of his knowledge that he is looking at a static inkblot only, often has a similar subjective feeling as

---

[9] Werner Wolff, *The Expression of Personality: Experimental Depth Psychology* (New York: Harper & Brothers, 1943), pp. 88–95.

[10] G. W. Allport, *Personality: A Psychological Interpretation* (New York: Henry Holt & Co., 1937), p. 487. In this context the question belongs whether gestures of hands, arms, and legs only—without the perception or the imagining of the trunk as being the center of, or participating in, the movement—are likely to be kinesthetic perceptions and should be scored M. The views of the Rorschach literature on this point differ, without discussing the relevant underlying questions. I suppose that the question has to be decided individually for each percept. It is one of the questions, though, for the solution of which more material is needed than research has made available so far.

in kinesthetic empathy: *as if* he were experiencing in himself a movement or posture which seems to take place at the same time outside of him in the inkblot. Because the subject in kinesthetic perception experiences in himself the feeling of the act he perceives in the inkblot, the quality of subjective conviction, the feeling of evidence a strong M response has for the person who gives it is of a different type and usually stronger and more deeply felt than the conviction that he feels, for example, about a well-seen, detached form response. While the latter is supported by outer evidence, the former is supported, in addition to that, by a feeling of inner evidence. Something within the subject identifies with what he believes to take place in the object. For this reason it is especially significant if kinesthetic responses show signs of uncertainty and wavering. These may consist in verbalized doubts about the percept or in the perception of different, especially of contradictory types of movement in the same figure. They often indicate difficulties in trusting one's own attitudes and feelings, one's intuition, difficulties in arriving at decisions and especially in knowing what one really wants, doubts about one's basic attitudes.

While in any feeling or attitude of which he is aware man has a direct experience of himself from within, the kinesthetic experience of oneself is characterized by the physical quality and by the content of the sensation, namely movement. Thus, kinesthetic experience of oneself and the inner experience of one's significant feelings and attitudes have in common the intimate relation to the self. But because of the physical quality of kinesthetic self-experience and because the content of this experience is movement it lends itself peculiarly well to the translation and projection into the visual perception of movement or posture.

In every act of kinesthetic and other empathy there is an element of projection. The subject understands the movement (in kinesthetic empathy) or the feeling (in other empathy) that he perceives in the other person in terms of his own inner experience of that movement or feeling. This experience is activated by the perception of the person (or object) toward whom the subject has empathy so that the subject undergoes, in the moment of empathic understanding, the actual experience of the movement or feeling as it has developed in himself on the basis of his own constitution and life history. This, his personal kinesthetic or other feeling, aroused by what he sees, is projected onto the person or object seen and merges completely, without the subject's being aware of it, with the percept of the person or object empathically perceived.

What varies in such acts of empathic perception and understanding is (a) the degree of congruence and kinship between the movement or feeling of object and subject. This variable is a function partly of the subject's openness and ability to perceive what is going on in the object, partly of the rigidity or flexibility of the pattern of those elements of his own experience which he projects on the object, partly of the degree of his preoccupation with himself. Of course, these three factors overlap and influence each other. (b) Another variable is the degree to which the mechanism of projection and the perceiver's own movement impulse or feeling is the source of the animation, the life, the feeling, the structure perceived in the object. In empathic perception of the sprinter or the dancer the object perceived lives, moves, and feels, and the subject, in the act of kinesthetic or other empathy, may actually share, to a greater or smaller extent, the experience going on in the person perceived. In empathic perception of an animal, a tree, a landscape projection has to carry an increasingly greater share of the animation of the object by the subjective experience and feeling of the perceiver. Nevertheless, even though they do not move, different forms and different inkblots, because of their differing dynamic qualities, *suggest* movement more or less strongly and some may suggest specific types of movement while others are more ambiguous with regard to the quality of the movements suggested. Rorschach discusses the fact that his inkblots differ in the degree to which they suggest movement.[11] In kinesthetic responses to the inkblots the form of the object perceived seems to stimulate kinesthetic innervations; these cause the perceiver to project something of his own inner experience onto the object, to give life to it, to animate it, and to endow it with movement. The mechanism of projection, thus, is essential for an understanding of empathic perception as well as of the kinesthetic responses.

## Projection and Kinesthetic Response

The concept of projection has to be defined differently from both the traditional meaning as developed by Freud and from the rather vague and broad meaning which it has assumed in the current use of the term "projective technique." In this presentation the term *projection is de-*

---

[11] Rorschach, *op. cit.*, p. 52.

fined as that psychic mechanism by which one attributes qualities, feelings, attitudes, and strivings of his own to objects (people or things) of
his environment. This may lead to the actual perception or to the assumption of the presence of these qualities in the objects of the environment, and it may help or hinder an understanding of the object.

Freud conceived of projection as a defensive mechanism by which
man externalizes that which becomes too difficult for him to deal with
within himself.[12] Thus, according to Freud, in a hysterical phobia the
instinctual demand from which no escape is possible is projected into
an outer danger which the subject then tries to avoid by precautions or
by flight. Or, in paranoia, the patient's own homosexual trends and hostility are attributed by him to others. In these examples and in Freud's
thinking in general, only those qualities or strivings are projected which
the person is not aware of in himself.

This latter condition, in my view, is not essential to the mechanism of
projection. While the person, as a rule, is not aware of the process of
projection as such, of the fact that he attributes something of his own
personality to the environment, he may or may not be aware that the
quality which he attributes to the environment is also a quality to be
found in himself. In other words, *while the content of the projection
may or may not be conscious to the person as being part of himself, the
process of projection usually takes place outside of awareness.*

The concept of projection developed here comprises the general human and the personal tendency to an anthropomorphic and, similarly,
to what I propose to call an automorphic view of the world—the tendency to perceive and think of others in one's own image, to expect and
to find one's own likeness in others. While the anthropomorphic concept refers to man's tendency to think of the environment and of the
universe in human terms, the automorphic concept refers to the individual person's tendency to think of the environment and of the world
in terms of his individuality, whether or not he is aware of it. Projection
comprises the tendency to attribute to the environment both such qualities of ourselves as we are aware of and such as we are not or only
partially aware of. While Freud always seems to have believed that one
projects only that which he is not aware of in himself, he did not originally restrict his concept to those cases where projection serves a defensive function, as he did in his later writings. Originally, he held that

---

[12] Freud, *Metapsychological Supplement to the Theory of Dreams* (1917)
[Standard Edition], XIV, 223–224.

"projection is not specially created for the purpose of defense, but . . . is a mechanism which has the greatest share in shaping our outer world." [13] Again, he implicitly comes closer to the view of projection developed here when he mentions that dreams are projections, externalizations of internal processes.[14] In dreams not only unconscious tendencies are projected into the dream images but also conscious ones in which the dreamer recognizes himself, his wishes and his fears. Only by assuming that the dream has the function of warding off a disturbance of sleep is Freud in a position to extend the defensive function of the mechanism of projection to dreams. However, in the course of the dream not only factors which might disturb the ego or the super-ego but also factors which are accepted by or known to the person as part of himself are projected into the dream images.

The *automorphic* view of the world by means of the mechanism of projection is only one particular kind of the *autistic* view of the world. Autistic thought and perception also comprise all the mechanisms by which the view of the environment and the world is organized according to the person's own needs, wishes, and interests. The tendency to perceive that which one needs or that which one fears—food if one is hungry, liquids if one is thirsty, the sights and sounds of danger if one is afraid—are examples of autistic perception.[15] Automorphic thinking, the tendency to invest others with one's own likeness by means of projection, is another type of autistic thought and perception.

Autistic thinking in general and the special type of autistic thinking that I have called automorphic thinking have to be distinguished from *egocentric* thinking. Egocentricity characterizes those states of mind in which the interests of the person obscure or blot out his capacity to think or feel about, with, and for others. While in psychiatric and psychological literature one often encounters a tendency to attach explicitly or implicitly a negative value judgment to autistic thought—just as in philosophy thinking that is anthropomorphic or motivated by the interest of mankind or of a particular human group often has been cen-

---

[13] Sigmund Freud, *Totem and Taboo* (1912–13) [Standard Edition], XIII, 64. For Freud's later viewpoint see his "*Metapsychological Supplement to the Theory of Dreams*" (1916) [Standard Edition], XIV, 223–224; and *Beyond the Pleasure Principle*, XVIII, 29.

[14] Freud, *Metapsychological Supplement to the Theory of Dreams*, 223–224.

[15] For examples of this kind of autistic thought and perception and an account of experimental evidence for it, see the chapter on "Autism" in Gardner Murphy's *Personality: A Biosocial Approach to Origins and Structure* (New York: Harper & Brothers, 1947), pp. 368–374.

sored—I believe that such negative value judgment is not justified. Both the anthropomorphic and the automorphic viewpoint can be a legitimate mode of thinking or it can become distorting. Just as every human trait, depending on its setting, its function, and its relative proportion with regard to other traits, can have positive or negative, healthy or pathological meaning, so can automorphic and autistic thinking. Indeed, it is quite impossible for man to avoid autistic thinking. Mankind cannot transcend human thinking nor can the individual person transcend the way of thinking which his personal history together with his constitution have developed in him. The progress of human thought depends on the contributions which individual persons make from their individual perspectives. All one can and should attempt to do is to become conscious of one's individual and group perspective and not to assume blindly that it is the only perspective from which the world may be seen.

Projection in the sense in which it has been defined here is a legitimate component of an understanding of others. Distorting projection constitutes one end of a continuous line at the other end of which genuine understanding of others has its place. In every act of understanding, something akin to one's own experience is felt in the other person. All understanding of others is made possible only by the fact that the other person is essentially like oneself, that, as Sullivan has formulated it, "we are all much more simply human than otherwise." [16] It is the essential likeness of man which is the basis of all real psychological understanding. This fact, correctly understood, makes it quite legitimate to understand one's fellow man in one's own likeness. In fact, one could well say that only to the extent that one has had an experience or a feeling will he be able to understand it in others. It is in this spirit that Goethe once remarked that there exists no crime of which he could not imagine himself capable. Understanding is real only to the extent to which it is possible for one to project from his own life experience such elements as he recognizes in the other person into the act of understanding. Projection becomes distorting to the extent to which (1) it has a defensive function; (2) tangential, partial, or otherwise superficial data from the other person's behavior are used to attach meanings taken from one's own life experience which do not correspond to the real and total picture of the other person's behavior; and (3) qualities are ascribed to the

---

16 Harry Stack Sullivan, *Conceptions of Modern Psychiatry* (New York: W. W. Norton & Company, 1953), p. 16.

other person the presence of which in one's own life is unknown to him or which he tends to deny in himself. That which one does not know about himself he cannot understand in others.

### Kinesthetic Responses and Basic Attitudes

It is not accidental that movement and kinesthesia should represent and be related to the factor which fuses the perceiver's own life experience, his own feeling with that of the perceived object by instilling something from his own life into the perception, the understanding of the object. Spontaneous movement—movement not propelled from outside but originating in the organism—is that which distinguishes the world of man and animal, of living beings, from the plants and the inorganic world. Movement may be said to be the character of life and the projection of movement to represent the living understanding—or, in the case of distorting projection, misunderstanding—of others.

What kind of movement does the subject project onto the inkblot in kinesthetic responses? Very often, although not always, that type of movement toward which he is most inclined. Every human feeling, attitude, striving has both a physical and a mental side and finds expression in physiological and neuromuscular as well as in psychic processes and conditions. The old, but still not quite dead discussion whether the physical, somatic determines the mental—or the mental the physical— is as futile as the question of whether the chicken or the egg existed first. The question itself—by postulating the alternative that one or the other, mind or body, must be primary and causative—is already misleading. They are different aspects of the same thing. This was known already to Goethe when he said:

> Nichts ist drinnen, nichts ist draussen;
> Denn was innen das ist aussen.
> So ergreifet ohne Säumnis
> Heilig öffentlich Geheimnis.
>
> (Epirrhema)[17]

---

[17] The poem has not been translated. The following is an approximate rendition of its meaning in English: Nothing is inside, nothing outside; what is inner is also outer. Go and grasp without delay the holy open secrets.

Another formulation of the same thought can be found in the writings of Novalis. Unfortunately I have not been able to find the passage which, if I remember correctly, reads: "*Das Aeussere ist das in Geheimniszustand erhobene Innere.*" (The outer is the inner elevated into a state of mystery.)

If a person has the tendency to react with a certain, typical attitude or striving to the world around him or to his own drives, then this attitude will also find expression in a neuromuscular set which could be described as the physical side of the attitude, a readiness to perform such motor activity as will be suitable to realize the goal of the attitude or striving.[18] This "goal" of a person's general attitude or orientation is either not at all in awareness or, at least, not in focal and full awareness. It is not a goal in the same sense as is the purpose which a person consciously wants to reach by a specific, consciously planned and executed series of acts. The neuromuscular set which is the physical aspect of a habitual, lingering readiness to react in a certain way to the world and to oneself is at the basis of both the inadvertent, expressive movements and physiognomic expressions of people and their kinesthetic responses.

Rorschach defined M as those responses which are determined by the form of the ink blot plus kinesthetic influences. He makes it explicit that the movement perceived must be felt, sensed, not merely named, in order to be scored M. The actual sensation or inner experience of movement or posture by the subject is essential for the kinesthetic response (both M and Mt). This means that in every kinesthetic response the subject experiences slight muscular innervations in the direction of assuming the posture or executing the movement perceived. Sometimes these innervations become sufficiently strong to lead to actual performance of the movement or, more frequently, to the beginning of such a performance which is then checked. Since the subject usually concentrates on the interpretation of the inkblots, the kinesthetic sensations are rarely if ever in focal awareness, and quite often the subject is not at all aware of them. The kinesthetic response, thus, is characterized by an accompanying innervation corresponding to the movement or posture perceived, but either this movement is not carried out at all or only partially or, in the rare cases in which the subject actually performs the movement or adopts the posture perceived, this is not done with as great an amount of energy as it would be done if the movement oc-

---

[18] This fact forms also the basis of Mira's Myokinetic Psychodiagnosis. He observes and interprets the blind execution of linear movements in space, assuming that the involuntary shiftings occurring in these movements express the person's attitudes and reactions, since every mental attitude implies a corresponding muscular attitude facilitating movements which would lead to the realization of the purpose contained in the mental attitude and blocking those that are opposed to that purpose. Emilo Mira, "Myokinetic Psychodiagnosis," *Proceedings Royal Soc. Med.* 33 (1940), 173–194.

curred as a spontaneous action. Another characteristic of the motor innervations in kinesthetic perception is that, in contrast to those in conscious action, they are not goal-controlled: he course which they take is not guided by the conscious purpose of effecting some change in the environment.

Rorschach realized that the correct identification of kinesthetic responses and their distinction from those in which movement is only named but not kinesthetically experienced can be one of the most difficult problems in scoring and that inquiry can overcome this difficulty only with intelligent subjects who "can generally say with reasonable certainty whether or not kinesthetic factors have contributed to the response." [19] The problem is even more complex than he assumed since intelligent subjects can have kinesthetic experience without being aware of it. Many postures and expressive movements which express strivings that are repressed are subject to what Sullivan has called "selective inattention" and thus are not in the awareness of the person of whom they are characteristic. Yet they must produce kinesthetic experiences even though the subject is not aware of them, much in the same manner as one is aware of only a fraction of the visual and auditory impressions which one experiences. The range between focal awareness, tangential awareness, and unawareness of an experience has room for many degrees and qualities of awareness and this holds true also for the kinesthetic sensations accompanying movement responses, in intelligent as well as in unintelligent persons. While the majority of kinesthetic responses are easily recognized, there will always remain quite a few in which it is difficult to decide whether a kinesthetic quality is present.[20]

In those kinesthetic responses in which movements or postures characteristic of the subject's own attitudes and strivings are seen,[21] the testee's characteristic neuromuscular "set"—that is, his own innervations toward a motor performance the actual execution of which is inhibited —is *projected* onto the inkblot in the form of a movement or posture which is similar to the one "intended" by these innervations. Either such inkblots or parts of inkblots will be seized upon by the subject for

---

[19] Rorschach, *op. cit.*, p. 26.

[20] The degree and type of awareness of the kinesthetic innervation leading to a movement response is an area which has not at all been explored. It may have significant bearing especially on the problem of covert self-reference in kinesthetic responses, which will be discussed later.

[21] This is the case in many, but not in all kinesthetic responses. The reasons for this will be discussed later.

interpretation as actually show an affinity to the posture or the movement corresponding to his own characteristic motor impulses, or he will project them even when the inkblot lends itself not at all or only with difficulties to such a percept. In the latter case an M minus (M—) response results which, as a rule, is typical of more pathological subjects in whom projection distorts reality.

This projection of the subject's own neuromuscular set or, rather, of the action "intended" by this set onto the inkblot, and the resulting perception or interpretation of the inkblot by the subject in terms of his own checked motor impulses furnish the theoretical explanation of that part of the diagnostic significance of the kinesthetic responses which is concerned with learning something about attitudes and strivings of a person from the specific quality of the movements and postures perceived by him in the Rorschach cards.

While the Rorschach literature has commonly accepted the finding that M responses represent the capacity for inner creation, it has ignored, with few exceptions, that they can be a valuable indicator of basic attitudes of the personality. I suppose that one reason for the neglect of so useful a diagnostic tool is that many clinical Rorschach workers have been interested in diagnosis according to the traditional classifications of different types of neuroses, psychoses, and so on, rather than in diagnosis of character structure in terms of basic attitudes and motivations. While the analysis of the specific quality of the movement perceived is of less importance for the diagnosis of different types of neurotic and psychotic disturbances, it yields highly significant material for the diagnostician interested in the person's basic orientation and attitude toward others and toward his own life.

Rorschach observed two types of movement, the stretching (extensor) and the bending (flexor) and found that the former is seen by people with an active, assertive striving, the latter by people whose attitude is passive, resigned, and so on. Piotrowski[22] has added to these the "blocked" movement indicating indecisiveness or what he calls "doubt neurosis."

On theoretical grounds it is difficult to see why only these two or three attitudes should find expression in kinesthetic responses. Binder, reviewing different kinds of movement percepts in Rorschach records, enumerates movements of battle, destruction, embracing, kissing, flee-

---

[22] Zygmunt Piotrowski, *A Rorschach Compendium* (Utica, N. Y.: State Hospitals Press, 1947), p. 32.

ing, seeking protection, seeking support, dancing, kneeling, extending the arms, and so on. He observes that they are either actions determined by drives or expressive movements.[23] While he does not mention any clinical evidence that the different drives expressed in the kinesthetic percepts play a significant role in the person perceiving them, he feels that the nature of the M responses must lie in their connection with the drives of the subject. Furrer[24] says in one of his formulations that the M responses are disjections or projections of the striving and attitude-taking ego or of its branches ("Abspaltungen," meaning literally *split-off parts*).

My own data lead me to the following conclusions. Comparison of kinesthetic responses with clinical, especially psychoanalytic material shows (1) that kinesthetic responses often express the person's basic attitudes toward himself, others, and the world around him, and (2) that not only active, passive, and indecisive attitudes are thus expressed, but that *any* significant attitude may find expression in kinesthetic responses. This does not mean that the kinesthetic responses are the *only* way in which such basic attitudes find expression in Rorschach records,[25] nor does it mean that *all* kinesthetic responses express significant attitudes of the person.

In order to interpret correctly the meaning of specific kinesthetic responses, it is essential to perceive and experience the concrete quality of the movement or posture seen by the subject. If one classifies the response too hastily as belonging to some general category such as extensor or flexor movement and then ascribes to this general category a fixed meaning such as extensor = active, flexor = passive, he will be prone to the same kind of faulty interpretation as the person is who uses the "dictionary" method of interpreting dream symbols and to whom, for example, a snake always means a penis no matter how the snake was experienced by the dreamer and what a snake means to him in his life. While it is true that certain types of movement or posture very often will have the same meaning—just as some symbols in the language of dreams have—it would be misleading to compile a catalogue of types of kinesthetic responses and to ascribe to them specific and invariable meanings. The temptation to use symbolic meanings

---

[23] Binder, *op. cit.*, pp. 47–48.

[24] Furrer, *op. cit.*

[25] They find expression in other factors, too, the most important of which are the symbolic form responses and the subjective definition of the test situation.

blindly and without discrimination seems to be considerable and wide-spread. I prefer, instead, to discuss some methodical viewpoints which I have found useful and relevant in interpreting kinesthetic responses and to illustrate them with concrete examples.

The central detail of card I of the Rorschach series frequently is seen as a person with arms and hands raised up. This is an extensor (stretching) movement in Rorschach's sense. The body is seen standing erect and the arms lifted above the level of the shoulders. Some people who see the figure in this way experience the gesture as an imploring one. They will see, for example, a woman stretching up her arms and asking for help, or somebody begging to be given something. Others see the gesture as that of a conductor directing an orchestra; still others see it as a person raising his arms to threaten somebody, or as a person throwing up his hands in surprise or in surrender. The perception of an extensor movement as a gesture of imploration, of asking for help, for mercy, or for some material gift occurs fairly frequently in card I as well as in other cards. It is characteristic of people with dependent needs, quite often of people with an expectant, "oral" attitude. It is not found in people who are very active or self-assertive.

People standing rigidly at attention, their bodies and heads very erect, their legs pressed closely together, their arms straight and held close to their bodies, are sometimes seen in the top detail of card VI or in the central small detail of the bottom area of card IX. The central figure in card I also is sometimes seen as just standing with legs pressed closely together. The kinesthetic emphasis in these percepts is on the erect posture and on the rigid tension with which the posture is held, keeping the body closed off against the world around. These percepts often express a quite unfree, rigidly controlled, and basically defensive attitude and are seen, among others, by people to whom spontaneous relations to others and the world around them are a threat. While the posture is an erect one, it would be misleading to classify it simply as an extensor movement. The main quality is that of rigid, tense, defensive control in order to keep up a certain appearance, a tense stability. What function this attitude has in the person would have to be seen from other factors in the test, among which might be other kinesthetic percepts.

Gestures of embracing, striking, begging, threatening, fleeing, attacking can all be seen in extensor movements. Yet the attitude of the person who sees mainly gestures of hitting, attacking, striking certainly is very different from that of the person who sees imploring and begging gestures in the stretched-out arms. *The concrete quality of the movement cuts across, and often is more important than, the general classification in stretching and bending movements.*

This does not mean that the distinction between flexor and extensor movements is not important. It is a very significant distinction if it is used with discrimination and does not blind one against more specific and therefore more significant meanings of the kinesthetic percept.

Suppose that two records both show prevailing kinesthetic percepts of "oral" movements such as receiving, begging, eating, asking for something, but that one shows a predominance of extensor movements and the other of flexor movements, such as people kneeling, inclining their heads, sitting in a hunched-over position; then it is safe to conclude that the person who sees the oral extensor gesture will more actively seek for or demand help, protection, nurture from others, while the person who sees the flexor movements is likely to sit and wait, perhaps resignedly, for such help. But neither of these two people can be said to have an active attitude. The basic attitude of both is that of dependence on others; they differ only in the way in which they expect to find gratification of their dependent needs. Still another person may see people grabbing things, animals or people trying to eat the same piece of food with each one trying to get the lion's share, people fighting over something in order to get it for themselves or pulling something away from somebody else, and so on. This person probably is of the oral-sadistic, aggressive type and, depending on other factors in the record, may also in his overt behavior be quite assertive, competitive, and aggressive. Yet, to think of him only in terms of the dichotomy active-passive, assertive-compliant, and to describe him as an active, assertive person would miss the most essential quality that he, too, is not a truly active person, but that his basic orientation toward the world, according to Fromm's typology of attitudes,[26] is an exploitative one which, "like the receptive, has as its basic premise the feeling that the source of all good is outside" of one and "that one cannot produce anything oneself."

Apart from the specific quality of the movement, tension, or posture seen, the way in which the person or animal seen is or is not related to others by his activity or state often yields relevant information concern-

[26] Erich Fromm, *Man for Himself,* p. 64.

ing basic attitudes. Are the people or animals by themselves, alone, or are two or more of them seen together? Especially in the cards which suggest two people (II, III, VII, IX, I, and X) it is significant if only one of them is seen and the other not. If two are seen, it is interesting to observe whether they are felt to be in some relationship to each other or not. The nature of the relationship, if any, is of interest, too. Is it a friendly or a hostile one? Do they turn toward each other or away from each other? Is the relation distant or close, dramatic or quiet, tense or relaxed, artificial or natural, veiled or open, playful, mocking, or serious? Often it is of as much interest to see what kind of relationship or activity is missing as to see what kind is present. There are records in which the avoidance of any aggressive movement or any hostile relation is an outstanding characteristic. Of course, one can speak of avoidance only when the subject gives a fair number and variety of kinesthetic responses and when, for example, he expresses aggressive tendencies in the animal but not in the human being responses, or in the symbolic form responses but not in the kinesthetic percepts.

Another significant aspect of the kinesthetic responses may be approached by asking oneself: How much energy does the movement or posture seen require and in what way or to what effect is that energy spent? This viewpoint, too, cuts across the distinction of extensor and flexor movements. Much or little energy may be spent in both extensor and flexor movements. From this viewpoint, active movements or postures in which energy is spent may be distinguished from inactive, static ones in which little or no energy is spent, but which, nevertheless, are not flexor movements—for example, lying outstretched, sleeping, or just standing and looking, and so on. Similarly, the attitudes expressed by flexor movements may show marked differences regarding the amount of energy involved and the quality of the experience undergone in them. One subject may see figures hunched over, bent from weakness, expressing feelings of exhaustion, weakness, being spent. Another subject may see figures burdened with a heavy weight which loads them down. Here, the experience is not one of complete lack of force, but of having to carry a greater load than one is able to. Still another subject may see flexor movements such as acrobats supporting their weight by neck and shoulders, legs bent parallel to the floor (sometimes seen in the upper lateral projections of card IV); here the expenditure of a great deal of energy, tension, and strain for the maintenance of a twisted position could be the experience expressed by the percept. A very tense and exhausting self-control by virtue of which the process of living becomes an acrobatic feat might be thus expressed. The described distinctions are helpful in showing something of the subject's feeling of the amount of energy available to him, the amount of energy spent in his living and whether this energy is felt to be needed for the mere maintenance of a precarious balance, of carrying on, or whether it is felt to be available for reaching some goal, for satisfying some drive, for some active achievement.

Other significant distinctions are those between tentative, exploratory movements or postures and definite decisive ones, between movements contemplated or initiated and those that are actually being carried out. These examples of various viewpoints from which the specific qualities of kinesthetic percepts may be examined and interpreted could be continued. There are other viewpoints and, of course, many more types of kinesthetic responses than the examples given here. As one pays attention to them, he will discover unfamiliar ones or new nuances of familiar ones.

So far the discussion has been concerned with the manner in which different attitudes, feelings, and strivings find an expression in the specific quality of the movements and postures seen in kinesthetic responses. This leaves two areas unexplored: (1) Is the extent to which the kinesthetic responses express character traits, attitudes, feelings, and strivings always the same or are there differences in degree? Are some kinesthetic responses more expressive of such traits than others, and do some express them more directly than others? Do all kinesthetic responses express such personal attitudes or are there some which do not? Finally, if they do not all express characteristic traits of the personality, how can one make diagnostic use of them? Is there a way in which to distinguish the diagnostically valuable and relevant responses from the diagnostically neutral and irrelevant ones? (2) Do the kinesthetic responses show anything, not only about what kind of attitudes, feelings, strivings are present in a person, but also what their place and function is in the personality structure and—as part of that question—what their relation is to the person's conscious ideas about himself?

Not all kinesthetic responses express individually characteristic traits or strivings of the person, nor does the absence of such responses mean that such traits are not present in the person. Empirically, one finds many kinesthetic responses in which the movement or posture seen does not seem to say anything about specific attitudes or strivings of the subject. This fact, of course, need not mean that these responses are not determined by the projection of a particular feeling or striving of the subject. It may mean that the determining attitude is expressed only in a very veiled or indirect way; or that the person trying to interpret the meaning of the response is not sufficiently astute or does not have sufficient information to recognize it. This is not different from dream interpretation in which some images do not lend themselves to interpretation because their meaning is too veiled, too obscure, or because the interpreter lacks sufficient information or insight. However, on theoretical grounds, too, one has to assume that not all kinesthetic responses have a personally significant, symbolic meaning, nor do they all express in a recognizable way specific attitudes of the subject.[27] The more kinesthetic responses there are in a record, the better is the chance that one or several will show in a recognizable way projections of personally significant trends. But if one thinks of the numerous records in which the only M response is the popular one to card III—for example, two waiters bowing, two men doing a dance, two comedians—and in which the Mt responses are restricted to such popular ones as "two animals climbing up a mountain" (seen in card VIII), it is difficult to see in what way these responses show anything of the personal attitudes of the subject. Those records with only few and conventional kinesthetic responses are mentioned here because they show up pointedly a factor which deserves consideration in the analysis of the kinesthetic responses of any record. The kinesthetic response, like any other type of response in Rorschach's test, is not a "free" association but determined, in part, by the objective stimulus material of the inkblots. The stimulus for giving kinesthetic responses—especially if the relatively infrequent cases with movement responses to unusual details (Dd) are excluded and only the much more frequent cases with movement responses to the

---

[27] Piotrowski (*op. cit.*, p. 32) seems to be of a different opinion when he says that "the M responses always reveal the subject's conception of his role in life." My doubts concerning the validity of this formulation are based on three factors: (1)There are purely conventional kinesthetic responses. (2) Some kinesthetic responses are too veiled or too complex to permit a clear view of the trend expressed by them. (3) The concept of life-role implies a relatively complete set of attitudes embodying the basic orientation of the subject to the world, to others, and to himself. This can be seen rarely from single kinesthetic responses, sometimes from a study of all the kinesthetic responses in a record, usually only from these together with the other factors in a record. What can be seen from non-stereotyped kinesthetic responses are usually single feelings or strivings or attitudes—in other words, elements which may furnish constitutive parts of what one might call the life-role of a person.

whole inkblot or to the more obvious details are considered—is much less strong and frequent than the stimulus for form responses. Some cards (VI, VIII) provide hardly any stimulus for M responses; in others the stimulus is restricted to a few areas. Some of these areas do not allow for a great variety of types of movement to be seen. For example, the black figures on card III can hardly be seen other than in a movement or posture where the upper part of the body is bent forward.[28] If, as often is the case, nothing more specific is seen than that the figures are animated, or that they are dancing, then the percept remains so conventional, so closely tied to the culturally stereotyped way of perceiving the objective stimulus that nothing personal can be seen from it. If all kinesthetic responses in a record are of this type, then the fact of the conventionality of the movement itself may be significant, but nothing about a particular striving projected onto the inkblot can be seen. From the standpoint of interpretation this is similar to handwriting which follows the pattern of school script quite closely and, by its lack of individually characteristic movements, can be evaluated only by asking oneself why the writer needs to follow the conventional pattern so closely.

While the purely conventional kinesthetic response is an extreme, although frequent, case, the fact remains that all kinesthetic responses, like all other responses, constitute a fusion between the objective stimulus, the culturally prevailing way of perceiving it and the personal factor of what is being made out of that stimulus. As in all adaptive behavior in which a person comes to terms with reality the different ways of reaction could be arranged, from the viewpoint under discussion now, along a continuous line one end of which would approach a quite impersonal reaction, almost wholly dominated by, and tied to, the cultural stereotype of dealing with the stimulus, and the other end of which would be a highly personal reaction. Obviously, kinesthetic responses will be the less expressive, or at least, the less recognizably expressive, of personal traits the more they approach the stereotype-

---

[28] Of course, in seeing them this way, quite a number of different possibilities still remain. They may be seen in the act of bending down or of straightening up, moving toward each other or away from each other, in a natural or in a strained position, in a conflicting or cooperating movement, in friendly or hostile activity, in balance or in danger of falling over, in play or in work, whirling around with no end or purpose in view or wanting to achieve something definite, and so on. This shows again that Rorschach's classification of flexor movement in terms of their bodies being bent over is insufficient and would in some of the examples quoted lead to misinterpretation.

determined end of that line, that is, the most conventional reaction. Rorschach, in the last two years of his life, felt that quite generally those M which are strongly suggested by the form of the blot do not require genuine empathy although they presuppose an Anlage for it; in this period he scored these frequently given M, which I call the conventional M, as FM (FB), for instance he scored the "waiters," often seen in card III, as FM.[29] This is consistent with his general view that "individual and original responses reveal more about the individual strivings of the subject and thus have more psychoanalytic meaning than the vulgar answers." [30]

Another factor which should caution one against assuming indiscriminately that every kinesthetic response reveals a basic feeling, striving, or attitude of the subject is the consideration that probably some kinesthetic responses express attitudes toward which the subject is capable of having empathy. This need not always mean that the feeling or attitude toward which empathy is experienced plays a basic role in the person's life. While it is true that in some people the capacity for empathy toward others is limited to feelings and attitudes which are basic in their own lives, others are capable of empathy also toward attitudes and feelings which play only a minor or occasional role in their own lives and toward which they are not habitually or compellingly inclined.

The practical question of how to select for diagnostic interpretation those kinesthetic responses which are projections of significant, personal strivings cannot be answered by any definite set of rules. Some criteria can be given, however, which usually are helpful in distinguishing the diagnostically useful from the neutral responses: (1) If there are several kinesthetic responses all showing the same or a similar type of movement, it is safe to assume that this movement expresses a striving of basic importance in the subject's character structure. (2) The

---

[29] G. A. Roemer, "Hermann Rorschach und die Forschungsergebnisse seiner beiden letzten Lebensjahre," *Psyche, Ein Jahrbuch für Tiefenpsychologie und Menschenkunde in Forschung und Praxis,* 1 (1948), 523–542. According to Roemer, Rorschach distinguished in this period (1) MM (BB) the great, purely introversive M which may occur in artistic and intuitive subjects, (2) the M (B) in their earlier meaning, (3) the secondary M among which he also counted movement responses given to very small areas, (4) the FM (FB) mentioned above; *ibid.*, pp. 536–537.

[30] Rorschach, *op. cit.*, p. 206. "Vulgar answers" is a not very fortunate translation of Rorschach's term *Vulgärantworten*, which means the very frequently given or "popular" responses.

more original, the more deviating from the conventional percept is the movement seen, the more likely it is that it expresses a personally significant trend. The concept "originality" as used in this context has to be distinguished from Rorschach's concept of the original response. The response may well be a popular one, yet the movement seen may deviate considerably from those that are usually seen. For instance, in card III the two usual human figures may be seen in danger of losing their balance; this movement is seen so infrequently that it is bound to have personal significance. Or in card VIII, the two usual animals may be seen; if they are seen as climbing a mountain or a tree and the movement of climbing does not, for some special reason, convey a particular significance, it is unlikely that it expresses a personally significant striving, for it is a movement so frequently seen in this card that it is usually a stereotype; if, however, the animals are seen trying to climb up the mountain but their hindlegs appear stuck, the movement ceases to be a stereotype and very likely expresses a personally significant feeling and conflict in the subject. (3) As in any interpretation of human behavior the psychologist must know what he is looking for, in what setting one trait is likely to be present and in which setting unlikely or impossible. Thus, in many cases the correct interpretation of the movement seen as well as the decision whether this movement carries recognizable, personal meaning at all will be possible only on the basis of other factors in the Rorschach record. Needless to say, *any* interpretation, even of the most telling movement, should always be made only within the context of the personality structure as shown by the entire record.

It has been shown that personally significant tendencies often are expressed in kinesthetic percepts and that automorphic projection of habitual, checked motor impulses onto the inkblot is the mechanism by which they have a determining influence on the movement seen. It is clear, then, that the movement perceived often has something to do with traits in the personality of the perceiver. The question remains *in what way* the trait or feeling expressed by the movement is embedded in the personality structure and whether the kinesthetic responses show anything about the structural place of the trait in the person. For example, a person may see repeatedly aggressive, hostile movements. According to what has been said so far, this means that aggressive hostile impulses play a role in this person and that he has projected them onto the inkblot. It would be of interest to know what role these impulses play in his personality structure. Is he aware of them? Does he accept them? Does he reject them? Are they partly or entirely alien to his idea of himself? I believe that in many cases it is possible to arrive at a correct or, at least, probably correct answer to those questions, sometimes on the basis of a careful analysis of the kinesthetic responses alone, in other cases by taking into account the context of the total record in which they appear.

The most important, single clue to this problem may be obtained by analyzing the quality of what I propose to call the *covert* (or implied) *self-reference* of the response. The term self-reference is usually employed to designate such phenomena as the delusional inclination of the paranoid patient to relate outside events which have nothing to do with him to himself. In the Rorschach literature, too, the term is used to designate the cases of patients who overtly indicate their feeling that there is some personal relation between them and the Rorschach cards. Self-reference, however, like all pathological phenomena, is present also in every normal person, the difference between the normal and the pathological being one of degree rather than of kind.[31] In many Rorschach responses, apart from the detached form responses, one can find by careful analysis of the response itself or of the feelings of the subject at the time when the response was given more or less covert traces of self-reference. This is especially true of the symbolic form responses and the movement responses, but in addition it is true of all other responses with a strong, emotional cathexis of the object seen. Of course, only the more seriously disturbed will feel that the inkblot actually has some intended or otherwise essentially personal relation to him. The normal and the average neurotic person will merely feel, especially when self-observation is asked of them, that their responses were given in such a way *as if* some personal relation might exist between them and the inkblot. For instance, as pointed out earlier, the person who tends to select forms of *shelter* in the inkblot and interprets them as cradles, nests, harbors, valleys, and so on, looks at the inkblot—with

---

[31] A completely "detached," objective view of others and the world around us is not possible to man. He tries to approach such a view in science. However, in every perception which is not artificially and purposely controlled there are elements of self-reference, sometimes quite overt, sometimes quite obscure. Man cannot help but perceive things as the person he is, with all his needs, interests, wishes, and fears. Inevitably, he relates what he sees in some way to himself although he usually is quite unaware of doing so. And even in conscious attempts at a detached, objective view of reality, even in the scientific laboratory, man cannot get rid of himself—that is, of observing things while being the kind of person, the kind of creature that he is and the participant of the kind of culture that he lives in.

some, however slight and unconscious, implication—as if it were a real object, not only an inkblot, and as if the areas seen in this way gave the promise of shelter to him. Consciously, of course, these people are perfectly aware that they are merely interpreting an inkblot. Nevertheless, there is the described, covert, not verbalized, and frequently not conscious self-reference. With regard to movement responses it is often possible to see something of the relation between the trait expressed by the movement and the person who gave the response by putting oneself in the place of the subject and asking oneself the following questions concerning the activity or motion seen in the inkblot: Am I doing this? Would I be likely to do this? Would I ever do such a thing? Am I just looking on? Is this happening to me? Do I fear that this might happen to me? Do I admire, despise, envy, condemn, feel indifference, condescension, and so on, to what is going on there? These questions which could be added to are suitable to bring into focus different degrees and kinds of self-reference which, in turn, tell something about the way in which the activity or event seen in the kinesthetic percept is related to the perceiver. Of course, the answer to these questions would be ideally reliable if obtained in an interview with a subject who has good awareness of himself, is a good self-observer, and has no resistance against communicating what had gone on in him. But in very many cases a skilled observer will be able to find the answer by analyzing the responses and the record with special attention to the style of verbalization, the expressive nuances of intonation, inflexion, and facial expressions, and so on, when the response was given and particularly by considering what the total record shows about the personality and the significant motivations.

A schematic classification of significant attitudes observable in the covert relation of the subject to the action, event, or situation seen in the kinesthetic percept would have to include the following viewpoints: (1) Does or could the subject, in phantasy, participate in, or identify with, what is going on or not? Or is there a counter-identification? (2) Is the type of his (imaginary, covert) participation active or passive, is he agent or victim? (3) Is his attitude to what is happening positive, negative, or neutral? Does he wish it would happen, does he fear it, is he indifferent to it? These different attitudes appear in various combinations. Participation (or identification) can take place in an active or in a passive role, and each of these roles can be hoped for or feared. Equally, in nonparticipation, the event or situation seen can be hoped for or feared and the subject, while feeling that he is not in the picture and can do nothing about it, may wish or fear to be actively or passively involved in such an event, or he may feel neutral about it. Not only do these attitudes appear in different combinations with each other, but they and their combinations also shade imperceptibly into one another.

If the subject *identifies* with—or thinks of himself as capable of participating in—the activity seen, it is an indication that there are no major obstacles to his becoming aware of the attitude expressed in the movement or that he may have some awareness of it. If, however, there is a marked counter-identification with the movement seen, a feeling that this is "not-me," [32] then the attitude expressed in the movement is likely to be dissociated. A fairly frequent example of this is to be found in the responses to the whole of card IV in which a huge man, a monster, gorilla, or giant is seen in a threatening posture. Usually the subjects giving this kind of response are afraid of what they see. The response, thus, is an example of counter-identification with, and dissociation of, the attitude seen and of implied fear that the subject may be the victim of the attack. Of course, other responses—especially the color reaction and kinesthetic responses dealing with, or avoiding, the theme of aggression—have to be taken into account in order to decide whether the subject in whose record this reaction to card IV appears is likely to have repressed all hostility and aggression, or whether the repression is only partial.

The *active or passive* role of the subject in his implied participation in the movement seen furnishes material significant for the question of whether the subject tends to feel the active agent in his life or the object or victim of life—of others. In the example just given the subject is by implication the potential victim of an attack by others. It is a response typical of the feeling that others—the world around one—are overwhelmingly stronger than oneself and that they constitute a threat. Thus, this response also shows the attitude of *fear* toward the activity seen. Altogether, this type of response is an example of projection in the sense in which Freud used the term: the subject's fear of his own aggressive impulses is dealt with by repressing these impulses and projecting them onto others of whom the subject then is afraid. Similarly, in this Rorschach percept the monster is experienced as "not-me" and as threatening.

---

[32] The concept "not-me" is taken from Sullivan's teachings. See Patrick Mullahy, *Oedipus Myth and Complex* (New York: Hermitage Press, 1948), p. 294.

In addition to this basic classification of types of self-reference indicating the subject's covert relation to the attitude expressed in the kinesthetic percept, quite a number of subtler gradations and nuances of the subject's feeling about his basic attitudes find expression in the movement responses and often can be recognized or inferred from an analysis of these responses. One may find more or less veiled feelings of compassion, self-pity, contempt, superior detachment, condescension, not taking anything including oneself seriously, and many other feelings about the traits or strivings expressed in the movement responses. They usually are the subject's feelings about these traits in himself and in others. Sometimes the subject may feel that he has contempt for the attitude in others and may not be aware of the fact that it is his own attitude too. While the trait, attitude, or striving always is expressed by the specific quality of the movement or posture seen, the feeling of the subject about it can often be seen by analyzing the relation between the quality of the movement and the content of the response, for example, the type of figure seen as moving and the attributes given to that figure. This is one of the significant relations between the formal pattern and the content of the response to which Rorschach calls attention.[33] For example, a man who had felt helplessly manipulated by a dominating parent in his childhood and who retained from this experience a deep fear of all close contact with people because he might again become the helpless, passive victim of somebody else, had in his more impersonal contacts with people in his work developed the opposite attitude and become an extremely efficient, brilliant organizer and executive. While his Rorschach record as a whole showed very marked signs of an unusually strong, active ambition and striving for achievement, in his kinesthetic percepts passive, helpless attitudes prevailed. He saw a child being dragged along a street helplessly, drunken women leaning against a lamppost with their heads lolling forward, women slumped in their seats, and so on. All these responses expressed his basic attitude of helplessness and passivity. In the response in which the child was seen, some compassion and probably self-pity about himself as a child were evident, while the reference to the drunken women showed his contempt for such a helpless attitude in himself and in others. The mixture of pity and contempt for his underlying, mostly unconscious attitude stands about halfway between identification and counter-identification with the postures seen. While he could still accept the idea of helpless-

---

[33] Rorschach, *op. cit.*, p. 207.

ness in a child, in himself as a child, he would have felt contempt for it in himself as an adult and thus had to see the helplessly uncontrolled posture in women toward whom he could feel superior.[34]

Even where the covert self-reference in the kinesthetic response points to active identification of the subject with the activity or posture seen, this does not mean that the striving or attitude expressed by the kinesthetic percept is actually carried out and realized in the subject's manifest behavior. All that one can say is that the strivings expressed in kinesthetic percepts are dynamically important tendencies in the personality structure. They may be needs and strivings of which the subject is aware, but that does not mean that they guide his purposeful behavior. I am inclined to assume that the expression of a striving in a kinesthetic percept usually indicates that there is some *unsatisfied tension* regarding this particular need, just as in Szondi's test the fact that a particular factor is "loaded" indicates such tension. The reason for my assumption lies in the inverse relationship between kinesthesia and motor activity. Rorschach assumed that the more kinesthesias a person shows, the less will he engage in motor activity and vice versa.[35] As has been shown, the kinesthetic percept is accompanied by arrested, checked motor innervations. Instead of being carried out, these innervations lead to empathy with movement observed in the environment, or to kinesthetic imagery as in kinesthetic percepts in Rorschach's test or as in dreams where also actual motor activity is suspended by sleep. The motor impulse is not carried out by activity but transformed into imagery. Instead of Rorschach's formulation, I would say that *in the act of kinesthetic perception or imagery motor activity is inhibited, and in the act of carrying out a motor impulse kinesthetic perception and imagery do not take place.* This does not mean that a person with many kinesthetic percepts will show little motor activity, nor that a person with much motor activity will have few kinesthetic percepts. It only means that the two states do not usually coexist in the same person at the same time. The fact that the motor impulse accompanying a kines-

---

[34] Hertzman and Pearce present interesting data from psychoanalytic exploration of Rorschach responses among which are also some examples of these finer nuances of the subject's feeling about his own traits and quite a number of cases showing identification of the subject with the human figure seen. While they relate these findings only to the content of the response, all their examples are either kinesthetic or dynamic (symbolic) form responses. The kinesthetic responses seem to prevail. Max Hertzman and Jane Pearce, "The Personal Meaning of the Human Figure in the Rorschach," *Psychiatry* 10 (1947), 413–422.

[35] Rorschach, *op. cit.*, p. 79.

thetic percept is not carried out but checked means that the drive leading to this motor impulse is not fully discharged or satisfied. Similar to many subtle, expressive movements in which an underlying attitude is expressed in small quantities, as it were, while the way to full discharge of this attitude in motor activity is blocked, the recurrent kinesthetic percept of the same movement or gesture indicates that full satisfaction of the drive expressed by this movement does not take place and that some tension remains in the need system to which the drive belongs. How much of it is discharged, in spite of this inhibition of full satisfaction, cannot be seen from the movement responses themselves, but can be estimated only on the basis of the other test factors, especially of the color and shading responses.

While the specific movements perceived in the kinesthetic responses usually are not representative of the testee's goal-directed, consciously purposeful behavior, they do represent significant, often basic tendencies in him and thus have a determining influence on the conduct of his life. They also influence his inadvertent expressive behavior, including expressive movements. They usually are "lived out" by him even though he may be not at all aware of this and might deny it if asked about it. In this respect they are no different from any unconscious drive or longing which may be denied, fought, overcompensated by reaction-formations, and yet exerts a clearly determining influence on the life of a person which becomes apparent to a competent observer. Rorschach's posthumously published case study is a case in point. His analysis of the quality of the movements perceived in the M and in some other responses that are kinesthetically co-determined shows the patient's pervasively passive attitude. Oberholzer's comment to this, quoted by Rorschach, is: "The M series is, therefore, what is 'lived.' I purposely avoided saying 'experienced' in order not to imply that the patient knows the nature of this experience. M is the compulsion determining what is lived and how it is lived." [36] This expresses clearly the well-known fact that unconscious attitudes are lived out in many ways which, to use Sullivan's term, are subject to "selective inattention" by the person who does the living out. As already mentioned, attitudes represented by the specific quality of the movements perceived can be, but need not be, unconscious. Whether they are or not, cannot always be decided on the basis of the test alone.

---

[36] *Ibid.*, pp. 207–208.

## The Problem of M, FM, and m

The psychological problem of the various structural ways in which the attitude or feeling expressed by the kinesthetic percept may be related to the self and the self-image of the subject furnishes also the frame of reference for a discussion of the attempt to differentiate movement responses according to the type of object which is seen as moving. This attempt has been made by Klopfer[37] and Piotrowski.[38] They distinguish human or humanlike movement which they score M, as Rorschach did, from animal movement which they score FM and from the movement of lifeless objects which they score m. They disagree with regard to details of scoring and to the meaning of the scores. With the following remarks I want to explore whether the ideas presented in the preceding discussion can throw some light on the differences between the three categories of movement proposed by these authors and to open a discussion regarding the evidence available for such a differentiation.

Rorschach took it as a rule that "answers may be considered as kinesthetically determined practically only when human beings or animals capable of motion similar to that of human beings (monkeys, bears) are seen in the figures." [39] But he observed that some subjects perceive movement also in all kinds of animals, plants, geometric figures, and even lines. These, too, he scored M; for example, the response to plate VIII "Resurrection—shows how the red animals are resurrected" is scored by him D M + A. In the posthumously published case study he introduces the category "F tending to M" for responses which "may have a kinesthetic determinant" and groups under this heading some responses showing nonhumanlike animal movement and the response "a skeleton in a light wrapping." I follow this suggestion by scoring all nonhumanlike kinesthetic percepts as Mt (Movement tendency).

Klopfer, Piotrowski, and their followers score animal movement *FM*. Klopfer says that "it is now quite safe to assume that they [the FM] represent the influence of the most instinctive layers within the personality." [40] His main reason for this assumption is that he has found that

---

[37] Bruno Klopfer and Douglas McGlashan Kelley, *The Rorschach Technique* (Yonkers-on-Hudson, N.Y.: World Book Company, 1942).

[38] Piotrowski, *op. cit.*, p. 40.

[39] Rorschach, *op. cit.*, p. 25.

[40] Klopfer and Kelley, *op. cit.*, p. 278.

"emotionally infantile" subjects "living on a level of instinctive prompt-ing below (their) chronological and mental age" invariably show a pre-dominance of FM over M responses. Piotrowski agrees with Klopfer's view and adds that the FM responses also (1) represent vitality and (2) are indicators of the subject's *past*, early childhood attitudes, whereas the M responses indicate the present attitudes.

My own observations lead me to a different hypothesis which hinges on the question of the subject's covert or overt identification with the movement seen. *Where overt or covert identification of the subject with the movement seen takes place, regardless of whether the movement be performed by an animal or by a human being, the striving or attitude expressed by the movement tends to be partially or entirely in aware-ness or accessible to awareness without major resistance. Where no such identification takes place, the striving tends to be repressed. The repression tends to be more severe where counter-identification takes place.*

As can be seen readily, the criterion of identification with the move-ment seen cuts across the distinction between human and animal move-ment. The threatening gesture of the giant in card IV, according to this criterion, may express an aggressive impulse as inaccessible to aware-ness as that expressed by the leopard stealthily stalking its prey which is seen sometimes in card VIII. On the other hand, two dogs lifting their heads to suck at a bottle (card II) may express an oral-receptive atti-tude fairly accessible to awareness, just as the children eating the cen-tral blue detail in card X may. In the first two examples the giant's and the leopard's activity probably is felt to be "not-me" by the subject (counter-identification); hence the aggressive impulses expressed by the movement are likely to be dissociated. In the last two examples there may be identification with the movement seen, at least there is no indication of counter-identification; hence the oral striving expressed by the movement is likely to be more easily accessible to awareness than the aggressive impulses of the first two examples were. (In order to find out whether the oral striving is or is not in awareness, more material would be needed than the two responses quoted.) It depends on the individual personality structure with what kind of activity, human or nonhuman, identification may take place.

While it is true that by and large people will identify more readily with human or humanlike activities, postures, strivings than with non-humanlike ones, this must not lead one to overlook the fact that the individual personality structure may place a strict tabu on *some* human activities which makes it even harder for the person to identify with these than with some animal activity which is more acceptable to him. With this important qualification in mind, the concept of *humanlike* movement is of some usefulness as one among several indications of the type of movement toward which one might expect an attitude of identification, although the mere presence of humanlike movement in a response does not justify, by itself, the assumption that the subject actually identifies with this movement; nor does the mere presence of non-humanlike movement justify the conclusion that the subject does not or cannot identify with this movement and that therefore the striving expressed by the movement is dissociated or repressed. The projection of an attitude or striving onto an animal, especially one that is not humanlike, rather than onto a human being may be, but need not always be, one of several ways in which repression of this attitude in the subject finds expression in his Rorschach responses.

What animal movement can be said to be humanlike? Rorschach seems to have applied anatomical criteria to this question. In mentioning monkeys and bears as the animals whose movements are humanlike he probably thought of the fact that they will walk, dance, stand, or sit sometimes on their hindlegs and use their forelegs much like arms. However, one encounters sometimes responses in which the subject quite obviously identifies, even consciously, with an animal movement and experiences it as humanlike, even though neither anatomy nor postural behavior suggests the similarity which is essentially a psychological one—a similarity of the inner attitude ascribed to the animal and expressed in its movement. Thus, one subject saw in the lateral red details of card III, on one side, a dog running away from another animal and turning his head to see whether his pursuer was catching up with him, on the other side, a dog putting up a front, pretending that he was going to fight, but actually just about to run for dear life. While both dogs are seen on all fours so that their posture is not humanlike, the subject was nevertheless speaking of his own conflict between anxiety and prestige, the wish to escape and the wish to maintain a façade of courage. The drives expressed by the animal movement were, at least partially, in his awareness. He was identifying with the animal movements seen. The dog's movements, while not anatomically humanlike, were psychologically humanlike (as well as doglike). This example also illustrates the point that animal movements cannot be said to refer more to the instinctive layers of the personality than human ones. Both human and animal movements can express drives and feelings of the personality. Because it is less likely that identification will take place with animal than with human movement, there may be a trend in the direction of animal movements tending to express more repressed, human movements less repressed, strivings and attitudes. However, such a trend—which it would be a useful task to investigate with statistical methods—does not relieve the psychologist of the task of examining each movement response individually with a view to determining whether the subject is likely to have identified with it, and on the basis of the answer to that question to draw his conclusions regarding the probability of the subject's awareness or unawareness of the particular trend expressed by the movement, regardless of whether an animal or a human has been seen as moving.

The viewpoint presented here is also in contrast to Piotrowski's assumption that the FM responses express past, the M present attitudes of the subject. On a priori grounds it is hard to see how an attitude, if it really is past history only, should still exercise a determining influence on the subject's present perceptions. Furthermore, *all* present attitudes of a person are usually products of his past, particularly of his early childhood. The fact that an attitude or striving is repressed does not mean that it is no longer present. On the contrary, repressed attitudes are usually more effective in determining present behavior than conscious attitudes are. While animal movements are, on the whole, although with many exceptions, probably somewhat more likely to express *repressed* drives than human movements are, they both express only such drives as are dynamically effective in the subject's present personality structure.

The score m is used by Piotrowski for the movement of inanimate objects caused by external and impersonal forces. The symptomatic significance which he attributes to them is that they express a role in life which the person feels "to be very desirable and gratifying but which to him is utterly unattainable because of both external difficulties and internal inhibitions" and which is not at all frightening to the person. Also, the m responses indicate, according to Piotrowski, self-observation, intelligence, and an "unwillingness to modify goals which originated in a period of lesser maturity." [41] Klopfer, who uses the score m

---

[41] Piotrowski, *op. cit.*, p. 43.

for inanimate movement and for a variety of other percepts only some of which are kinesthetically determined, ascribes to them a meaning almost opposite to that named by Piotrowski—namely, that they represent inner promptings which are experienced by the subject "as hostile and uncontrollable forces working upon him." [42] What both authors seem to have in common is the assumption that the m responses express drives about which the subject is or feels incapable of doing anything. They differ in that Piotrowski assumes that the subject feels these drives or their goals to be very desirable, whereas Klopfer assumes that they are felt to be very undesirable or hostile.

If one applies the viewpoint developed here to the problem of the m responses, the essential question, again, is not what kind of object is seen as moving but what the implied attitude of the subject is to the movement seen. One of the typical and significant attitudes to be found in kinesthetic perception is that the subject does not feel that he could actively participate in the movement or activity seen and that he is quite incapable of influencing what is going on. It is the attitude of the impotent spectator. This attitude may refer to events which take place in the world outside of the person, with little or no reference to him, or to events which greatly affect him. It may concern wished-for as well as feared happenings. Again, this attitude may be found toward human movement as well as toward inanimate movement; for example, in the percept of the threatening giant in card IV the subject usually does not have the feeling that he could do anything against the threat. However, if an object is seen as moving due to the influence of external and impersonal forces such as gravity, explosions, and so on, active participation or identification in the subject's phantasy is less likely to occur than in human movements. It is more likely that the subject perceives this movement as a spectator who cannot do anything about it. While there may be identification with the movement seen, it is usually not an active one. Rather the subject feels as if this were happening to him without his making any effort for or against what is happening. In schizophrenic patients the feeling that the movement seen takes place in, or happens to, their own bodies without their being able to do anything about it becomes as vivid occasionally as the passive, synkinetic experiences of some schizophrenic patients who, as Rorschach reports,[43] feel

---

[42] Klopfer and Kelley, *op. cit.*, p. 279.

[43] Rorschach, "Reflexhalluzination und Symbolik," *Zentralblatt für Psychoanalyse und Psychotherapie* 3 (1912–1913), 121–128.

in their own bodies movements they perceive outside of them, such as the opening and closing of a door, or the wiping of the floor by another patient.

The reasons for which a subject needs to feel or feels that he cannot do anything for or against something, that he is an impotent onlooker, can be of various types. Typical and significant reasons are: (1) The activity or striving is dissociated. If it takes place outside of the subject and if he cannot do anything about it, then he cannot be held responsible. For example, the percept of a bullet tearing through a body, sometimes seen in cards VI or VIII, may express dissociated hostility, aggression, murderous impulses. The projection of the dissociated impulse onto the impersonal bullet serves to maintain the dissociation by not connecting the activity with a person. In this case the object movement serves the same purpose as human movement seen with counter-identification, as "not-me," or as nonhumanlike animal movement. (2) The subject feels impotent toward life, incapable of protecting, defending, or asserting himself. This leads to two typical situations: (a) He feels that he cannot ward off the dangers threatening him. The feared event takes place anyway. For example, in the response "a bullet tearing through a body," identification may take place with the body. The impersonal quality of the bullet and its movement may be necessary either to express the inevitable, inexorable course of events feared and/or because the subject cannot permit himself to hold another person—for example, a parent—responsible for the threatening danger, since that might arouse his hatred of that person, which, in turn, would arouse too much anxiety in him. Another example of a feared, inanimate movement are the responses in which houses, rocks, and so on, are seen falling apart or tumbling down (not infrequent in card VII). They often express the subject's feeling of severe insecurity, his fear of falling apart or of having no ground under his feet—feelings against which he feels impotent to do anything. In more pathological, especially schizophrenic patients, one will encounter occasionally such a response with H or Hd content—for example, a body falling apart or disintegrating. In less disturbed people this percept is too fear-arousing and too much in contrast to their daytime, rational modes of thought, so that for this reason they project the feeling onto inanimate objects. Again, a similar feeling may occasionally be expressed in an M response—for example, a person being crucified, split in two, and so on—if kinesthetic empathy is felt with the victim. There, too, the attitude is one of impending danger or disaster or death against which one is helpless. (b) The subject has wishes or hopes, but feels helpless and incapable of making concrete efforts toward their realization; for example, the fairly frequent responses in which objects or people are seen as rising, soaring, floating, not through their own efforts but lifted by nonhuman forces. These responses often express the wish to rise to some higher or better state or to break away from obstacles or chains in one's life, or to escape from some sort of confinement; but at the same time they express the feeling that one cannot do anything about this, by projecting this striving onto nonhuman forces. This type of response is frequent in people who, consciously or unconsciously, expect some kind of miracle which will change their life or bring the satisfaction they want. Sometimes, these responses also express phantastic or grandiose notions about oneself which usually also contain an element of magic wish-fulfillment. (a) and (b) may be combined in the same response. For example, explosions or volcanic eruptions often express at the same time the subject's wish and his fear to release some inhibited, repressed impulse which is felt to be outside of his control. Sometimes the wish, sometimes the fear will be more emphasized or more repressed. Also in responses in which primarily a fear is expressed—for example, the fear of falling, losing one's hold, and so on—there may be present an element of wishing for the feared event, of wanting to give up active effort and to surrender to the disintegrating forces.

Inanimate movement, thus, is particularly suitable to express the subject's feeling that he is not responsible for what is going on and that he can do nothing about it. This feeling may serve the function of maintaining dissociation of the striving expressed by the movement, or of expressing the subject's helplessness with regard to either the fulfillment of his wishes or the defense against the dangers that he fears. However, the particular fitness of inanimate objects or forces to attract the projection of strivings toward which the subject has one of these attitudes must not lead one to overlook that human and animal movement may and do sometimes serve the same purposes. The decision on what kind of striving a kinesthetic percept expresses as well as on what relation this striving has to the subject, to his awareness, to his self-image, and to his feeling of what he can or cannot do, can be made only on the basis of an analysis of the concrete percept in its context with the total record, not on the basis of what kind of object is seen as moving, nor merely on the basis of whether the movement is flexor or extensor.

In Klopfer's scoring, facial expressions are considered as "additional m." If the faces or masks seen are frightening, he assumes that the subject projects his fright onto the mask and, according to him, all facial expressions "clearly indicate that some tendency to M has been repressed," but that this is "a superior—i.e., more adjusted—form of inhibition to that represented by the usual m." [44] The word "projection" is used by him in a sense different from its usual meaning. The subject does not project his own feeling—namely, fright—on the face or mask seen as one does in what is usually considered projection and as is true of kinesthetic percepts. If the subject projected his feeling of fear, one would expect him to see a frightened rather than a frightening face.

While facial expressions, thus, are not projections as kinesthetic percepts are, I agree with that part of Klopfer's statement in which he says that the seeing of fear arousing facial expressions very often indicates the subject's fear and anxiety. The psychological mechanism involved, however, is a kind of autistic perception different from that involved in projection. It is not seeing the environment in one's own image, but seeing that in the environment which one expects—fears or hopes—to see. Facial expressions recurrently seen or seen in an original way seem to be indicative of the attitude which the subject expects other people to have toward him. This hypothesis is in agreement with Murray's experimental findings that fear makes people attribute maliciousness to faces in photographs.[45]

## M and the Capacity for Creative Experience

The peculiar aliveness which distinguishes the true work of art from other products of human skill and endeavor, and the relation which exists between the artist creator and his creation are the subject of three stories, one a Greek myth, one an ancient Chinese fable, and one a modern fable. In the Greek myth, Pygmalion, the artist, having hewn the image of a woman out of stone, falls in love with her and moves Aphrodite to give life to her. In the Chinese fable Wu Tao-Tse, one of the illustrious painters of landscapes which have no counterpart in the painting of any other nation, having reached old age paints for the last time "mountain and water" which is the Chinese word for landscape.

---

[44] Klopfer and Kelley, *op. cit.*, pp. 116–117, 280–281.

[45] H. A. Murray, "The Effect of Fear upon Estimates of the Maliciousness of Other Personalities," *Journal of Social Psychology*, 4 (1933), 310–329.

He mounts his donkey, rides into the mountains of his painting, and is never seen again. The modern fable is told in Jean Cocteau's motion picture *Le sang du poète*. The hero is shown drawing a human face. The mouth in the face starts to speak. He wants to silence the voice of his creation and puts his hand over the mouth. But now a replica of the mouth appears on the palm of his hand and tells him to go through a mirror on the wall. He follows the command and finds himself in a long, dark hallway where, peering through the keyholes of the rooms on this corridor, he sees a series of scenes which seem to represent terrifying and significant events in his past life, his childhood and adolescence.

What the three stories have in common is that the artist has given life, real existence to his work: Pygmalion has achieved this through his prayer; the Chinese painter can ride into his own painting where he will continue to be till the end of time; and the young draftsman finds himself compelled by the voice of his own work to delve into the dark corridor of his past. This last story, told with modern sophistication and explicitness, expresses not only the life-instilling quality of the creative process but also points to the dark well of the personal past, of the subconscious into which, as E. M. Forster says, man, in the creative state, lets down a bucket and "draws up something which is normally beyond his reach. He mixes this thing with his normal experiences and out of the mixture he makes a work of art." [46] Cocteau's story, then, tells us that it is not only life in the abstract which the artist gives to his creation, but life itself—a voice that leads to and comes from his own past and is part of his own life. The story has its application to the theory of the kinesthetic response. The life, the movement with which the perceiver animates the percept is his own life, his own movement. Therefore it is possible, as has been shown, to see something about the significant, personal attitudes of the perceiver from the kind of movement with which he endows the percept.

When one disregards specific attitudes and pays attention only to the general process of enlivening the percept by looking at it, not detachedly, but by putting oneself inside of it in imagination, by feeling from inside (*erfuehlen*) how it moves and lives, then one is concerned with those general qualities of the movement responses which make them representative of what Rorschach called the capacity for inner creation

---

46 E. M. Forster, "The *Raison d'Etre* of Criticism in the Arts," in *Music and Criticism*, edited by Richard F. French (Cambridge: Harvard University Press, 1948), pp. 9–34.

and what I believe to be a factor in man's capacity for creative experience. The faculties operative in this way of perceiving things are part of man's equipment for relating himself to the world around him and understanding it. They are not peculiar or restricted to the artist. They have to do with a particular type of relatedness to the world rather than with any specific gift or talent. While these faculties tell us something about how the person experiences the world around him or is capable of experiencing it, they do not tell us whether he is equipped to communicate his experience to others through the medium of special skills and talents such as painting or writing. They refer to a creative factor in the act of experiencing, to that factor by which man puts something of himself, projects himself into his experience, brings his own life in touch with the life around him. They do not refer to what is more usually understood as the creative personality—namely, the person who creates some work of art or poetry or fiction. This is one of the reasons why statistical research as to the frequency of M responses is not likely to show any significant difference between artists and other people who do not have the gift of communicating their experience in a permanent form to others.[47]

While Rorschach felt that the capacity of inner creation, represented by the M responses, is identical in its highest development with artistic inspiration, religious experience, and so on, in his discussion of imagination he comes closer to the meaning of the M factor as it is described here—namely, as a creative factor in experience rather than in production, in the type of relatedness in the act of experience rather than in the act of producing a work of art.[48] In defining his concept of imagina-

[47] Another reason has been well stated by Roe in her work on painting and personality when she says that, perhaps, "a creative personality is not a prerequisite to success as an artist in our society" [Anne Roe, "Painting and Personality," *Rorschach Research Exchange* 10 (1946), 86–100]. If one reads the list of the winners of the Nobel prize in literature for the last 30 years most of whose names are forgotten today, he wonders whether the kind of success represented by this and similar signs of public recognition does not express the astonishingly sure instinct of the public for that which is conventional, hence easily digested, or fashionable rather than for that which is creative, hence demands some effort. Many people are so pleased when they feel they understand a piece of music or a painting that the praise which they accord to its author expresses this pleasure with themselves rather than a tribute to the artist. Since they are the more pleased the easier they understand, their applause is really intended for that with which they are already thoroughly familiar, not for that which may open a new experience or a new insight to them.

[48] While the factor represented by M is by no means identical with what E. Fromm calls the productive orientation but is only *one* of several factors in the

tion he says that while usually only people with creative imagination are described as imaginative, the question of "whether the imagination creates in a receptive or in a productive way is of secondary importance" and that "many subjects who believe that they have no imagination of their own, yet admit that they greatly enjoy the imaginative productions of others, who—in other words—have only a *receptively creating* [italics mine] imagination react in the test in such a way that it is either impossible or difficult to distinguish them from those with productive imagination." [49]

In Rorschach's distinction between productive and reproductive intelligence, too, the concept of productivity does not refer to the capacity to produce something in the sense of artistic, scientific, inventive, or other productions, but only to an "inner creation" in the sense that productive intelligence enables the person to understand and experience something in *his own way*, to assimilate it to his own life rather than to learn and reproduce a cliché. That the creativity represented by the M factor refers to a particular way of experiencing, and relating oneself to, others, himself, the world, and the problems that he wants to understand and solve, and not to any particular talent or skill needed for artistic or other creation, is shown also by the fact that under hypnosis the number of M responses can be increased by the suggestion to live more within oneself, in one's own world of thought and phantasy, to rely on one's own imagination and intelligence,[50] while no hypnotic suggestion will endow the subject with gifts or talents that he does not have in the state of waking.[51] In an abbreviated way, one might say that the M responses refer to the capacity for *creative experience*, not to the capacity for *creative production*. Creative experience is a prerequisite

---

productive type of relatedness, Fromm's concept of productivity has that in common with the meaning of the M factor that it, too, does not refer to the act of producing something as much as to a way of relating oneself to the world.

[49] Rorschach, *Psychodiagnostics*, p. 102. The above is my translation of Rorschach's original text; the English edition of *Psychodiagnostics* omits or changes several nuances of the German text which are relevant to the point discussed here.

[50] See the interesting experiment reported by Lane in which the number of M responses was increased from 3 in a waking state to 13 in a record taken in deep hypnotic trance in which the suggestions mentioned above had been given to the subject. Barbara M. Lane, "A Validation Test of the Rorschach Movement Interpretations," *American Journal of Orthopsychiatry* 18 (1948), 292–296.

[51] It is possible that the realization and employment of gifts may be inhibited in a subject and that hypnotic suggestion can temporarily remove these inhibitions so that the appearance may be created as if the subject had acquired a talent by hypnotic suggestion.

for creative production, but it is not the same. If creative experience takes place in a person's encounter with a work of art, he is, to quote E. M. Forster again, "rapt into a region near to where the artist worked," the beholder or listener undergoes "a change analogous to creation," but he does not become a creator.[52]

The M responses represent a factor essential for creative experience; they do not represent all that is necessary for creative experience. In order to make an experience creative, it is necessary that the person is not merely a mirror reflecting whatever image is thrown onto it, but that his own life, his own attitudes, his own experiences meet and merge with the object of his experience. Only thus is something new created—namely, *his* experience of the object. If the subjective element, the aliveness of the perceiver's own attitude is missing, then there will be a cliché or a vacuum instead of an experience. If the objective element, the essential qualities of the object perceived, is overshadowed or distorted by the preoccupation of the subject with himself, then there will be autistic distortion instead of real experience. Creative experience presupposes openness and sensitivity toward the world around one as well as the capacity to bring to bear one's own aliveness and attitudes, one's own life perspective, on that which one is open to perceive. As I have formulated it elsewhere: "The desirable relation of the person to the world is a twofold one. He must be receptive for the impressions of his environment, not merely in the role of the detached observer, but sensitive to the persons and things around him, able to be affected and impressed by them. His self must not merely reflect an ever changing environment to which he adapts and reacts, but it must also be a center in itself which is capable of its own expression and realization and thus affects the world around him." [53] The capacity to project one's own life on the object perceived and thus to have empathic experience of the object represents that side of man's relation to the world which contributes something of his individual personality to the complex act of experience.

This capacity to project one's own attitude into the act of experience and thus not merely to remain re-acting but also to contribute to that which one perceives, probably is represented in Rorschach's test by the M more than by the Mt. Hardly any concrete data are available as yet on this question and no satisfactory, explanatory concepts. It is an area

---

[52] Forster, *op. cit.*

[53] E. Schachtel, "On Color and Affect," *Psychiatry*, 6 (1943), 393–409, p. 409.

in which it is possible to raise questions, but not to formulate more than tentative hypotheses to answer them. I want to suggest as such a hypothesis that only those attitudes are available to the subject to use creatively in his experience which are entirely or partly accessible to awareness, in other words the attitudes with which, in his kinesthetic percepts, he is able to identify actively. By and large, as has been shown, these are more likely to be the human and humanlike movements than the others, the M rather than the Mt. In Lane's experiment the hypnotic suggestion inducing a "creative" attitude led to a very strong increase of the number of M, not of FM (animal movements).[54] She used only one subject in her experiment; yet this result underlines the relevance of the question even if it does not answer it.

On theoretical grounds, too, one might expect that those movements and attitudes with which the subject is capable of identifying actively are more likely to be indicative of his capacity for creative, empathic experience than those with which he cannot identify, due to repression, dissociation, and so on. Since the M responses, with the exception of those in which counter-identification with the movement seen occurs, are more likely to represent the attitudes with which the subject identifies or is capable of identifying actively than the Mt, the M responses are also more likely to represent the creative factor in the capacity for experience than the Mt. Intensive rapport which, according to Rorschach, is characteristic of the M type—while extensive rapport is characteristic of the C (extroversive) type—is a concept which is helpful in throwing light on this problem. The projecting and at the same time identifying and empathic process which is characteristic of the M responses (excepting the counter-identification M) is also the most important factor in intensive rapport, be it with a person, a landscape, a piece of music, architecture, a tree, a word, a poem, the movement or posture of an animal, and so on. This active projection of one's own, felt attitude into the understanding (or misunderstanding), the experiencing of a person or object of the environment obviously is possible only with regard to those attitudes which are accessible to the subject, with which he can identify himself. An attitude which is tabu, which is "not-me," which is dissociated, one cannot actively identify with. The state of intensive rapport with another person can be described as feeling inside of oneself as one believes the other person to feel. To avoid mis-

---

[54] Lane, *op. cit.*

understanding I want to emphasize again that this subjective feeling of empathy or identification in intensive rapport is not identical with actual, empathic or other, knowledge of how the other person feels. Misunderstanding of the other person may well go along with the conviction that one knows and feels inside of oneself what is going on in the other person. Whether empathy in intensive rapport distorts or conveys the other person's feeling to the subject depends on his openness, sensitivity, receptiveness toward the other person or, in terms of Rorschach categories, on his color and shading reaction and on his F+%. It also depends on the range and variety of attitudes and feelings which one is capable of identifying oneself with and toward which, consequently, one can have intensive empathy. This is the reason why a variety of different types of movements seen in M responses can be, as Piotrowski observes,[55] an asset in the intuitive understanding of other people. The M responses as such are merely indicative of the capacity to project, rightly or wrongly, the alive quality of one's own inner attitude into the act of experiencing the other person; the types of M responses will indicate something about the range of attitudes toward which the subject is capable of having empathy. Thus a person with a considerable number of passive, resigned, bent-down M responses will be capable of intensive rapport, but is likely either to be limited in this rapport to people of the same type or to attribute these qualities to, and experience them in, people who do not have them or of whom they are not particularly characteristic.

The attitudes and feelings toward which one is not capable of active identification because one has dissociated them or because they seem outside of one's reach—in other words the attitudes that are more frequently represented by the Mt than by the M—are unlikely to be available for projection in the act of creative experience. Toward those that are repressed the subject is blind, he does not know and experience them in himself. While his experience of the world is affected by them nevertheless, he is unable to feel them inside of himself, hence also unable to have conscious, empathic experience of them in others, because it is essential to such experience that one feels the attitude seen in the other person in oneself, that one is capable of reproducing the attitude in oneself. This does not mean that one does not attribute dissociated attitudes to others. One is very likely to do that. It merely means

---

[55] Piotrowski, *op. cit.*, p. 36.

that such attribution will not have the quality of empathic, identifying experience. The seeing of a dissociated attitude in others hence lacks an essential quality of creative experience, the quality of inner relatedness, of recognizing in others that which one knows in himself. This is the reason also why paranoid projections do not have the quality of empathic identification. In paranoid projection the subject does not identify with the hostility attributed to the other person, because he is blind toward the hostility in himself. He does not recognize the other person as related to himself by empathic identification as one does in any act of creative experience. Since his own hostile attitude is dissociated, it is an attitude not available for active identification and empathy with the hostility attributed to the other person. The paranoid projection is characterized by counter-identification, by experiencing the quality attributed to the other person as alien to oneself, not by empathic identification.

The capacity for kinesthetic perception and imagery is not restricted to those who give kinesthetic responses in Rorschach's test, but is part of everybody's equipment. Man would be unable to see things the way he does, without kinesthetic perception. Zenon, in the famous Eleatic paradoxon of the flying arrow, has first called attention to that. If one thinks of the arrow, he can think of it only as being at a definite point at any given moment. How then is it possible, asks Zenon, that the arrow is flying? The answer to the problem probably lies in the fact that only because man experiences movement in himself, due to his aliveness, can he perceive movement. If he could do nothing but think about the arrow, he probably would be unable to arrive at the concept of continuous movement. In the work of Melchior Palagyi, Ludwig Klages, G. Revesz, Erwin Straus, and others the inseparable connection between human perception and movement has been demonstrated.

Rorschach mentions that giving no M responses is only a relative measure of the capacity for kinesthetic perception, since the seeing of movement purposely has been made somewhat difficult in his inkblots. Most people who do not give M responses in Rorschach's test see human movement in the Levy Movement Blots in which kinesthetic perception has been facilitated by the design of the blots and by the task given to the subject in which he is asked to say what the figures on the blots are doing.[56]

---

[56] The Levy Movement Blots have been developed for experimental and clinical purposes by David Levy and have not yet been published.

Thus the absence of M does not mean that the person without M lacks the capacity for empathic projection and for creative experience. The absence of M in depressed people is easily understandable, because in the state of depression one is temporarily cut off from the capacity for creative experience since one is both not open toward the stimuli around one (absence of color responses) and incapable of projecting oneself in empathic understanding of the environment. The absence of M in those coartated records which are characteristic of the rigidly defensive and repressing personality does not mean that these people are not potentially capable of both openness toward the world and intensive, creative rapport. Their rigidity is a safety device which may lead to the kind of muscular armature that blocks even the slight, involuntary motor innervations which are necessary for empathic, kinesthetic experience.[57] Not sufficiently developed differentiation of the capacity for experience may be another reason for the absence of M. The question whether such lack of differentiation may not have some relation to the educational background and socioeconomic status of the person has not even been raised by the literature. Yet comparative Rorschach data from low-income groups and from educated middle-class groups are suggestive of such a possibility. This would be consistent with the assumption that the absence of M responses says something about the apparatus for experience that is actually available to the person at the period of his life when the test was given, but does not say whether the limitations and the lack of differentiation of this apparatus are constitutionally inherent characteristics of the person and how the potentialities of the person might have developed under different conditions.

The absence of M responses in the records of *very young children* poses a different kind of problem. The fully matured and highly differentiated adult mind is capable, up to a certain extent, of voluntarily assuming different attitudes in his perception and experience of the environment. He can be at one moment the detached observer; the next moment he can open himself receptively to all the impressions from the environment and the feelings and pleasures aroused by them; and in the next he can project himself in empathic experience of some object

---

[57] This constitutes merely one of several mechanisms which can lead to the absence of M responses in defensive coartation. Others are the obsessionally exaggerated demand for exactness, the tendency toward a too narrow and too literal subjective definition of the Rorschach task, and so on.

of the environment. In looking at a tree, for example, he can in one moment be the detached botanist who observes, compares, classifies what he sees; in the next moment he may surrender to the color of the foliage and bark, the sound of leaves rustling in the breeze, their fresh scent after a shower of rain; and in the next moment he may try to feel, inside of himself, kinesthetically, how slight or solid the trunk stands and rises up, how calmly the branches spread, or how gracefully they move and yield to the wind. He can combine these different ways of experiencing the quality of the tree or he can separate them and concentrate on one or the other. This differentiation and specialization of attitudes and capacities in experience is a quite late development. The young child is neither capable of detached observation nor of voluntary maintenance of, and concentration on, one or the other of the described attitudes. Also, the sense of the self, of his being an entity separate from the environment is developed only gradually by the child. He lives much more directly with and in the objects of his environment as they affect his needs, wishes, and fears than the adult does.[58] The capacity for kinesthetic perception and the type of relatedness represented by it is not missing in later childhood, but it is gradually developing into a distinct and separate mode of experiencing things. That in young children's Rorschach tests kinesthetic perception tends to appear with regard to animals before it appears with regard to people probably has to do with the attitude of small children to animals (and also to objects, toys). The animal means something different to the young child than to the adult. The whole view of the world is much more animistic in the child. Most children have had significant emotional experiences with toys or real animals. The animal, as a rule, is a more important denizen of the child's than of the adult's world and the child identifies more with the animal and does not make as sharp a distinction between animal and man as most adults do. Because of these differences between especially early childhood and adulthood, the meaning of the Rorschach scores is somewhat different for children than it is for adults, and this holds true for location and content as well as for the determinants.[59]

The analysis of the processes in kinesthetic perception of the Ror-

---

[58] For a more detailed description of the tremendous change in the mode of experiencing the environment that takes place during infancy and childhood, see also Schachtel, *Metamorphosis*, pp. 279–322 and *passim*.

[59] It is probable that dynamic form perception precedes, and takes the place of, kinesthetic perception in the Rorschach reactions of young children.

schach inkblots has led to the following conclusions and hypotheses, some of general psychological significance, some of particular interest to the Rorschach diagnostician and research worker.

## General Theses

1. Just as there is a tendency in man to view the world in an *anthropomorphic* way, in his own image, so there is a tendency in the individual person to view others and the environment in an *automorphic* way, in his own likeness.

2. The main psychological mechanism in the automorphic view of the environment is the mechanism of *projection*. Projection is defined as that psychic mechanism by which one attributes qualities, feelings, attitudes, and strivings of his own to objects of the environment (people, other organisms, things).

3. While the *process* of projection usually takes place outside of awareness, the *content* of the projection may or may not be known to the person as part of himself. In this respect the concept of projection developed here is wider than Freud's who assumed that the content of the projection always is repressed and that the function of projection is to enable the person to deal with an outer danger when it becomes too difficult to deal with an inner danger which therefore has to be repressed and projected.

4. Projection can serve constructive as well as defensive purposes, can be a normal as well as a pathological process.

5. Projection becomes distorting to the extent to which (a) it has a defensive function (projection in Freud's sense), (b) tangential, partial or otherwise superficial data from the object are invested with meanings from the subject's own life which do not correspond to the real or total picture of the object, (c) qualities are ascribed to the object the presence of which the subject denies and is unaware of in himself (projection in Freud's sense).

6. Projection plays a role in every act of *empathic understanding* since the subject cannot have an inner understanding of another person's feeling except in terms of his own experience of that or a similar feeling. In empathic understanding the projection of the subject's own feeling merges inseparably with the perception of the other person's feeling.

7. Such projection need not be distorting since men are basically similar and akin to each other and so are their experiences.

8. Empathic projection presupposes that the subject is aware that the

feeling or attitude which he perceives in the other person is part of his *own* life and his own experience. In the act of empathic understanding the feeling or attitude perceived is activated in the perceiver. A relation of kinship is established by the projection of the subject's feeling on the object. In contrast to this, in paranoid projection, the object is perceived as alien because the subject denies and even abhors the idea that the quality or feeling projected could be part of himself.

9. Empathic projection can help or hinder the understanding of the object, depending on the degree of congruence or discongruence of the subject's and the object's feeling.

*Rorschach Theses*

1. In the processes underlying the kinesthetic responses, the projection of checked motor impulses, of which the subject may or may not be aware, onto the inkblot plays a significant role (in addition to form perception).

2. This particular kind of projection is characterized by the facts that (a) the feeling projected is a kinesthetic sensation and (b) in contrast to kinesthetic perception of an actually moving object the movement is *entirely* projected onto the static inkblot. In other words, the share of the mechanism of projection in the perception is greater in the kinesthetic response than in kinesthetic perception of an actually moving object.

3. The attitude typical of kinesthetic perception of the Rorschach inkblots is not that of a detached, outside observer but one in which the subject experiences in himself the movement perceived in the inkblot. The degree of awareness of this experience varies. When there is marked awareness of the kinesthetic experience, the subject has the feeling that he knows from inside how the object perceived moves (kinesthetic empathy).

4. Since kinesthetic sensations are the only way in which man has direct, inner, physical experience of himself and his characteristic movements, postures, and tensions, they are deeply and intimately connected with the central layers of the personality.

5. In kinesthetic perception the subject, stimulated by the perception of the object, projects *his* sensation of movement or posture onto the object, thereby establishing a type of relatedness in which he may feel inside of himself the movement or posture seen in the object.

6. Because of this mechanism of projection in kinesthetic perception

the subject is likely to project and perceive such movements and postures as he himself is inclined to perform. This inclination is embodied
in neuromuscular "sets" which may be described as a lingering, habitual
readiness to perform certain movements or adopt certain postures. Usually the actual performance of these movements is inhibited and the
subject is unaware of his neuromuscular set. The latter is a physical
aspect of the subject's basic attitudes. In kinesthetic perception this set
is activated and leads via projection to kinesthetic imagery in which the
subject may become aware of acute innervations toward the performance of the movement which, however, usually is not carried out.

7. Kinesthetic percepts, due to the described processes leading to
them, often express basic attitudes of the subject. Not only active, passive, and indecisive attitudes, but *any* attitude may be expressed in kinesthetic percepts.

8. Extensor movements do not always express active, nor flexor
movements passive attitudes. The specific, concrete quality of the
movement perceived often is more significant for the interpretation of
the attitude expressed by the movement than such general qualities as
extensor or flexor.

9. Not all kinesthetic responses express personally significant, basic
attitudes. Some are culturally determined stereotypes, others may express attitudes toward which the subject is capable of empathy and
which may play a minor role in his life but are not basic in his character
structure. The main criteria for selecting the responses expressing personally significant, basic attitudes are (a) the recurrence of the same or
a similar movement in several kinesthetic percepts, (b) the originality
or deviation from the culturally determined pattern of the commonly
given movement responses, and (c) the total setting of the record in
which the kinesthetic responses occur.

10. Dynamic (symbolic) form and kinesthetic responses are usually
accompanied by covert self-references of which the subject may or may
not be aware and which the observer often can discover by a careful
analysis of the response in its relation to the total record. Identification
(actual or potential) and counter-identification with the movement
seen, active or passive (imaginary) participation in it, positive, negative or neutral attitudes to it are the main types of such self-reference.
They occur in various combinations and gradations. From them it is
possible to draw conclusions regarding the degree of awareness or repression of the subject with regard to his basic attitudes and regarding

the type of relation between his self-image and the event or activity expressed by the movement.

11. The types of covert self-reference in kinesthetic responses throw light on the attempts to differentiate movement responses according to the type of object seen as moving (M, FM, m). They are more basic than, and cut across these distinctions.

12. The perception of facial expressions probably is not a kinesthetic response nor is it based on projection. It probably comes about by man's tendency to perceive that which he expects (hopes or fears) to see.

13. The M responses do not represent the capacity for creative production; they represent one factor in the capacity for creative experience. This factor is the capacity for *empathic projection.*

14. Most Mt (nonhumanlike movement) responses do not seem to represent this factor. The reason for this probably is that man is capable of empathic projection only with regard to such attitudes which he can recognize as part of himself and with which he can actively identify. The Mt responses often do not refer to such attitudes, but many M responses do.

15. The absence of M responses does not necessarily indicate the lack of capacity for creative experience.

# 10 / NOTES ON SHADING

On the original inkblot cards made by Rorschach the dark areas were a uniform gray or black. It was only in the printed cards that, due to the poor work of the printer, differences in shading and the more or less vague forms to be glimpsed in these nuances appeared. When Rorschach saw the proofs of the printed cards, in June 1921, he soon realized the possibilities this new feature offered.[1] In the first edition of his book shading is not mentioned, but in his paper on the test of Oberholzer's patient, early in 1922, a few weeks before his death, Rorschach had already formed some impressions about the significance of the shading responses. In this paper, which has been added as Chapter VII to the later editions of his book, he says that the shading responses "have something to do with the capacity for affective adaptability, but an anxious, cautious, unfree type of affective adaptation, a self-control in the presence of others and particularly a tendency toward a basic depressive mood and the attempt to control this in the presence of others." A little later he speaks of the "cautiously adapted and consciously controlled affectivity" indicated by the shading responses.[2]

Since Rorschach's few remarks, the literature on his test has distinguished a greater variety of shading responses than of any other determinant. Both their scoring and the meanings attributed to them vary considerably.[3] In contrast to the variety of scores and of the meanings

---

[1] Ellenberger, *op. cit.*, p. 206.

[2] Rorschach, *op. cit.*, pp. 195 and 200; translation somewhat changed in order to render more accurately the original text.

[3] See the comparative tabulation of the various shading scores in Maria Rickers-Ovsiankina (ed.), *op. cit.*, pp. 452–461. For our purposes it is not necessary to

assigned them by various authors is the paucity of attempts to validate these meanings empirically or to develop a rationale that attempts to explain why they might have these meanings.

The main exception to this is to be found in the work of Binder.[4] He distinguishes two types of shading responses: one in which a diffuse, total impression of shading as *darkness* leads to a *dysphoric* response (scored by him as Hd—*Helldunkel*—and F Hd or Hd F, where it is combined with form as a determinant); the other where two or more different, discrete nuances of shading are used to build up the impression on which the response is based; according to him, these occur only with form as the predominating determinant; hence he scores them F(Fb). He develops a rationale for the meaning of these two types of shading responses based on his distinction of central feeling tones or moods and peripheral, reactive, discrete feelings.[5] He considers the former related to the Hd, the latter related to the F(Fb) responses. We shall return to his rationale for the Hd responses later, when we consider those responses which show a reaction to darkness. A less elaborated, detailed and explicit, more aphoristic rationale than Binder's and one that is intended to apply to all shading responses is contained in a brief statement by Klopfer, who has developed the greatest number of different scores for shading responses. He believes that the shading response shows how the person deals with his need for *affection;* that shading creates in the testee some kind of "contact sensation" which evokes the need for basic emotional security (to be held, to belong), and that the different types of shading responses represent different ways of handling this need.[6] While I believe that an imagined contact sensation plays a role in some texture responses, I do not believe that it applies to all shading responses, nor do I share Klopfer's view that all shading responses are directly related to the need for

---

consider all of these different scores. I use the score Ch for all responses to over-all shading, that is to say, for the responses to over-all darkness (Binder's Hd) as well as those to diffuse shading. They usually are given to the whole blot or to a large area of the blot. For the responses given to two or more discrete nuances of shading I use the score (C). Ch as well as (C) occur pure or in combination with other determinants, especially form. For their combinations with form I use, analogous to Rorschach's differentiation of color responses, the scores FCh, ChF and F(C)—identical with Binder's F(Fb)—and (C)F.

[4] Binder, *op. cit.* A brief English synopsis of his book by Ewald Bohm is available in Rickers-Ovsiankina (ed.), *op. cit.*, pp. 202–222.

[5] *Ibid.*, pp. 203–206.

[6] Klopfer *et al., op. cit.*, I, 580.

affection although, again, this need probably does play a role in some shading responses and often it may have an indirect relation to other shading responses as well as to other determinants.

We still know less about the shading responses than about most others. Hence, I shall have to limit the following discussion to the attempt to describe some perceptual qualities which occur in shading responses and to explore those experiential-perceptual attitudes which are likely to lead to the perception of these qualities or are activated by their perception. As with the other determinants, I believe that an understanding of these attitudes offers a promising approach to our understanding of what the shading responses mean and why they mean it. Before examining various types of shading responses, I want to discuss briefly the role of shading in the perception of the Rorschach blots whether it leads or does not lead to shading responses.

If the shading of the achromatic blots were absent and they consisted only of outlines and perhaps some lines within the outlined areas, their visual impact would be much reduced. The fact that the expanse delineated by the contours of the blots is filled with shading (or with color in some of the cards) creates a much more striking contrast between the white background and the darker figure. We can assume that it is this *contrast* that is most immediately striking for most people when they first glance at a Rorschach card and that draws their attention to the figure.[7] The majority of testees, after this first impact, no longer attend to the white areas of the card, which to them become mostly background; they concentrate on the figure and its qualities, its form and, sometimes, on the quality of its shading.

In the perception of a relatively small area such as the Rorschach blots, most people, of course, notice the achromatic colors, just as they notice the chromatic ones. But to most the over-all shading of the achromatic blots will not be sufficiently impressive to become a determinant or to disturb them. An exception to this are those responses in which shading is seen as over-all *texture*, especially the popular animal-skin, rug, or fur responses to cards IV and VI. The texture responses will be discussed briefly later. Where, aside from the texture responses, the *over-all* shading does become a determinant, this presupposes a particular susceptibility or inclination of the person to be impressed by

---

[7] For the significance of contrast in perception compare above, Chapter 7, especially pp. 151–155, where the role of contrast perception in ontogenetic development is discussed.

it.[8] The perceptual attitude of the person in the Ch responses presupposes this inclination.

Two different perceptual qualities and two correspondingly different perceptual attitudes can be observed in these responses. One is the response to the *darkness* of the shading when it is perceived with a dysphoric mood quality. The other is the response to the *diffusion* of the shadedness. By this I refer to the perception of shading as a film rather than a surface color, combined with a quality of pervasiveness and the absence of clear boundaries and structure within the over-all shaded area. Often these two qualities, darkness and diffusion, are both present and experientially inseparable in a Ch percept, as for example in the response "night" to card IV; but sometimes only one or the other determines the response.

The dysphoric reaction to *darkness* may occur to gray as well as to black or to a mixture of gray and black, seen as over-all shading of the whole blot or a relatively large area of it. It is similar to sensory-affective color responses in that the perceiver is passively impressed by the darkness and experiences it with a certain feeling tone, in this case a dysphoric one. An example of such a response to darkness, as distinguished from diffusion, is the "scarecrow," a W FCh response to card IV, in which the dysphoric feeling tone probably is one of something scary or ominous. Other examples of dysphoric feeling tone experienced in the perception of darkness are sad, mournful, threatening, depressive, barren, just as a chromatic color may look exciting, threatening, gay, warm, cool, fresh, and so forth. But in contrast to most color responses in which a discrete, specific color strikes the perceiver, responses to over-all darkness usually convey a feeling, in varying degrees, as if the testee had been plunged into or enveloped by a darkling mood and, as Binder has shown, point to pervasive (in his terminology "central") dysphoric moods that are readily triggered even by such a small stimulus as the Rorschach blots.

This sounds as though the dysphorically affected perceiver were the passive victim of a dark, depressing world or, in the Rorschach situation, of the darkness of the blot. But often this is not entirely so. We can observe that depressive patients seem to look for those factors in the environment which fit into their depressive mood and sometimes seem almost disappointed when something good happens to them, as if

---

8 This has been pointed out by Binder for those responses which show a dysphoric reaction to darkness, his Hd responses. Binder, *op. cit.*, pp. 64 and 119.

it interfered with a wish to prove how dark everything is. Similarly, those Ch responses that are primarily a reaction to darkness (rather than diffusion) often point to an *assertive* quality. This quality may be described as an assertive (though often only implicit) complaint, a calling attention to how black, unpleasant, depressing everything is, an insistence on the dysphoric qualities all around. The people who show this behavior not only attend selectively to whatever in the environment seems to them syntonic with their depressive mood (as, for instance, the gray-black in the Rorschach blots), but they also want to let others know about it and, directly or indirectly, call their attention to their black mood and to the "blackness" of the environment. It is as if they were saying: "There you are: another of these dreadful, depressing blots." Typically, this does not happen in severe depressions, where Ch responses rarely occur and where a lifeless, laborious quality prevails in which every effort is too much and its result is expected to be inadequate. Rather it appears in milder depressions where the reproach and anger which play such an important role in the general dynamics of depression are manifest even though not always acknowledged by the patient. Rorschach wrote that responses determined by black and by white as color values are found in epileptics and "in normal people who suffer from *half wanted, half unwanted* . . . depressive moods.[9] "Half wanting" the depression expresses well the assertive function of the depressive mood, namely, the assertion of its angry and reproachful quality.[10]

The reaction to over-all shading as *diffusion* is different from that to shading as darkness; it is a different perceptual experience which takes place in a different perceptual attitude; it may or may not occur together with the experience of darkness. Diffuse shading, as mentioned earlier, is perceived as film color rather than as surface color. The blot is no longer seen as a solid object but as diffuse matter which offers no

[9] In E. Schneider, "Eine diagnostische Untersuchung Rorschachs auf Grund der Helldunkeldeutungen ergänzt," *Zeitschrift für die gesamte Neurologie und Psychiatrie*, 159 (1937), 1–10; italics mine. In my experience, this is true of the response to over-all darkness or blackness but of responses to whiteness only where white is seen as coldness (e.g., in some snow or ice responses) or otherwise in a dysphoric way.

[10] Compare also Piotrowski, who differentiates two groups of shading responses: the dark or black and the light or nondark shading responses. He stresses the assertive meaning of the dark shading responses and believes that the people who give them deal with anxiety by overt motor activity, are doers such as antisocial psychopaths, adolescents, pioneers, leaders, etc. Zygmunt A. Piotrowski, *Perceptanalysis* (New York: Macmillan, 1957), pp. 262–263.

hold; it seems to dissolve and to have no internal stability or solidity. Sometimes this goes together with a lack of definite contour—as, for example, in such responses as fog, smoke, steam—or else with a contour that lacks firmness and can change any moment, as sometimes in the response "clouds." Not only the contour, but also the surface is dissolved. In all the examples quoted there is no definite surface, at best a nebulous one. When over-all shading is perceived as water, as it sometimes is in cards, I, IV, or VI (also sometimes in the blue area of card VIII, where color and diffuse shading may combine as determinants of the "water" response), the water usually is not felt to have a definite surface or boundary, or else it is one that undergoes constant change, like the sea.

To experience in the small area of a Rorschach blot this perceptual quality of lack of stability, firmness, definiteness, of lack of hold presupposes a susceptibility to such experiences, just as does the dysphoric reaction to darkness. This susceptibility exists in conditions of more or less conscious, overt, diffuse *anxiety*. The subjective experience of anxiety is characterized by a lack of hold, by mild or severe disintegration or disruption of the secure and taken-for-granted hold on one's place in relation to the environment, especially to other people. It is also characterized by similar feelings about oneself: as though the hold in oneself gave way to a lack of direction, an *absence* of any hold or direction. To speak of feelings *about* oneself when trying to describe the experience of overt anxiety is somewhat misleading because the loss of objects and the loss of self in anxiety tend to prevent any *"feeling about"*; the more severe the anxiety state, the more objectless and subjectless it becomes. Instead, it causes a feeling of nothingness, of nothing to hold onto, whether in oneself or in the environment.[11] The person prone to or actually experiencing diffuse anxiety (as contrasted to fear), because of the described experiential nature of anxiety, seems to be particularly susceptible to perceiving shading as diffusion, to be vulnerable to its objectless, nebulous, vague quality so similar to what he feels in himself when anxious. And, depending on the degree of anxiety and on the

---

[11] This phenomenological description of anxiety holds true regardless what theory of anxiety one may believe in. It is essentially in agreement with Kierkegaard's and Heidegger's view that anxiety, in contrast to fear, deals with nothingness, and with Goldstein's concept of anxiety as the catastrophic situation which he describes as a "breaking down or dissolution of the world and a shattering of (the) own self." Kurt Goldstein, *op. cit.*, p. 295. Compare also May, who gives a detailed survey of the various concepts and theories of anxiety in which "the distinction between subject and object breaks down"; Rollo May, *The Meaning of Anxiety* (New York: The Ronald Press Co., 1950), p. 193 and *passim*.

defenses available to him against it, he may feel more or less helpless and unable to take hold of and structure what he sees in such diffuse shading. It will be recalled that anxiety tends to interfere with the capacity to give well-perceived form responses. The stronger the anxiety, the more likely the occurrence of pure Ch or Ch F responses of the diffusion type, or of FCh in which the form is vague or poorly seen.

Rapaport considers cards IV, VI, and VII—which, due to their prominent shading, tend to stimulate more shading responses than the other cards—grossly articulated. He assumes that it is "not the shading and the anxiety, but the gross articulation and the articulation difficulty which are at work" and have the effect that "anxious people fail on these cards more readily than do non-anxious." [12] I believe that both a specific readiness to perceive shading in the way just described and the general impairment of perceptual hold in overt anxiety account for the Ch, ChF, and FCh responses of the anxious. The Ch of the anxious do not have the insistent, quasi-assertive, directly, or veiled reproachful quality of the depressive Ch, nor do they show the veiled and usually denied satisfaction which mildly depressed people often experience when they feel that they can point to reality factors as responsible for their suffering and which they also sometimes show, more or less explicitly, when they can point to the bleak, dark, dull, or otherwise dysphoric quality they perceive in and ascribe to the shaded Rorschach cards. Rather, diffuse, overt anxiety seems to make people particularly susceptible to the perception of things nebulous, foggy, diffuse; it decreases and impairs their capacity and energy for active grasp and structuring; this in turn makes them prone to feelings and percepts in which vagueness and a lack of firm anchorage and firm grasp are conspicuous.

The meaning of the diffusion Ch and the rationale of this meaning, as discussed here, bear a close relation to a remark which Rorschach made about the emphasis on *perspective* and *depth* in shading responses. He writes that "a special talent for the perception of the spatial, of depth and distance seems to correlate . . . often, perhaps always, with certain feelings of insufficiency the content of which is a sensation of lack of hold, instability, going out of joint" (*Aus-den-Fugen-Gehen*).[13] What Rorschach describes here is the experience of anxiety and insecurity, so often linked with feelings of insufficiency, which, in my opinion, corre-

---

[12] Rapaport, *op. cit.*, pp. 284–285.

[13] Rorschach, *op. cit.*, p. 201. Translation changed to correspond more closely to the original text, in which there is no reference to "being out of joint with the times," as the English edition has it.

lates with the perception of diffusion in the Ch type of shading. Actually, the responses to which he refers seem to combine perspective with the perception of darkness and diffusion. They are: (1) "a wide parkway, lined by beautiful, dark trees, which ascends and is lost in the distance, in a parapet," seen in card II, the trees in the large, dark D, the parkway in the white space between the dark D; (2) "again like a parkway, the dark trees, and in the middle the path which leads far, far away," seen in X, the trees in the dark inner part of the top central gray figures, the path in the white space (and possibly the center of the top gray?). The percept of leading far, far away seems related to the one in the response to card II of the way that is "lost in the distance." It is worth mentioning that this theme recurs in another shading response in this record, given to IV, W: "A column of smoke which shoots up powerfully in the middle, then divides and only up there, inside loses itself" (*verliert sich*).[14] Although the dark shaded areas in the responses to II and X are seen as the trees lining the parkway, they are not seen as concrete, individually perceptible trees but as a mass of trees, as their diffuse darkness, as one might see a distant forest where the form of the trees is lost and only their dark mass is perceptible. It is interesting that in these particular responses the perspective is one of far distance where the way is "lost in the distance." This seems to go together with the feeling of a loss of reliable hold characteristic of the diffusion Ch. I doubt that all responses in which perspective plays a role can be interpreted as indicators of anxiety. One might say that the inkblots are felt to be most simple and solid when seen as clearly outlined two-dimensional figures and that they lose some of that simplicity when a third dimension is added. However, I do not think that the mere fact of seeing something as three-dimensional points to anxiety; examples would be the perception of a rounded cheek in the face or head seen in the top third of card VII, or the apple sometimes seen in the two outer D of the bottom pink area of card IX. Nor do I believe that a perspective, clearly and palpably perceived, indicates the presence of diffuse anxiety of the kind that Rorschach describes as a feeling of "going out of joint." Only where perspective dissolves or "gets lost" in the distance (in some respect similar to the experience of diffusion) it may point to the presence of anxiety.[15]

---

[14] *Ibid.*, pp. 187–189; translation changed slightly to render more accurately some relevant words of the German text.

[15] The record discussed by Rorschach contains two more diffusion Ch responses,

The perceptual attitude in the (C) responses—comprising the F(C), (C)F and (C)—, that is to say, in those responses in which not the over-all shading but *discrete, different nuances of shading are used as* determinants, differs markedly from that leading to Ch responses. This difference does not consist primarily in the role of form as a determinant which, in Binder's usage, is always predominant and to which the (C) show a greater affinity than do the Ch. The difference consists mainly in the detailed attention to the fine nuances of shading. In contrast to the different chromatic colors, the different nuances of shading are not striking. They have to be sought out; they become significant only when attention is focused on them. In that respect they resemble form responses. But they are different from them in that the attention concerns the color values of the achromatic scale, in addition to whatever attention is paid to the form of these differently shaded grays and blacks. The perceiver attends to and often feels into the tonal quality of these different nuances, he responds to them; but he has to seek them out in order to respond to them because, by and large, they form not striking but rather subtle contrast patterns; perceptual sensitivity is required to discover them. The difference between color and F(C) responses may be illustrated by that between paintings and etchings. Whatever else is involved in seeing an oil painting, its colors stand out immediately because of the inherently striking quality of color. They call attention to the painting. Of course this does not preclude the detailed attention to and "tasting" of the finer nuances of color which occurs in a different attitude. An etching cannot be seen without detailed attention, except as a gray or dark mass of shading. But to see what is in the etching, more detailed attention to the nuances of shading and form has to be paid than in order to see what is in a painting. The latter can be taken in at a glance although, of course, it cannot be fully appreciated in this way. The quality of attention and sensitivity to the different nuances of shading required for the perception of F(C) finds its parallel, in another area of behavior, in the attention and sensi-

---

smoke, seen in cards II and VII. Oberholzer's patient, in whose record these responses occur, suffered indeed from the insecurity and anxiety feelings described by Rorschach. Ainsworth's and Klopfer's hypothesis of the meaning of structured perspective in shading responses (scored by them FK) is that they indicate "an attempt by the person to handle his affectional anxiety by introspective efforts, by an attempt to objectify his problem by gaining perspective on it, by putting it at some distance from himself so he can view it more dispassionately." Klopfer *et al.*, *op. cit.*, I, 268. This sounds like a direct translation of visual perspective into gaining distance from anxiety and seems to me without foundation.

tivity to the emotional overtones and undercurrents in the human environment required if it is important to one to sense or know what the attitude of the other person is. The person who is sensitive to the mood and the unspoken emotional undercurrents in the human environment may be said to have antennae or feelers out to pick up the indications of these undercurrents in physiognomic or gestural expressive nuances, in intonations and manner rather than manifest content of speech, and so forth. The underlying perceptual attitude of the person who has his antennae out, as it were, to feel out the hostile, indifferent, or friendly, disapproving or approving, forbidding or accepting, anxious and tense or secure and relaxed quality and other attitudes or moods of the other person or the social environment is similar to that of the person who carefully explores and pays attention to the different nuances of shading: they both pay attention to, try to feel into something that is not apparent to one who listens only to the content of what is being said to him or who looks only at the obvious or striking features of the ink-blots.[16]

Binder differentiates two types of F(C), those that manifest a dysphoric feeling and those that show a pleasurable enjoyment of the finely differentiated shading tones. He restricts Rorschach's interpretation of shading to the former and feels that the latter represent an intimately accommodating, tenderly compliant adaptation.[17] The difference in feeling tone of the various F(C) is obviously as significant as it is in the color responses. However, the basic perceptual attitude in both types of F(C) is the same: the stretching out of feelers in order to explore the nuances. Whether such sensitivity is an asset or becomes also a liability depends on whether it is in the service of appropriate response or leads to the unfree, guarded approach mentioned by Rorschach. The two need not exclude each other. Only careful consideration of the whole record, especially of the feeling tone of the shading responses and of their relation to the color responses, will show whether

---

[16] Genetically, the perception of emotional tone and of tension and anxiety by the infant and young child precedes, of course, the learning of language and the understanding of spoken content. It develops from the perception of the infant's own comfort or discomfort in contact with the mothering one and her moods and tensions. However, at a much later stage of development, the attention to the obvious, visually, and to content, verbally, often overshadows and, in quite a few people, all but extinguishes the capacity for perceiving the finer visual and, more important, the emotional nuances of the environment.

[17] Binder, *op. cit.,* pp. 38–39 (*"intim entgegenkommende, zärtlich-schmiegsame Anpassung"*). See Bohm, *op. cit.,* p. 212.

we deal with sensitivity in the positive sense of the word or whether this is overshadowed by oversensitivity leading to excessive caution. As a crude rule of thumb one might use the quantitative relation of the (C) to the color responses. Where the former are more numerous, we might hypothesize that the F(C) represent excessive dependence on the other person's mood and expectations, resulting either in compliant fitting in or in cautious, anxious, guarded, and unfree adaptation which usually has the function not to expose oneself and not to arouse disapproval or antagonism.

The quality of anxiety in the records with more (C)-type shading than color responses is, I believe, different from the already-described quality of anxiety represented by the diffuse shading perceived in the Ch responses. Numerous F(C) responses point to *anxious tension* rather than to vague, diffuse anxiety. Often the person who suffers from such anxious tension is not aware of it, or he may be aware of tension but it may never have occurred to him that this tension has to do with anxiety regarding his relations to other people and their attitudes to him. Such anxious tension leads to the "anxious, cautious, unfree type of affective adaptation" described by Rorschach as represented by the shading responses. In the shading responses discussed by him, in the record of Oberholzer's patient, both Ch and (C), combined with form, occur as determinants; hence we can assume that the patient suffered from anxious tension as well as from diffuse anxiety and insufficiency feelings.

Binder's and Rorschach's shading responses do not include all of those in which shading is seen as *texture* and which are scored separately by a number of authors, including Beck and Klopfer.[18] Where texture is seen in such a way as to be based on discrete differences between several nuances of shading rather than on an over-all impression, it would correspond to Binder's F(C), as in a response to a detail of card VI quoted by him: "Here the lighter shadings—like a recently, freshly grown coat of fur—there the delicate extensions form a transition to the older parts of the fur skin with here and there some darker, more woolly spots. And in the middle, on the back, a darker stripe has been dyed in—a pity: here (the two light gray spots in the center) it

---

[18] Compare the comparative score tabulation in Rickers-Ovsiankina (ed.), *op. cit.*, pp. 458–461. I score the texture responses, as I do all shading responses, depending on whether they are a response to two or more discrete nuances of shading—F(C), (C)F or (C)—or a response to undifferentiated, diffuse over-all shading—FCh, ChF or Ch.

looks as if the hair had been pulled out," which he classifies as one of the pleasurable F(C).[19] Some other texture responses overlap with his Hd responses, for example the W response to card VI, reversed: "The spread-out legs of an animal skin, in back the tail—all spotted, rather old and worn," which he scores as Hd.[20] But many texture responses do not fit into his classification. Ainsworth and Klopfer suggest that texture responses "as . . . the other shading responses relate to the handling of affectional need and to the basic expectation of affection to be received from the environment." [21] I do not see a sufficient basis for such a generalization regarding texture responses, much less, as already mentioned, regarding all shading responses. But I do believe that some texture responses have to do with the wish for pleasant and comforting skin contact, some others with the fear and discomfort of unpleasant skin contact. However, texture can also be perceived in a detached way, as it often is in the popular animal-skin responses, resembling in this respect the "cognitive" type of surface color responses. It can be perceived as pure surface, as in many responses in which stone, polished wood, iron, etc., are seen. Or it can be seen as fur, wool, etc.— i.e., with a soft surface which "gives" and thereby changes the contact sensation in a significant way. It is among these responses that the need for and/or pleasure in gratifying tactile contact seems to find expression. Similar to a distinction important in the color responses, the difference between pleasurable and unpleasurable contact is significant in the interpretation of the texture responses. There is a difference between the person who sees in the shading a soft, warm fur and the one who sees a slimy snail, usually the difference between pleasure and disgust. There is also a difference between seeing a hard and a soft surface. But the interpretation of this difference is more complex than that of the pleasurable and the disgusting texture. The hard surface may be experienced with positive or negative overtones, as may the soft, although there more usually the pleasurable tone predominates. It would go beyond the scope of this book, however, to discuss in detail all the possible meanings and interpretations of these various kinds of texture responses.

*Disturbances* in performance (marked increase in reaction time, rejection, breaks in sequence, marked decrease in number of responses,

---

[19] Binder, *op. cit.,* pp. 68–69. I would score this (C)F.

[20] *Ibid.,* p. 68.

[21] Klopfer *et al., op. cit.,* pp. 270–271.

verbally expressed negative reactions, poorer form level, etc.) on the heavily shaded cards are not necessarily due to the shading. For example, in card I the disturbance may be orientation shock rather than shading shock, or a combination of both, in card II it may be red shock, in card IV it may have to do with the massiveness of the figure, in card VI with the frequently seen sexual organs. Where the disturbance is due to the shading, it has different meanings, depending on the quality of the shading which disturbed the testee. In my experience the most frequent and pronounced shading shock occurs in card IV and is due to shading perceived as combined darkness and diffusion or combined darkness and massiveness. Where it is due to the perception of darkness and diffusion, it resembles and may derive from the young child's fear of the dark, the night, being alone in a dark room. In the dark the reassuring presence of familiar objects is lost. Hence, children's anxiety and longing for comforting reassurance, as in the child Freud overheard calling out from a dark room: "Do speak to me, Auntie! I'm frightened!" "Why, what good would that do? You can't see me," to which the child replied: "If someone speaks, it gets lighter." [22] Card III is characterized by relatively small, well-articulated, discrete areas of shading and by its impelling and familiar suggestion of two people, a popular response. Card IV, in contrast, has a much larger expanse of dark shading within which there is no clear articulation. Hence it offers for those susceptible to it the strongest stimulus for the perception of darkness and diffusion in which no clearly defined, familiar object appears. Where not diffusion but massiveness combined with darkness becomes the disturbing stimulus of card IV, the blot is usually perceived as a threatening or otherwise foreboding, powerful figure and the shock reaction is likely to derive from the testee's conscious or unconscious fears of such figures which, in turn, may derive from the fear of a powerful, actually or potentially threatening parent of his childhood, either father or mother or a parent-substitute.

---

[22] Freud, *Introductory Lectures on Psychoanalysis* (1916–17) [Standard Edition], XVI, 407. Lorenz goes even further and assumes that the fear of the dark is innate in man. He writes of primitive men: "They were obsessed by the fear of the unknown which, engraved in bygone eras into the convolutions of our brain, renders even today the darkness of night a source of terror to the child and, to the adult, a symbol of all things evil. This is an age-old memory of the time when the powers of darkness, in the form of flesh-eating beasts of prey, sprang out of the night upon human beings. For our forefathers the night must indeed have held unlimited terrors." Konrad Lorenz, *Man Meets Dog* (1953) (Baltimore: Penguin Books, 1964), p. 3.

There are, of course, still other causes and forms of shading disturbances of which I want to mention only one, because of its similarity to a
phenomenon described in the discussion of color responses.[23] Some records with no Ch, or at least no pure Ch or ChF responses, but with
marked shading disturbance, are essentially very similar, in their diagnostic significance, to records with one or two Ch or ChF responses.
Both these reactions point to marked difficulties or inability in coping
with anxiety or depressive feelings. The absence of the shading response, in the context of this kind of shading disturbance, is not a denial
of the shading but expresses the helplessness in relation to the task of
integrating it with form; it expresses the momentarily disabling impact
of the shading, just as the pure Ch response, in the same context, expresses the inability to integrate shading with form, the giving in to the
impact of the shading.

---

[23] Compare above, Chapter 8, pp. 185–186.

# 11 / ON CONTENT, SYMBOL, SCORE,
AND PERCEPT

Rorschach wrote in his book that only occasionally does the *content* of the responses offer indications about "the contents of the psyche," but he cautioned that conclusions from such indications should be drawn only after a consideration of the psychogram, the over-all findings, and the attitude of the testee in giving the relevant responses. By "contents of the psyche" he refers to the testee's *interests*. This is shown in his illustrations of an engineer repeatedly seeing parts of machinery or a housewife dress patterns.[1] The conclusions he draws from such content in conjunction with the over-all picture refer to the degree of energy the person invests in his work, the amount of pleasure he gets from it, and the degree of his adaptability to working conditions; they refer to the dynamics of the person's relation to his work rather than merely to the fact that he does work of the particular kind indicated by the responses. He goes on to emphasize that responses referring to unconscious contents deriving from repressed, emotionally charged complexes are strikingly rare and that his test is not suitable to explore the unconscious.[2] In his 1922 case study he modified this position somewhat and dealt rather extensively with the relation of the test findings to the unconscious of the patient. In doing so, however, his interest was focused not so much on content interpretation as such as on the problem *which types of responses are likely to refer to unconscious or dynamically central problems of the testee and which are not.* His answer to this question concerns mainly the relation of the various deter-

---

[1] Rorschach, *Psychodiagnostics*, p. 122.
[2] *Ibid.*

minants to the functions of consciousness and to the unconscious. The form responses represent the conscious functions; the M, especially the specific quality of the movement perceived, come closest to central, unconscious attitudes; the C and CF he considers closer to the unconscious than the F. He also makes the point that unique responses and genuinely original ones tell us more about psychoanalytically significant material (namely, individual strivings and preoccupations) than do popular ones. Finally, he makes the observation that the F responses do not always exclude material deriving from unconscious complexes, and that whether they do or not depends on the degree of repressiveness of the person and on the temporary variations of repressiveness.[3] Thus, in Rorschach's thinking, content interpretation is always closely linked to the specific perceptual quality of the response as well as the total configuration of the test record. There are good reasons for not using specific content outside of this linkage for interpretation.[4]

These reasons do not include any assumption that the content of responses is unrelated to drives, impulses, affects, interests, defenses, and individually characteristic ways of adaptation to reality. By and large, content seems to be related more to adaptive and defensive structures than directly expressive of drives and impulses. The reason for this lies in the fact, already stated by Rorschach, that his test does not elicit a "free flow from the subconscious" but demands adaptation to given, external stimuli. Such adaptation is "an activity of the 'fonction duréel.'"[5] However, in many severely disturbed people and in normal people with relatively little and nonrigid repressiveness, content often is also directly expressive of drives, impulses, and their derivatives. Furthermore, since the publication of Rorschach's book ego psychology and similar developments have taught us to view adaptive and defensive structures also as a continuum with and not only as in contrast to and in conflict with drives and their derivatives and to pay more attention to the individually characteristic styles of adaptation. Indeed, the test often permits an instructive view of the relation between drives, relatively autonomous goals, and adaptive and defensive efforts.

The reason that content, by itself, is of relatively little value and un-

---

[3] *Ibid.*, pp. 204–214.

[4] I am not referring in this section to the use of content as indicator of stereotypy, as in the A%, but only to the use of content as symbolic representation of drives, conflicts, and interests related to the specific quality of the content.

[5] Rorschach, *op. cit.*, p. 123; translation somewhat changed to render more closely the original text.

reliable as a diagnostic indicator lies in the fact that Rorschach's test was not constructed and not intended to use verbal content of the responses as a basis for diagnostic conclusions regarding personality structure and dynamics, unconscious trends and personal interests. There are other instruments available and more suitable for the exploration of possible symbolic and other meanings of verbal content. Furthermore, content is more subject to conscious control than any other factor of the test and it is very difficult—most of the time impossible— to decide on the basis of content alone what the relation of this content to drive, defense, adaptation, and so forth is. This is especially true of the content of a single response. Some, but not all, of the pitfalls of content interpretation can be avoided by a thematic analysis of the major trends in the content of all the responses, as some authors have proposed.[6] However, such an analysis presupposes a relatively rich record with regard to both the number of responses and the quality of their content. In other words, the sample from which a quantitative, thematic content analysis is drawn has to be fairly large in order to approach anything like representativeness of the ideational productions of a person and some measure of reliability within the anyhow considerable limitations of content analysis. Also, it must be kept in mind that the content of any *single* response may or may not be related to the particular drive or defense classifications that its content suggests to the tester. For instance, the response "lips" is likely to be classified in such content analysis under the general heading "oral." But its personal significance may well be different from and unrelated to the psychoanalytic concept of orality.

Similarly, any of the content categories usually used in scoring content may have entirely different meanings and point to entirely different perceptual experiences in different testees or in the same testee in different responses with seemingly the same content. Take, for example, anatomical content which Rorschach scored Anat. and considered indicative, in people who are not physicians, of either an "intelligence complex" (that is, the attempt to impress the other person with one's

---

[6] George DeVos, "A Quantitative Approach to Affective Symbolism in Rorschach Responses," *Journal of Projective Techniques*, 16 (1952), 133–150; Schafer, *op. cit.*, pp. 114–139. Compare also Holt and Havel's "Summary of Primary- and Secondary-Process Variables." Robert R. Holt and Joan Havel, "A Method for Assessing Primary and Secondary Process in the Rorschach" in Rickers-Ovsiankina (ed.), *op. cit.*, pp. 263–315. Both Schafer and Holt do not interpret content independently of the perceptual factors.

learning or intelligence) or of hypochondriacal ruminations.[7] Some anatomical responses are given with complete detachment from the content, others with an air of worry or with implications of disease or physical defect, others in a mood of a cramped attempt to say *something* when nothing really comes to mind, still others with the underlying concern about the wish for or the fear of the lack of a firm hold in oneself, as sometimes is the case with such responses as spine or backbone.[8] Obviously, the perceptual experience is a very different one in these different examples. It is the different, experiential quality, indicated by the determinants and by the emotional tone of the response rather than the abstract classification of its content as anatomical and the score based on this abstract classification which furnishes the decisive clue to the interpretation of the response as indicating, for example, a detached, possibly ambitious solution of the test task, or a worrying, hypochondriacal preoccupation, or a vague, anxiety-ridden attempt to cope with the task, or an unconscious identification with or wish for a firm hold in oneself, as the case may be. Of course sometimes several such meanings may be present and overlap in a single response.

Unfortunately, many students and quite a few professionals tend to "interpret" the content of single responses not only without considering the perceptual qualities of the response and the relation of its content to the over-all themes in the content of other responses, but by assuming a fixed symbolic meaning, in dictionary fashion, for a particular content, either whenever this content appears or when it is seen in a particular inkblot. In addition, many assume that a particular inkblot has a specific content, for instance the center detail of card I a woman, the top detail of card VI a penis, the vertical center of the large detail of the same card a vagina, card IV a male, and card VII two female figures, or even more specifically a father- and mother-symbol, respectively. If the testee does not respond to these blots with this content, they assume that the actual content of all or some of his responses has to be interpreted *as though* it referred to the assumed "content" of the blot, for example as though the testee were "denying" the presence of this content or as though what he said or felt about the content actually seen by him referred to the presumed "objective" content of the card. Such fixed procedures would certainly simplify the task of interpretation if they were valid, and they also may meet the common human and especially

---

[7] Rorschach, *op. cit.*, pp. 198–199.

[8] Compare above, pp. 39–40.

the student's needs for certainty, security, and simple rather than complex "answers." However, they lead inevitably to the mistakes to which every dictionary type of interpretation is prone. Unfortunately, this kind of content interpretation is encouraged by the writings of some authors.[9]

In contrast to such practice it is essential to emphasize that the primary data elicited by Rorschach's test are not concepts but percepts, that the raw material for our diagnostic work is not associations that come to the mind of the testee freely but associations of objects (animals, people, lifeless objects, and so forth) which he feels look like the blot or parts of it. This description itself is too abstract and pale to do justice to the data furnished by the test. The data we study in Rorschach's test are what the testee saw in the blots and how he saw it, in the full concreteness of the percept and with all the emotional overtones and undercurrents that color what he saw, and all the intellectual and emotional effort, its quality, its process, its smoothness, or conflicts which entered into the work of perceiving, associating, and judging the fitness of the percept. From his words we try to reconstruct his experience. The score is merely an abstraction of this experience, and the verbal content of the responses is also an abstraction. While, of course, we eventually have to abstract from the totality of the record what is most significant, such abstraction will be both more accurate and richer if its basis is the concrete perceptual experience of the testee and its genesis as reconstructed on the basis of his responses and his total behavior. Only within this framework is it of interest that one object rather than another (which also might have fitted the blot) came to the mind of the testee and was selected as a response, or that one area or aspect of the blot rather than another attracted his attention and became the basis of his response, perhaps because it could be seen as an object with which he was preoccupied or because he found it easier to think of something in connection with this rather than with another area.[10]

---

[9] Robert M. Lindner, "Analysis of Rorschach Test by Content," *Journal of Clinical Psychopathology*, 8 (1947), 707–719; Fred Brown, "An Exploratory Study of Dynamic Factors in the Content of the Rorschach Protocol," *Journal of Projective Techniques*, 17 (1953), 251–279. For a critical evaluation of these methods of interpretation as contrasted with thematic content analysis, see Schafer, *op. cit.*, p. 118, note.

[10] I am not implying that the choice of location is dependent primarily on the two reasons mentioned above. Usually other reasons are more important and several factors work together in determining location.

The inclination toward pure content interpretation has, among other consequences, frequently a subtle effect which gets in the way of the Rorschach worker even if consciously he intends to use, in addition to content analysis, the classic method of interpretation. The effect I have in mind can be described as a shift from a perceptual and experiential to a verbal level of looking at and dealing with the test data. The word used by the testee to refer to what he saw and the tester's associations to and thoughts about that word, that concept tend to become the focus, and the way in which the testee saw the blot tends to disappear or to become less important. Rorschach was aware of the temptation to substitute words for percepts and cautioned explicitly against it in his discussion of the M response; he warns not to consider a merely verbally named movement as a kinesthetically felt one, a warning that very often is no longer heeded.[11]

Indeed, it takes a great deal of time and effort to learn to *see* what the testee *saw* and how he saw it rather than merely to hear or read what he *said*. Of course the words of the testee are what is immediately available to us and the most salient words are usually those by which he tells us what he saw, that is, the words giving the content of the response. This fact probably plays no small role in the widespread inclination of many students of Rorschach's test to use content by itself, or without sufficient consideration of the percept. However, the words used by the testee, both in the spontaneous performance *and* in the inquiry, are relevant only as signposts toward what he saw and, additionally, insofar as they tell us something about his style and pattern of communication or his failure to communicate adequately. The temptation to rely on mere words has deep roots in our culture, but the verbal expression often distorts, veils, renders incompletely, or comes to replace rather than signify the actual percept, both for the testee and the tester. Man's greatest invention, language, has helped him immeasurably to articulate his experience and thus not only to communicate it but also to become more fully aware of it. But language also often comes to substitute for, prevent, and obscure experience,[12] quite aside from the fact that it can be used and often is used to omit, change, deny, or edit what actually has been going on. Thus, the use to which language is put cannot only enlarge awareness, but can also uphold the

---

[11] Rorschach, *op. cit.*, pp. 25–26.

[12] For a more detailed discussion of this aspect of language see Schachtel, *Metamorphosis*, pp. 158–165, 237–248, 279–322.

limitations of awareness which all men, in varying degrees and more often inadvertently than otherwise, tend to perpetuate. This limiting and obscuring use of words occurs in tester as well as testee and is of interest specifically with regard to the relation between word and percept.

People differ a great deal in the extent to which they are able and willing to communicate and articulate what they see and experience. Nobody can do this fully, at least not in the relatively short time of a Rorschach test. Many factors interfere with or prevent accurate communication of experience. One factor is that we often are not fully aware of our experience because we focus on one aspect of it and are selectively inattentive to or repress others. Other factors are the general and the personal limitations of language to convey all that one sees, feels, experiences. Awareness of these limitations may or may not be present; the person may sense that he has not been able to say quite what he wanted to say, he may consciously struggle to find the right words; but it may also happen that the facile availability and use of words is one of the ways by which what is potentially available to awareness and communication gets barred from both.

It is astonishing to observe how little many people are really aware of what they see in their everyday life and how much they fail to see. They may pass a house daily on their way to work, they can tell you that they have seen it, but they cannot tell you how it looks. They see, as it were, the concept "house"; they immediately classify it as such and henceforth "see" only the thing so classified, not the actual house, its structure, color, its doorway, style of architecture, roof, and so forth. The person who responds to the Rorschach blots is in a somewhat different position, because the test task usually tends to mobilize his attention more than do the objects he sees on his way to work. Nevertheless, there are of course for everybody a lot of things in the inkblots that he has not attended to and not seen and to which therefore he has not responded. However, in the present context another fact is of more interest, namely, that people who have responded to certain aspects of the inkblots often are only marginally or not at all aware of what exactly it was they have responded to. This is usually the case with their responses to the general qualities of the inkblots and to the "perceptual themes" inherent in the different structures of the individual inkblots.[13]

---

[13] See Chapter 3.

Similarly, the obvious difficulty some people encounter with the unexpected appearance of color and the task to integrate color with form
may not have come to their awareness. Often they are unaware that
they seek out certain dynamic forms or avoid others. They may repeatedly see similar kinds of movements or postures, but since they pay
attention primarily to the content they saw, they are not aware of this.
In most of the examples cited so far, the words used to describe *what*
they saw, the attention of the testee to the varying content, may veil or
remove altogether from his awareness the underlying theme that becomes apparent only if we look at *how* he saw these different contents.
It is no coincidence, of course, that the examples given concern aspects
of responses which frequently refer to unconscious tendencies or to
tendencies which have never come into focal awareness of the person as
being peculiar to him, and not shared by everybody.

The instances mentioned so far deal with perceptual experiences
which usually are not explicitly named and not noticed by the testee,
yet become apparent if not in a single percept then in trends common
to several percepts, such as recurrent dynamic forms, or recurrently
similar emphases in the patterning of the structure of the blots in the
responses. As every Rorschach worker knows, there are numerous other
occasions in which the content of a response does not tell us exactly
what the percept was, does not, for example, indicate where and how
this particular content was seen, what the determinants were, whether
a genuine kinesthesia was involved or only a word naming a movement,
and so forth. If the Rorschach worker is not satisfied with pure content
analysis, as a minority sometimes seem to be, he will try to find out in
the inquiry those aspects of the percept he needs to know in order to
score location and determinants of the response. But, as Rorschach
pointed out,[14] some people do not know or are unable to decide whether
kinesthetic factors played a role in their response, or whether and to
what extent color was a co-determinant, together with form, of their
response. The same often holds true for other perceptual aspects of
their responses such as the role and quality of shading as a co-
determinant or the delimitation of the area to which the response referred. Thus, the testee may be quite clear about the content of his
response, but unclear about how he saw it, about the percept on which
the response was based. One not infrequent reason for this is that the

---

14 Rorschach, *op. cit.*, pp. 26 and 30.

percept was based on a fused or global impression of several aspects. Another possibility is that the percept was rather vague to begin with. The testee, in these cases, knows more or less that the blot looked like the object (content) he named, but the content is much clearer to him than the percept. Like so much of our experience, the testee's experience, in such a case, may have been more comprehensive and less clear than his words indicate. In such cases it is the task of the tester to arrive at some judgment, based on the particular response in comparison with other responses and with the testee's general style of perception and communication, what the percept probably was like, or else to be aware of the fact that he cannot know what it was like. Another example of a significant difference or discrepancy between verbal content and perceptual experience can be found in the case of some quite verbose people who give verbally elaborate responses, but what they actually saw may have been either quite vague or much simpler and more primitive than the content led one to expect.

It is important to be aware of the fact that in the *inquiry*, too, the content of the information given to the tester's questions regarding the percept may or may not be a reliable guide to the actual percept. Even when great care is taken to avoid all leading questions in the inquiry, many testees will form their own notions of what the tester does or does not want to hear and will have their own reasons for what they do and do not want him to know. These notions and reasons may be conscious; more often they are not or only peripherally in the testee's awareness. But they lead to a conscious or unconscious editing of the information given, be it in order to please the tester, to maintain a certain self-image, or for other reasons.[15]

The tester who is not alert to the differences between content and percept runs the risk of taking the content for the percept, the word for the perceptual experience, or of constructing his own version of the percept on the basis of an uncritical acceptance of the testee's words rather than of a careful reconstruction of his percept. A more important danger lies in the fact that the tester, like the testee, is subject to the temptation to substitute words for experiences, ready classifications for the richness of reality and, in his particular work, diagnostic clichés for the complexity of the living person. The temptation to take the content as verbalized by the testee or the content score for the percept is not

---

[15] This "editing" depends largely on the testee's subjective definition of the inquiry situation.

only due to the testee's limitations in articulating what he saw and to the tester's own readiness to use and accept words for the perceptual experiences to which they point but which they often blur rather than illuminate. They are often due also to an unwillingness, reluctance, or inability to get into contact with the actual, living other person and with what is going on in the other person's experience, and to an inclination to look at the other person and his experience from a too narrow and/or depersonalized perspective, in the present context from the perspective of the content label or the content score. People differ a great deal in their ability and willingness to look with an open and receptive mind at the world around them and at another person, really to hear, listen, read, see, empathize. They may feel safer when they deal with a "case" rather than a person; or they may feel more secure with a closed system of definite labels, scores, content-symbols, and so forth, rather than with the full actuality of what is before them. In the service of these and other biasing tendencies the tester may see only certain aspects of the responses because he looks for these and may not arrive at the actual percept. Even the scoring itself, indispensable as it is, may be misused in the service of such tendencies. The tester, especially the beginning one, may be so driven to find the correct score that he does not have the freedom to look at the actual percept, which is always more than its score, or that he feels he has to score even when neither the response nor the inquiry offers sufficient information for complete scoring. He may not see the percept because his focus on scoring obscures rather than illuminates it. By this I do not mean that scoring and interpreting the score have this effect, but that the *function* the score may serve in an individual tester may obscure the actual percept. While the psychogram with its abstracting summary of all the scores is an important diagnostic instrument, the scoring also should help to make vivid and articulate the individual percept underlying a particular response. But some testers do not use it that way. Even though they had to analyze the response in the process of scoring it, they fail to synthesize the result of such an analysis into a thus enriched and more articulately visible percept. Instead, they use the score only in its abstracting function, its summary implications. Often the people who are prone to do this also are prone to pay insufficient attention to the finer perceptual differentiations which disappear if only the one score common to them is attended to. Two F+ or two FC responses may, in spite of their common score, show significantly different nuances of form perception or of the role of color and the way it is integrated with form. The tester may also, in his turn, "edit" the responses, without being aware of it, in order to fit them to his particular bias. He may do this with the content as well as the percept, and with the symbolism which he ascribes to the content.

Nobody is entirely free from the described or similar biasing tendencies. The best we can do as clinicians[16] using Rorschach's test is try to become aware of such tendencies in ourselves, control them, and attempt to get as concrete and rich a picture of the perceptual and experiential qualities of the person's responses and of the processes leading to them as possible.

[16] The researcher, depending on his goal, is often in a different position, for example in studies involving statistical validation of the meaning of a certain score.

# 12 / THE INTERPERSONAL MEANING OF
# THE RORSCHACH-TEST SITUATION

All perception takes place as an encounter between the perceiver and his environment in a life situation in which the perceiver relates to the environment at a particular moment, now, in a particular situational configuration of which he and the environment are constitutive. Neither perception nor any other act of a living organism takes place in a vacuum, or in a neutral field, or ever in the same field for two different perceivers or for one perceiver at different times. This holds true also for artificially controlled and standardized conditions of the experimental laboratory. That this has often been overlooked has led to many errors and faulty theories based on the evaluation of data obtained in such experiments.[1]

Perception of the Rorschach inkblots, too, takes place in a life situation of which it is an inseparable part and which I shall call the Rorschach-test situation or, briefly, the Rorschach situation. We have

---

[1] The systematic and thoughtful criticism of Pavlov's work by Erwin Straus is an example of the far-reaching insights to be gained by the methodical consideration of the life significance of the situation in which organism and environment interact. Erwin Straus, *op. cit.* Since the publication of the article on which the first part of this chapter is based (1945), more attention has been paid to some of the factors which have the effect that for animals as well as (especially) for people no two situations are completely alike. For the role of the tester's as well as the testee's influence on the Rorschach-test situation compare Schafer, *op. cit.*, especially Chapter 2, pp. 6–73. For a general survey of recent research on the effect of the experimenter or the tester on the results of the experiment or test see B. L. Kintz, D. J. Delprato, D. R. Mettee, C. E. Persons, and R. H. Schappe, "The Experimenter Effect," *Psychological Bulletin*, 63 (1965), 223–232; for a survey of the recent literature on the interpersonal aspects of so-called projective testing see Joseph Masling, "The Influence of Situational and Interpersonal Variables in Projective Testing," *Psychological Bulletin*, 57 (1960), 65–85.

learned from modern biology to consider the organism not in isolation but to understand its living and functioning only in interaction with the environment. Similarly, modern psychology and psychiatry have taught us to study and understand man only in interaction with his environment, particularly with the most important factor of it, the human environment.

To understand a Rorschach record it is essential to be aware of its interpersonal aspects and implications. This means primarily that we must never forget that the Rorschach performance and the experiences of the testee in the Rorschach situation are an interpersonal performance and interpersonal experiences. I use the term interpersonal in Sullivan's sense,[2] comprising not only the interpersonal relations of the people present in the Rorschach situation, namely, the tester and the testee, but also those who are mentally part of the Rorschach situation because they play a role in the tester's and, more important, in the testee's mind, either in parataxic distortions of the tester's personality and attitude or because they figure in the testee's ideas and phantasies, conscious as well as unconscious, of what he "ought" to do, what is expected of him, and what effect his performance might have on the tester and on significant people in his past and present life.

Since the Rorschach situation is constituted by two people[3] and the perceptual object (the inkblots), both these people will influence the situation and what happens in it. But the share of the testee in the situation is usually greater than the share of the tester. The testee, not the tester, encounters the inkblots and reacts to them. Also, the testee brings with him a whole set of conscious and unconscious expectations and attitudes concerning people who do diagnosis or testing or whatever he expects the tester to do, and concerning what he himself will want to do or have to do. As a rule, this set is independent of the personality of the tester, although occasionally it may be influenced by what the testee might have heard about him from others. When the testee meets the tester and when the tester explains the test task to him,

---

[2] H. S. Sullivan, The Interpersonal Theory of Psychiatry (New York: W. W. Norton and Co., 1953).

[3] The term "Rorschach situation," as used in this book, applies to the standard individual test situation. The group test situation is in several respects different from the usual Rorschach situation. Records obtained in a group test not only yield fewer data than those obtained in the standard test situation, but the interpretation of such records should take into account the different situation if the interpretation is made to obtain a detailed personality picture and not only for screening purposes.

this set of expectations will undergo certain concretizations and transformations. These, in turn, are likely to be affected by the testee's previous experience with and reactions to significant people in his life of whom, consciously or unconsciously, the tester or something he says or does reminds him. Our diagnostic interest, of course, is concerned with the testee's experience of the test situation. The personality and behavior of the tester become relevant only insofar as they affect this experience and as we are in a position to gauge their effect on test performance. Therefore, we shall first consider the *testee's subjective definition of the Rorschach-test situation* and the influence this definition has on his performance.[4] Then the problem of the influence of the tester's personality and attitude and of other variations in the situational configuration will be discussed briefly insofar as they may influence the testee's reactions.

### The Testee's Definition of the Rorschach Situation and Its Influence on Test Performance

In the psychiatric interview some of the most significant and revealing material is obtained by the attempt to explore carefully how the person interviewed experiences and reacts to the situation in which he finds himself during the psychiatric interview. Freud, in developing the technique of analyzing the "transference," has opened the main road to such exploration. In psychological testing, however, this source of insight, on the whole, has been neglected, disregarded, or purposely excluded. Even in the field of personality tests the tendency has been either to obtain through questionnaires material similar to the data supplied by a patient's anamnesis of his life history and to evaluate this material by quantitative methods, or to have the subject perform certain tasks and to evaluate his performance of these tasks by quantitative and, more recently, occasionally also by qualitative methods.

By far the greater part of the literature and practice of personality testing seems to rest on the assumption that the way in which the subject experiences the test situation is irrelevant to the results of the test, and therefore need not be considered in the evaluation of the results.

---

[4] The following discussion of the testee's definition of the test situation is largely taken from E. G. Schachtel, "Subjective Definitions of the Rorschach Test Situation and Their Effect on Test Performance," *Psychiatry,* 8 (1945), pp. 419–448, with some additions.

Quite often the thought that there is such a thing as a personal experience of and reaction to the test situation has not occurred to the inventor or user of a psychological test. Yet to treat the subjective experience of the test situation as nonexistent or as irrelevant can only lead to errors in the evaluation of test results.

There are two ways, it seems to me, to deal intelligently and rationally with the very complex factors and processes designated here by the concept of "test situation." One can regard these factors as a source of disturbance of the attempt to obtain "objective" results. If one takes this attitude, it does not help to deny or to ignore the fact that each person will define, consciously or unconsciously, the test situation according to his own needs, wishes, and fears, and that his definition of the test situation will affect his performance. One can try to reduce the stimuli which may provoke and strengthen such subjective definitions of the test situation, although one can never exclude them entirely. And one can try, in addition, to evaluate the influence of the subject's definition of the test situation on his performance in order to be able to discount it, although only a very approximate discount will be possible since most tests offer little or no opportunity to study the quality and the degree of influence which the subject's personal definition of the test situation will have on the test results.[5]

The other rational way of dealing with the subjective definition of the test situation is to regard it not as an unavoidable nuisance, a disturbing source of mistakes, which has to be considered only in order to eliminate it, but to use it as a valuable source of insight into the subject's personality structure and attitudes. If one really knows how a person experiences and reacts to a certain situation, one knows a great deal about this person. And it seems a pity for the student of personality to discard rather than to explore such significant material.

By a person's definition of the Rorschach situation I do not mean merely, and not even predominantly, the conscious ideas of this person about what is going on in his taking a Rorschach test. Rather I want to designate by this term the person's total experience of the test situation, whether he is aware or unaware of the elements comprising this experience. Very many people are consciously of the opinion that they take a personality test in order to find help of some sort, while unconsciously

---

[5] This approximately is the method suggested for intelligence tests by Richard Sears, "Motivational Factors in Aptitude Testing," *American Journal of Orthopsychiatry*, 13 (1943), 468–492.

they take the occasion as an examination in which they have to get perfect marks, or as a competitive race with unknown rivals, or as a trial in which they have to defend themselves against unknown charges, or as a battle in which they have to defeat or outwit the person who gives the test.

The testee's definition of the situation becomes visible only against the background of the objective elements in the situation—that is, those elements that are present in all Rorschach-test situations, which belong to the common and more or less standardized conditions of Rorschach's experiment. How the testee experiences these common elements of the test situation, and how he reacts to this experience—which reaction in turn influences his experience of the situation—constitute *his* definition of the test situation.

The most important common elements of the Rorschach situation are:

1. The *togetherness of two people*, the tester and the testee, in the relationship of the test situation.

2. The fact that a *task* is given to the testee by the tester, which in turn establishes one specific aspect of the togetherness of these two people.

3. A fairly constant element of the task situation is the usual awareness of the testee that the tester—or someone else—will draw certain conclusions concerning him from the way he handles the task. Of what general type these conclusions are, what their significance for the testee and for the tester might be, and on what, specifically, they will be based—these are questions the answers to which differ widely in different testees according to their definition of the test situation.

4. The specific qualities of the test task. The most important of these are the newness and strangeness of the task, which is due mainly to the unfamiliar and ambiguous nature of the inkblots and the relative lack of rules and directives; in other words, it is less of a task in the sense of a narrowly prescribed type of effort being demanded of the testee than are most other tasks in a test situation and in many work situations.

The following discussion of subjective definitions of the Rorschach-test situation is based on and refers to the testing of adults and adolescents. It would exceed the scope of this book to discuss the interesting question how the test situation is experienced by *children* at various developmental stages. I want to mention only two points in which most children's experience seems to differ from that of most adults. The youngest group of children (preschool) probably are not aware or do not much think about the fact that the tester will draw conclusions from their test performance; much less do they give thought to what these conclusions might be. They may consider the test a new kind of game or something akin to looking at pictures. This or similar notions are actually most suitable to lead to a productive performance in this age group. Most children (up to ten or twelve years?), furthermore, are probably convinced that the blots do represent or are supposed to represent something and that therefore there are right and wrong answers.

All the described elements in the Rorschach-test situation, the togetherness of two people, the fact that one poses a task to the other, the nature of this task, and the awareness of the testee that his performance will furnish the basis for another person to form certain opinions about him the nature of which is not known to him in any detail: all these elements are inseparable and influence each other. When one considers them as being constant, objective, identical elements in all Rorschach tests, he must be aware of dealing with mere abstractions, with empty vessels which have to be filled with the reality of the concrete test situation and into which, above all, the testee will pour *his* feelings, ideas, wishes, needs, and fears, defining the test situation as he experiences it.

Rorschach, on two occasions explicitly, in other passages implicitly, refers to these differences in the subject's definition of the test situation. He mentions that for the M-type—the introversive—the test is play; for the C-type—extroversive—it is work.[6] In several passages of his book he discusses the particular reactions of those people who "take the experiment very seriously."[7] He was aware, then, of differences in the subjects' attitudes to the test and also of correlations between such attitudes and test scores. When he states that people who take the experiment very seriously also take everything else in life very seriously,[8] he must feel that in their attitude to the test situation these people behave as they always behave; in other words, that they transfer to the test situation the attitudes, strivings, defenses, needs, fears, wishes, and interests which they characteristically show in other situations of their lives, which have been formed by their previous experiences, and which are part of the structure of their personalities. Among the people who

---

[6] *Psychodiagnostics*, p. 81.

[7] *Ibid.*, pp. 43, 57.

[8] *Ibid.*, p. 43.

"take the test very seriously" Rorschach numbers pedantic and "school-master" personalities, as well as depressed persons with inferiority feelings, anxious persons, and melancholics.[9] These are very different types of people, who may have markedly different personality structures. The way in which the pedant "takes the test very seriously" is different from the way in which the anxious person or the melancholic does.

Rorschach's *aperçu* on the people who take the test very seriously certainly has a bearing on the question of the psychological significance of the test situation; but he did not attempt to deal explicitly with this problem of the subjective definition of the test situation and the light it sheds on character structure. In order to do that it will be useful to discuss first frequent and typical definitions of the test situation and their relation to personality structure.

The role of *authority* in a person's life exercises as central an influence on his definition of the Rorschach situation as it does in shaping all his reactions and behavior. Particularly fear of, submission to, admiration for, or rebellion against irrational authority,[10] in other words, all the various forms which an inner dependence on such authority may take, usually have a profound and visible effect on the way in which people experience the Rorschach situation. The reasons for this are to be found in the objective elements of the Rorschach situation, which tend to activate the strivings, needs, and fears comprising a person's attitude to authority. When Rorschach's test is used outside of institutions in order to help people with their difficulties and problems and when such help is sought by the person concerned, then the relation between tester and testee, considered apart from the specific task posed in the Rorschach situation, is in some aspects not dissimilar to the relation in a first interview between analyst and analysand. Psychoanalytic literature frequently discusses the problem of the irrational authority ascribed by the analysand to the analyst whose help he is seeking. There is no need to repeat these familiar discussions here. It is sufficient to remember that the person seeking help or advice very easily may be inclined to vest in the person of whom he is asking help the attributes of some kind of irrational authority or power, and to react not so much to the person before him as to the attributes with which he has endowed him, both consciously and unconsciously. In institutions such as hospitals,

---

9 *Ibid.*

10 For the concept of irrational—or inhibiting—authority see Erich Fromm, *Escape from Freedom* (New York: Farrar and Rinehart, 1941), pp. 164–178.

schools, prisons, colleges, the Army or the Navy, the Rorschach situation may be changed appreciably by the fact that usually the test is not given because the inmates, charges, or members of the institution have asked for it but because they are asked by someone "in authority" to take a Rorschach test or to "cooperate" in taking a Rorschach test, quite often without being given specific reasons. These possible differences between "free" and "institutional" Rorschach tests should be kept in mind by those who analyze and interpret the test records. Regardless of these differences, the relation between tester and testee, *without* consideration of the specific task which the tester asks the testee to perform, is a largely unstructured jumble of possibilities resembling the scattered pieces in a kaleidoscope, the colors, shapes, and numbers of which determine a certain range and choice of patterns but which will assume definite shape only as the kaleidoscope is turned and then held in one position until it is turned anew. The turn of the kaleidoscope is the introduction of the specific Rorschach task into the interpersonal relation between tester and testee. It is the Rorschach task which at once narrows and gives structure—variously to be filled, enriched, impoverished, adorned, or simplified, made flexible or held rigidly—to the Rorschach situation.

The Rorschach task—the task of telling the tester what the Rorschach inkblots might be or what they look like—has been examined by Binder with the purpose of applying to it general laws governing the mental processes of people confronted with and trying to solve a given mental task. Binder, following Selz,[11] notes that the determination to solve a mental problem results in the activation of such intellectual operations as are suitable—or, it should be added, *deemed* suitable by the subject —to realize his aim. He then describes the Rorschach task as consisting, first, of the demand to perceive the inkblots and, second, to find an object which will be similar to the particular aspect under which the inkblot has been perceived—that is, similar to the individual perception of the inkblot. There is no need here to discuss the validity of this description and of Selz's laws governing the solution of mental tasks, since obviously this type of law will not help in learning something about the *individual* definition of the task in the Rorschach situation but refers to general laws which are supposed to apply in the same way to anyone

---

[11] Binder, *op. cit.*, p. 20. Binder refers to the exposition of such laws by Otto Selz, *Ueber die Gesetze des geordneten Denkverlaufes* (Stuttgart: W. Speman, 1913).

who tries to solve the Rorschach task—or any other mental task—and which, therefore, have to abstract from rather than to observe and consider minutely the specific meaning of the Rorschach task to the *individual* person.

In considering the variety of special meanings which the Rorschach task may assume in lending itself easily to a variety of transformations by, and integrations with, people's attitudes to authority, it is useful to be aware of some factors and patterns peculiar to Western civilization. The meaning of a mental task, and more specifically of a mental task in a test, is predetermined by all previous experience of the person who is about to perform the task. This comprises his previous experience with mental tasks and with tests. The quality of the demand which a person feels to be made on him when he is confronted with such a task may be considered as consisting of a culturally determined general idea of what he is asked to do, and of the personally determined concretization of this idea. His attitude to the demand corresponds to both these factors, to the broad meaning of "test-task" as determined by cultural patterns and to the personal meaning, that is, to his own way of experiencing situations in which such a task is given to him. In concrete experience, of course, such a distinction between cultural and personal factors determining the quality of an experience would be artificial; the two are completely merged. The culturally determined meaning of test situations and of the tasks set in them are usually more conscious to people, although they do not think of them explicitly as peculiar to their culture, than the personally determined meaning, of which they often are quite unaware and usually at least partly unaware.

In Western civilization, tests and test-tasks have close affinities to authority, status, competition, and to the market on which one may or may not be able to sell his working power, experience, special aptitudes and gifts, and even his "personality." Tests are given in school. The authority of the teacher, supported by, and partly successor to, parental authority, the authority of the whole educational system, and ultimately of society, determine much of the meaning of these tests for the child and the adolescent who passes or fails them. These authorities give urgency to the tasks, the right or wrong solution of which will determine the outcome of the test. Tests will often be instrumental in deciding whether an applicant shall be admitted to college or to a job. Written and oral school examinations are tests which to many mean the difference between misery and happiness, failure and success, being praised or condemned, being accepted or rejected by the powerful authority or by that internalized image of the authority which has become part of the personality and which Freud has designated by the term "super-ego."

The more dependent a person is on authority, on any or all of its manifold embodiments, manifestations, and expressions, on its real or imagined, apparent or veiled pressures, demands, and expectations, the more he will be inclined to experience tests as a kind of examination and judgment by authority, and to be particularly sensitive to those cultural implications of test situations which refer to the aspects of authority and its real or imagined power over the person's life.

The sensitivity toward the authority aspect of test situations in general may lead to a considerable variety of subjective definitions of these situations and in particular of the Rorschach situation, depending upon the specific development and structure of this sensitivity in the individual person which finds expression in his attitude to authority. However, these various "authoritarian" definitions of the Rorschach situation have some common elements which affect the responses to the Rorschach inkblots and the test behavior. Two of these are particularly important and often have marked consequences. First, the test situation is experienced as a *pressure* situation; and, second, it is defined as being in some way or other governed by more or different rules, directions, restrictions, or standards than it actually is, which leads to a more narrow and rigid definition of the test-task than the one given in the instructions to the subject.

The *pressure* to which the person sensitive to and dependent on authority feels subjected in the Rorschach situation is qualitatively and quantitatively different from the mere *demand* implied in any task which a person is asked to perform. In the dependent person's definition of the Rorschach situation a major influence is exercised by his feeling that someone else, who is placed by him in a position of irrational authority, expects him to do something. He does not feel that he wants to do something; he is *supposed* to do something. The scale of this pressure may extend all the way from a slight feeling of uneasiness to a profound and harassing conviction that he must under all circumstances and at whatever cost "live up to" the expectations of the other person. Whenever the attitude emphasizing the necessity to fulfill certain expectations is the dominating trend in the definition of the Ror-

schach situation, the relationship to the tester usually is largely parataxic.[12]

If the testee combines personal ambition with a rebellious or depreciating attitude, or if he senses in the tester personal qualities which
make it impossible for this particular testee to ascribe to him attributes
of authority, then the tester may be more or less excluded from the
authoritative aspects of the Rorschach situation. In this case those aspects may be represented by the testee's own ambition, by that image
of authority which he has internalized, which drives him to do his
utmost, because otherwise he will feel that he has not met his own
standards, that is, the standards of the internalized parental or similar
authority. It does not make an appreciable difference in the test performance, the responses to the inkblots, whether the testee's attitude to
authority is crystallized, as it were, in his image of the tester or in the
anonymous demand of the test situation, that is, in himself as he has
come to internalize the personal authorities of his life history. These
two foci of authority, the seemingly external one in the person of the
tester, on whom the testee projects his image of authority, and the internal one in the testee's super-ego, are always active and complement
each other in varying proportions. The role of an external focus of authority may also be assumed or shared by someone who is going to
learn the results of the test, a psychiatrist, a relative, a teacher, or a
counselor.

An important part of the pressure felt in the Rorschach situation by
people dependent on authority derives from their ideas and feelings,
vague or definite, unconscious or conscious, of what is going to happen
or what it is going to mean if they do not meet the demands and standards which they have introjected into the Rorschach situation. Someone
—a non-existent figure created by them and variously projected on the
tester, on other people, on an indefinite number of people's opinions
about them, on some more or less mythical agency, or else their own
self-feeling complementing or more or less replacing such outer
"judges"—is going to judge them, to decide on their success or failure.
Actually the concepts of success and failure are quite out of place and
unsuitable to designate the results of a test which is constructed to elicit

---

12 For the concept of parataxic interpersonal situations see Harry Stack Sullivan,
"A Note on the Implications of Psychiatry, the Study of Interpersonal Relations,
for Investigations in the Social Sciences," *American Journal of Sociology,* 42
(1937), 848–861; p. 855.

information about structure, conflicts, and difficulties of personality. Nevertheless, the enormous cultural role and the impact on people's lives of the facts designated by these concepts of success and failure affect a very great number, probably the majority, of testees in such a way as to give to the ideas of success and failure an important and quite often a dominating role in their definition of the Rorschach situation.

The pressure caused by a person's ideas about what is going to happen if he does not meet the demands made on him in the Rorschach situation varies in degree and quality. Two variables of this pressure may be denoted as the power ascribed to the imaginary judge and as the scope and weight of his judgment. The words "judge" and "judgment" are chosen because they characterize roughly a widespread parataxic distortion of the test situation. The *power* of the judge refers to the quality and degree of dependence of the testee on the opinions of the personally significant people about him. The *scope* of the judgment refers to the testee's definition of the test outcome as having significance only for certain limited spheres of his personality—such as intelligence or creativity or some special difficulty with which he is concerned—or as concerning his entire personality and life. The *weight* of the "judgment" concerns the degree to which he is ready to accept it, regardless of its objective validity, or to adopt a critical attitude toward it, which in turn may be one of valid criticism or of irrationally conditioned resistance.

The degree to which the Rorschach situation is defined as being under authoritative pressure determines the degree to which the testee responds to the test in order to fulfill certain expectations and in such a way as he thinks he is supposed to respond. On the other hand, when the Rorschach situation is experienced as being free from authoritative pressure, the testee will respond not because he thinks he has to meet certain demands but because he wants to respond, and his response will not be determined by what he feels he is supposed to do, but by the spontaneous interest and mental activity which the inkblots stimulate in him. In the pressure situation the testee feels: "I have to do this." In the free situation his attitude is: "I want to do this." Others' expectations—real or imagined—govern the pressure situation; the testee's own decision and interest shape the free situation.

Another aspect of these contrasting attitudes is that the pressure situation is more or less subject-centered, while the free situation is object-centered. In other words, in the pressure situation feelings about what the other person expects, what he will think, what his attitude to the testee and his opinion about him will be, what he will do to the testee, constantly influence the development of the test situation and are of major interest to the testee. In the free situation, the task itself, the inkblots and the images and ideas they arouse form the major interest of the testee. He is able to apply himself in a relaxed way to the test-task and to develop an interest in it, while the authoritarian testee applies himself to the task in a forced manner, and the development of object interest, that is, of interest in the inkblots, is constantly interfered with by his preoccupation with the imagined attitude of the "authority" and with the relation between him and the authority.

The authoritarian definition of the Rorschach situation means not only that the testee "works"—he does not play as some nonauthoritarian testees feel they do when responding to the Rorschach inkblots— and works under pressure. It also means that his definition of the Rorschach situation restricts the Rorschach task and the possibilities of performing it to his or the imagined authority's satisfaction. This *restriction* of the Rorschach task not only has the general quality of anything done under pressure which implies that the testee feels unfree to do as he pleases—he is not relaxed; he cannot use his capacities fully and freely —but, in addition, it quite often leads to specific transformations of the Rorschach task, which is then felt to imply certain demands and to be subject to certain rules and prohibitions which have no basis in the actual instructions given to the testee. The testee may feel that certain minimum achievements are required of him, for example, that he must not give less than a certain number of responses to each plate or that the more responses he gives the better his achievements will be or that he must respond very rapidly and not delay his response beyond a certain time. He may feel that certain types of responses are not permissible or that they are not so good as certain other types of response. He may feel that he must be quite accurate about his responses or that, on the contrary, he has to let his imagination run wild. He may feel that he has to respond to the inkblot just as it is given to him, that he must not look at it from another angle and must not turn it. He may think that he has to be complete in his interpretations and must not omit any part of an inkblot. He may feel that he must continue to respond as long as possible, to the point of exhaustion, or that he must not take too much of the tester's time. These examples could be continued and will be discussed in greater detail when the effects of the definition of the Rorschach situation on the score of the test and the behavior of the testee are examined.

To appreciate the significance of a subjective definition of the Rorschach situation, which more or less drastically restricts the freedom of response invited by the objective Rorschach situation, it is necessary to consider the nature of the Rorschach task and particularly those factors which constitute its most marked differences from other test-tasks. Practically all psychological and psychometric tests, whether they be of the question-and-answer variety or performance tests, language, arithmetic, or manual aptitude tests, whether designed to measure intelligence, other mental and emotional factors or physical abilities, not only have a clearly defined task but also leave no doubt in the subject in which direction he has to look for the solution; and in very many tests—particularly intelligence and performance tests—he also has a definite knowledge of the factors which will decide whether his performance is a good or a poor one. The testee knows, for example, that he has to answer certain questions or that he has to find the one correct solution for an arithmetical, logical, or linguistic problem, for a puzzle, for the way out of a maze, or the completion of a picture, of a phrase or of a story. Quite often he is told that he is to work as fast as he can or that he has to be as accurate as possible. All these tests resemble work under definite directions. This may be work of a routine character, as in many manual performance tests, or work in which success depends on finding the correct solution to a quite specific problem. It is usually non-creative work and practically always a definite assignment with no or very limited choice in the way of fulfilling it, an assignment governed by definite directions and rules, in which one can either succeed or fail or in which one's performance will be rated and will receive good, fair, or poor marks, as in school. In contrast to these tests, the Rorschach task to say what the inkblots might be, what they look like—does not have one correct or, for that matter, any correct solution. There is no "wrong" or "right," no "good" or "poor." The testee is not given any directions, nor are any rules of procedure or qualitative or quantitative standards of achievement announced to him. He is free to do what he likes, to give few or many responses, to go slowly or fast, to look at the inkblots from any angle he wishes, to interpret whatever part of them he pleases or not to interpret at all, if he is not interested in a particular inkblot. Moreover, compared with the tasks in other tests, the Rorschach task is strange and unusual. It does not imply its own one-way pattern of solution as do most other test-tasks; it gives a wide scope of possible responses, in fact, an unlimited scope. In most tests the problem or task presented is identical with or similar to the problems and tasks which the testee is required to solve in his work or in school. They demand manual performances of various types, knowledge of various types, logical thinking, linguistic proficiency. Thus, even without explicit directions, these tasks by their very familiarity imply a pattern of response and point the way in which the response is to be sought. They correspond to a cliché which is already well known to the testee, if not in its specific content, at least in its general qualities. The accidental Rorschach inkblots with their more or less phantastic shapes, shades, and colors do not provide any such cliché. The testee is free to develop as much spontaneity as he can, to discover and wander in this strange land of unknown shapes, to stop and linger where he likes, to follow what interests him, and to leave aside what bores or repels him. He may hurry or take his leisure, he may become absorbed or may react superficially, he is free to do as he pleases. For once, he is not told that he must observe directions, not trespass, maintain an even speed, achieve a minimum, not transgress a maximum limit. This freedom of the Rorschach situation, one might think, would be welcome and invite a free and spontaneous reaction. But in the majority of Rorschach records, in my experience, this silent invitation to a free and spontaneous response is not accepted and is quite often not even noticed by the testees. Frequently it makes them uneasy, occasionally to the degree of profound distress. They seem to prefer the well-ordered prison life of routine under definite and familiar instructions to the embarrassing and frightening freedom of following their own interests, thoughts, and feelings in a spontaneous undirected response. Instead of finding relief in the absence of rules governing every step of their performance, they make or demand rules, and if they are told that there are no rules, they invent and introduce their own rules, thus limiting the scope of their responses by following the path that seems safer to them because it is fenced in and has signposts so that they cannot lose their way or be surprised by unexpected destinations.

The anxiety aroused by the relative absence of rules and directions in the Rorschach-test situation is related also, as has been pointed out before, to the "dizziness of freedom" in the face of its many possibilities.[13]

---

[13] See above, Chapter 3, p. 23–24.

Just as many adolescents and young adults escape from the anxiety and the burden of the choice what to do with their lives, what career to choose, and so forth, by—often more or less resentfully—following the real or imagined preferences or demands of a parent or teacher, so the tester in the Rorschach-test situation often serves as the focal figure on whom the testee may shift, usually without being aware of it, the burden of choice by imagining that the tester expects one type of response or behavior rather than another.

Thus, the authoritarian-dependent attitudes are always directly related to the problem of *responsibility*. The conscious or unconscious, overt or covert assuming of responsibility or shifting it onto another person, institution, or onto a situation is one aspect of independence (responsibility to oneself) or dependence (somebody or something else is responsible). Responsibility, in this context, is understood as the basic responsibility for one's life, one's decision, and actions. An extremely conscientious person who does his job in the most meticulous, thorough, and faultless way, and therefore is often described as a "responsible" person, may actually be not at all responsible in the sense in which the word is used here. He may unconsciously feel that his life is not his own, but that his whole purpose in life is to do as the authority tells him in order to win the authority's protection, love, and approval. In thus handing his life over to the authority he loses both the freedom and responsibility of choice. Such loss is usually accompanied by conscious or unconscious resentment and by shifting both credit and blame for one's life and what one has done with it onto the "authority." These attitudes, which can be sketched here only very briefly, crudely, and in a much oversimplified way, inevitably also determine the testee's experience and definition of the Rorschach situation and are often apparent from his reactions. The more independent the testee is, the more he will feel that he can structure the Rorschach situation and that what he does with the inkblots is *his* choice, decision, accomplishment, manifestation of *his* way of experiencing and handling the situation and of *his* encounter with the inkblots. The more dependent he is, the more he will feel that he is only doing what somebody else, the authority, asks him to do and that the other person or the situation determines his every move. The conscious or unconscious implication of this attitude often is that the tester is responsible for the testee's reactions, even where the predominant conscious feeling may be one of insufficiency, self-blame, or failure. For example, a person may feel and say that he is not doing well, that he has no imagination, that he is no good, and the same person may also feel and say, perhaps in a tone of reproach and indignation: "But you did not *tell* me that I could have turned the cards" or "But I thought that you wanted me to look at the whole blot only and not to take parts of it" or "I thought you did not want me to take too much time." "I thought this is the kind of thing I was supposed to do" or "How can you do anything else with this kind of material or in this kind of situation?" are the spoken or unspoken tenor of attitudes in which responsibility is shifted from the testee to some other "agency." There are, of course, many different and often very subtle ways in which this shift is brought about and expressed.

The uneasiness and helplessness of the basically dependent and authoritarian character in the face of the nondirective, nonauthoritative Rorschach task may or may not reach awareness. I have the impression that the less conscious his dependence and lack of spontaneity are, the more readily and automatically will the testee tend to introduce his own rules and prohibitions into the Rorschach task, never doubting that they define what he is supposed to do. The more he is aware of his helplessness and fear in such a "free" situation, the more he will either be inclined to ask for directions or to discover how other people behave, or will feel angry, puzzled, bewildered, and helpless. Even the imaginary rules by which the testee tries to define the task more narrowly and strictly than it is given to him do not always suffice to allay his fears, misgivings, and doubts. For the authoritarian-dependent type of personality the ultimate pattern of the Rorschach situation as he experiences it unconsciously—and sometimes also consciously—bears the closest resemblance to a situation which has nowhere been described with greater penetration and lucidity than in the novels, stories, parables, and aphorisms by Franz Kafka, a situation which is most significant for modern man. He is being examined by the authority. But he does not know who the authority is. Is it the man sitting opposite him? Or is this man only a minor functionary behind whom arise the images of a hierarchy of other unknown authorities? He is called upon to do something. But he never quite knows what it is that he is expected to do. There are laws, there must be laws which say what to do. But he does not know them or he is not sure that he knows the right ones. He feels accused, but by whom and of what? How is he going to defend himself against a charge the content of which is unknown to him, and who will tell him what the proper defenses are? He does not know what effect his words will have nor according to what standards they will be judged. Perhaps it is best to do what everybody does, but what does everybody do? And, being accused, should he not do better than everybody? But what is better? Or is it safest, after all, to take refuge in the protective coloring of personal anonymity, to lose oneself entirely and try to be exactly like all the others? Then perhaps one will be overlooked and the threat will pass. Maybe one can even hope to be accepted as one of them, hope to belong. If only one knew what all these others would do in this situation and if one could be sure that the hidden searching eye of the authority will not discover him nor find out his weakness.

The attitudes to authority are closely related to the *strivings for status* and to *competition*. These, too, may affect a subject's definition of the Rorschach situation. It is a relationship deeply rooted in Western cultural institutions. The powerful authority decides who wins in the competitive struggle for superior status. The parental authority will accord the status of favorite, or good or bad child, and thus decide the rivalry of the siblings. The teacher will decide the competitive struggle between his students. The anonymous authority of society, of the market, of public opinion, or of "fate" will decide who wins the battle for success. Even when seemingly the people who are, or have been, the significant representatives of authority in a person's life are regarded by him as rivals in competition whose better he has to prove to be; even when thus no visible authority is left, the desire to "come out on top," to beat everyone else, usually includes the desire to gain or to force acceptance and recognition by an anonymous authority, which may exist only in his own unconscious.

Since the construction of most tests designed for so-called measurement of intelligence or other mental or physical qualities, aptitudes, and personality traits is based on the very principle of competitive comparison, and since these tests also are often closely connected with the subject's competitive experience in school and similar situations, the test situation is likely to activate and spotlight the competitive strivings for superior status and achievement. Persons vary in the emphasis which their experience makes them place on the competitive rivalry with others, or on the judgment of the authority which will decide this competition. In some the authority-aspect will prevail, in others the competitive aspect. The two cannot be entirely separated, and for this reason the attempt to single out the competitive striving for status and achievement in order to discuss its influence on the definition of the

Rorschach situation artificially isolates a trend which cannot be understood entirely in isolation.

The more irrational, neurotic, and indiscriminate the quality of a person's competitive striving for status and achievement becomes, the stronger will it affect his definition of the Rorschach situation. Seen from this angle the Rorschach situation is extended to include an indefinite number of imaginary competitors. The testee's definition of the Rorschach task in competitive terms creates an interpersonal situation in which he tries to compete ambitiously, hopefully, compulsively, anxiously, in despair, or as the case may be, with an indefinite number of others, trying to emerge best, fearing failure, wondering how he is doing. Sometimes such competition may be unconscious, the competitors a shadowy, vague driving force in the back of the testee's mind. Sometimes the indefinite crowd of rivals may crystallize in the conscious image of one or two people, or in the composite image of all the other people whose Rorschach tests the tester has seen, and in the question of what their "achievements" in the same situation were.

Dependence on authority causes the testee to define the Rorschach situation in such a way that he has to follow imaginary authoritative rules. Consequently, he has to be alert and observe these rules and to seek approval of the authority. He is not free to devote his undivided attention and interest to the matter before him. Pronounced competitive strivings cause the testee to define the Rorschach situation in such a way that he has to do better than others, to defeat others. Consequently, he has to imagine the character of the performances of others and try to surpass them. Again, he is not free to devote his interest wholly to the task with which he is confronted. The authoritarian definition of the Rorschach situation tends to restrict it by the introduction of rules to be observed or by the helplessness due to the lack of such rules. The competitive definition of the Rorschach situation tends to restrict it by focusing attention on imagined yardsticks for measuring achievement, on the basis of which the testee believes his performance will be compared with others' performances. Just as the imaginary commands and prohibitions governing the authoritarian Rorschach situation may find various concrete expressions, so the imaginary standards governing the competitive Rorschach situation are conceived by different testees in different concrete ways. In other words, the competitive testee will arrive at some idea, more or less explicit, of what really matters in his responses to the Rorschach inkblots, according to what scale they will be weighed, from what viewpoint they will be judged. The more explicit such an idea is, the more he will then concentrate on that aspect of his responses which, according to his idea, will decide how much better or worse he is doing than others.

Rorschach's observation of the difference between quantitative and qualitative ambition[14] is relevant for this process. Pronounced quantitative or qualitative ambition both often result from a definition of the Rorschach situation in terms of competition. They correspond to two typically different yardsticks according to which different types of competitive testees believe their performances will be judged and will compare favorably or unfavorably with others. *Quantitative* ambition is fostered by the belief that the more responses one gives, the better his performance will be. This belief, in turn, may rest on the idea that a great number of responses will indicate much imagination, industriousness, energy, prolonged concentration, cooperativeness, conscientiousness, or whatever seems important and related to quantity to the testee. Perhaps even more often the testee may have the culturally conditioned idea that quantity as such, a great amount of anything, is better than a smaller amount, and that this applies also to the Rorschach responses. *Qualitative* ambition results from a definition of the Rorschach task according to which certain types of responses are supposed by the testee to be better than others. He attempts, therefore, to produce these "better" responses. An example of this type of ambition is to be found in the attempt to give very original responses. The testee may expend great effort to produce what he believes to be an original or a "different" kind of interpretation, and often he will ask to make sure that no one else has ever given such a response. Or he may worry whether his interpretations are not too banal, whether he can produce something original. Another type of testee will try to satisfy his qualitative ambition by producing only Whole responses—interpretations of the entire inkblot as opposed to those in which only part of the blot is interpreted—because he believes those to be more valuable.

At first glance it might seem as though a *resistant* attitude in the Rorschach situation were equally far removed from, if not opposite to, the authoritarian as well as the competitive definition of the Rorschach situation. Instead of trying to find and follow closely the imaginary rules governing the "authoritarian" Rorschach task, or instead of trying

---

[14] *Psychodiagnostics,* p. 21.

to do one's best in surpassing others in competition, the resistant attitude usually leads to a conscious or unconscious, more or less pronounced reluctance to see anything in the Rorschach inkblots or to develop any interest in them. It may also lead to a type of reaction which the testee, consciously or unconsciously, feels to be the opposite of what he thinks he is expected to do. Despite the manifest difference, even contrast, between Rorschach performances based on an authoritarian or on a competitive definition of the Rorschach situation, on the one hand, and performances due to resistance to the Rorschach situation on the other hand, some of the attitudes to and definitions of the Rorschach situation leading to resistance are closely related to the authoritarian and the competitive attitudes.

The problem of resistance in the Rorschach situation is an exceedingly complex one which cannot and need not be fully discussed here. It is sufficient to designate some typical definitions of the Rorschach situation which imply or lead to resistance. The most effective resistance obviously is the refusal to take a Rorschach test when it is suggested. This refusal may or may not be the result of a perfectly rational decision. One occasionally encounters Rorschach performances which are only a slightly disguised refusal. For example, a boy in a reformatory, who probably felt that the psychologist making Rorschach tests had no business asking him to cooperate and who yet was under institutional pressure, showed his hostility and contempt toward the whole procedure by giving to each card a response with sexual content couched in a wide and, from plate to plate, varying assortment of slang terminology. He had defined the situation in such a way that he was in the role of defending himself against unwarranted intrusion and showing the other fellow where he "got off." Quite a few perfunctory test performances, usually somewhat more effectively disguised, are based on similar attitudes; and their interpretation according to established Rorschach procedure without taking into account the personal meaning of the test situation and its influence on the performance would be entirely misleading. On the other end of the scale of resistance are those people who consciously want very much to cooperate but are unconsciously resistant. They and all others who vary between the points of complete—disguised or undisguised—resistance and that of complete conscious cooperation furnish the considerable reservoir of *ambivalent* attitudes to the Rorschach situation.

When competition is concerned with status rather than with achievement, the Rorschach situation will be defined by some testees as a kind of battle in which they have to prove their superiority to the tester. One way of doing this may lead to the attempt to defeat the imagined purpose of the tester. "You are not going to get anywhere with me" is the unconscious slogan of such performances. While his conscious will to cooperate makes it necessary for the testee to respond, the unconscious satisfaction which he derives from defeating the tester leads him to various kinds of limitations of his responses. He may try to make them as noncommittal and neutral as possible. This usually leads, among other things, to a relative or total absence of H—human being—responses. He may feel that nothing occurs to him. He may feel driven to give responses which he thinks are rather nonsensical or ludicrous. Quite often he will remark on this by saying, for example, "I really don't see how you possibly can get anything out of this."

This is essentially the same attitude as the one encountered often in the psychoanalytic situation where, too, the patient's compulsive need for prestige may temporarily be stronger than his wish to find help and where he unconsciously prefers the satisfaction of defeating the analyst to the help which he seeks consciously but which at the same time he cannot seek wholeheartedly because there would be too much anxiety and resentment aroused in him if he became fully aware of the extent of dependence which seeking help means to him.

Profound feelings of insignificance, weakness, or guilt may lead to a strong fear of being "found out." This may lead to a definition of the Rorschach situation as a trial in which the tester is prosecutor and judge and the testee the defendant who has, above all, to avoid the judge's discovering anything about him, because whatever he finds, the defendant will be doomed. Such a definition of the Rorschach situation often will affect the Rorschach performance in a similar way to that caused by the unconscious desire to defeat the tester in order to prove the testee's superiority.

Another not infrequent definition of the Rorschach situation leading to an ambivalent attitude belongs to the group just discussed of "authoritarian" definitions of the Rorschach situation, with this difference, that rebellion against authority is added to dependence on authority. Hence, the Rorschach situation is defined as one in which the testee is faced with an authority, the task governed by authoritative rules. But, while he feels caught in this situation and somehow dependent on its imagined demands and rules, he wants at the same time to rebel against the authority and the situation. Thus tendencies to cooperate—to "submit"—and tendencies to resist—to "rebel"—are intermingled in individually varying proportions and ways. It depends on the proportional weight and structure of these ambivalent strivings and on the degree to which either one or the other is more or less conscious what their concrete effect on the definition of the Rorschach situation and on the performance will be.

In some cases the contradictory strivings of the ambivalent attitude are expressed in contradictory features of the Rorschach record. For instance, one can often see how the wish to be accepted and appreciated alternates or is mixed up with the wish to defy, with an "I don't care" attitude, and how both these tendencies combine in an authoritarian definition of the Rorschach situation in which the compliant trends determine some, the defiant other features of the record.

The preceding descriptions of various attitudes and of their effect on the experience of the Rorschach situation resulting in various subjective, conscious, and unconscious definitions of that situation are by no means complete or exhaustive. Not only will the observer of Rorschach test performances or the student of Rorschach records have an opportunity to explore variations and combinations of the described examples of definitions of the Rorschach situation, not only will he be able to elaborate them with many finer nuances and an infinite variety of detail, he will also encounter many other attitudes leading to different definitions of the Rorschach situation. Only a few are listed: the attitudes of indifference, indolence, listlessness, depression; the overcritical, minimizing, deprecating attitude; the attitude of withdrawal; different attitudes to the tester in the sense of wanting to exclude him from awareness in order to feel reasonably free and able to concentrate on the test-task, or of wanting him to participate, wanting to include him in the test situation. The definitions of the Rorschach situation described in more detail were selected for two reasons chiefly: first, because they seemed suitable to illustrate the meaning, significance, and effect of what I call the "definition of the Rorschach situation"; and second, because they are typical and very frequently encountered in Western civilization.

While the subjective definition of the Rorschach situation, directly and indirectly, in obvious and in subtle ways, influences the entire Rorschach performance, this influence is not always traceable, not in all the channels through which it is transmitted and not in all its effects. This is not peculiar to the processes described, it is due to the dullness of one's perception. In this respect the instrument of the Rorschach test, while very sensitive and revealing, shares the shortcomings of all one's instruments for the observation of human character and behavior. All that is seen are fragments from which experience and skill have to construct a reasonably likely and rounded picture. Also the categories which Rorschach uses for the analysis of Rorschach performances and which are mostly contained in his different scores do not seem to be equally strongly nor equally directly affected by the testee's definition of the Rorschach situation. This is due to the complex and manifold nature of the processes going on in Rorschach tests and furnishing the material to be studied by the Rorschach method. Some of these processes are more immediately related to the testee's experience of the test situation, to his definition of that situation and the task presented therein. Others concern more directly his perceptual and comprehending apparatus, on which Rorschach's theoretical interest was focused.

The following discussion will consider various factors used in the customary analysis of Rorschach records, such as time, number of responses, certain of Rorschach's scoring categories and other elements of his psychogram, and will explore some of the ways in which they are affected by and susceptible to the testee's definition of the Rorschach situation. In other words, instead of analyzing definitions of the Rorschach situation as entities, as I have done so far, I shall now discuss some of Rorschach's categories in order to explore their relation to the definition of the Rorschach situation. The purpose of this exploration is twofold: first, to pursue further the study of the effect of the definition of the Rorschach situation on the test performance and the test score, thereby making available for the practical interpretation of Rorschach records the methodical tool of exploring and diagnosing the testee's definition of the Rorschach situation; second, to contribute to the understanding of the processes which are expressed in the various Rorschach scores and in the other factors used in traditional diagnosis.

The *number of responses* is strongly affected by the subject's attitude to the Rorschach situation. This is especially true of the very short—below 15—and of the very long—above 60—record. However, an equal number of responses in two records by no means justifies the conclusion that the two testees defined the Rorschach situation in a similar way, nor does a pronounced contrast in the number of responses between two records mean that the two testees had entirely contrasting attitudes to the Rorschach situation. For example, a definition of the Rorschach situation in competitive terms may lead to a record with only 10 responses but also to a record with more than 100 responses, if one subject competes by trying to make his responses definite masterpieces and the other by trying to show that his imagination, his astuteness of observation, his diligence or whatever he believes he is exhibiting by his performance, is inexhaustible.[15] On the other hand, a record with only 10 responses may derive from a definition of the Rorschach situation in terms of competition—qualitative ambition—but also from a definition of the Rorschach situation in terms of a battle between tester and testee, in which the testee wants to defeat the tester—resistance—or from an attitude of indifference and listlessness, by which the Rorschach situation is defined as one more boring, dull, and not-worth-bothering-about event, toward which the testee has the feeling, "It's all the same anyway, and why go to all this trouble?" Often such seeming listlessness is only the cover for an unconscious quite active resistance, which chooses to manifest itself as indolent resignation in order to fight more easily all attempts to overcome it. All forms of resistance may lead—although not necessarily—to a small number of responses. These examples show that no one-way track leads from any single isolated symptom to any single subjective definition of the Rorschach situation. It is necessary to consider the total configuration of many or all elements of a Rorschach performance, the score and psychogram, as well as the single responses and the behavior of the testee, to reach reasonably valid conclusions regarding the testee's experience and definition of the test situation. In this respect, the use of the subjective definition of the test situation as a tool to enrich the understanding and diagnostic value of Rorschach performances is no different from the traditional use of the Rorschach method or, for that matter, from any other method for the diagnosis of personality structure and personality difficulties.

Rorschach enumerates various types of "normal" people—who, in his terminology, include the neurotics—who characteristically give markedly fewer or markedly more responses than the average.[16] The list of those giving few responses comprises depressed, sullen, unobliging persons and those who are ambitious to give responses of the highest qual-

---

[15] These descriptions refer to Rorschach's concepts of qualitative and quantitative ambition. Compare *Psychodiagnostics,* p. 21.

[16] *Ibid.,* p. 21.

ity. The list of those giving many responses consists of cheerful subjects, subjects in good humor, those who enjoy phantasy, those who are interested in the test, those with quantitative ambition, the "model pupils" and similar types. One does not need much experience, imagination, and empathy to see at once that in quite a few of the types enumerated in these lists the paucity or abundance of responses derives directly from their definition of the Rorschach situation and their corresponding attitude to the Rorschach task, and not, or only in secondary ways, from a manner of visually perceiving and comprehending peculiar to them. The sullen and the unobliging give few responses because of their resistance to the test situation as they define it; the people with qualitative ambition because of the particular concept of competition and perfection which they transfer to the Rorschach situation. Those with quantitative ambition give many responses because they define the situation as a competition and the yardstick of success in competition as a quantitative one. The "model pupils" define the Rorschach situation as an authoritarian one in which they want to gain approval and recognition by the "authority," usually with some competitive feeling that they want to get higher credits than others.

The situation is more complicated as far as the few responses of the depressed person and the many responses of the cheerful and good-humored are concerned. A depressive mood operates in various ways at the same time, which all tend to decrease the number of responses to the Rorschach inkblots. It directly affects perception, visual and otherwise; and it also affects the depressed person's definition of the Rorschach situation. The depressed mood severely restricts the general capacity for experience, for being impressed or stimulated by anything; it blunts and retards the receptive processes by which the senses and the mind receive stimuli from the world around them; and it affects in a similar way the reaction to such stimuli and all activity. Visual impressions become dull; perceptiveness is diminished. This leads to a less rich and differentiated perception of the inkblots, as well as to less vivid, slower, and fewer associations to them and thus to fewer responses. In addition to that, the depressed person experiences and defines the Rorschach situation, similar to his entire life situation, as burdensome, unsolvable, weighing down on him. The Rorschach task is changed into one more burden, into a problem which it is laborious and hopeless to tackle and which thus is approached with all the heaviness and plodding effort with which one approaches a problem that one has neither the hope nor the interest to solve, but which is unavoidable. This attitude, too, makes for fewer responses. And finally, the hostility against the self, the severely self-critical and negativistic attitude characteristic of states of depression, leads to an over-critical negativistic attitude to the ideas occurring to the depressed person while he looks at the ink-blots. He tends to reject these ideas because he feels that all he does will be inadequate. He defines the Rorschach situation as a serious, difficult, burdensome task, which will be unsolvable for him or for which, despite laborious effort, he will find only a poor and inadequate solution. Thus, both the depressed person's changed visual perception and comprehension and his definition of the Rorschach situation tend to decrease the number of responses.

The opposite tendency of the elated, cheerful mood to increase the number of responses operates in a similar way. The increased zest and active interest in life characteristic of a cheerful mood have an activating influence, increase the capacity for experience, and open and make richer the sensory and comprehending processes. Thus, the Rorschach inkblots are perceived with greater richness and variety, they stimulate more interest and more associations. The Rorschach task is defined as an interesting experience or as a task which the testee feels confident he will be able to solve.

*Time* is another factor which often is quite markedly affected by a subject's definition of the Rorschach situation. This refers less to the average reaction time per response in any given Rorschach record than to specific time phenomena, which altogether are an interesting and valuable element of Rorschach performances.

Rorschach's remark about the increased reaction time per response of depressives and the shortened reaction time of manics[17]—which applies also to the depressive and the elated mood in "normal" persons—can be explained in the same way as the difference in number of responses between these two groups. Also, people who take the Rorschach situation very seriously tend to have a longer reaction time per response than people who "make light of it" or who are only quite superficially interested in it.

Apart from the rather meager information which the average reaction time per response gives, Rorschach paid attention to time only with regard to the *delay* of response to Plate VIII, the first all-colored plate,

---

[17] *Ibid.*, p. 22.

as an indicator of color shock. In other plates also an increased amount of time elapsing between the exposure of a plate and the first response often indicates shock, such as orientation shock in Plate I, red shock in Plate II, dark shock in Plate IV, and shock caused by the perception of consciously or unconsciously censored material. All these shock reactions have a relation to the testee's definition of the Rorschach situation. They do not occur in people who react freely, spontaneously, and in a relaxed way. They do occur in people who for defensive purposes have to formulate a certain routine of reaction, who have to feel *prepared*, and to whom, therefore, the new, the strange, the unexpected, comes as a shock. Any definition of the Rorschach situation and the Rorschach task which tends to transform them into something to be dealt with according to familiar and definite rules and routine exposes the person so defining the situation to shock whenever he feels a radical or unexpected change. The delay in time is needed in order to regain composure, to mend the damage inflicted to the armor of routine and preparedness, and to make the readjustment which has become necessary since the situation had been defined in too rigid and too narrow terms.

An initial delay of response may also occur without the shock produced by the impact of the first plate, the red, the darkness or the color, when a too narrow or rigid definition of the Rorschach task and a correspondingly rigid method of dealing with it encounter obstacles which do not permit the use of this method. Thus, a rigid intention to begin with a W response to each plate may cause a marked delay if the testee does not succeed in finding a suitable response. It is often not easy or else impossible to decide whether initial delay, for example in Plate VI, is due to the difficulty of finding a W response or to shock caused by the perception of sexual symbols or to shock caused by the pronounced, diffuse, dark shading of the large lower part of the plate.

Often the lapse of time between the last response to a plate and the act of returning the plate or putting it down has a significant relation to the testee's definition of the Rorschach situation. There are quite a few people who find it difficult to part with a plate even when they are unable to see anything more in it. They contrast with those who know when they are finished and put down the plate simultaneously with, or a few seconds after, their last response. Sometimes this delay in relinquishing the plate after the last response is so marked that it shows a considerable strain on the testee, who thinks he ought to find something more to say and yet is unable to do so. If such *end-pauses* occur fairly regularly in each plate, they usually indicate that the testee feels under pressure to produce more responses than ideas occur to him. Such pressure often results from a definition of the Rorschach situation—authoritarian or competitive—in which the testee either feels that certain minimum requirements are imposed on him or in which he feels for some other reason that he will be judged inadequate however hard he tries. End-pauses usually indicate that the testee is not yet satisfied with his performance. It is always worthwhile to try to discover the source of this dissatisfaction. If marked end-pauses occur regularly regardless of the type and number of the preceding responses, then an irrational and compulsive quality of the described dissatisfaction may be assumed, which makes it the more significant for the personality structure. Sometimes the occurrence of the end-pause will be limited to plates to which fewer responses have been given than to those with no end-pauses. In this case the definition of the Rorschach task probably contains a minimum clause. Sometimes the end-pause will be linked with responses which the testee for some other reason considers unsatisfactory; for example, he has failed to find a W response, he has not succeeded in interpreting all parts of an inkblot, or he finds his response too vague. If it is possible to perceive such a connection, it will often contribute to a clearer and more concrete understanding of what the testee felt he ought to do, of his definition of the Rorschach task. A comparison of the time spent on rejected plates or after "unsatisfactory" responses with the time spent on plates which the testee feels he has interpreted successfully, will often give a clue to the testee's intensity of feeling about success and failure and to the weight of pressure to continue an effort when the flow of ideas has ceased.

The *sequence of modes of apperception*—in short, sequence—is one of the most delicate and informative Rorschach tools provided that it is not handled in a mechanical, purely statistical fashion. It responds significantly to the testee's definition of the Rorschach situation as well as it often indicates significant shifts in the testee's experiences throughout the test performance. By sequence Rorschach understands the pattern in which W, D, Dd responses follow each other throughout the ten plates. His description of the various types of sequence is based on a fictitious "standard" of reaction, according to which the subject would start in each plate with the attempt to interpret the inkblot as a whole —W response, then proceed to the interpretation of the more obvious details of the inkblot—D, and finally conclude with one or more of the smallest, less obvious details—Dd. Such a procedure, repeated throughout the ten plates, would result in a rigid sequence. As this procedure is less and less strictly followed, the sequence becomes orderly, then loose; and finally, when no semblance of an organized sequence remains, it is called scattered. The reversal of the usual procedure, starting with D and proceeding to W, is called inverse sequence.

It is obvious that the more or less strict adherence to such a pattern of interpreting inkblots throughout the ten test plates has no direct relation to the particular quality of the usual everyday visual perception and visual experience of a person. In this respect sequence differs profoundly from, for example, the reaction to color in the Rorschach inkblots, which often has a direct relation to the person's general everyday reaction to color. What is it, then, that one is observing when studying "sequence" in a Rorschach record? Rorschach and the literature on Rorschach do not provide an answer as far as I can see. It is the way, I think, in which a subject tries to organize, automatically or consciously, successfully or unsuccessfully, his activity in performing the Rorschach task or—mostly in instances of scattered sequence—does not try to organize his activity. In other words, in sequence one observes largely the method, or lack of method, by which the subject divides the over-all task, to say what the ten inkblots might be, into the concrete tasks of dealing with the individual inkblots and their component parts. The different types of sequence mentioned by Rorschach, however, do not merely represent different plans or methods of procedure. They have to be viewed from various angles. First, they indicate the attempted method, or lack of it, of approaching and dividing the over-all task. Second, they indicate the degree to which the testee has carried out his attempted approach. He may deviate from it for various reasons. It may not be too important to him to follow the same approach in all the ten cards. He may find it too difficult. He may be distracted. He may be so disturbed—shocked—that he cannot do as he would like. Any one of these and other reasons may lead to a sequence other than rigid. For the diagnostic evaluation of the sequence, it is helpful if one is able to discover the specific reasons for the deviation from the fictitious example of the rigid sequence. Loose sequence, for example, may be the outcome of a compulsively rigid method of approach repeatedly disturbed by unexpected shocks and difficulties; it may be the product of an unmethodical or an easily distractible mind, unable to concentrate for more than a few minutes, but it may also be the outcome of a free and easy approach in which the testee does not take the task too seriously and responds to what interests or fascinates him rather than to something to which he feels he is supposed to respond. The variety of possible determinants for each of Rorschach's categories of sequence, a variety greater for the ordered, loose, and reversed than for the extremes of rigid and scattered sequence, accounts for the variety of personality types and disorders which have an affinity to these categories. The description given of two or three entirely different configurations leading to loose sequence explains the fact, observed by Rorschach, that, among others, neurotics as well as artists and imaginative persons often show a loose sequence.[18]

It is apparent from this discussion of the processes underlying the phenomenon of "sequence"[19] that they have the closest relationship to the subject's definition of the Rorschach situation. How someone experiences, comprehends, and feels about a task given to him, how he defines the task, inevitably determines the way in which he sets out to tackle it and very often it also affects the extent to which he can carry out his approach to the task. Rorschach's observation that the most rigid sequence is found among those people who take the test very seriously, and not only the test but everything with which they are confronted in life,[20] emphasizes this close relationship between definition of Rorschach situation and type of sequence. They are the people who feel, consciously or unconsciously, that they are put to a test by a strict authority and that they have to endeavor with great seriousness and with all their mental resources to pass this test, to find recognition by the authority. Hence, they feel that they must not progress as they please but that they have to follow stringent rules; and the rigid observance of an orderly and systematic method in dealing with the ten inkblots is one of those rules which they are likely to impose on the task and on themselves. Rorschach mentions pedants as belonging to this group of people who take the test very seriously, as well as "schoolmaster" personalities, depressed persons with inferiority feelings, anxious persons, and melancholics.[21]

---

[18] *Ibid.*, p. 43. Rorschach says that many neurotics, imaginative persons, and artists show a loose sequence. The English translation makes of this: "many imaginative, neurotic artists."

[19] The discussion is by no means complete. An exploration of the very interesting problem of the "scattered" sequence of many schizophrenic personalities, which would lead away from the main topic of this chapter, would show still other factors involved in "sequence."

[20] *Psychodiagnostics*, p. 43.

[21] *Ibid.*, p. 43.

The pedant and the "schoolmaster," dependent on authority and authoritative rules, define the Rorschach situation in authoritarian terms. At the same time they usually derive a good deal of satisfaction from the "excellence" of their performance because they enjoy unconsciously the tyrannical and pedantic mastery to which they subject the material before them, in their turn; and, feeling that they have done well, they seem to share the power of the authority whose imagined rules they have upheld in following them. In this satisfaction they differ from the depressives, the melancholics, and the anxious. These experience only the difficulty of a task governed by all the rules which a strict authority expects them to follow. It would lead too far to pursue the interesting and rewarding problem of the great variety of definitions of the Rorschach situation related to the other types of sequence. The reader acquainted with Rorschach's test will be able, on the basis of what has been said so far, to continue such an exploration.

Provided a certain minimum of intellectual equipment, any person can interpret the Rorschach inkblots in a rigid sequence if asked to do so, that is, if he determines to do so and directs his attention and will accordingly. Sequence, in other words, is one of the factors in Rorschach's test which can be easily influenced by volition.[22] It shares this quality particularly with the *clarity of form perception*. If an intellectually normal person is asked to see to it that his interpretations of the inkblots are confined to really accurate likenesses, he can increase the percentage of clearly and accurately seen forms—F + %—in his responses.[23] The reason for this is that both methodicalness of approach to a given task and accuracy in perceiving, comparing, and selecting objects of similar shapes are conscious intellectual functions—which does not prevent them from becoming more or less automatic and being exercised habitually in varying degrees by most "normal" people if no special attention is called to them. Both play a prominent role in the training and education of the intelligence. To recognize things, and later to recognize the shapes of letters and words in learning to read, is one of the most continuously trained faculties in childhood. And the tasks given in school are replete with the demand to deal with them in a systematic, methodical way. Accuracy—F + %—and method—sequence, thus, are not only amenable to conscious purposeful manipulation, they cannot only be "improved" to a rigid 100 per cent standard

---

[22] *Ibid.*, p. 67.
[23] *Ibid.*

of perfection; they are also faculties which have become intimately associated, through the whole intellectual training of childhood and adolescence, with the sphere of authoritative rules and tasks. The demands to be attentive, to concentrate, to be accurate, to go about one's work methodically are explicitly and implicitly major demands of this early period of training. Most people have quite often been told by some "authority" or other that they could meet these demands if only "they put their minds to it," if only "they really wanted to do it." It is not surprising, then, that those people who experience the Rorschach situation as a situation in which, once again, they are asked by some "authority" to do something and in which they will be judged according to how well they do it, are likely to transform the Rorschach situation into a familiar "school" scene and, in their endeavor to give a good account of themselves, act according to rules and try to "work" along lines which have the closest association or are identical with the rules and authoritative demands which have governed such an important part of their lives and their mental training. Their high F + % does not derive, as it does in some others, from their perceptiveness, their gift of seeing and observing; neither the depressive nor the pedant has these gifts. It derives from their definition of the Rorschach situation, which, in turn, expresses their general attitude to life. They are the people who, in Rorschach's words, take the test "very seriously." They are the people who feel that they are tested and judged by a strict authority, which is the "serious" situation par excellence of their whole life. It is for these reasons that one finds both the tendency to strict sequence and the tendency to a high F + % with particular frequency and most pronounced among those people who, because of their character structure —pedantic and "schoolmaster" personalities, or the mental state in which they are—depressed, define the Rorschach situation as an examination by a strict authority according to exacting rules and standards.

The already discussed production of a great quantity of responses and the rigid endeavor to respond to each and every part of the inkblots, not to omit any detail especially if no W response has been found, to exhaust the given task completely, are other types of behavior in which the subject reverts to such consciously manipulatable standards of "excellence" as may have governed his earlier experience in school and similar situations, and transfers them to the Rorschach situation because he experiences and defines it in the described way.

Rorschach observes that the same group of people who show the tendency to strictest sequence and highest $F + \%$ also are the ones who are most acutely and often painfully conscious throughout the test of the fact that they interpret inkblots and do not "recognize" pictures.[24] While, as a rule, only psychotics, oligophrenics, or people with low although still normal intelligence may believe that they recognize definite pictures in the inkblots and that nobody could see anything different from what they see in them, the usual "normal" awareness of interpreting rather than recognizing is in only the background of the average person's mind, especially the more he becomes interested in and absorbed by what he is doing. In the depressive and the pedantic personality, however, attention is focused on what they tend to define as the essential requirement of the task: doing systematic accurate work rather than letting their imagination play. They tend to doubt all the time whether their interpretations are sufficiently accurate likenesses of the inkblot shapes. They tend to be disturbed by their feeling that nothing they can think of really seems to fit the inkblots, a feeling which may lead to angry criticism of the "shortcomings" of the inkblots in some pedantic people, or to a feeling of their own inadequacy in most depressive people. But both groups are alike in that they are never "carried away" by their interpretations, and never forget that they cannot quite achieve the desired congruence between interpretation and inkblot although they do their utmost to achieve it. They are, in Rorschach's words, most aware of the assimilative effort in interpreting the inkblots. I believe that this behavior is a manifestation of a lack of relatedness to the world around them and of a corresponding definition of the Rorschach situation which does not permit the establishment of any spontaneous relation to and interest in the inkblots. In terms of Rorschach's categories, this lack of relatedness to the world, characteristic of the "pedantic" and the "depressive" group, also appears in their coarted—or coartative—experience type: in the absence of color and movement responses. In terms of the meaning of the Rorschach situation to these people a few more words are needed to give at least a general description of their attitude. Neither the pedantic nor the depressive type experiences himself as part of the world and the life around him but as pronouncedly separate from it, although in different ways. To both the world outside them appears as a tremendous force with which they have to cope, in different ways. They are not part of the

---

[24] *Ibid.*, pp. 17–18, 23.

stream of life around them. They are in opposition to it, not because
they want to oppose it, in an active way, but as the victims of a superior
force are opposed to it, because they feel that this force threatens to
engulf them. Their separateness, aloneness, lack of relatedness, are
their main common characteristics. The depressive personality tends to
feel that he is helpless, that he cannot do anything, that every step he
takes is really a hopeless step, that the situation confronting him is quite
beyond his ability and power. Every act, every attempt to do something, every gesture to cope with the overwhelming weight of the world
around him, appears enormously difficult, laborious, and also quite use-
less and futile to him. He cannot hope to do anything adequate. The
pedantic personality usually has repressed the feeling of strangeness
and helplessness toward the world around him and is conscious only of
his devices to cope with the world. Yet these devices are mostly a defense against the threat of being engulfed by the chaotic turbulent life
around him. He must unfailingly follow his pedantic ritual which keeps
these chaotic forces from him and gives him the feeling that he has
imposed order on chaos, a feeling which may even permit him to enjoy
his mastery and domination. But whenever he is unprepared, whenever
he encounters life without being able to subject it to his protective system of order, routine, and minute preparedness, he feels threatened. A
strange and new situation, like the Rorschach situation, brings the described feelings and tendencies of the depressed and the pedantic personality into play. They both tend to experience the Rorschach task as
something that is imposed on them. It comes from the outside. They are
confronted with it. They have to cope with it. It does not become their
own, they do not develop any genuine and spontaneous interest in it. It
remains part of the strange and threatening outside world. The depressive personality feels that he will not be able to cope with it, the pedantic personality starts at once to look for the magic rules and rituals
which govern this situation and tries to apply the ones that he is accustomed to apply. It is the fact that both the pedantic and the depressive
personality's definition of the Rorschach situation emphasizes the
strange task which is imposed on them from the outside which makes
them remain conscious all the time that they are not doing something of
their own but that they are trying to find the correct way to deal with
an unknown potentially dangerous situation. They have to check constantly whether they are really on the right track, the depressive considering this unlikely, the pedantic making sure that he has followed the
correct protocol. Their increased awareness of assimilative effort, em-

phasized by Rorschach, is but an expression of their fundamental unrelatedness and of their feeling of being caught in a strange and threatening situation, being confronted with a strange task of unknown portent, rather than feeling that they participate actively in a situation which stimulates their interest and which they can mold according to their particular interest. They remain aware, often painfully and self-consciously, that someone else, someone in authority, is asking them to do something strange, which they do not feel sure how to handle; and therefore their interpretations of the inkblots are given under the strain of doubting or of having to discover whether they really do conform to the imagined requirements of the task, particularly to the requirement of accurate likeness. The task never becomes their own, as it does with those people who are fascinated by it, who enjoy the discoveries they make in interpreting the inkblots, and do not experience the task as something imposed on them nor the inkblots as difficult problems which they might fail to solve correctly. There is a direct and positive correlation between the feeling that the Rorschach situation involves a strange and difficult task, imposed from the outside by an authority—personal or impersonal, and the awareness of assimilative effort. From the maximum oppressive awareness of assimilative effort to a minimum or even to complete unawareness of it, there is a scale of transition which shows such a variety of degrees and qualities of that awareness and of corresponding feelings about the Rorschach task, that it would be impossible to describe them adequately in limited space and without considerable repetition.

Not only the sequence of *modes of apperception* but also the various modes themselves are frequently influenced by, and related to, the testee's definition of the Rorschach situation. It has been mentioned previously that an authoritarian or a competitive definition of the Rorschach situation may lead to the belief that some types of responses are better than others, and that it is, therefore, important to concentrate one's efforts on the production of those responses. The most outstanding example of this is the *Whole* response—W. Rorschach's "W+ type" is a good illustration. He responds to the inkblots with 10 or approximately 10 W responses, one for each plate. As Rorschach states, these performances are somewhat artificial feats.[25] He has encountered them mostly

---

[25] *Ibid.*, 41. Rorschach's word *Kunststück* for such a performance is not a "work of art"—*Kunstwerk*—as the English translation has it, but rather a trick or stunt performance, a *tour de force*. It always has something more or less forced and artificial about it.

in intelligent people who suspect the test to be one of the ability to make abstractions and combinations and who seek to excel by a brilliant performance.[26] This describes a typical part of a definition of the Rorschach situation in the sense of this chapter. But essentially similar definitions of the Rorschach situation leading to an exclusive or predominant production of W responses may be based on other varieties of the belief that W responses are "better" than others or are the only ones that count. Performances of the W+ type may be based on the idea that W responses are more inclusive than others. I have seen records in which Rorschach's question asked with the submission of the first plate: "What might this be?" was defined by the testee as meaning that one W response only was required and permitted. This is a typically authoritarian-ambitious definition of the Rorschach situation, in which the testee at the same time narrows the Rorschach task by quite stringent requirements to which he feels bound and makes those requirements such that they can be met only by the ambitious performance of the W+ type. The W+ type, thus, shows varying mixtures of submissive ambitiousness, aggressive will to give a brilliant performance, usually some kind of perfectionism, and sometimes a narcissistic pleasure in his own performance.

Next to the W response, the *Dd response* has a close relation to the definition of the Rorschach situation. By Dd response—small detail response—Rorschach understands interpretations of all those details of the inkblots which do not belong to the statistically most frequently interpreted details. They are usually not selected for interpretation by the average person, mostly because they are too small to attract his attention. About their symptomatic significance, Rorschach says that the more grumbling, faultfinding, pedantic, or petty a person is, the more Dd responses will appear in his record.[27] As far as the "normal" personality—which includes the neurotic—is concerned, this symptomatic significance of the Dd response, in my experience, is too narrow. There are many persons who give a good many Dd responses without being particularly faultfinding, pedantic, or petty. The reason for this becomes more apparent if one examines the Dd response in the light of the subject's definition of the Rorschach situation and of his experience in giving Dd responses. Two types of "Dd-attitudes" emerge from such an examination. One is the Dd response given on the basis of quantita-

---

[26] *Ibid.*

[27] *Ibid.*, p. 40.

tive ambition, of the striving to give many responses, whether this desire takes the form of setting oneself a minimum standard of the number of responses to be given to each plate, or whether it takes the form
of wanting to give a great many responses, as many as possible. The
other type is the Dd response given on the basis of a particular kind of
"accuracy," a concern about the minute, the unessential, the smallest
detail of everything. Chiefly, this latter type has the significance which
Rorschach attributes to all Dd responses given by "normal" subjects.

The "quantity" Dd is an almost inevitable result of the desire to give
a great number of responses. This is due to the objective fact that there
are only ten whole inkblots, a considerably larger but limited number
of ordinary details—D, but an infinite number of Dd. In addition, the
people who have a strong quantitative ambition always feel under some
pressure. This pressure, usually of competitive or authoritarian origin,
inevitably leads to a restriction of their imaginative, creative, inventive
powers, to a more or less cramped attitude, which hampers the richness
and the free flow of ideas and associations. Hence, they are usually not
able to give a great variety of responses to the limited number of W
and D. Thus, both the objective and the subjective limitations of W and
D responses tend to make these people resort to the interpretation of
Dd's, the limitless number of which would permit them to continue
forever. Of course, such an attitude also leads to a very stereotyped
kind of response which is characteristic of these performances. The
"quantity" Dd results usually from the same psychic tendencies which
have been discussed in connection with quantitative ambition. It tends
to appear near the end of the responses to each plate after the testee
has more or less exhausted the other possibilities of interpretation—W
and D, yet feels obliged to continue.

Dd responses may also result from the qualities which Rorschach believed to be their only source in "normal" persons, namely grumbling
and pedantry. The attitude leading to these Dd is not one of quantitative ambition but one of overconcern about and interest in the unessential, the petty. It often combines traits of obstinacy, pedantry, pettiness.
Instead of dealing with the essential aspects of a situation, a problem,
an experience, these people cling to minor considerations, indicate
small deficiencies, and are worried if not everything is 100 per cent
consistent. Sometimes their interest in the Dd parallels an interest in all
the deviations from exact symmetry in the inkblots. Whereas the quantity Dd is mostly a function of the subject's definition of the Rorschach

task and has little or no direct relation to his characteristic manner of visual perception and comprehension, the "petty" Dd is related to both the individual processes of visual—and other—perception and comprehension *and* to the individual definition of the Rorschach situation. The "petty"-Dd type of person, in looking at paintings, at the furniture in a room, at a building, will be equally likely to detect "flaws," or to be interested in minor things which strike him as "curious" or inconsistent, as he is likely to concentrate on the minor details—Dd—of the Rorschach inkblots. At the same time these Dd are very often the expression of a definition of the Rorschach situation—and of the subject's life situation in any other interpersonal relationship—in ambivalent terms. On the one hand, he "submits" to the situation defined in authoritarian terms; on the other hand, he evades or rebels against the "authority" and tries to *assert* himself by clinging to minor details instead of dealing frontally with essentials.

The examination of Rorschach responses from the viewpoint of their function of serving as an act and expression of the testee's *self-assertion* makes it possible to find the common denominator for both the "quantity" and the "petty" Dd, and thus, extending Rorschach's findings, to define the general symptomatic significance of Dd responses in "normal" subjects. The self-assertive quality of Rorschach responses is largely a function of the definition of the Rorschach situation in terms of a proving ground of the testee's value, personality, status. The more he tends to define the situation in authoritarian or competitive terms, in terms of having to prove himself in order to meet authoritative or competitive standards, the more his responses will assume for him the function of having to assert his personality in terms of the values and goals which he introjects into the Rorschach situation. Since the "normal" person usually tends to feel that the Dd response is not so adequate and satisfactory a means of dealing with the Rorschach inkblots as are W or D responses, the attempt to assert himself by offering Dd responses has the quality of a *substitute* for a more complete, more direct self-assertion. Rather than not respond at all or stop responding, the testee resorts to a Dd. This quality is equally apparent in the quantity Dd as it is in Rorschach's petty Dd. The traits represented by the latter—grumbling, pettiness, pedantry—have the function of asserting oneself in a negative or petty way where insecurity and fear block an open and direct self-assertion. Similarly, in the quantity Dd the testee tries to assert his capacities by resorting to more and more Dd since he cannot find any other responses. Here too the Dd response is produced to defend himself against the pressure and insecurity of the test situation and to overcome the feeling of inadequacy. Since his W and D responses, due to his insecurity and incapacity for direct and open self-assertion, are felt by him not to be sufficient proof of his "value," and since he cannot produce any more of these, instead of deciding to finish with a Rorschach plate he resorts to Dd responses. Even if these become obviously quite stereotyped and meaningless, he will often go on and on, since their meaning to him is not contained in the significance of what he sees in the inkblots but in the mere fact that he keeps on responding and thus asserting and proving that he does not "fail." [28]

The *content* of responses is another area which is quite often directly influenced by the testee's definition of the Rorschach situation. This influence may be a positive or negative one; it may lead to the selection of or emphasis on certain types of content or to elimination and censorship regarding other types of content. The most frequent example of the latter is the conscious suppression of sexual content. The testee defines the interpersonal situation in the Rorschach test in such a way that sexual content would be embarrassing to him. With subjects who are more or less familiar with psychoanalysis, one often gets the opposite reaction: they define the situation with reference to their idea of psychoanalytic free association and feel not only free but quite often obliged to give as many responses with sexual content as they can bring themselves to discover in the inkblots.

A definition of the Rorschach situation in authoritarian or competitive terms leads some people to a preference for such areas of content as they feel will best meet the standards of the authority, or of the imagined decision on the competition. From Rorschach's own discussion of the significance of the content of responses, the anatomy responses are examples. He found that many morons, especially morons with hysterical features, who feel that they have to show "intelligence" give anatomical responses.[29] This observation can be extended to cover

---

[28] This discussion of the symptomatic significance of Dd responses and of their relation to the definition of the Rorschach situation does not apply to the typical schizophrenic Dd, which comes from other sources. It applies to the majority of "normal Dd" responses. Occasionally Dd in "normal" people will have other origins and accordingly other significance. See also Furrer's remarks on the significance of Dd. Albert Furrer, *Der Auffassungsvorgang beim Rorschach'schen psychodiagnostischen Versuch* (Zürich, 1930), pp. 6, 55–56.

[29] Rorschach, *op. cit.,* p. 45.

a considerable number of quite "normal" people in whom the Rorschach situation induces a sort of school-attitude. They seem to feel that certain types of responses will be more appreciated by the "teacher"— and therefore by themselves. Usually, these responses are taken from the fields of anatomy, biology, geography, and sometimes art. They are intended to be "scientific" or simply "educated" responses.

If in the definition of the Rorschach situation the desire "not to be found out" plays a considerable role, the content of the responses may be influenced in the direction of neutrality and lack of personal significance. This type of testee will try to limit his responses to such objects as he feels to be noncommittal. Quite often this leads to the reduction or exclusion of responses in which human beings are seen—H responses.

Besides such direct influence of the definition of the Rorschach situation on the content of responses, one can frequently observe an indirect one. Stereotypy of the content of responses or poverty of ideas may be due not to a lack of intelligence, as it often is, but also to a tense, defensive, or in other ways rigid attitude and a corresponding definition of the Rorschach situation which do not permit a free flow of associations.

With the discussion of number and time of responses, modes of apperception and their sequence, $F + \%$, and content of responses, those factors of the Rorschach psychogram have been examined which are directly affected by the testee's definition of the Rorschach situation. On some other factors the subject's definition of the Rorschach situation seems to have an indirect influence only, or else the influence is not so apparent and traceable as in those discussed. These other factors are the movement, color, and shading responses. Phenomena of shock, inhibition, and disturbance which occur with regard to these responses seem to be the main way in which the indirect influence of the definition of the Rorschach situation on the occurrence of these responses becomes visible. The more rigid and tense the definition of the Rorschach situation, the more likely does it lead to an inhibition of M responses and to color and dark-shock or other color disturbances. Shading responses, with the exception of Ch, may have another relation to the definition of the Rorschach situation. More than color and movement responses, though usually less than form responses, their number often increases disproportionately more than the total number of responses. If a subject tries to find as many responses as possible, if he goes "out of his way," forcing himself to look for responses, he can always find more form responses and also more shading responses than color and movement responses. This is partly due to the fact that color responses are usually given either to the whole inkblot or to those parts of one inkblot which are covered by one color, and that these uniformly colored areas usually coincide with the normal detail—D. In contrast to that, shading responses can be given and are frequently given to minute areas of shading—Dd areas, and there is, for all practical purposes, an unlimited quantity of such areas. Moreover, the attitude in giving shading responses very often is one of *looking for* minute things in the shading, whereas in color responses the subject is usually *impressed or struck by* the impact of color. Movement responses also do not occur, as a rule, in Dd areas but typically only in W or D areas. Thus, a definition of the Rorschach situation in terms of quantitative ambition may lead to a disproportionately strong increase in the number of shading responses for the same reason as it often does with regard to the number of form and Dd responses.

One of the difficulties in diagnostic work with the Rorschach method, as with other methods of psychiatric and psychological diagnosis, arises from the fact that every single element of the score and the psychogram —every single "symptom"—may be caused by several different psychic dynamisms. Even syndromes of several symptoms—several factors in score and psychogram, although of greater diagnostic value because they may point from several directions to the same dynamism—do not always come from the same causes and therefore do not always have the same meaning. In this, among other things, lies the weakness and the danger of all "sign" methods of diagnosis which rely on the combined occurrence of several symptoms—"signs"—in one record for their diagnostic conclusions. Ultimately, this difficulty traces to the fact that observation of human behavior always is observation of fragments only of human behavior, out of which the observer has to construct a reasonably probable and coherent picture of the total personality structure or of such personality dynamisms as are relevant to the special problem in which he is interested. One is in no different position if one tries to gain insight into a person's definition of the Rorschach situation on the basis of his Rorschach responses, their score and the psychogram. Only by careful consideration of all factors and their total configuration, by paying attention to contradictory factors in the total picture and trying to account for them can one arrive at a reasonable hypothesis. The fragments of the subject's reactions which one gets to see in his Rorschach responses often are supplemented in an illuminating way by the observation of his *behavior in the Rorschach situation*. Rorschach has already emphasized that it is helpful to observe and record not only the responses of the testee but also his facial expressions, voluntary and involuntary movements, and signs of possible color shock.[30] This material is of particular value for an accurate picture of the subject's definition of the Rorschach situation. The manner of speech, intonation, changes in speech behavior, the postural behavior, the way of sitting in the chair, the manner of handling the Rorschach cards, the questions asked and the remarks made, the conversation between tester and testee, all this is helpful in arriving at a better understanding of the way in which the testee experiences the Rorschach situation, especially if such observations are checked against the material derived from the score and psychogram. The evaluation of the testee's behavior need not be discussed here. The technique of such evaluation is not different in the Rorschach situation from that of the interview situation.

One aspect of the manipulation of the Rorschach cards, however, deserves some attention because it is peculiar to the Rorschach situation: the *turning*, or not turning, of the cards by the testee so that he may look at the inkblots from various angles. Some Rorschach workers tell the testee before or while they hand him the first plate that he may turn the plates and look at them from different directions. I believe that it is more informative if, in this respect as in all others, one introduces as few directives, instructions, rules, and suggestions as possible into the situation, so that the testee may have the greatest possible scope for a spontaneous undirected performance. Rorschach seems to have had the same principle in mind when he wrote that it is essential to avoid coercion and pressure as much as possible.[31] If left to themselves, subjects will vary a great deal in their card-turning behavior. To some the idea of turning the cards will never occur. To some it will occur; they will start to turn one card quite tentatively only to return it to the original position. Sometimes this is done almost surreptitiously, as though it were something forbidden. I have seen quite a few people who either showed an amazing ability to see things upside down or who turned their head in order to look at the card from a different angle but did not dare turn the card. The position of the card as it was handed to them

---

[30] *Ibid.*, p. 54.
[31] *Ibid.*, p. 16.

must have seemed sacrosanct even when they were looking at it from a different angle. Others will ask whether they may turn the cards and do so when they are told that they can do as they please. Some, even after receiving "permission" to turn the cards, will not turn them, or, having turned them immediately after having been told that they may do so, will forget about it and look at all the following cards only in the original position. Many will turn the cards spontaneously, without asking whether they are permitted to do so. Some will turn all cards upside down demonstratively before the first response or even before they have looked at the card. It is useful to pay attention also to the moment at which a testee either asks whether he may turn the cards or starts turning them spontaneously. It may be a moment of stress, when he feels he should give more responses but cannot see anything more in the original position, or when he has not been able to see anything at all in the card. Others want to begin prepared, knowing exactly what they are supposed to do and not to do, and ask the question about turning before, or right after, they have received the first card; the same behavior, of course, might also have motivations other than preparedness. While occasionally some card-turning behavior seems to speak for itself, it is as important here as with any other factor in the Rorschach test to remain aware of the fact that any isolated element of behavior may have more than one possible explanation and may originate from quite different motivations. On the other hand, two seemingly widely different kinds of behavior may come from the same motivation. Thus, the testee who defines the Rorschach situation in markedly authoritarian terms, as a task governed by stringent rules and to be handled "correctly," may arrive at two seemingly quite opposite types of behavior with regard to turning the card. He may be profoundly convinced, possibly without being aware of it, that one has to accept every situation just as it presents itself at first, that there is no way of influencing or changing any situation in life. His conviction makes him incapable of looking at any problem or anything from a "different angle" and this applies, quite literally, to the Rorschach inkblots. The angle at which they are presented to him, their original position, is *the* position in which he has to look at them; nothing can be changed about that. He has to accept and to comply with the situation as it is presented to him. But a testee of quite similar character structure, who also feels that the Rorschach situation is governed by a severe authority and strict rules, may decide that in order to solve the problem correctly and completely and to make a really thorough job of it, he has to turn and look at each plate religiously from all angles, or at least in the original and the reversed positions, and to try and find some responses for each of these positions. On the other hand, not turning the plates is, in itself, by no means an indicator of an authoritarian character. These examples are given only to illustrate the need for a comprehensive study of all available material in a Rorschach record before arriving at a diagnostic interpretation of any single factor in the material.

Awareness of the testee's definition of the situation does not only contribute substantially to the diagnostic evaluation of his Rorschach performance and thus to a better understanding of his personality, it is also important for a correct evaluation of the information which the testee may give when asked how and where he has seen what he mentions in his response to an inkblot. Such an *inquiry* may be necessary when the response itself is not sufficient to indicate clearly the percept on which the testee's response was based. Rorschach workers differ in the extent to which they carry out this inquiry. Rorschach himself seems to have asked only where he felt a need for further clarification, and I find this practice usually quite adequate. Some others, however, feel that an inquiry should be made into all responses, and Klopfer, the chief proponent of this group, has written at some length about the technique to be used in such an inquiry.[32] However, neither he nor other adherents of the practice of a complete or extended inquiry seem to be aware of the need to interpret and evaluate rather than to take at face value the information given in the inquiry by the testee. This need arises not only from the fact, to which Rorschach pointed with regard to color and movement responses,[33] that many people do not know, or are not able to indicate reliably, whether and how their percepts were affected by color, kinesthesia, and other factors. It is at least as much due to the fact that *the testee's definition of the inquiry situation may lead him, consciously or unconsciously, to change his original spontaneous percepts.* The inquiry situation differs markedly from the Rorschach situation in its objective aspects; it is a new experience, a changed situation for the testee, who will define it in a way characteristic of his personality.

To understand and interpret correctly both the information and additional responses given by the testee in the inquiry or in the procedure

---

[32] Klopfer and Kelley, *op. cit.*, pp. 40–51.
[33] Rorschach, *op. cit.*, pp. 30 and 26.

known as "testing the limits" (Klopfer's term), it is essential to be aware of the meaning which these situations have for the testee and in which ways this meaning differs from the meaning of the spontaneous Rorschach performance where the testee first encountered the inkblots and responded to them and to the Rorschach task. The significance of the subjective definition of the inquiry situation will become apparent if we consider some examples, typical of different attitudes.

Two frequent, seemingly opposite ways of experiencing and defining the inquiry situation are (1) as an attack, a criticism, a calling to account; (2) as a reassuring and supporting contact with the tester. Both these definitions of the inquiry situation are often parataxic distortions of the dependent variety,[34] the first a defensive reaction, the second a support-seeking reaction. Both occur mostly among people who defined the Rorschach situation in an authoritarian way.

The definition of the inquiry as an *accounting for* and *justifying* of responses can be observed very frequently.

In the Rorschach situation the testee is free to see, to discover, and to say whatever he wanted. In the inquiry he is asked to explain his responses, to describe them in greater detail. Many people tend to experience this changed situation in such a way that they feel called upon to account for their responses in one way or another. If they have felt from the beginning that the Rorschach situation was some kind of examination or other, their suspicions are now confirmed. No matter how convincingly the tester may try to explain to them that he is interested in their responses and he wishes they would tell him some more about them, they will interpret it, unconsciously if not consciously, that now they have to justify what they have seen. Others will feel deceived. First they were made to believe that everything they saw was all right, and now they have to explain what they saw. So the tester must have found something the matter with their responses. Both these attitudes will inevitably foster the wish to show that their responses were quite "all right," quite "good" responses, and the explanation of the previously given responses will tend more or less to describe them in terms which, in the eyes of the testee, will show that they were quite "good" responses. Since the instructions and the Rorschach inkblots themselves invite imagination, the concepts formed on the basis of the inkblots, the

---

[34] Sometimes they are not distortions but due to the conscious or unconscious attitude of the tester. This aspect will be considered later in the context of the role of the personality of the tester in the Rorschach situation.

things perceived in them, usually are not and cannot be accurate likenesses and frequently they are quite vague if measured by standards of realistic accuracy. In the inquiry situation the spell of the Rorschach situation is broken. If he has been fascinated by these phantastic inkblots, the imaginative person may well feel that now he is required to explain pedantically each flight of his phantasy. And the countless people with an always ready reservoir of guilt and inferiority feelings may now feel embarrassed or ashamed, because in the cold light of critical observation the puzzling or elusive image that seemed to have some likeness to the inkblot when they first perceived it, suddenly has lost all such likeness. Sometimes this change in attitude is so great that people really do not recognize any more what they have seen before.

The general effect of the defensively experienced inquiry will be restrictive. The restriction may occur along the lines of having to be more careful and accurate, of having to defend or better one's "record." This may also lead to the giving of additional responses in the inquiry. Often additional responses arising from this type of motivation will show the marks of constriction because too much effort to find a "good" or an "unassailable" response has gone into their perception.

The inquiry may be experienced as *support* and *reassurance,* for example by some of the people who feel helpless, insecure, or anxious in a situation in which they are free to do what they want. As soon as questions are asked, they feel they have something to go on and they can form some idea, correct or mistaken, of what the tester wants them to do. Also they feel more in contact with the tester if an exchange of questions and answers takes place and this may have a reassuring effect. They are often people who find silence difficult to bear. Even when the tester has the desirable attitude of a genuine interest in them and their way of seeing the Rorschach cards, they need some "activity" which will prove a contact, a sharing that they cannot experience when the other person is silent. Their attitude is similar to one often found in the psychoanalytic situation. There this type of analysand wants above all some kind of "cue" from the analyst, a question, a remark, a behavioral cue which will permit him to orient himself along the lines of the analyst's real or imagined "expectations" rather than feel, think, and express his own feelings and thoughts. This kind of person sometimes will be more productive in the inquiry situation than in the spontaneous Rorschach performance and, with the support experienced in the inquiry situation, feel freer and therefore able to see more and to see in a less constricted, more personally meaningful way.

The same person may feel both called upon to account for his responses, to prove that they are good, and encouraged because he feels no longer alone and interprets the tester's questions in such a way that he can use them as some kind of directive or approval.

The inquiry may also be experienced as *boring*, especially if a systematic inquiry into each response is made. This may be a rational, justified, or irrational reaction. Where the responses of the testee have been reasonably clear, the inquiry is often superfluous and therefore experienced by the testee as obtuseness and lack of understanding on the part of the tester. Even a pertinent question may be experienced rationally in this way if it concerns, e.g., a determinant that is important for the percept and not to be ascertained from the original response, but if in terms of everyday communication the testee is justified in feeling that he has made sufficiently clear what he saw. The testee's feeling that the inquiry is boring and the tester obtuse is diagnostically significant only when it points to a disturbance in communication. For example, the testee may assume in an *egocentric* way that everybody sees things the same way as he does and that therefore what he sees should be quite apparent to anybody else. Or the testee may express himself in a cryptic or autistic way so that objectively he does not communicate while subjectively he is convinced that he does and reacts with disappointment, hurt, anger, etc., when he feels that his communication has not been understood. Such faulty communication or breakdown of meaningful communication is of course diagnostically very important and often becomes apparent in the reactions of the testee to the inquiry. The feeling of being bored because the tester is so stupid as not to understand what the testee has said is not the only reaction to be found in such cases. Reactions may range all the way from annoyance and arrogance to despair and anxiety.

There are, of course, many other attitudes and feelings, besides these frequent and typical ones, that may determine the testee's definition of the inquiry situation. It may be used for a withholding and being-prodded kind of relationship, it may offer an opportunity for narcissistic display, or cause feelings of insufficiency. Instead of being experienced as reassuring it may activate suspicion, fear, and distrust.

One concrete example may serve to illustrate the problematic nature of the information received in the inquiry, and the kind of mistakes to which the acceptance at face value of such information may lead. Many people see in Plate I and in Plate V a bat or a butterfly. When they give such a response, they usually have in mind that the whole inkblot more

or less looks like a bat or a butterfly. Their response is a Whole response
—W. If an inquiry is made, they are asked to show to the tester the bat
or butterfly they have seen before. In this changed situation they will
restudy the plate and through the minds of many of them some thought
such as this may pass: "Well, it does not really look altogether like a
butterfly. How does a butterfly look? Does he have these things sticking
out at the side? I don't think he has. I suppose what I meant was that
all this looked like a butterfly but not those things at the side." And with
perfect sincerity or, as the case may be, with a more or less faint awareness that they are changing something which surely does not matter
much one way or another, they proceed to delineate to the tester on the
inkblot that by butterfly they meant all of the inkblot with the exception of the two lateral extensions on each side of Plate V. The changes
may be considerably greater and more important than the one just described. But even this change would lead some Rorschach workers to
give to such a response the score of cut-off Whole response instead of
Whole response.[35] In reality these responses are as good an example of a
real W response in Rorschach's sense as any. In many instances the original percept is a W percept, in which no particular thought is given to
the question whether this or that smaller part of the inkblot should or
should not be included. The feeling is that this thing more or less looks
like a butterfly. Only the changed situation of the inquiry raises the
question in the mind of the testee whether the thing they saw really
looked in all respects like a butterfly. Of course, there are other instances in which a great deal of thought and doubt precedes the decision that the whole blot looks like a butterfly and still others, although
probably not very many, in which the original percept explicitly excluded one or several small protrusions of the inkblot. But if the inquiry
is to elicit valid information regarding the original percepts of the
Rorschach performance, it is essential to be constantly aware of and
alert to the many changes which testees will make, sometimes deliberately, more often inadvertently or quite unconsciously, due to the
profound change of the situation and their definition of the changed
situation.

The analysis of Rorschach records can be enriched considerably by a
correct interpretation of the inquiry. This presupposes an analysis of
the interpersonal situation in the inquiry. The significance of additional

---

[35] Klopfer and Kelley, *op. cit.*, p. 83.

responses, e.g., can be understood only if we know what the inquiry situation meant to the testee as compared with the test situation. Only from such an understanding is it possible to form a reasonably valid conclusion concerning the significance of the testee's ability and will or readiness to give responses in the inquiry that he did not give in the spontaneous performance. Similarly, the correct evaluation of information concerning the responses in the spontaneous performance is possible only if the significance of the inquiry situation for the testee has been grasped.

### The Influence of the Tester, the Social Situation, and the Purpose of the Test on the Test Situation

We have discussed so far some of the many different meanings which the combination of the elements common to the Rorschach-test situation may have for the testee, due to his personality, his life experiences, and the resulting set of expectations, fears, hopes, ambitions, and so forth with which he approaches the test task. The multitude of such differing meanings would be present and would have to be considered in the test interpretation even if it were possible rigorously to standardize these elements. Actually this is not possible. The social setting in which the test is given, the circumstances under which it is given, the way in which the test-task is posed differ widely. These differences cannot be obliterated and therefore must be taken into account. Even the attempt to standardize the test instructions, that is to say, the posing of the test-task, for example by uniformly using Rorschach's words "What might this be?" in presenting the inkblots to the testee, does not effectively standardize the task. Both the situation and context in which these words are spoken and the manner in which they are spoken by different testers, or by the same tester at different times and to different people, are bound to affect the testee's experience of the test situation and thus the meaning it has for him and the way he will define it. Similarly, the verbal and nonverbal behavior of the tester after the test instructions are given, during the test performance and the inquiry, will affect or change the test situation and its meaning for the testee in various ways. These differences in the meaning of the test-task and test situation tend to affect also the test performance and they may and often do affect the formal test score, i.e., the uninterpreted test results.

If the statistical concept of test-retest reliability were a valid criterion of the usefulness of a test, these facts would throw serious doubt on the usefulness of Rorschach's test. I believe, however, that the way in which the concept of test-retest reliability is widely used as such a criterion is open to serious methodological question. It is a valid criterion only to the extent that tests are supposed to be measurements of unchanging factors. One of the main purposes of Rorschach's test is to throw light on the way in which people experience the world, their life, themselves. The test would not be the sensitive instrument it is if it did not reflect the fact that the quality of experience fluctuates depending on the person's mood and on his changing reactions to different situations. It is the character of life (as contrasted—roughly—with the phenomena studied in physics) that it never repeats itself exactly. It is the task of test interpretation to differentiate between temporary fluctuations, reactions to specific situations, and relatively more enduring reaction patterns. It is also the task of the test interpreter to be aware of the (fluctuating) limitations of the test instrument and to decide when the test material is sufficient and when it is insufficient to make these differentiations. No test should be relied on blindly. The tester ideally should always make an informed decision whether any specific test in the specific circumstances of its administration allows or does not allow him to draw the conclusions from it that, according to the "rules," it seems to indicate.

The consideration of the social situation, the circumstances under which the test was given, and of the tester's personality and behavior serves several purposes. It can help us avoid mistaking the testee's behavior and performance, caused by something in the specific situation, for a quite generally representative example of his reactions under any and all conditions. It can especially caution us to remain aware of the limitations of the test which, in certain situations, may allow us to see only or primarily the testee's defenses without permitting us a reasonably accurate estimate whether this defensiveness is his essential characteristic or whether, given other circumstances, we might discover other aspects of his personality. It can, in other words, teach us to know when we do not know or when we cannot tell whether we know or do not know the essential dynamics of the testee's personality and when, thus, we cannot rely on Rorschach's test for a reasonably rounded exploration of the testee's personality. The evaluation of the total test situation can also serve as a source of insight provided that the tester is aware of, for example, the defensive quality of the testee's reaction and of the special circumstances or factors that have caused or contributed to his reaction. In such a case it can help us understand why the testee reacted the way he did to these particular circumstances.

I shall review briefly some of the relevant factors that are likely to affect the testee's experience of and performance in the Rorschach test situation; they concern the personality and behavior of the tester, the circumstances under which the test is given, and the sociopsychological implications of specific test situations. Not only the testee but also the tester has a subjective definition of the Rorschach-test situation which, as in the testee, is largely a function of his personality and his experiences and which, in turn, is affected by the personality and behavior of the testee. The *tester's definition of the test situation,* like the testee's, is partly conscious and partly either repressed and unconscious or not in clear awareness. He is aware of the fact that—in one way or another— he is engaged in his professional work when giving a test. Often his work takes place in a situation in which he gives and interprets the test not for his own use but for somebody else as, for instance, in a hospital or clinic setting for the psychiatrist or psychologist who is treating or will treat the patient or who will decide whether, in what way, and by whom the patient should be treated; or, in private practice, for the professional who referred the patient to him for diagnosis and evaluation. In these cases the tester's relation to the person or persons who are going to use his report will play a role in his definition of the test situation, even if he is not aware of it as is the case quite often. Also if—as happens not infrequently—the test is just required routinely and filed away routinely without really being used, this will affect the meaning of the test situation for the tester, for instance by giving him a feeling of futility and lack of seriousness and purpose. What the conscious as well as the unconscious meaning for the tester of his professional work and of its concretization in a particular setting and in a particular test situation with a particular testee will be varies from one tester, one setting, and one test situation to another.[36]

In his relation to testees the tester is likely to be motivated, too, by attitudes of which he may not be sufficiently aware. For example, he may, consciously or unconsciously, feel and act like an omniscient authority, feel superior to the testee, pride himself on his diagnostic prowess, or feel like a detective who is not going to miss any "tricks." On the

---

[36] For a detailed discussion of the "Dynamics of Testing" see Schafer, *op. cit.,* pp. 7–32.

other hand, he may feel that, while giving a test, he is being tested himself. He may feel insecure as a person or in his competence as a psychologist and thus experience that he is on trial. Even though he may feel on trial he may at the same time feel that he is a judge and that the testee is on trial. These attitudes center around the theme of irrational authority and, thus, concern only one cluster of dynamic trends which, if present, are likely to affect the tester's definition of the test situation. There are many others.[37]

Expressed in descriptive rather than dynamic terms, a tester's warm or friendly versus a cold, harsh, and demanding attitude is likely to affect the testee's definition of the test situation. This is true whether warmth or coldness are enduring personality traits of the tester or whether they are purposely adopted attitudes. In the latter case there is some experimental evidence that a warm attitude of the tester is likely to increase the number of responses and to lead to more imaginative and creative responses than a cold, authoritarian attitude.[38]

However, the same personality trait or attitude of the tester may affect testees of different personality types in different, sometimes opposite ways. For instance, a friendly, outgoing, and somewhat effusive tester may have an encouraging effect on people with a need for demonstrative contact but a frightening effect on schizoid personality types, paranoid or schizophrenic testees, and may cause them to withdraw and impoverish their performance. Conversely, a more reserved tester may arouse anxiety in some people, relief and a chance to express themselves more freely in others. A tester with an authoritarian attitude which he may consider benevolently encouraging although it also may be patronizing and domineering may give to one testee a feeling of being guided and encouraged and, because of his dependent needs, may make him feel secure and arouse in him the wish to please this "benevolent" authority-figure. This may lead to a quite productive test performance, influenced by what the testee imagines would be "good" responses in the eye of the tester. Another testee might bristle at the same attitude, sensing the condescending and controlling features of the tester's personality, and might react to them with resentment, resistance, or defiance.

The tester's personality is likely to affect not only the testee and his

[37] For examples see *ibid.*

[38] Edith Lord, "Experimentally Induced Variations in Rorschach Performance," *Psychological Monographs,* 64 (1950) (Whole No. 316).

experience and definition of the test situation but also the tester's interpretation of the test results. For example, some testers tend to put an
exaggerated emphasis on those of the testee's traits and conflicts which
also constitute difficulties in their own lives and therefore, in testing
and elsewhere, may loom larger in their view of other people than they
actually are.[39] Many testers, especially at the beginning of their professional career, look so eagerly for signs of pathology, sometimes of a
specific type such as schizophrenia, that they find it even where a more
balanced perspective would show that it is not present. The French
have an apposite word for this kind of bias, which they call *déforma-
tion professionnelle* and which all professions have to guard against.

Of course, the tester's behavior and attitude is not a function of his
personality only but is, in turn, affected by the testee's personality and
behavior. For example, a hostile or contemptuous testee may antago-
nize a tester in a variety of ways which may affect the tester's attitude
and behavior. This may not only reinforce the testee's hostility but, if
the tester is not sufficiently aware of and in control of his reactions, also
may lead to biased interpretations. Furthermore, not every negative
reaction of the testee can be interpreted uniformly as indicating, say,
general hostility or rebelliousness. Actually, such reactions of the testee
may in some cases be legitimate, in some others they occur when the
tester's personality or utterances touch on a specific, vulnerable area of
the testee without signifying over-all hostility. If the tester, for reasons
in his personality, is particularly vulnerable to negative reactions to
him, he may overreact to them, in his behavior or in his test interpretation or in both.

The general social *background* and the *situation* in which the test is
given also affect the testee's experience and definition of the test situation. While they cannot be separated in reality, I distinguish here the
situation and the circumstances in which the test is given and which led
to the test from the test situation in the narrower sense—i.e., the situation created by the giving of the test itself that we have examined so
far. The background situation is determined, among other factors, by
the function and purpose the test serves, the way in which these have or

---

[39] Hammer and Piotrowski found this with regard to the trait of hostility in test
reports on the House-Tree-Person drawing test. Testers who were rated as more
hostile than others tended to rate the hostility of the testees higher than did less
hostile testers. E. F. Hammer and Z. A. Piotrowski, "Hostility as a Factor in the
Clinician's Personality as It Affects His Interpretation of Projective Drawings
(H-T-P)," *Journal of Projective Techniques,* 17 (1953), 210–216.

have not been communicated to the testee or in which the real purpose of the test has been disguised by a pseudo-purpose that is told to the testee,[40] by the social class and status of the tester and testee and—as has been mentioned earlier—by the general meaning of tests in the culture or the particular social group or by the absence of such meaning. For example, tests given in a hospital in connection with the decision whether a patient should or should not be committed to the hospital are likely to have a different meaning from those given in private practice in connection with the decision whether or not psychoanalytic treatment is advisable. Both these situations are different from tests given to a delinquent in connection with his trial or with the question of probation. Tests given in a prison or reformatory for research purposes are likely to have a different meaning to the testee than do those given to volunteers, for the same purpose, in an academic setting. Tests given or suggested by a person already known to and trusted by the testee may have a different meaning than those given or suggested by a stranger. Tests given when the testee has been told, in a general or specific way, why they are given, will have a different meaning from those where the testee has either been told nothing about the purpose of the test or something that is not true. In anthropological fieldwork—where Rorschach's test has been used frequently—the culture is likely to have no general concept of the meaning of tests. Obviously, the meaning of the test situation will depend heavily on the relation between the fieldworker and the community as well as the particular testees. Interpretation of the test, in these circumstances, is even more dependent on a correct evaluation of the meaning of the test situation for the testee than it is in Western civilization, and particularly in the United States, where testing is ubiquitous.

Just as in different cultures the meaning of the Rorschach-test situation is likely to differ in as yet unexplored ways, so it is likely to differ in *different social classes and groups* within the same culture. These differences stem partly from the influence of differences in social class that may exist between tester and testee and from their effect on the testee's as well as the tester's definition of the test situation, partly from the fact that the particular quality of the Rorschach test-task is likely to have a different meaning to different social classes and groups. The complicated, important, and interesting questions how these differences

---

[40] This is often done in experimental use of the test and—unfortunately—sometimes also in its clinical use.

affect test results and how to take them into account in test interpretation have hardly been touched upon, much less answered by the literature.[41] To answer them would require a combination of sociological and test data which, so far as I know, is not available. Therefore only some questions and speculations which might stimulate further thought and research can be offered.

As we have seen earlier, a productive and rich test performance presupposes, among other things, an openness toward and interest in the blots and the capacity for imaginative, intellectual play. The potentiality for this attitude and for this kind of activity probably differs, in ways unknown to us, because of genetic and similar constitutional factors. Furthermore, the realization and use of whatever potentiality people have for such mental activities are bound to differ drastically depending on how much opportunity and incentive the early (preschool) and also the later environment provided for the exercise and enjoyment of such capacities. Incentive and opportunity for imaginative, intellectual play are relatively lacking in the lower class (workers, unemployed, the majority of underprivileged minority groups such as Negroes). Most of the members of this class are likely to look upon inkblot play or inkblot tests or similar activities as silly nonsense of no use, just as intellectual play is likely to be of little use to them, hence neglected, derided, or unheard of. Thus whatever inherent potential a member of these classes or groups may have for such activities is likely to remain undeveloped. This implies that the Rorschach and similar tests may not be instruments or vehicles suitable for the fullest and richest expression of the personality of members of these groups because they lack experience and interest in the kind of activities that would allow them to make use of such vehicles. If this is so, it would be impossible to decide on the basis of Rorschach's test whether, say, a coartated and stereotyped test performance is due to a generally impoverished, constricted, or relatively undeveloped personality or

---

41 Some of the relevant questions have been raised by Frank Riessman and S. M. Miller, "Social Class and Projective Tests," *Journal of Projective Techniques,* 22 (1958), 432–439, with further references to the literature. Fiedler and Stone have tested a group of children, age six to eleven, of low socioeconomic status and found striking differences between this group and a group of children from a high socioeconomic status background tested by Ames and her associates. Miriam Forster Fiedler and L. Joseph Stone, "The Rorschachs of Selected Groups of Children in Comparison with Published Norms: II. The Effect of Socio-Economic Status on Rorschach Performance," *Journal of Projective Techniques,* 20 (1956), 276–279.

whether it is due to the test not being a suitable instrument for these people to use and to permit an adequate view of their personalities. As Riessman and Miller have put it, "The workers' Rorschach response may be characterized by lack of interest and involvement." [42]

The work of Haggard and Davis on intelligence tests and social class has shown that, to some extent, the difference in degree of incentive, motivation, and practice between different social classes for the kind of activity demanded by the test-task makes these tests unsuitable for a measurement of intelligence of lower-class children that would be comparable to such measurement among middle- or upper-class children.[43] Thus the usual intelligence tests are not as suitable vehicles for the lower-class child to express and show his intelligence as they are for a middle-class child.[44] Rorschach believed that his test permits, among other things, a "finely differentiated examination of intelligence . . . almost entirely independent of education and memory." [45] While this is probably true insofar as the differences in education between different countries within Western civilization are concerned, I doubt that it is true for the differences in education between different social classes. While the test does not require specific knowledge, as intelligence tests do, it offers much richer material for a much fuller interpretation where the testee has had "education" in the "play" of his intelligence. Similarly, the test by and large does not permit as differentiated an examination and picture of the dynamics of personality structure in members of the lower class and of some other social groups as it does in members of the educated and sophisticated metropolitan middle and upper classes and comparable groups.

The possibility that a coartated and stereotyped Rorschach performance with relatively few responses may be due to the meaning of the test situation for certain social classes and groups and to the consequent relative unfitness of the test instrument for differentiated personality exploration among members of this class or group does not preclude

---

[42] Riessman and Miller, *op. cit.,* p. 437.

[43] Ernest Haggard, "Social Status and Intelligence: An Experimental Study of Certain Cultural Determinants of Measured Intelligence," *Genetic Psychology Monographs,* 49 (1954), 145–186. A. Davis, *Social Class Influences upon Learning* (Cambridge: Harvard University Press, 1948).

[44] I omit here any discussion of the important and problematic question what the concept of intelligence is that underlies the measurement of intelligence in these tests.

[45] Rorschach, *Psychodiagnostics,* p. 66.

that such a performance also may have a *defensive* function, just as it
often does in other people. The general human tendency toward what I
have called embeddedness[46] in the familiar and accustomed habits, environment, way of life, and the anxiety when confronted with the challenge of the strange and unknown that would require a measure of
leaving such embeddedness are likely indeed to mobilize defenses to
ward off and avoid the challenge presented by the inkblots. This is
likely to be the case even more in people who have had no or minimal
experience with the kind of activity that can lead to the exploration and
enjoyment of the world of the inkblots than it is in people who have
had such experience. But even if we were to consider the socially conditioned lower-class coartation primarily from the viewpoint of defense
against the unknown, it is very important to be aware of the fact that
this "defense" has a different meaning and function than it does in a
person of the educated middle or upper class. In the case of the former
I would expect it to be the average and in that sense normal reaction, in
the case of the latter the pathological (neurotic) aspect would be more
striking since the person most likely has had opportunity and incentive
to develop the skills and activities which would lead to a richer performance.

The problem of the area of usefulness of Rorschach's test for a differentiated personality diagnosis is not confined to the questions raised by
the Rorschach records of testees from a lower-class background. A population such as that described in the Lynds' *Middletown*, comprising
the whole range of socioeconomic classes and particularly the middle
class and its values, seems to me as likely to produce coartated and
rather stereotyped Rorschach performances as those from members of
the working class. This is not the place to discuss whether—if this should
be true—it is due to a shift in the meaning of the classes and in the
social stratification or whether it is due to a difference between a more
sophisticated metropolitan and a less sophisticated country and urban,
other than metropolitan, middle-class population or a combination of
these. I just want to mention the possibility that it might also be due to
the "religion" of a crude materialism indoctrinated at present by our
culture and especially our mass media in all classes, which preaches
that only what one can buy and how much one can buy and activities
that enable one to buy things are important. Such an attitude, too,

---

[46] Schachtel, *Metamorphosis*, pp. 22–77.

might lead one to consider as silly and futile the kind of intellectual, imaginative play that provides the key, among many other things, to the world of the inkblots.

While social class or group is one of the factors that may cause a definition of the test situation which, in turn, leads to a coartated and stereotyped test performance and thus makes a differentiated diagnosis of personality dynamics difficult or impossible, it does not interfere, as a rule, with the diagnosis of severe pathology, especially of psychoses. Psychotic states, especially acute schizophrenic states, in all social classes seem to be incompatible with the consistent, defensive, impersonal attitude which underlies the kind of coartated and stereotyped performance discussed here.[47] Another exception to class- or group-conditioned coartation probably are some test performances of the youngest group of children, say, in the range of three to four years.[48] In schizophrenic states the breakdown of defenses and the manifest activation of primary process thought interferes with a stereotyped attitude of indifference, lack of involvement, and impersonality, and leads to a more personal, though sick, performance. In the youngest group of children it may be that they are not yet caught so completely in the stereotyped reactions of older members of their class or group and that it takes time to suffocate the spontaneous life of the child in the deadening routine of hopelessness of a fairly narrowly circumscribed attitude.[49]

The tester's definition of the test situation may be affected by *social bias.* Haase reports that essentially similar Rorschach records were interpreted consistently as more maladjusted if the testee belonged to the working class than if he belonged to the middle class.[50] Whether social

---

[47] Psychotic depression often produces an entirely coartated and stereotyped performance. But it differs from the tests discussed here in several respects, especially in the laboriousness, slowness, self-rejecting attitude which also leads to an implicit or explicit critical or otherwise negative attitude toward the depressed person's performance.

[48] This is an impression based on acquaintance with only a small number of records.

[49] More data would be needed to confirm or refute my impression that the records of the youngest children do not have the impersonal quality of the kind of adult record discussed here. If my impression proves valid, the hypothesis discussed above would be consistent with the "broken ego" theory of what I expect the average record of the total adult population to be like. (See above, Chapter 7, p. 96.) The developing ego of the youngest children would not yet be "broken."

[50] W. Haase, *Rorschach Diagnosis, Socio-Economic Class, and Examiner Bias.* Unpublished doctoral dissertation, New York University, 1956, quoted by Riessman and Miller, *op. cit.,* p. 433.

bias does or does not manifest itself in such gross ways in test interpretation, wherever it exists it is bound to influence the relation, for example, between a middle-class tester and a working-class testee and their mutual definition of the test situation in many ways which affect the attitude and behavior of tester as well as testee.[51]

The way in which the testee and his definition of the test situation are affected by the tester and the circumstances of the test, including its social setting, can be a limiting or an illuminating factor for the diagnostic purpose of testing. Whether it is one or the other depends to some extent—not entirely—on the tester. Insofar as it depends on the tester, the decisive variables are his behavior and the degree and quality of his awareness: awareness of the testee's reactions, of the possible and actual implications of the test situation, and especially awareness of and insight into his own behavior, motivations, and his reactions to the testee and the test situation. The keener and wider the tester's awareness and his ability not to be deflected and blinded by his own emotional reactions, the more illuminating will be the use he can make of the implications of the test situation. If, as happens not infrequently, a testee's reaction to his definition of the test situation is a blanket defense, leading to a coartated, stereotyped performance, perhaps to only a few and impersonal responses, this defensive attitude is significant but it may not permit the tester to see more than just this defense. Hence it becomes important to gain access to the testee in some other way.

Sometimes a thorough inquiry and testing the limits will be sufficient since, as we have already seen, the inquiry constitutes a marked change in the test situation. If the inquiry permits a fuller view of the testee, it will be important to understand what the inquiry situation as contrasted to the test situation meant to the testee, in order to appreciate correctly the significance of the fact that the inquiry yielded more data than the test itself. Sometimes asking the testee which blots he likes and which he dislikes and then asking him why he likes or dislikes them will be illuminating. This constitutes a radical change of the test situation. It no longer requires the finding of a likeness and the judgment of the

---

[51] These factors are being recognized, recently, more frequently and clearly in psychotherapy and psychoanalysis of working-class people where there is more opportunity to become aware of them than in the relatively brief contact of testing. Psychoanalytic psychotherapy has developed in a middle-class milieu, with all the limitations this implies. We are just beginning to become aware of these limitations and to overcome them.

likeness implicit in the test-task. Instead, we ask for a personal, emotional reaction of like and dislike. Some people will experience this as permission to tell the tester how they felt and feel about the blots and, in this context, communicate, implicitly or explicitly, important impressions of the blots which, because of their definition of the test situation, they either did not allow themselves to experience before or, if they did experience them, rejected them as inadmissible or irrelevant for the fulfillment of the test-task. Thus, a testee might have perceived card IV as something dark and big and threatening. But he may have defined the test situation in such a way that it did not allow for the development and integration of such a feeling with the task of finding a good likeness to the blot, whereas when asked about his dislikes he may feel free to say that and why he disliked card IV. Another person may experience the question which blots he likes and which he dislikes as a formidable task, possibly even more formidable than the original test-task, and he may feel incapable of making a choice or be reluctant to communicate it. This in itself is a significant finding and its meaning has to be evaluated. In any case, in order to appreciate the data elicited by the question about the testee's preferences and dislikes, we have to understand the testee's definition of this situation of personal choice as compared with his definition of the Rorschach-test situation.

Whether such approaches do or do not yield significant additional data, it cannot be stressed sufficiently that Rorschach's test—and any other test—should not be used as the only diagnostic tool, but always in connection with other tests and a diagnostic interview. Only such a variety of perspectives permits us to gain a reasonably complete and rounded picture of a person and compensates for the distortions that the meaning of the situation created by a single approach and the view from a single perspective (through a particular tool: interview, test, etc.) may create. If such a multiple approach does not yield data sufficient for diagnosis and insight into the essential personality dynamics, a retest by another person different in personality type and sex from the first tester may elicit a fuller and richer performance.

# INDEX

Abilities, achievement and, 6–7
Abnormality, 64, 66
Abstraction, form perception and, 90–91
Achievement, abilities and, 6–7
  measurement of, 286
  response as, 6
Activity, 58–59
  strained, 45
Adolescents, coartation of, 96 n.
Adults, children and, 127–128
  perception of, 68
  (see also Parents)
Advertising, mass-media, 104
Affection, need for, 244
Affective adaptation, 253
Affective liability, color responses and, 163
Affectivity, color response and, 165, 168, 178
Affects, 164–165
  ambivalent, 169
Aggression, 135–136, 215, 218, 233, 304
Aggressive-sadistic tendencies, 135, 209
Agoraphobia, 100–101
Ainsworth, Mary D., 251 n., 254
Allport, Gordon W., quoted, 197
Ambition, 287, 292–293, 304–305
Ambivalence, 169–170, 172, 288–290, 306
Ames, Louise Bates, et al., 157, 182 n., 323 n.
Anderson, Harold H. and Gladys L., 10 n.
Animals, kinesthetic perception of, 238
  movements of, 222
  sensory perception of, 143
Anlages, 150, 214
Anxiety, 32, 227, 320
  defenses against, 118
  diffuse, 248–250, 253
  escape from, 48
  freedom and, 23, 282–283

  perceptual hold and, 106–107, 112, 117–118
  reactions to, 48
  about the unknown, 22–25, 46–48, 51, 100
Anxious persons, 298–299
Apperception, 12
  sequence of modes of, 296–303
Aristotle, 89
Arnheim, Rudolf, 33 n., 90 n.
Art, color response to, 173
  creative experience and, 229–231, 233
  (see also Paintings)
Artists, 114, 174, 179, 298
  and creative experience, 229–232
Associations, 44
  color responses and, 180–181
  form responses and, 93–94, 181
  free, 54, 111–113, 116, 180–181, 212, 307–308
  loosening of, 56
  openness toward, 53
  perception and, 53
  range of, 16–18
    limitations on, 18, 54
  response and, 14–15
  stereotyped, 56
Associative activity, energy of, 35
Associative processes, 71
Attention, receptive, 45, 58
  to shading nuances, 251
Attitudes, 50–51
  active, 59–61, 241
  toward authority, 187
  basic, 198
    kinesthetic responses and, 203–229
  careful, 185–186
  changes in, 78
  childhood, 223
  differentiation of, 237–238
  toward environment, 200, 233, 252
  kinesthetic perception and, 226, 234, 241

329